THE PARLIAMENT OF CANADA

The past fifteen years have seen more changes to the institutions and processes of the Canadian government than any previous period. Central agencies and the policy-making process have been drastically reorganized. A constitution with an entrenched charter of human rights has been adopted. Resources have been strengthened, procedures tightened, public accessibility enhanced through the televising of proceedings. The staff of Parliament has become more professional.

But in spite of this formidable list of changes, there is intense dissatisfaction with the way parliamentary government functions in Canada. A recent Gallup poll found that a majority of Canadians had little or no interest in Parliament. And many eminent Canadians, including Robert Stanfield, Michael Pitfield, Pierre Trudeau, and a host of academics, have criticized the institution. Parliament is considered neither important nor effective.

In this insightful study of Parliament today, C.E.S. Franks considers the successes and failures of reform from three perspectives. He examines first the theories of parliamentary government to explain the gap between Canadians' expectations of Parliament and the reality. Next he explores the effect of recent reforms on parliamentary government, including the utility of debate and question period, the accomplishment of committees, changes in the role of the MP, and the impact of television. Finally he considers proposed reforms to the Senate and the electoral system within the context of the system of parliamentary government.

The central institutions of Canadian government come into clear focus in Franks's analysis, as they have evolved to now and as they may develop in the future.

C.E.S. FRANKS is Professor of Political Science, Queen's University. In 1977 he founded the Canadian Study of Parliament Group, and was its first president.

C.E.S. FRANKS

The Parliament of Canada

UNIVERSITY OF TORONTO PRESS
Toronto Buffalo London

© University of Toronto Press 1987
Toronto Buffalo London
Printed in Canada

ISBN 0-8020-5735-7 (cloth)
ISBN 0-8020-6651-8 (paper)

Canadian Cataloguing in Publication Data

Franks, C. E. S.
   The Parliament of Canada

   Includes bibliographical references and index.
   ISBN 0-8020-5735-7 (bound) ISBN 0-8020-6651-8 (pbk.)

   1. Canada. Parliament. I. Title.

JL136.F72 1987   328.71'07   C87-094110-0

Contents

Acknowledgments

This book could not have been written without the help of many people. S.H. Beer, Alan Cairns, and Senator John Stewart gave encouragement in the early stages. J.E. Hodgetts, John Meisel, Eugene Forsey, and Mary Anne Griffiths, Clerk Assistant (Research) of the House of Commons, and her staff read through the manuscript and offered many helpful criticisms and suggestions. J.E. Hodgetts in particular subjected the manuscript to his perceptive editorial scrutiny at two separate stages, a labour well beyond the call of duty. The three readers of the manuscript for the University of Toronto Press were admirably helpful in both encouraging and warning, and perceptive comments on sections were offered by Ray Duplessis, Law Clerk of the Senate, and Ian Stewart, former deputy minister of finance. Alistair Fraser and Bev Koester have given encouragement and help over the years. Financial support was provided by the Queen's School of Graduate Studies and Research, and the Ontario Arts Council. Virgil Duff of the University of Toronto Press gave support at every stage. Ms B. Endersby was copy editor. Beverley MacLean helped unravel the mysteries of the Senate. Jill Harris and Shirley Fraser did the typing.

I would like to follow in the footsteps of another professor and say that, with all this help, the faults in the book must belong to someone else, but I know that isn't so. Books on a subject as big, important, and dynamic as the Canadian parliament can never be definitive or even correct; the research is never completed; manuscripts are merely reports on work in progress, or on work already abandoned. The faults in the book are my own.

I should like especially to acknowledge two more general debts of gratitude: to the late Dr J.A. Corry, who inspired my interest in politics and parliamentary government; and to the men and women who serve Canada in parliament. They make our government and our country work, at a cost to themselves and their families far greater than is generally realized.

THE PARLIAMENT OF CANADA

1

Introduction: Parliament in an Age of Reform

Ours is an age of reform. In 1979 the privy council office, in its submission to the royal commission on financial management and accountability, claimed that 'during the last twenty years ... more change has occurred in the way the government orders its machinery for getting things done, and in the variety and pervasiveness of the programs it delivers, than in any comparable period in our administrative and social history.'[1] Parliament underwent more reform in those twenty years than in any previous period, and arguably more than in its entire previous existence. And the process of reform did not stop in 1979. The study of procedure of the House of Commons by a special committee in 1982 led to many important reforms. Further changes were made in 1985–6, and the special committee that proposed those reforms claimed that its recommendations were 'the most ambitious attempt to pursue major and comprehensive reform in the more than one hundred-year history of the Canadian House of Commons.'[2] The Senate also has been the target of innumerable studies, and Senate reform remains one of the more written-about topics in Canadian politics.

The record of the reforms of the past decades is not one of unblemished success. As we shall see, many reforms have not accomplished their stated objectives, while others have had unanticipated and undesirable consequences. Reforms that are not solidly grounded in reality are not likely to succeed. Quite the reverse, they are likely to create unreasonable and unreal expectations which cannot be met. The resulting failures lead to disillusionment, pessimism, and a loss of legitimacy for the public and participants. Constant reform can become as much a habit as immobility and can be as inappropriate a response to problems.

The purpose of this book is not to make more proposals for reform. The themes of reform have not changed. The same complaints of excessive partisanship, government domination, lack of influence of the private member and the need for improved committees and accountability, for a greater role for parliament in policy-making, and for reform of the Senate continue despite the passage of time and the many changes that have been made. Similarly, the list of proposed reforms has changed little. Rather, the purpose of this book is to place discussion of parliament and its reform solidly in its context – the Canadian society, economy, political culture – and the stresses and demands to which Canada and its political system are subject. A secondary purpose is to examine the various proposed and implemented reforms in the context of this broader look at parliamentary government and its functioning in Canada. This examination will, I hope, illuminate some of the obstacles to reform, some of the ways in which criticisms and attempts at reform have been misguided, and some of the strengths (which are often neglected and sometimes difficult to see) as well as the weaknesses of the Canadian parliamentary system.

The Canadian parliamentary system is based on the British prototype. Like the Canadian House, the British House of Commons has changed in many ways during recent years. However, in some areas, such as strengthening committees and giving MPs more independence from party discipline, the British House has been more successful. The comparison of Canadian and British experience helps illuminate some of the obstacles to reform in Canada, and the importance of many underlying factors that are usually not taken into account in proposals for reform. For these reasons I have used British experience as basis for comparison and as an illustration in several key places in this book.

I have used the example of the U.S. congressional-presidential system less often. This system, because of its high visibility, and the power and influence of the United States, inevitably becomes a basis for comparison in the discussion of parliamentary reform in Canada. On some issues our institutions have been caught between the constraints of the basic principles of the parliamentary-cabinet system and the beguiling image of the U.S. system, with its powerful committees and highly visible and influential senators and congressmen. But the U.S. system is very different, both in terms of representation and in terms of control and use of political power. There are no positions in the U.S. system in which power and responsibility are concentrated to the extent that they are in the prime minister and cabinet in Canada. Nor is there any forum in which the U.S. president and political executive are subjected to the sort of continual gruelling scrutiny that the Canadian prime minister and cabinet receive in question period and debate. The structure of elections is different in the United States, as is the role of the party. The kinds of policies that emerge from the U.S. system are different from, and not necessarily better than, those that come from the Canadian parliamentary system. I agree with the recent observation that 'the U.S. model is misleading and irrelevant for Canadians.'[3]

Four essential functions of parliament in the Canadian system are: first, to make a government, that is, to establish a legitimate government through the electoral process; second, to make a government work, that is, to give the government the authority, funds, and other resources necessary for governing the country; third, to make a government behave, that is, to be a watchdog over the government; and fourth, to make an alternative government, that is, to enable the opposition to present its case to the public and become a credible choice for replacing the party in power. Parliamentary activities of legislating and policy-making are largely aspects of the function of making a government work, and parliament's role in them is not now, nor has it ever been, the dominant one. In comparison, the U.S. Congress has virtually no role in the functions of making a government and creating an alternative government, and has a very large role indeed in the function of policy-making.

There are two further functions of parliament which are so important that they deserve to be identified in their own right, though they might also be subsumed under the general rubric of making a government work. The first of these is the function of parliament as a recruiting and training ground for political leaders; the second is the function of political communication, where the processes of parliamentary discussion, in Bagehot's terms, express the mind of the people, teach society, and inform both government and citizen of grievances and problems.

In structure this book progresses from a general look at the form and rationale of parliamentary government to an examination of how the system works in Canada. Chapter 2 introduces some conceptual issues and underpinnings. After a review of some fundamental principles, it shows that discussion of reform in Canada chooses one particular way of looking at parliament, and one which, it will be argued throughout this work, is at odds with how the system actually works and with the policy orientation of successive Canadian governments. Chapters 3 to 5 consider aspects of the central and essential basis of parliamentary government, the processes of representation in the House of Commons. The role of parties and the electorate, the members of parliament, and the parliamentary workworld are examined in turn. These three chapters place the House of Commons in the context of Canadian political culture and society, and illustrate the very real problems in the role and position of the member of parliament. Chapters 4 to 9 look at how parliament operates, and its work and activities. Procedure, debates and question period, and committees are examined successively and the constraints placed on them by the realities of representation are illustrated. Chapter 9 examines the Senate; chapters 10 and 11 examine two key functions of responsible government: policy-making (or making a government work) and accountability (or making a government behave). In these functions parliament and government interact, and committees, debates and question period, cabinet ministers, opposition leaders, and private members make their impact. Here many of the strengths, as well as the weaknesses, of the parliamentary system are identified. The focus of this book, therefore, develops progressively from questions of theory, to the basis of representative government in the electorate and nation, to parliament and its workings, to the relationship of parliament to government. The final chapter returns to the question of reform, and assesses its success in fulfilling the very demanding functions it is expected to perform.

The fundamental argument in this book is that reform of parliament is not simply a technical matter of making parliament more effective and efficient, although it is often presented in those terms. Reform is also a question of the purposes for which political power is to be used in Canada and how various interests and viewpoints succeed or fail to influence political choices and outcomes. The balance between parliament and government affects the balance between an emphasis on the particular and on the general welfare. There are many collective, public goods that can only be provided by government, and will only be adequately ensured if a strong voice defending a general public interest is heard in politics. Fundamental and often competing goals of equality, freedom, justice, private and public goods, and economic growth and stability must be balanced in the political processes. The parliamentary system, with a concentration of power in the cabinet and competition between parties in parliament, provides a powerful means of asserting a collective interest over and above the particular. The rhetoric of reform argues for a parliament-centred structure of power; the reality of Canadian politics is an executive-centred system. The differences between the two are not merely questions of who has power, but of what kinds of policies we want. The executive-centred system has enabled a collectivist voice to be expressed in Canadian politics that would be diminished if the system were to become strongly parliament-centred.

The second argument is that parliament has two modes of operation, the adversarial and the consensual. The adversarial mode is most prominent in question period and debates, the consensual in committee work. Each mode has its strengths and weaknesses. The rhetoric of parliament-centred reform argues for more emphasis on the consensual. It exaggerates the strengths of this mode, and understates its weaknesses, while at the same time it ignores the real and important virtues of the adversarial elements.

The third argument is that there is a severe problem in the role and position of the member of parliament in Canada. This problem is normally discussed in terms of the constraints of party discipline. This focus is wrong. Party discipline is a product of the root problem and is not the cause. The underlying problem is that the processes of representation, of parties, of electoral attitudes and behaviour, of demographic change and many other factors, all contribute to creating a House of

Commons composed of amateur and short-term members who are asked to perform a very difficult and underappreciated job. MPs generally have little political experience before being elected to the House and stay there only a brief time. Senators, in comparison, have more previous experience and longer tenure. Parliament, and the cabinet too for that matter, can be no more effective and influential than resources of manpower permit. The constraints of manpower affect all aspects of parliamentary government: the executive, in limiting the range of choices and quality of potential cabinet ministers; the opposition, in being effective critics of government and creating a plausible alternative to the government; committees of the House, in rapid turnover and sometimes ineffective chairmanship and members; the value and interest of debates and question period; the capacity of members to understand and use procedure; and the speakership. The position of the individual member in terms of career, workworld, future expectations, and personal satisfaction is crucial to the working of the parliamentary system, and to the possibilities for reform. It is also unsatisfactory.

Fourth, there is a paradox that at the same time as the parties are so influential and powerful within parliament, they are weak outside it, both in terms of gaining consistent strong allegiances within the electorate and in terms of generating ideas and policy proposals. It is a well-known and often criticized fact that the parties are the most important control over an MP's voting behaviour within parliament. Not so much appreciated is how important party is to the entire career of an MP, from election, through every aspect of parliamentary tenure, to post-parliamentary life. At the same time, the weakness of parties outside parliament is one of the reasons why MPs are amateur and transient. It is also one of the reasons why political discussion in Canada often lacks both thoughtfulness and power.

Fifth, parliament and the parliamentary system are under severe stress because of the growth of government. Where the theory of parliamentary-cabinet government postulates two systems – a parliament and a government, with the cabinet as the link between them – there are now three systems, with the emergence of a huge and in many ways autonomous bureaucracy. Ministerial control over departments and agencies is now as much an issue as parliamentary control over ministers. The role of parliament is also changing in an increasingly complex and growing system of government and government–interest-group relations. These problems are exacerbated by the increasing importance of federal-provincial relations in Canadian politics, and the domination of these relations by executive federalism, in which political argument and negotiation is between levels of government rather than between parties in parliament.

Sixth, communication through the media plays a particularly important role in explaining and interpreting parliament in Canada because of the weaknesses of the parties as policy-creating and -discussing bodies. The media tend to be superficial and critical in their presentation of government and politics. While parliament and parliamentary committees are often insightful and thorough in their studies and discussion, little of this gets reported. There is a huge gap between serious discussion of policy within government, or even in parliament, and what gets reported. As a result, public understanding and the mobilization of consent are now big problems.

The final argument is that despite its faults the parliamentary system in Canada works better than the literature would lead one to believe. The system was transplanted to this country a century and a half ago, and since then has grown and adapted in the Canadian environment. A century and a half is not a long time in the perspective of the development of parliamentary institutions, and it is not surprising that the Canadian system still suffers from growing pains. But there is a vast difference between growing pains and the death throes some observers claim to see in looking at the Canadian parliament.

Reform has focused on the obvious and easy things to change, such as parliamentary committees, procedure, and the Senate, while many of the real problems lie elsewhere, in leadership, parties, the media, and political culture. Institutions have, to a large extent unfairly, borne the brunt of dissatisfaction, while the causes and remedies lie in less structured and less malleable parts of the political system. Perhaps, too, concentration on institutional reform has misdirected too much political discussion towards administration and away from content, away from substantial issues of policy.

It would require unrealistic expectations for the possibility of perfection in human institutions to hope that parliament would completely fulfil all the demands and hopes laid upon it. Parliament has many faults. It is also central to the use of power in society. The size and scope of modern government and government's intimate involvement in the economy, society, and the lives of individuals mean that government cannot be regarded as a neutral instrument. Government harms some, benefits others, and its powers and actions are legitimated by parliament. Citizens, fully aware of how their lives are affected by government, do not regard politics or political institutions neutrally. Violent passions, including greed, aggression, hate, anger, even idealism, are intimately and understandably involved in politics, and political institutions as well as leaders are the targets of these emotions. Many of the criticisms of parliament and the parliamentary system are legitimate, and relate to procedures and structures which can and need to be improved. Others arise from unreasonable expectations of what politics and political institutions can accomplish, or from dissatisfaction with outcomes. The Canadian parliamentary system has been created and is made to work or fail by human beings, with all their warts and imperfections. Institutions are not perfect, any more than people are.

To defend parliament this way is not to imply that the institution does not need reform, but to warn that caution is needed in advocating change. Government and government institutions are inevitably going to provoke some hostility and criticism, and often the institutions bear the brunt of unreasonable criticisms, or criticisms more properly directed elsewhere, perhaps at the individuals the electorate has chosen to run those institutions. One challenge is to identify the criticisms that are reasonable, that address problems that can be corrected, and to distinguish those problems from ones that would be more properly resolved through political action and change, or that arise from the uncertainty and difficulties that are part of the human condition. Another is simply to understand and appreciate parliament and its place in the processes of representation and governance. Parliament is not just a background for an agenda of reforms. It is a lively and vital part of the living constitution.

2

Approaches to Parliamentary Government

There is room within the Westminster model of parliamentary government for many different configurations of power. The key actors are the government, the House of Commons, and the nation as electorate and as groups and organizations interested in and affected by government. At some periods in the evolution of the British parliament, the Crown and government were dominant, at other times the Commons. Sometimes both were controlled by powerful interests and influential individuals. Two basic principles emerged, however, which structure the broad relationships between government, parliament, and the people. These are that parliamentary government is 'responsible' and 'representative.' This chapter will examine three configurations of power and conceptions of parliamentary government and will relate them to the Canadian political system and some of the issues in reform of parliament. But, first, these basic principles of responsible and representative government need to be explained.

The parliamentary system means government in and with, but not by, parliament. The innovation of an elected representative assembly as the means by which government is controlled, and through which governments change, is the fundamental contribution of Britain to political theory and practice. The various meanings of 'responsibility'[1] define the link between parliament, the elected representative assembly, and government. 'Responsible' in its first sense means that ministers and the cabinet have power and are responsible for its use. Individually, ministers are by law assigned responsibility for the administration of departments and the exercise of discretion. With few exceptions (although they are growing in numbers), public servants exercise power in the name of, and on behalf of, the minister. In most other political systems, including those of continental Europe and the United States, much of the responsibility for day-to-day administration, and much discretionary authority, is by law assigned to public servants. Collectively, the prime minister and cabinet are responsible for the overall management and direction of government.

In a second sense, 'responsible' means that the government is expected to be a trustworthy steward of the nation's affairs. In L.S. Amery's words, responsibility

connotes a state of mind, which weighs the consequences of action and then acts, irrespective, it may be, of the concurrence or approval of others ... A British government is not merely responsible to those who have appointed it or keep it in office in the sense in which an agent is responsible to his principal. It is an independent body which on taking office assumes the responsibility of leading and directing Parliament and the nation in accordance with its own judgement and convictions.[2]

A modern cabinet is, of course, responsive to many real pressures and does not and cannot act solely in accordance with its own judgment and convictions, and one would be quite justified in mistrusting a government that was so self-centred as to do so. The cabinet must balance particular pressures from interest groups and other sources with its concept of the public interest, and in this difficult balancing act its judgment and convictions are inevitably, and usefully, tempered by necessity.

Through cabinet ministers the Crown and government are represented in parliament, and to a large extent determine what parliament does. In the cabinet, as Bagehot described, there is a 'close union, the nearly complete fusion, of the executive and legislative powers.'[3] The cabinet and ministers are responsible for planning and making policies, overseeing administration, raising and spending revenues, drafting all major legislation, preparing budgets, making appointments to boards, commissions, and other senior government posts, preparing and signing contracts for public works, purchasing supplies, legal services, advertising, etc, managing the public service, drafting and promulgating subordinate legislation, administering and applying the law, and even invoking the War Measures Act, which suspends all normal civil liberties and rights. This list is far from exhaustive. Money bills, those recommending expenditures or programme changes which would entail expenditures and bills affecting taxes, can only be introduced into parliament with the recommendation of the Crown.[4]

These enormous centralized powers of the cabinet, part of the monarchical heritage, are more like those normally associated with an autocratic dictatorship than with a democratic government. The safeguard against their abuse lies in the relationship between parliament and government. In the third sense of 'responsible' government, ministers are not only responsible *for* the use of these powers, but are also responsible and accountable *to* parliament. Parliament, and particularly the House of Commons, is consequently the central forum for discussion about the use and abuse of political power, and is the source of the legitimacy and authority of a government. Government and parliament live and die together. They are bound to each other. A cabinet must have the support of a majority in parliament. If it loses this support on a question of confidence it must resign or ask for an election. If it loses an election, it loses its right to remain in office. The awareness of scrutiny through processes of being held responsible and accountable by parliament also helps to make ministers and governments responsible in the sense of serving as trustworthy stewards.

Ministers are expected to have seats in parliament, and normally these seats are in the elected House of Commons rather than in the appointed Senate. This requirement is a matter of convention, not of law, and ministers have, on occasion, not been members of parliament. When John Turner became prime minister in 1984 he was not a member of parliament. In 1975 Pierre Juneau, who had been chairman of the Canadian Radio-Television Commission, was made minister of communications though he had no seat in parliament. Soon after, he ran for parliament in a by-election, and he lost. He then resigned from the cabinet, although he was not legally required to do so. Prime Minister Trudeau thereupon made Juneau deputy minister of communications – the supposedly non-political permanent head of the department of which he had been ministerial head. Whatever this shows about the attitude of the Trudeau government to the electorate and the public service, and whatever it shows about the number of ways to skin a cat, it does show the strength of the convention that ministers must have seats in parliament. Only then can they be held responsible and accountable.

The real threat to responsible government in this era is not that ministers will try to avoid responsibility and accountability (although this does sometimes happen, especially when there is a rapid turnover of ministers) but that ministers cannot exercise effective control over their departments. We shall examine these questions more closely in the later chapters on policy-making and accountability. The central issue is whether the doctrine of ministerial responsibility asks too much of a minister, who in reality can direct and control only a minuscule portion of a department's business, and too little of the civil servants, who in reality exercise a great deal of discretion and use power with a great deal of autonomy. The opposition in parliament is a most vociferous advocate of full ministerial responsibility because the doctrine makes the government the legitimate target of attacks on any weakness in policy or administration. But whether the doctrine in its absolute form accurately describes present realities or is the proper basis for accountability for routine administrative and financial details is doubtful. There is no argument, however, over the desirability of the cabinet's and ministers' responsibility for leadership, policies, important decisions, and general steward-ship of the nation.

The parliamentary system is a representative one. The essential base of representation is the individual member of parliament, elected in nation-wide elections from single-member constituencies on the basis of universal adult suffrage. Elections are held in Canada when the prime minister asks the governor general to dissolve parliament and call one. Elections are normally called after four years, or at the most five, although if the government is defeated on a vote of confidence (as happened in minority parliaments in 1963, 1974, and 1979) they can be held sooner. Representation through MPs is an exceptionally complex subject (as are the intricacies of votes of confidence and the role of the governor general in calling elections) and its various ramifications take up the bulk of the next three chapters of this book. What is important to note here is the principle, and the reality, that every Canadian is directly represented in the House of Commons through an elected member of parliament. In this sense, as well as many others, the House of Commons is the true voice of the nation.

In modern government there are many other systems of representation which compete for legitimacy and power with the elected members of the House. In practice the electorate more normally votes for a party and party leader than for the local candidate. The parties also, for the most part, determine and control the parliamentary activities of elected members. As a result, the political parties have in many ways become more important parts of the representative system than the individual elected members. This is particularly true for the government side, where the prime minister and cabinet hold positions of enormous responsibility, and where a vast gulf exists between backbencher and minister. The prime minister, himself, represents the nation and is the most powerful person in politics.

Interest and pressure groups are another system of representation. In the United States they are now almost treated as part of the institutions of central government. In Canada there are proposals to make their status formal through a system of registration. For the most part, pressure groups work behind the scenes with civil servants and cabinet ministers, but when their persuasions fail in private they will lobby members of parliament and committees. There is an uneasy tension in politics between these groups, which express the views of particular interests and concerns in the country, and the system of elected representation in parliament.

The public service has its own views on the public good and the policies that would be most beneficial for Canada. Because it is so large, and because of its intimate contacts with the clientele it serves and the interest groups concerned with government, the public service often has a more informed and useful understanding of policy issues than do politicians. It serves as the spokesman within government for many groups, and sometimes regards itself as the defender of those without other access to power. In this way, the public service also has become a system of representation.

Provincial governments are a further system of representation. The division of the power to legislate between two levels in the Canadian federal system is our way of overcoming the obstacles of an enormous land mass, a dispersed population, two major languages and cultures, and other important regional variations.

Regardless of the extent to which law-making competence was historically divided into watertight compartments, the most pronounced feature of modern Canadian federalism is the interpenetration of the two levels of government, so that federal-provincial relations have become perhaps the most contentious and written-about aspects of Canadian politics and government. Provincial governments often argue that they more accurately express the interest and concerns of citizens than do members of the federal House.

Each of these groups – federal politicians, parties, interest groups, public servants, and provincial governments – has its own particular biases and concerns. There are often disagreements between subgroups, among pressure groups or provinces, or between different departments of government. Policy decisions arise from relationships and trade-offs between competing actors and interests, and the system of elected representation through parliament is not always the most powerful and legitimate. In fact, it rarely is. This dissonance between theory and reality is the source of much of the discontent with parliamentary government in Canada, both among observers and among MPs.

The media, television and newspapers in particular, are a crucial part of representative government. Though not a system of representation themselves, they provide most of the information by which the public interprets, forms its opinions, and decides, in politics. The media have their own biases, and inevitably select and colour the information which the public receives. They also affect how politicians and interest groups behave and argue in their efforts to get attention and to persuade successfully.

The principles of representative and responsible government are only the bare bones of the parliamentary system, and many other principles and factors contribute to the working system of government. One of these, which describes a key linkage between government, parliament, and the electorate, is that government is by consent. To consent does not necessarily mean to want. It can mean to acquiesce or to agree. For the system to work, losers as well as winners must accept outcomes. As J.A. Corry wrote, 'democracy is as much a matter of gaining the consent of minorities as it is of giving effect to the will of the majority.'[5] Compromise and accommodation are essential to consent.

The role of parliament in the representative and consent-creating processes is strongly affected by the division into government and opposition. In nineteenth-century Britain 'Her Majesty's Loyal Opposition' emerged as part of the constitution. Although we tend to take the existence of an opposition for granted, the fact that it is not only there but is identifiable, constitutionally legitimate, and lively is most unusual in the world's array of political systems. Governments are more noted for their tendencies to suppress opposition than to hallow it. But in modern parliamentary government the driving force in holding the government responsible is an official opposition motivated by desire to prove the government incompetent or worse, and itself as better. The process of contest and confrontation should ensure that the government, to overcome and forestall criticism, produces policies that have the widest possible acceptance. The opposition, in its turn, should attempt to win comparably wide support for its side. A weak opposition will not be able to ensure accountability, nor will it be a credible alternative. A strong, effective opposition is essential to good parliamentary government.

The format of parliamentary discussion is adversarial. It assumes that multi-sided problems can be reduced to two viewpoints: in favour and opposed. Often the truth is that many on the government side are opposed or lukewarm, while some in the opposition are in favour. But these subtleties disappear in parliamentary debate. This system is similar in structure to our law courts, which are adversarial rather than inquisitorial. Consent is mobilized through the parliamentary struggle: the government, by withstanding the attacks of the opposition and by putting forward its proposals with conviction and vigour, proves the sincerity and the justness of its cause. This process is neither rational nor scientific, but it achieves consent, though through conflict rather than co-operation. It also has an element of gaming and gamesmanship in it, which helps to make politics the popular spectator sport it is, although this gamesmanship can trivialize issues and sometimes repels people.

The parliamentary processes are only a small part of the mobilization of consent. Other aspects include government consultation with interest groups before formulating policies, study by royal commission so that the public, media, and interest groups participate in and influence the policy-making process, and public information campaigns to gain support for the government's position. In these processes compromises, and moderation of demands, are essential to arriving at decisions which accommodate varied competing interests to the point of achieving consent.

Words and discussion are the core of effective parliamentary government. In parliament the government explains and defends its policies and actions to the nation; the nation through its representatives tells the government what it likes, doesn't like, wants, and doesn't want. This complex dialogue teaches and informs both nation and government. Sometimes the discussion is carried out at an abysmally low level; at other times it is of very high quality indeed. But the fact that it exists at all, and that it is a continuous, peaceful dialogue and debate, is what makes our government the mutual endeavour of a free people rather than the arbitrary exercise of power by a despotic force.

CONCEPTIONS OF PARLIAMENTARY GOVERNMENT

The inheritance of Canadian political institutions is the British parliamentary system; the environment is the northern half of a continent, nearly twenty-five million people, including two major language groups and many regions, subcultures, and other linguistic minorities, most of whom live in a narrow band along three thousand miles of border shared with the most powerful nation in the world. The tension between this vast and diffuse environment and the inheritance of a highly centralized form of government developed within a small island nation-state has not been easy to resolve, and the process of resolution is still going on. Political institution-building and nation-building go hand in hand.

Crucial to political institution-building are the ideas and concepts we have about our government and politics, how the processes of representation ought to function, and how institutions ought to work. Either written or unwritten (and usually unwritten), the constitution of a country contains a conception of the interests that are legitimate and ought to be recognized and influence the use of political power, a sense of the processes and structures through which power ought to be exercised, and some description of the ideals, values, and vision of the public good that ought to be achieved through politics.

Over the centuries during which the parliamentary system evolved in Britain, there were striking changes in the configurations of power, representation, and policies, and corresponding changes in the conceptions of how parliamentary government ought to work and what policies government ought to adopt to create this society. These conceptions are also expressions of theories of representation, of who ought to wield power, how they ought to be chosen, through what processes of representation and decision-making the general interest is defined, and when the general interest ought to prevail over the particular, or the particular over the general.

The history of Canadian parliamentary institutions is so brief that the sort of massive change from one conception of representation to another, which took centuries in Britain, has not occurred here. Nevertheless, there are competing conceptions which are important for understanding both Canadian parliamentary government and discussion of its reform. Three such conceptions will be used in this study: the executive-centred, the parliament-centred, and the collectivist. These are analogous, respectively, to the Tory, Liberal, and collectivist notions which S.H. Beer applied to various stages in the evolution of the British parliamentary system.[6] 'Tory' and 'Liberal' have, however, such different meanings in Canada from those intended by S.H. Beer that it is best to choose less politically loaded terms. Others have suggested, also drawing on British experience, the use of the terms 'court' and 'country.'[7] In other words, the difference is between ins and outs. This approach shows that many of the differences in how things look depend on where you sit. I find the three-part distinction more useful, however, because the questions involved are more than just differences between ins and outs. There are also differences in the kinds of policies which emerge from the system, and this distinction is best illustrated by including the third, collectivist conception. The use of three conceptions also highlights some of the unusual features of the Canadian parliamentary system.

The Executive-Centred Conception

The British progenitor of the executive-centred system is Toryism, old and new. In old Tory thought society was corporate and hierarchic. It was divided by degree, with the monarch at the pinnacle as head of church and state, the lords, knights, burgesses, and others below. The monarch at the head was responsible for the governance and well-being of the nation. The role of parliament was primarily the redress of grievances, bringing the problems of constituencies before the court, considering private bills, and in return for these favours from the Crown, granting subsidies to pay for the burden of administration and the numerous wars. Most policy-making, and all administration, was the prerogative of the Crown and outside the purview of parliament.

It was an age and a theory of strong government and paternalism. The emphasis was on community rather than the individual. Many members of parliament were dependent on the influence of patrons, the great lords of the realm. 'For themselves the magnates sought power, prestige, and material advantage – great offices of state, the grant of manors, even the supreme prize of the Queen's hand; for their followers, lesser offices and perquisites. In addition to the hopes of future favor there were ties of personal loyalty and traditional sentiment. It was a politics not of principle and program, but of honor and interest.'[8] Members of parliament were usually powerful and influential people in their own right. As parliamentarians they furthered their own, their patrons', and their constituencies' interests in the small, closed society that governed Britain.

Modern Tory thinking also believes in a concentration of power at the centre. Though rank and degree in the earlier sense are outdated notions, a similar attitude persists in the concept of class. Society is still hierarchical, and the realm should be governed by an élite, a ruling class of the few who are able to acquire the art of governing. This élite is formed through both heredity and the co-opting of those of merit from the lower classes to the higher. Mass suffrage is accepted but the electorate is passive, not active. Their participation is limited to voting and support of the party. The party does not offer a programme spelling out the policies it will adopt when it achieves power. Policies will be the responsibility of the prime minister and cabinet. There is a strong emphasis on leadership. Party discipline is rigid. Parliament discusses and supports a government. It is composed of leaders, the ministry; followers, the government backbenchers; and the opposition.

Tory thinking includes not only strong but big government. It professes the belief that the élite leaders, the wealthy and the advantaged, have a responsibility for the welfare of the others. Thus state education, universal health-insurance schemes, and welfare programmes are quite compatible with Toryism. So also is a strong role for government in planning the economy and restructuring industry. Tory thought is a vast distance away from the individualism of the modern conservatism of a Reagan or a Thatcher.

Canada also has an executive-centred, Tory, strain in politics. G. Horowitz and others have identified this strain as an ideology. But it also exists as an approach to institutions and the practice of government. Not unnaturally, the government, the 'court' party, is the more articulate in defending this approach. The privy council office has argued, in perhaps the strongest expression of this approach in Canada, that 'constitutionally, the power of the state flows from the Crown and generally speaking may only be exercised by or on the authority of the Crown.'[9] Parliament has a relatively small role if this viewpoint is accepted.

The Parliament-Centred Conception

The British parliament reached an apogee of influence in the nineteenth century, when the liberal theory of government was dominant. A member of parliament in nineteenth-century liberal doctrine was not merely a delegate from his constituency or party who reflected the will of those who sent him to parliament, but a representative charged with deliberating on and seeking the common good. There was consequently a strong role for parliament and parliamentarianism. Liberalism was the philosophy of the emerging property-owning middle class. Walter Bagehot, a strong liberal, wrote that 'the masses of Englishmen are not fit for an elective government.'[10] J.S. Mill proposed a system of suffrage in which additional votes would accrue to persons of merit, defined to include those occupying positions of power and prestige, having university education, etc.[11] Liberalism, like Toryism, was in its origins élitist rather than democratic.

Liberals mistrusted both interests and parties. Members of parliament as independent rational human beings ought to think for themselves, free, unlike members of the earlier unreformed parliament, of allegiance to interest groups and powerful patrons, and free also from the bondage of party discipline. The liberal parliament controlled the cabinet, which Bagehot described as 'a board of control chosen by the legislature, out of persons whom it trusts and knows, to rule the nation.' It was a 'committee of the legislative assembly,' though an extraordinarily powerful one, which had the power to 'dissolve the assembly which appointed it.'[12]

Liberalism was the philosophy of laissez-faire, of small government and a free, market economy under the 'rule of law' established by tradition and parliament. 'The sole end,' according to Mill, 'for which mankind are warranted, individually or collectively, in interfering with the liberty of action of any of their number, is self-protection.'[13] Government exercised a police function, protected property, enforced contracts, provided essential public services, defended the realm, and collected only enough taxes for these limited activities. The public business of parliament was small. The legislative processes and policy-making were slow and gradual, and the policies embodied in major public bills ripened over many years of public and parliamentary discussion before being enacted as legislation.[14]

A substantial proportion of legislation – more than half in the first part of the nineteenth century – was private bills, affecting railways, joint stock companies, land, canals, cities, etc. Debate on most of these private bills was not along party lines; rather disagreement was between competing interests seeking the power to accomplish their commercial ends, for instance, a corporation seeking the authority to build a railway, purchase the right of way with compulsion if necessary, and reap the huge profits of such an enterprise. Many of the most violent conflicts in parliament were between the supporters of competing railway and other interests. Members, despite the liberal ideal of an unattached, disinterested representative, all too often had a pecuniary or other interest in the outcome. MPs were normally eminent and distinguished men, and many were successful business entrepreneurs. 'It is because I have made a fortune and am independent, that I come here to ask for your suffrages to send me to Parliament,' one railway king told the voters when first standing for the House.[15] These private-bill functions were gradually transferred to the executive in the second half of the century. There they were exercised in a quasi-judicial manner, and the substance of parliamentary legislation became more focused on public bills as the age of laissez-faire faded.

Nowadays the liberal, parliament-centred notion has attraction in both Britain and Canada as a direction of reform. It has special force in Canada because of the proximity of the U.S. example, which is legislative-centred in the extreme.

The Collectivist Conception

Collectivist politics developed in the nineteenth and twentieth centuries as an alternative to individualistic liberalism. With the extension of the franchise, the Labour party, which expounded socialism, emerged as a strong force. It was organized on the basis of a powerful extraparliamentary structure and an ideology which, like Toryism, recognized class differences, only here the class which was to be represented was the working class rather than the élite. The Labour party supported strong government intervention in society and the economy to reduce inequalities and improve general welfare. The party was a social movement, and an instrument of social change. Toryism and collectivism, curiously enough, have closer similarities with each other than either has with liberalism.

The Labour party's views on the role of party, parliament, and government were not dramatically different from Toryism; quite the reverse, over much of the spectrum they were compatible. By the twentieth century, the Tories, like the Labour party, supported the general structure of modern parliamentary government: universal suffrage, periodic elections, freedom of speech and press, an elected legislature, and a career civil service. Their belief in strong, disciplined parties, as well as their support of large, interventionist government, set both parties apart from nineteenth-century liberalism.

Both socialists and Tories developed large, broadly based party organizations outside of parliament. Collectivist politics rejected the parliamentarism of the previous century. Members of parliament again became delegates rather than representatives, but delegates of parties instead of constituencies. Party discipline in the House became rigid, and there was a diminished role for both parliament and its members, as the one was replaced as a consultative assembly by the pluralist network of interaction with interest groups, and the others were chained by the whips and party lines. But there still were fundamental ideological differences between the parties. The Conservatives' vision continued to contain hierarchy, social and economic inequality, and government by an élite; Labour was egalitarian, and believed and practised participation and democracy within the party. Canada, as we shall see, has a pronounced collectivist orientation as well.

THE CANADIAN EXPERIENCE

Each of these conceptions of parliamentary government includes a sense of what the important divisions in society are, and how these various divisions ought to be represented and find expression in politics. They postulate the structure and role of, and power relationships between, parliament and government. These, like the description of important divisions in society, vary substantially from one conception to another. The conceptions also establish roles and structures for other political actors, parties, pressure groups, and the public. These too vary substantially. Each includes a rationale and a process by which both general and particular interests are expressed and balanced in decision-making. And each conception embodies a sense of the kinds of issues, problems, and policies with which politics ought to be concerned, and these too vary. It can be seen, then, that the role and power of parliament, within the framework of responsible and representative government, far from being established and immutable, is dependent on a complex series of factors which, like parliament itself, have changed over the centuries as society and the parliamentary system have evolved together. Our challenge now is to disentangle these factors and relationships in Canada.

Because both our society and our parliament are young and transplanted, they do not show the slow historical evolution from one conception to another of their English progenitor. In Canada the evolution of parliamentary institutions was compressed into a very short time period in the nineteenth century and was interwoven with the progression from colony to nation. The beginnings were certainly Tory in the United Empire Loyalist colony of Upper Canada, but Toryism, even when it was predominant, was not without its critics, as the continuing pejorative connotations of the term 'Family Compact' illustrate. From the outset, liberal strands from both Britain and the United States mixed with Toryism, and radicalism, with its insistence on democracy and participation, was also a strong element and made British North America receptive ground for collectivism. A socialist strand in Canadian political culture has contributed to the collectivist orientation as well. These different strands affected the structure of power, the policies, and the rhetoric of Canadian parliamentary government.

The Structure of Power

The structure of power in Canada is executive-centred. It became moulded in this form soon after confederation, and has retained the form to this day. Though Sir John A. Macdonald and his Conservative party ruled Canada for most of the first thirty years after confederation, this apparent stability masks considerable development and change. In the early years especially, Macdonald's government was by no means secure in power. During the session of 1867–72 there were, according to Eugene Forsey,[16] 171 occasions (apart from procedural votes) when supporters of the government voted against it. The dissidents included many prominent supporters of the government, and were sparked by many important issues. The government was frequently defeated, but did not resign.

Macdonald quite naturally sought to strengthen the security of his government, and spent a large proportion of his time and energy in ensuring the support of members, many of whom were 'loose fish' and 'shaky fellows,' whose support was not guaranteed but had to be wooed or bought. Though independent, members of parliament were not the disinterested representatives of liberal theory. Much government activity was involved with the details of services: the location of post offices, railway stations, and harbours, wharves, and ferries and the appointment to positions in government. Many members were 'ministerialists' who would not commit themselves to a party until they had won a seat in an election, after which they would join the winning side.[17] Macdonald not only had to attract individual members to his side, he also had to get and maintain the support of regional leaders, such as Joseph Howe from Nova Scotia and Sir George Etienne Cartier from Quebec. Majority-building and -maintenance within parliament was a large part of the business of government. Macdonald's government was engaged in the task of nation-building through the acquisition of territory, the creation of communications and transportation links, and, later, his National Policy for encouraging the growth of industry. It was also engaged in party-building. By 1878 the government's hold on its supporters was secure. There was little major public legislation. Politics involved the widespread use of funds and other resources by the government to consolidate its power and reward its supporters:

Since there was little government, the burdens of administration and law-making were light, and the leaders of the political party in power, the cabinet, devoted most of their time and energy to the intricate task of holding together a majority in the legislature and of employing, for this purpose, the patronage at the disposal of the government ... the principal role of political life was not the administration of existing law and the making of new laws, but the rewarding of those who took part in public life by the distribution of patronage. Patronage was a natural currency of public life, and the power to dispense it was what, for the most part, gave a cabinet minister the authority and prestige that he desired. The distribution of patronage, Sir Wilfrid Laurier's biographer wrote of the Laurier administration, was the most important single function of the government.[18]

This patronage function was quite un-liberal. It bound member to party, and made him dependent on the largesse of his leaders. It created a pre-liberal, Whig or Tory, patron-and-client relationship which is still of importance in Canadian politics.

Legislative control of the executive was weaker in Canada than in Britain. The legislative assemblies of the colonies and the new western provinces emerged not as a counterbalance to a domineering executive power within the same system, but as a means of wresting power from foreign imperial control in London and later Ottawa; in this struggle the basic structure of responsible parliamentary government was created without the legislatures themselves developing a strong identity separate from the executive.[19] The normal structure of power in Canadian government, particularly at the federal level, but in most of the provinces as well, became a cabinet which controls a majority in the House through rigid party discipline. A party once in power is likely to remain there for a long time, and there is a vast inequality in resources and power between government and opposition. Patronage, which only a governing party can use, has remained a powerful adhesive, bonding government, party workers, and electorate.

The member of parliament, even on the government side, in this structure of power has only a small role in formulating policy. His main task – apart from supporting the party in debates, votes, and committees – is constituency business, both getting government projects in his riding and handling grievances of constituents. The member accepts the yoke of party discipline with little public complaint. Regardless of what his real feelings are, when a vote is recorded in the

House he is loyal to party first and a representative of the people confronting the executive second.

Within government, there is a pronounced emphasis on leadership, and particularly on leadership by the prime minister. Neither his nor the cabinet's role is to implement policies created by the party outside of parliament. The parties outside parliament exist, apart from the New Democratic Party (NDP), primarily as instruments for electoral purposes – for getting and keeping power. Their policy-creating capacity and their ability to control the party's parliamentary leadership, particularly for a government party, is usually so weak as to be non-existent. The prime minister and his cabinet fulfil and are expected to fulfil a central initiating, energizing, and directing role. The structure of power is executive-, not parliament-centred.

The reality of this power structure can be illustrated by using a measure of the experience in office of prime ministers and members of parliament. Tables 1 and 2 compare these for Canada and Britain. It can be seen that there is a marked difference. Canada is characterized by long-term prime ministers and short-term members of parliament, while Britain has the opposite: long-term members of parliament and short-term prime ministers.[20] Four prime ministers have governed Canada for 60 per cent of our history. It takes twice as many, eight, to reach 60 per cent in Britain. No British prime minister has held office even as long as the fourth most durable of our prime ministers, Sir Wilfrid Laurier. Tenure in office has been even shorter in the twentieth century in Britain, where no prime minister has held power for more than 8.8 years, while four Canadian prime ministers in this century have held power for a longer time, including the all-time record setter, Mackenzie King, with 21.5 years. In Canada there is a strong contrast between a few long-term prime ministers at one end of the pole and many short-term ones at the other; British prime ministers are much more clustered near a mean of about six years. A comparably striking contrast would be found between the longevity of governments in the two countries, with Canada being marked by long periods of dominance by one party: the Conservatives for most of the nineteenth century, the Liberals for most of this one. The durability of prime ministers and parties is, of course, interrelated. Both indicate the strength and centralization of power in Canada.

The contrast between parliamentary experience of MPs is equally remarkable. More than half of Canadian MPs have had fewer than five years in parliament; only 23 per cent of British. More than half of British MPs have more than ten years' experience; only 23 per cent of Canadian. The average Canadian member of parliament is a newcomer who is likely to leave before he has served ten years, and is most unlikely to serve for fifteen years. The average British member has been in the House for at least ten years, and is very likely to serve for at least fifteen which,

TABLE 1
Comparison of parliamentary experience of MPs in
the UK and Canada

Years of experience	Percentage of MPs*	
	Canada	UK
0–4	53	23
5–9	24	22
10–14	14	18
15–19	6	17
20–24	2	9
25–30	1	7
over 30	–	4

*This table is based on data from *Dod's Parliamentary Companion* (UK) and the *Canadian Parliamentary Guide*, for 1961, 1971, 1981. There is no significant difference for either parliament between the decades.

bearing in mind the average age of first election to parliament, is not far from retirement age.

This comparison of parliamentary experience of MPs and of time in office of prime ministers shows there is a very different relationship of power between the two bodies in Britain and Canada. In Canada a strong, solidly entrenched prime minister faces an insecure and transient House of Commons; in Britain an insecure and transient prime minister faces a strong and solidly entrenched House. Power is more centralized within the political executive, particularly the prime minister, in Canada than in Britain.

This analysis of MPs and prime ministers is a powerful illustration of the consolidation of power within the political executive in Canada. Many other indicators point in the same direction. For example, as we shall see later, in chapter 5, party discipline has become looser in Britain, and there are many recent examples of government measures being defeated, even important ones, by the defection of their backbenchers. No comparable trend has developed in Canada. Another example: although Britain was behind Canada in creating a comprehensive system of specialist committees in the House of Commons, these committees have already proved to be more autonomous than those in Canada.[21] The British House of Commons is a far more independent-minded and -acting body than the Canadian House.

The imbalance between the power of the executive on the one hand, and

TABLE 2
Comparison of time in office of prime ministers in the UK and Canada since 1867

	Canada			UK		
Rank	Name	Years*	%†	Name	Years*	%†
1	W.L. Mackenzie King	21:5	18	M. of Salisbury	13:9	12
2	Sir John A. Macdonald	19:2	16	W.E. Gladstone	11:11	9
4	P.E Trudeau	15:5	13	W. Churchill	8:8	7
3	Sir W. Laurier	15:3	13	H. Asquith	8:8	7
5	Sir R. Borden	8:10	8	H. Wilson	7:9	7
6	Louis St Laurent	8:7	7	Margaret Thatcher	7:4	5
7	John Diefenbaker	5:10	5	B. Disraeli	6:11	6
8	R.B. Bennett	5:3	4	S. Baldwin	6:10	6
9	L.B. Pearson	5:2	4	J.R. MacDonald	6:9	6
10	Alexander Mackenzie	4:10	4	H. Macmillan	6:9	6
11	John Thompson	2:1	2	C. Attlee	6:2	5
12	Brian Mulroney	2:1	1	D. Lloyd George	5:10	5
13	A. Meighen	1:8	1	E. Heath	3:8	3
14	J.J.C. Abbott	1:4	–	A. Balfour	3:5	3
15	Mackenzie Bowell	1:2	–	N. Chamberlain	2:11	2
16	Joe Clark	0:9	–	Sir H. Campbell-Bannernan	2:4	2
17	Sir Charles Tupper	0:4	–			
18	John Turner	0:2	–			

*Years:months (as of October 1986)
†Per cent of years since 1 July 1867 (Confederation)

parliament and party on the other, which was marked in the nineteenth century, has become even more pronounced during the twentieth with the growth of the civil service. During the 1940s and 1950s Canada developed one of the best civil services in the world. This service had close links with the Liberal government. Many senior civil servants, including Bud Drury, Mitchell Sharp, J.W. Picker-sgill, and Lester Pearson, later became Liberal cabinet ministers. The executive was the focus of political creativity. Policy initiatives did not come from the party outside of parliament, though the extension of the franchise made it more important to appeal to a mass electorate. Some initiatives in the welfare and social services sectors were borrowed from the platform of the Co-operative Common-wealth Federation (CCF) party. Many, including such fundamental innovations as the adoption of Keynesian economics and the stimulation of industrialization, communications, and transportation, found their origins within civil service and cabinet. A Liberal-party and civil-service élite led and guided the transformation of Canada from an agricultural to a modern industrial and welfare economy.

Despite Prime Minister Trudeau's early commitment to participatory democracy and strengthening parliament, the most important institutional reforms of his
government were to strengthen the central agencies of administrative and political
power, particularly the privy council and prime minister's offices. These reforms
have only accentuated the executive-centred aspects of the structure. Prime
Minister Mulroney's tenure has entailed a further strengthening of these central
agencies.

Policies

Because of its origins and geography, Canada always has had an active,
interventionist government. French Canada was an offshoot of the powerful
monarchist state in Europe, and expressed in its society and institutions the
hierarchical society of France, led by the church and hereditary élite. Much of the
older parts of English Canada was settled under the stimulus of the loyalist exodus
from the United States, with the British Crown taking an active role in providing
the infrastructure of settlement and the basic necessities for pioneering families.
From the beginning of settlement, government in what has become Canada
accepted the responsibility of creating the means of transportation and communication – roads, bridges, canals, railways, etc. The image associated with the
American frontier is one of the pioneer coming first and creating settlements, with
government following after; the image associated with the Canadian frontier is of
the surveyor and government coming first, the pioneers after.

The Canadian economy has been capitalist and market-oriented, but with
intervention by government. Sir John A. Macdonald's National Policy encouraged
domestic industry, and the mammoth Canadian Pacific Railway, one of the largest
capitalist corporations in the world, could only have been built because it was
supported by the resources of the national government. But at the same time
government, through other programmes of support for agriculture, fisheries, and
small-scale industry, affected the lives of individuals, families, and small
communities.

Particularly in the post Second World War period this double-barrelled policy
mix of the federal government became a pronounced feature of national life. On
the one hand the government was concerned that the Canadian economy should be
in better shape at the end of this war than it had been at the end of the First World
War, which had not so much reorganized as disorganized the economy. During the
Second World War the government had consciously used the arguments of war
production to create an industrial infrastructure. Some of the new firms were
Crown corporations, others government-supported but private. As a result Canada
ended the war no longer as only an agricultural and staple-product economy, but as
one of the larger industrial forces in the world. Direct support of big business has

continued to be a pronounced feature of Canadian tax, regulatory, and expenditure policies.

At the same time the government introduced important collectivist welfare and labour programmes. Like the policies of industrial support, these had roots in the pre-war period. It was the Conservative government of R.B. Bennett in 1930–5 which first proposed the shift from laissez-faire to the welfare state,[22] and the socialist CCF party which later proposed the same shift in a more orderly and coherent form. The pre-war Rowell-Sirois Commission had made an exhaustive study of the questions of equity and participation in a modernizing economy. During the Second World War the powerful and able federal civil service developed a programme of welfare and labour policies which they hoped would avoid a post-war depression like that which had followed the First World War, and which would ensure prosperity and full employment. This agenda became the basis of the social-policy thrusts of the federal government for more than two decades after the war ended. Its results are impressive. For example, government-financed and -managed hospital and medical-care insurance schemes in Canada mean that for a much smaller proportion of gross national product than in the United States Canadians receive better medical care that is more evenly and equitably distributed and delivered across the nation and social classes.

The policy orientation of Canadian governments has been positive and interventionist, and more in line with collectivism than with nineteenth-century liberalism. In so far as party lines and discipline are rigid in parliament, and the government depends on the support of a mass electorate, the structure is also collectivist. But an essential ingredient of collectivist politics is missing in Canada: active mass parties creating proposals for pragmatic action to move from a laissez-faire to an interventionist government. We have achieved collectivist policies without collectivist politics. A large part of public expenditure is now directed towards welfare, health, and other sorts of collectivist programmes. This collectivism reflects a sense of society which is more socialist and Tory than liberal.

Canadian governments have been strongly pluralist, with close connections with business and commercial interests. But the parties outside of parliament have been weak, and have had neither mass membership nor impact upon policy development. Collectivist policies were not adopted as in Britain through the growth of a mass party which implemented its reform programme when it became government. Rather it was a top-down development, with conceptualization and innovation centred in the civil service and ministry. On the one hand governments have responded to particular interests through pluralist processes of interest-group accommodation. On the other, they have introduced collectivist policies through a dialogue with a mass electorate, although this dialogue has not been conducted through collective political action, but through electoral appeals and mass communication.

The Rhetoric

The time of the growth of responsible government in the colonies of British North America before 1867 coincided with the time of liberal parliamentarism in Great Britain. Lord Durham, who began the process with his report of 1838, called by R.M. Dawson 'the greatest constitutional document in British colonial history,'[23] was a Whig with liberal tendencies. The rhetoric of the struggle for responsible government was liberal and parliament-centred.

Even though the practice moved towards an executive-centred power structure, the rhetoric for the discussion of the Canadian parliamentary system remained, and still is, nineteenth-century liberal and parliament-centred. Edward Blake, in running for parliament in 1867, made it clear to the electorate of South Bruce that he was rich:

He wanted the last fact known; he was totally independent. He had made the resolve, he announced, that he would not enter politics until he had gained a competence of a hundred thousand dollars. Office meant nothing at all to him as a source of personal income; it would be what he felt it should be, a sacrifice and a service. He earned now annually more than the combined salaries that would be paid to a provincial cabinet. All this he hammered home to gaping electors ...[24]

Blake was contrasting his financial independence to the dependence of Macdonald's ministers on railway magnates. Nevertheless, he echoes the arguments of the British candidate quoted earlier. The ideal remained the independent MP of liberalism. R.M. Dawson in his *Government of Canada*, first published in 1947, described the role of members: 'The ideal relationship is one where, as Macauley said, the electorate choose cautiously and confide liberally; then, after the term has expired, they will review the conduct of the member and pronounce on his stewardship as a whole.'[25] Party, which even when Dawson wrote had more effect on re-election than a member's conduct, does not enter into this idealized evaluation.

Both great early textbooks of twentieth-century Canadian political science, R.M. Dawson's *Government of Canada* and J.A. Corry's *Democratic Government and Politics*, were imbued with the spirit and essence of nineteenth-century liberalism. Corry said the basic ideal of government was respect for the individual personality, which was achieved through the ideals of universal freedom, belief in rationality, and ideals of equality, justice, and rule by law. The liberal-democratic legislature is an institution 'constructed under the compulsion of these ideals, and designed to promote their realization.'[26] The cabinet is 'an executive committee of parliament,' and it is 'through the cabinet that parliament effects its criticism and surveillance of daily administration.' Similarly, Dawson states that 'the House of Commons does control the cabinet – rarely by defeating it, often by criticizing it, still more often by the cabinet anticipating criticism before subjecting itself and its acts to the House, and always by the latent capacity of the House to revolt against its leaders.'[27] Even when Dawson was writing the House had not revolted against its leaders for many years. R.J. Van Loon and M.S. Whittington thirty years later nevertheless echo the same view: 'In the British parliamentary system, not only is there no real separation of powers, but the legislative branch directly controls the executive branch.'[28] These views are far from the Tory theory of the relationship between Crown and parliament.

Recently, the special committee on reform of the House of Commons claimed that 'the purpose of reform of the house of commons in 1985 is to restore to private members an effective legislative function, to give them a meaningful role in the formation of public policy and, in so doing, to restore the House of Commons to its rightful place in the Canadian political process.'[29] The recent royal commission on Canada's economic union received many briefs and submissions proposing reform to parliament. All of these argued for movement towards a more parliament-centred approach.

There are many reasons for this overwhelming dominance in rhetoric of the parliament-centred view. There is the historical fact that this was the mode of discourse when the system was created and has remained so. There has been the proximity and strength of the U.S. example, where senators and congressmen are independent and powerful, and because of the saturation of Canadian awareness with products of U.S. mass communication, there has developed a strong belief that members of parliament ought to be much more independent. A recent Gallup poll found that only 7.9 per cent of Canadians felt members should vote as their party requires, a belief totally at odds with the reality that Canadian MPs vote as their party dictates nearly 100 per cent of the time. The rhetoric indicates a direction that change ought to take to persons dissatisfied with the present workings of the parliamentary system. And, even if they were strongly opposed to whole-scale movements towards the U.S. congressional system, few would argue against at least a little more autonomy and freedom for the individual members of parliament. But the contradictions between the parliament-centred rhetoric and the executive-centred reality create obstacles to reform.

The Canadian Parliament and Its Reform
In the company of the world's legislatures, the Canadian parliament is old and stable. This fact is often obscured because comparisons are normally made with

the British parliament, which is venerable indeed, and the U.S. Congress, which would also rank among the top handful of legislatures in terms of age. Not only is the Canadian parliament itself old, but the executive-centred structure of power crystallized into much its present form in the first decades after confederation. And activist government which at the same time aids individuals and supports big business and large-scale corporate enterprise was part of Macdonald's policies and can be traced back even earlier, to colonial times.[30]

This pattern of power and policies does not, however, fit into Beer's categories. Whereas in Britain parliamentary government evolved over the centuries, with one configuration of parliamentary government gradually replacing another as society, culture, and the economy changed, in Canada the development of parliamentary institutions was compressed into a short period, in which there was no easy fit between the theory and practice of government. The parliamentary system developed under the influence of liberal rhetoric which postulated one form of behaviour, a power structure emerging out of colonial times which created another, and needs, problems, and a political culture which pushed towards policies from still another style of parliamentary government. There is in Canada, consequently, a mixture in which we have identified three strands: a parliament-centred rhetoric, an executive-centred power structure, and a collectivist approach to policies.

These three strands do not compete with one another in the electoral arena. Parties do not consistently propose one conception of policies and representation. Rather, the different conceptions are, to a large extent, outside and independent of parties. The NDP is certainly most collectivist in its view of policies and party structure, but its views on the role of parliament and the structure of power are not now strongly collectivist. The Liberal party and the Progressive Conservatives do not espouse a coherent conception of parliament, power, and policies. An opposition party normally talks about reform in parliament-centred terms, but when in government does nothing to weaken the strong, centralized executive power. Conceptions of representation do not so much *compete* for legitimacy as approaches to governance as *conflict* in terms of theory and practice. The conflicts in approaches to representation are not articulated and visible between parties, but are embedded and hidden within the whole complex structure, practice, and understanding of parliamentary government. The Canadian parliamentary system, in short, has a parliament-centred rhetoric and mode of thought, but without the reality of independent MPs, parliamentarian or small-government allocative politics. It has an executive-centred structure of political power, without the accepted élitism and ordered hierarchical society of Tory ideology. And it has collectivist policies without mass parties and collectivist politics.

This is not to say that the Canadian parliamentary system is at fault because it fails to reproduce more closely what exists or has existed in Britain, any more than that it should copy the U.S. system. The stability and continuity of the Canadian pattern are evidence that it not only functions but enables a great many needs and demands to be satisfied. But there are some worrisome features in the conflicts and contradictions, particularly in the discrepancy between the rhetoric and the practice.

The rhetoric fails to describe or explain how the Canadian parliamentary system actually works. It creates an anomaly between how people think parliament and members of parliament ought to behave and how they actually do behave. It is inherently critical, and less concerned with understanding or explaining what we have than with proposing change. It is not surprising that Canada has not found a fulfilling, purposeful role for parliament and its members. The rhetoric demands that the individual MP should think for himself, be independent of party, and that parliament be where great decisions are discussed and made. The power structure gives members a subordinate role and disciplines them to party lines, puts the focus for discussion as well as decision in the executive rather than in parliament, and assigns government the role of benevolent paternalism. Collectivist policies make government big, activist, and interventionist, but neglect the mechanism of strong mass parties which link citizens to government. The individual MP is caught between a rhetoric telling him to be independent and think for himself, a power structure which leaves him with little to do except work on constituency matters and worry about re-election (which, with the 40 per cent turnover at elections, is a real concern), and policies with widespread appeal, but with which he has little connection, and which link government directly with citizens, bypassing MPs and parliament.

Virtually every proposal for reform of parliament contains, either explicitly or implicitly, the goals of members with greater autonomy and independence and a parliament which is a decision-maker as well as a decision-discusser. The focus of reform is on such items as encouraging more free votes, creating stronger and more independent committees, and giving MPs greater resources for research. But despite twenty years of reform there is still dissatisfaction with parliament. Reforms have caused only a slight, if any, shift of power from the executive towards parliament. The British comparison shows that party discipline can be weakened, and committees made more autonomous, without deviating in any serious way from the principles of responsible parliamentary government. But even with intensive efforts at reform, Canada has not shown a comparable change. The reasons for the failure are powerful. They lie in the contradictions between the rhetoric and reality.

Parliament-centred theory postulates strong independent members of parliament. But, as we have seen, Canadian MPs are, on average, short-term members whose parliamentary careers are in all likelihood brief. This turnover militates against both strength and independence. Influence and the capacity to exert power in any organization to a large extent come from the quality of manpower, length of tenure, knowledge of the system, creation of informal contacts and relationships, obligations, and quid pro quos. In dealing with the prime minister, cabinet, and civil service, the short-term Canadian MP is at a disadvantage. He is weak because his past experience and future security are limited. Similarly, because his tenure is brief, his independence is lessened. Support, comfort, and tangible rewards from their party are often important to the well-being of members after they leave parliament. These rewards are, in turn, related to the extent to which the MP has been a loyal party man, that is, has not exhibited contrariness and independence. The rigidity of party discipline is closely related to the insecurity of seats, and the former is not likely to change without change in the latter.

A strong, independent legislature is more compatible with pluralist than collectivist policies. Its business is that of distribution of resources between private groups rather than an expression of an overriding public interest. Strengthening of parliament, and making members more independent, might well have the unwanted consequence of making Canadian politics more sensitive to private interests and less responsive to the more general interest. This consequence could, in turn, be harmful, not only to the collective public, but also to the government, which would gain the support of powerful interests with few members but lose the support of the public at large, whose perceived interests would be opposed to those of particular groups. This is an especial risk in a country like Canada, where political parties, because they are not organized on a mass basis, cannot express a collective public interest, and the organizations which have a large membership and attempt to express a general interest are weak, while groups with a narrow concern are strong and well organized.[31]

The peculiar problems faced by the Progressive Conservative party when it assumes office are directly related to the sensitivity of parliament to particular interests. Two crucial issues which cost the 1979 Clark government public support, the decision to 'privatize' Petro Canada and the decision to move the Canadian embassy to Jerusalem, both had been decided while the party was out of office. In opposition a party is especially sensitive to discontented minorities and is all too likely to confuse their shrill persistent voices with the more general public interest. The Mulroney government has found the same difficulty in putting forward policies that support a general public interest rather than particular and advantaged groups. The perception of what ought to be done has varied between government and opposition in Canada, not so much because of deep-seated ideology as because of position: government must express and try to respond to a perception of a general public interest; a long-term opposition will hear above all the voices of special interests whose demands have not been met by the government.

This analysis shows that there are deep-seated obstacles to creating a much stronger parliament in Canada. Problems in the security, independence, and role of the member of parliament put him in a position of weakness and dependence that cannot be changed either by wishful thinking or by procedural reform. The structure of parties and interest groups would likely mean that the greater the voice of individual members and committees in policy decisions, the more these decisions will move away from attempts to express a general, collective interest. This shift would not please the electorate. The rhetoric of parliamentary reform is frustrated not so much by the stupidity and obstinacy of those in power as by real constraints within the system of representation and by a policy orientation that is incompatible with parliament-centred rhetoric.

These factors will be examined more extensively in later chapters. The important points to bear in mind are:

1 Proposals for reform are ideological as well as technical. There is a close relationship between the kind of parliament Canada has, the kind of political parties, the role of MPs, and the policies of government. If the conventional rhetoric were to be translated into practice, and Canada were to move towards a parliament-centred configuration of parliamentary government, we would also move towards more emphasis on pluralist, interest-group politics and away from a centrally expressed collectivist public interest.

2 A parliament more in line with the parliament-centred rhetoric must have strong, secure, independent MPs who can follow their own path. They must be able to choose and enjoy a career path as a parliamentarian outside the paths of advancement controlled by parties and whips. Members are not in this position in Canada, nor are they likely to be unless a massive change takes place in how the electorate makes its decisions.

3 Collectivist policies in Canada, such as universal pre-paid health and hospital insurance, welfare programmes, old-age pensions, and family allowances, are a product of the centralized power structure as well as of the collectivist and socialist strains in Canadian political culture. A consequence of a pronounced move towards a parliament-centred system would be the likelihood of a change in policies away from this collectivist orientation.

The Canadian habit in making reform has been to ignore the interdependence and interrelationship between policies and structure of power. Reform of parliament has attempted to move in one direction, reform of policy-making in another. The sources of failures both to and of reform and of many of the problems of policy-making and government are to be found in these incompatibilities and contradictions. To be successful reforms must be made in a broader context of understanding. An important challenge is not (to paraphrase Marx) to propose reforms to parliament, for countless critics and observers have done this, but to understand it, for only through understanding can a better system be made. In the past, the expectations and hopes of reformers have all too often been frustrated because they have failed to appreciate the reality of how the Canadian parliamentary system works, and the forces that determine the behaviour of members and government.

3

Parliament and the Party System

The most important determinants of the control and use of power in the Canadian parliamentary system are the political parties. Elections are more a matter of voters choosing between parties and party leaders than between individual candidates. The winning party becomes the government, with a monopoly over executive power and domination of parliament. Within the House of Commons, the basic structure of proceedings is the adversarial format of contest and debate between the government and opposition parties. Issues, representation, elections, and proceedings are all structured around, and dependent for their functioning on, the existence and strength of the political parties. The political parties are not only powerful, but also long-lived. The Liberals and Conservatives have been with us since soon after confederation, while even the young NDP and Social Credit party came into existence (recognizing that the NDP evolved from the CCF) well before the birth of most of the electorate.

The dominance of party and partisanship in Canadian politics means that Canadian MPs vote in parliament as their party dictates. This they do faithfully, to the point that for more than a hundred years no government in Canada has been defeated in the House of Commons through the defection or abstention of its members. Nor is faithfulness in the opposition much weaker. This guarantee of support by its MPs enables a majority government to rule with security and comfort. Though the discipline of party is at times confining for members of parliament, parties also organize members into cohesive units which provide the satisfaction of collective action. This chapter will examine the parties and party system in Canada. The two succeeding chapters will look more closely at the elected members and their place in the processes of representation.

THE PARTY SYSTEM

The two-party system has often been viewed as a natural product of the parliamentary form of government. The division of the House into government and opposition sides, so the argument goes, leads to a comparable reduction of opinions and allegiances to two teams, as does the simple plurality, single-member constituency basis of representation, with its tendency towards rewarding the larger parties at the expense of the smaller.[1] In Canada, however, experience has confounded this traditional theory. Since 1921 there always have been more than two, and as many as five, parties represented in the Commons. From 1957 on, in particular, there have been many minority governments, in which the third and fourth parties were important not only because of the numbers of their elected representatives, but also because they held the balance of power: only with their support could one of the major parties maintain the confidence of the House. Six of the eleven elections since 1953 have resulted in minority governments. This fact has led many observers to argue that Canada has changed from a two-party system to a multi-party system[2] in which no single party can be assured of, or is ever likely to get, a majority of the seats in the House. Minority government, a situation likely to arise under a multi-party system, has sometimes been seen as a problem and an aberration from the classical model, and sometimes as a natural and not unhealthy form of parliamentary government.[3]

However, in spite of the fact that most federal elections in recent decades have produced minority parliaments, the further fact remains that most of the time Canada has not had a minority government. For eighteen out of the twenty-eight years between 1957 and 1985, or nearly two-thirds of the time, the government has had a majority; for only ten years has it been a minority. Further, for twenty out of the twenty-eight years the Liberal party has formed the government, continuing a domination in federal politics which it has enjoyed since 1896. At no time did a Liberal government in a minority parliament form a governing coalition. Rather, it retained power exclusively in its own hands, relying on the reluctance of third parties to defeat a minority government too soon, or making whatever concessions or bargains it needed to retain minor-party support covertly. There was no open sharing of power.

This dominance of the Liberal party, and its virtual monopoly over executive power, has led many analysts to argue that Canada has neither a two – nor a multi-party system. Rather, it has a 'one-party dominant' system in which the Liberals, to use R. Whitaker's phrase, are 'the Government Party.'[4] This system, it is argued, is quite different from either the classical two-party or the multi-party system because there is, regardless of how many political parties are recognized or hold seats in the House, in reality only one essential party, the one that forms the government. It is long-lived and monopolizes political power. The opposition parties are, even in the long run, weak and unimportant. The existence of a 'government party' is a manifestation of the executive-dominant power structure.

These interpretations of the Canadian party system contain different viewpoints on how political power ought to be controlled in Canada. The two-party–system interpretation suggests that there ought to be fairly evenly balanced 'ins' and 'outs,' each with a solid base in cultural, economic, and regional groups, which compete with one another for the support of a volatile, floating portion of the electorate. The success of a party ought to depend on its ability to retain its base support and devise policies and programmes, and on leadership that will attract and capture the volatiles. The parties ought to alternate in government at frequent intervals. The two parties should be more or less evenly matched, and their success should depend upon the skill with which they play the political game. The electorate is the real wielder of power through its ability to make a free choice in elections.

The multi-party interpretation suggests that the differences between various groups and factions in the nation are too great to be integrated into two parties. More are needed. The third and fourth parties can represent many different sorts of bases. The CCF-NDP developed as an ideologically based party, although one with support from a social class (labour) and geographical regions (British Columbia, Saskatchewan, Manitoba, and parts of Ontario). Social Credit also professed an ideology, although the dominant characteristic of their support was regional (Alberta and later Quebec). The Progressives were primarily an agricultural and western party, although they also had support in rural eastern Canada as well.

In the past, defenders of the parliamentary two-party system have viewed the multi-party system as inferior because it leads to divisiveness and weak government.[5] More recently, however, many analysts have come to view the multi-party system as valuable in its own right, with virtues the two-party system does not share. A. Lijphart in particular has argued that, contrary to the parliamentary format, majoritarian government is a consensus model in which there are many political parties, no single one of which dominates or monopolizes the use of power.[6] Power is shared between parties through a coalition government. The parties can be based on any combination of cultural, economic, regional, religious, or other factors. Integration and consent come through the open compromises and sharing of power in the governing coalition. In the consensus approach, the individual citizen has influence over government because he belongs to a political party closely aligned with his central concerns and interests, and this party participates in the exercise of power through membership in a coalition. The parties left out of the coalition at one point will likely participate at some future time. Thus, power is dispersed through many parties representing varied interests and groups, rather than being concentrated in a single party which forms the government. Lijphart argues that consensus rather than majoritarian government is appropriate in non-homogeneous, plural societies, where there are many groups and interests which will inevitably be left out and neglected by a ruling majoritarian party.

The complexity and variety of Canada make Lijphart's view appealing here. Nevertheless, in spite of the multiplicity of groups and cleavages[7] and their representation by multiple parties at the federal level, political power has continued to be controlled in the majoritarian, parliamentary manner. We have had, for much of the recent period, the numerous parties of the consensus format of democracy, but not the attendant power sharing. Further, at the federal level, power, for most of Canada's history, has been controlled by a dominant governing party. Canada has had neither a balance of two parties alternating in office nor a sharing of power in coalitions between several parties. The balance of power in parliament is uneven, and the various parties have quite different characteristics, depending upon their place in the hierarchy. With its concentration of power in the cabinet, the parliamentary system requires a strong government. This Canada has had. The parliamentary system does not require a strong opposition, and Canadian oppositions have often not been strong.

The Government Party

The government party, as described by Whitaker, is a 'cadre' party.[8] It is dominated by its parliamentary leadership (the cadre), and the members of the party outside parliament, whether rank-and-file or constituency officers, have little say in policy or party finances. There is a strong emphasis on the role of the leader, who personifies the party as a powerful governing vehicle. The party forms the government, and much of its organization, functions, and characteristics are related to getting, using, and maintaining power. The parliamentary branch of the government party dominates the party outside and is in turn dominated by the prime minister and cabinet. A major instrument for accomplishing this domination is government patronage. Loyalty to leaders and party is rewarded through appointment as judge, ambassador, member of board or commission, or other position of emolument and prestige. In this tradition, Prime Minister Trudeau, on his leaving office, ensured that several hundred of his supporters in parliament and of the functionaries who served his government gained this sort of reward. Other party supporters are rewarded with government contracts or part-time jobs.

Within the government, ministers serve as the spokesmen for regions and interests. Not the least of their functions is the 'ministerialist'[9] one of ensuring that their regions, and party supporters within their regions, receive an appropriate share of rewards and government goods and services. The relationship between politicians and the populace consequently becomes one of patron-client, with the personal relationship, including services and favours, becoming an important factor affecting the use of government powers and the distribution of resources.

The government party occupies the centre of the political spectrum. It exists in a polity where there are multiple cleavages – linguistic, religious, regional, class – but where the class cleavages (which could otherwise be represented by nation-wide class parties) are not dominant. The party becomes a means of accommodating the various élites, and satisfying the wants of the special interests they represent.[10] The ministerialist character of the government enables interests, particularly regional ones, to be represented. The government party must perform a delicate balancing act. On the one hand, it must satisfy powerful economic and commercial interests whose financial and other support is vital to survival. On the other hand, it must satisfy enough of the electorate to remain in office. One way it satisfies the electorate is through patron-client relationships. Another is through welfare and other redistributive and equality-oriented programmes which have a wide popular appeal. The government's policies can be and even are likely to be directed both towards support of wealthy business interests and towards the mass electorate.

The governing party has no explicit or consistent ideological or philosophical framework. Rather, it straddles the middle and assimilates whatever it is expedient to include at either, or both, sides of the centre. Opposition parties, left, right, or centre, have a problem in defining their own position because the government party occupies all desirable ground. Arguments between parties as a result become squabbles over details rather than arguments over direction and principles. Policy-making, because of the weak party organization outside parliament and the absence of serious debate between parties, becomes centralized within the government. Policies are made within the bureaucracy, or between bureaucrats and ministers, rather than through public discussion. Politics turns into bureaucracy. The electorate does not participate in policy-making either through party membership or through other channels. Rather, it is the passive recipient of government programmes, policies, and, for those who have served the party, rewards. The dominant political values in the electorate become deference and unreflective loyalty.

Whitaker's analysis produces a reasonably accurate picture of the federal Liberal party, and of other dominant government parties such as the Ontario Progressive Conservatives, between 1942 and 1985. The kind of politics it portrays does not have intellectual depth or excitement, but appears 'provincial' and 'sordid.'[11] Patronage and details rather than policy are the focus of public attention. The electorate is passive, at best 'quasi-participative,' and even if it is active within the governing party it has little say in the decisions that affect it. The party is powerful and dominates the political scene. However, there is an obverse to that power. The basis of its strength is that it holds office and can use the resources of government for its own purposes. When it loses power it no longer has these resources available (although some, like Senate appointments, can endure for decades), and is in danger of losing not only its power but also its support. Success is its *raison d'être*.

This sort of party system, Whitaker argues, finds fertile soil in a country with multiple cleavages and a federal structure. The government party does not transcend federal-provincial differences and serve to integrate the two levels. Rather, the federal government party deals with the provinces through executive federalism outside party politics. Provincial parties of the same name as the government party at the federal level do not work closely with it. It even prefers to deal with provincial governments of another name. The government party is powerful and survives partly because it has a perpetual opposition in the provinces, and for provincial governments to have the same name could prove to be a handicap.

The 'government party' analysis is not entirely satisfactory. It does not adequately explain why opposition parties remain weak, or why politics with substance and dignity does not replace the often sorry spectacle of Canadian politics. Nevertheless, Whitaker's interpretation is powerful and advances our understanding. His conclusions encapsulate much of modern Canadian politics:

The curious lack of definition of Canadian parties, which has troubled so many observers of our politics, is only reinforced as the evidence concerning their structure is marshalled. The Liberal party was an organization seeking not so much to consolidate its distinct partisan identity as to embed itself within the institutional structures of government. Its fulfilment was not so much organizational survival as it was institutionalization as an aspect of government: control over recruitment channels to senior levels of office. The deadening of political controversy, the silence, the greyness which clothed political life at the national level in the 1950s, were reflections of a Liberal ideal of an apolitical public life. In place of politics there was bureaucracy and technology. This in no sense meant that Canada stood still. Profound changes were taking place in the nation's political economy. But these changes tended to take place outside the realm of traditional political debate. Instead, it was between the great bureaucracies, whether public (federal and provincial) or private (Canadian and American), that debate and policy refinement took place. The Liberal party had truly become the Government party – an instrument for the depoliticization and bureaucratization of Canadian public life.[12]

A dominant governing party is characteristic of the Canadian experience at the provincial as well as the federal level. The Progressive Conservative government of Ontario by 1985 had held power for more than forty years, since before most of the electorate was born. Like the federal Liberal party, the Ontario Progressive Conservative party spread octopus-like through the institutions and processes of government, and had established countless and profoundly important interconnections and relationships between itself, the bureaucracy, and the private sector. It too had shown an amazing ability to regenerate itself through new leadership and new policies. And it as well benefited from a divided opposition.

Perhaps the most important unanswered question is not *how* a government party operates, for Whitaker has done a good job of describing this, but *why* the party system is so asymmetrical. After all, our parliamentary system is based on competition between parties, and competition only exists, at least in the longer run, when there is some measure of equality and balance in power between the contestants.

The Opposition

An effective opposition is crucial to the operation of parliamentary government. Without a strong opposition, the parliamentary system will perform the function of creating a legitimate government but it is unlikely to make the government behave and cannot produce a credible alternative to the governing party. The blame for many of the apparent problems of our parliamentary system can be attributed to the weakness of the opposition. It is in large part their inability to present serious and attractive policy alternatives, to develop leadership, to disclose the flaws in the government, and in short to persuade the electorate that they are more fit to hold power than the government party, that makes our parliament and provincial legislatures ineffective and irrelevant to the major decisions and issues in politics.

A pattern which crystallized soon after confederation has persisted to the present.[13] Sir John A. Macdonald's government was a coalition of various elements which his skills as leader brought together. They included the conservative French-Canadian Catholic *bleus* under Cartier, the Ontario Tories and anti-Catholic Orangemen, the large business interests of Montreal under Galt, and others, including Hincksite Reformers under Baldwin from Canada West (southwestern Ontario). This disparate collection was held together by the National Policy, with its double thrust of protection of Canadian industry and expansion of Canada and the railways to the west, and ample small-scale patronage at the local level to maintain commitment and electoral support. Both big business and individuals and small business gained from supporting the government. Macdonald's governing Conservative party straddled the centre geographically, economically, and socially. The opposition was made up of what was left over, including the Clear Grit radicals of Canada West, the anticlerical *rouges* of Quebec, and other fringe elements.

A challenge constantly facing Macdonald was to maintain the allegiance and support of elements and leaders already within his coalition, and to lure in others. The 'ministerialist' politics of the early parliaments enabled individual MPs and factions to be bought by patronage and position, and under these influences Macdonald's Conservative party became the prototype for Whitaker's 'Government Party.' The opposition was not really a party: it was united by neither philosophy nor organization nor leadership nor demographic homogeneity. The only unifying factor it possessed was that it was against Macdonald's government. The Conservative party ruled for thirty years after confederation. Its one loss of power came in 1873, when its support in parliament disintegrated through the defection of groups because of the scandals relating to railway construction. The Liberal party under Alexander Mackenzie, which replaced it, never became an effective government. It had no clear policies. The party's leadership was weak and marred by conflicts between Mackenzie and Edward Blake. Its loss in the election of 1878 consigned it to opposition status for nearly twenty years. It remained a loose collection of incompatible elements, as little able to use and retain power as it was able to find agreement among its parts.

These same imbalances and contrasts between government and opposition have characterized the Canadian parliament in most of the twentieth century, only with the Liberals as the governing party; and while the Progressive Conservatives have remained the major opposition party, since 1921 there have been at least one, and as many as three, other small parties in the opposition. The Progressive Conservative party in particular has been marked by weak and transient leadership.[14] When it gained office under Diefenbaker in 1957, and soon after, in 1958, obtained the largest majority up to then in Canadian history, it had severe internal problems and was unable to use power effectively. The large French-Canadian element felt, and was, alienated from the party leadership, and in the election of 1962 dwindled from fifty to fourteen MPs. From 1963 to 1984, the Liberal party to all intents and purposes governed Canada. Its support in parliament was predominantly from Quebec and Ontario. The opposition was composed of the elements left out of that dominant central coalition. The Progressive Conservatives became concentrated in the west.

The NDP has been a small persistent group of the left, more sympathetic to the Liberals than to the Progressive Conservatives (especially in a minority parliament), but unwilling to join with either major party. The Social Credit party, originally based in the west, reached a peak of thirty MPs in 1963. The Quebec Créditistes separated in 1968, and after the party had played a key role in the defeat of the Clark Progressive Conservative government in parliament in 1979, it lost all its representation in the election of 1980.

Whether the opposition has been two or four parties, it has retained important characteristic features. First the opposition, as began in Macdonald's era, has been made up of what has been left out of the dominant coalition. For modern Liberal governments, this coalition has included Quebec and the prosperous and big-city parts of Ontario. The west, the poorer and rural constituencies in Ontario, and parts of rural Quebec have been opposition, as have been the Maritimes and Newfoundland, where the Progressive Conservatives have won more seats than the Liberals in all elections since 1963 except in 1980. In more ways than one, the Liberals have represented the affluent comfortable centre in Canada, the opposition the periphery and have-nots. Although recent Liberal governments have had their power base in a coalition of Ontario and Quebec, historically, the majority of Ontario MPs have often been on the opposition side, much more often than have been Quebec MPs.

Second, there was no cohesiveness or common denominator to the opposition. The fact that it was divided into several parties is one proof of this. The ideological split, with the NDP to the left of the Liberal government, the Progressive Conservatives to the right, created a situation where each opposition party had more in common with the government than with the other opposition parties.

Third, the major opposition party, the Progressive Conservatives, was itself seriously divided. Its main block of seats in parliament was in the west. The average number of seats the party has won in the west since 1962 is forty-five, in Ontario, thirty-three, in Quebec, four, in the Maritimes and Newfoundland, eighteen. The western Progressive Conservative members of parliament have not only been chronically out of power, but they represent a region which historically has held a grudge against central Canada, a region which under recent Liberal governments had virtually no representation in the cabinet, which has been a federal-provincial battleground in energy policy, and which, despite its affluence has a boom-and-bust economy and has felt alienated and victimized by other regions. Demographic and electoral realities make it obligatory that any party that wishes to govern Canada must create a viable long-term coalition between several regions, and that these must include substantial portions of Quebec and Ontario. The attitudes and policies which western Progressive Conservative MPs bring to Ottawa do not, in many instances, fit with those of central Canada. For example, the energy policy devised by the Conservatives in opposition became the policy of the short-lived Clark government of 1979, and the attempt to implement it was the most important single policy leading to the government's downfall. The problems of creating an energy policy acceptable to central Canada as well as to the western branch of the party had been ignored while the party was in opposition, but could not be avoided by the party as government.[15] Difficulties with language policy have bedevilled the party. Its western branch, if it wishes to remain inside a government party, must temper its peculiarly western outlook to make a workable coalition with parts of central Canada under a discipline which it could neglect in opposition. Frequent changes of leader, and continuing internal divisions, have handicapped the party for generations.

The main factor uniting the opposition, and in particular the Progressive Conservatives, has been that they are in opposition, and critical of the way power is used by the central government. H. Thorburn has admirably summed up the differences between the parties:

Taken globally, we can hypothesize that Canada has three types of parties: the normal government party (Liberal), the normal opposition party (Conservative) and the third party that has virtually no chance of forming the government or official opposition, but which has continuing strength (NDP, and perhaps Social Credit) ... Hypothesizing further, we can say that the Liberals are perceived to be the successful party and therefore draw to themselves those people who most want to be on the winning side, to be close to power, and who are most prone to accept the status quo. Conversely, the federal Tories draw those people who seek to take issue with the government in an ideologically conformist manner, and who are prepared to be on the losing side most of the time (in federal politics).

Extending the hypothesis further, one can say that the third parties will attract those who are reconciled to being on the losing side for the present and foreseeable future, and who take their critique of the status quo beyond the point of ideological conformity. The NDP supporter is, obviously, prepared to accept and advocate a greater degree of ideological deviance (socialism) than the Liberal or Conservative supporter.[16]

Thorburn's analysis suggests that the main policy differences between the parties are not ideological, regional, economic, or cultural, but in their attitude towards the way political power is used by government: supportive, critical, or reformist. This sort of attitude, the unarticulated emotional substructure of the party, permeates MPs, party workers and organizers, supporters and sympathizers. Because it is so firmly embedded, and so fundamental to the meaning of political participation to members of the party, it is difficult to change.

The Problem of Inequality
Even if the Thorburn hypothesis that supporters of the different parties have different attitudes towards power is someday proved incorrect, there is no question that relationships of MPs to power vary widely, depending on which party they support. If there were frequent alternations of government, the imbalance of power between government and opposition would be redressed over time. But one-party domination means that there is an inequality of expectation as well as position.

This inequality of expectation is profound. It is likely that at some point in his career an MP belonging to the dominant party will participate in the exercise of power. About 20 per cent of the governing party will be members of the cabinet. One will be speaker. Another, government whip. Twenty or so will be parliamentary secretaries. Another twenty will be committee chairmen. The caucus will include some former cabinet ministers and more future ones. Because parliamentary secretaries rotate in office far more rapidly than ministers, there will be many former parliamentary secretaries in the party. In all, about seventy MPs, or one-third to one-half the caucus of the governing party, will hold a position of some power in government, and many more will either have held power, or will hold it some time in the not too distant future. In addition, members of the government caucus have a peculiarly privileged position because they hear legislative proposals before they are introduced into parliament. Although this preview does not often produce changes in legislation, and functions more as a means of generating and organizing support within caucus than as a policy-making device, it does give all government MPs an opportunity to discuss government proposals in private with cabinet ministers. The weekly sessions of both caucus and caucus committees thus enable government backbenchers to participate in and influence the processes of governing. An MP on the government side has a good chance of holding a position of power; those left out have a good prospect of achieving a position of power someday, and backbenchers have more direct contact with cabinet. Nor should the prospects of future rewards be neglected. A very high proportion of government MPs will someday, when their parliamentary career ends, obtain a position of reward (patronage) as judge, member of board or commission, senator, or ambassador. These sorts of rewards and promises of future rewards make the expectations of government MPs great indeed.

Of the positions open to opposition members, the most important are those of party leader, House leader, whips, and other officers of the party in parliament, including the opposition frontbench spokesmen. Of these, only the party leaders and House leaders receive additional pay. An opposition member usually becomes deputy speaker. The chairman of the public accounts committee is an opposition member, as are, on occasion, the deputy chairmen of committees, and in a recent innovation, some of the chairmen of the new legislative committees. These rewards are far fewer than those available to the government, whether measured in terms of numbers, power and influence, or proportion of MPs benefiting or likely to benefit from them. In addition, the opposition caucus has no special advantaged position in looking at government legislative proposals, which it receives at the time they are made public, that is, after they have been considered by the government caucus.

In Britain, there is less inequality of position and expectation. The speaker is often from the opposition side, as are a large proportion of committee chairmen. Government backbenchers, unlike Canadian practice, do not receive and discuss legislation before it is introduced in the House. But, above all, power frequently shifts from side to side in elections: since the Second World War there have been six changes of government, and the Labour party, the less dominant of the two major parties, has held power (as of 1984) for seventeen years, or nearly 40 per cent of the time. These seventeen years were in three periods, none of which lasted fewer than five years. Over the years, power has been reasonably evenly shared in Britain, and MPs on both sides have comparable expectations of someday being on the winning side and obtaining a post in the ministry. This expectation is all the more realistic because the average British MP remains in the House far longer than his Canadian counterpart, and perhaps is one of the reasons they choose to stay in parliament.

In Britain, an MP on either side of the House will belong to a party which has actively participated in formulating many policies and programmes. His party while in power will have been responsible for administering even those programmes which it did not initiate. Regardless of his party affiliation, he will have a commitment to much of what the government does. In fact, the range of policies about which there is great disagreement between the two sides in Britain is not large, and there is a consensus between both parties in support of the bulk of government activities. Disagreements between the parties centre on a narrow band of cleavages, representing for the most part ideological and class differences.

Although party links in the u.s. Congress are very loose, both congressmen and senators actively participate in the processes of policy-making and control of government. Legislators from either party, simply because they wield power, have commitments to the activities of government. There is more equality of position than in Canada, and more commitment to a political career.

In contrast, the inequalities between the two sides in the Canadian parliament affect attitudes and commitments to government. The government side supports. The government is the author of virtually all programmes, policies, and administration; what it does not like it can change. The Progressive Conservative opposition, in comparison, was responsible for virtually nothing. It was a spectator, vocal and normally critical, while policies were made and the business of government carried out. Its role was to attack and criticize, not to create and make successful.

Politics is, with good reason, called the art of compromise. Governance is a continuous balancing act between competing and conflicting interests, where limited financial and human resources must be juggled to satisfy unlimited and often opposing claims. An expenditure in one area will raise complaints in another. Labour versus capital, east versus west, big city versus small town, welfare versus lower taxes; the whole, enormous gamut of government services and programmes is constantly being disputed. A government must continually make a mix of trade-offs and compromises between these competing interests which will ensure that the electorate, although never entirely satisfied, is satisfied enough that it will return them to power.

Criticism is a different art. It involves pointing out the inconsistencies and partial commitment involved in compromises. It includes proving that one group is neglected, another favoured. It does not, however, necessarily involve compromise and the melding of diverse viewpoints and interests into workable, cohesive, and responsible policies. In Canada, it rarely does this. The Conservative party has been accused of having an 'opposition mentality,' or 'opposition syndrome,' of constantly opposing, rarely supporting or proposing, without a consistent ideological or interest basis for the positions taken, and without recognition or acceptance of the compromises necessary for political success.[17] The party has been essentially negative, united only in agreeing that the government was bad. Its positive policy proposals were, in comparison with its criticisms, few and unimportant.

Opposition mentality has developed because of the imbalance between the long-lived, dominant government party and the weak opposition. Because of the inequalities of position and expectation, the opposition is not subjected to the discipline of compromise, as is the government. Groups within it are able to express their views without the opposition being forced to answer the question of whether they too would have to make the compromises involved if they were in government. This tendency is exacerbated by the adversarial format of parliament, which makes it perforce the role, and even the obligation, of the opposition to criticize and oppose. The press and its own supporters are highly critical if an opposition appears to agree too much with the government. Most opposition members normally have never held power, and have little commitment to making the government work.

Opposition mentality has been counterbalanced on the government side by 'arrogance,' the 'Liberal assumption that their party was the only one capable of governing in Canada.'[18] Parliament, by 1984, became to the Liberal government an unpleasant and unfortunately not always avoidable last step in the policy-making process. Its purpose was to rubber-stamp decisions made elsewhere, after serious discussion in the important national forums – the civil service, federal-provincial meetings, private consultations, and the upper reaches of the party leadership. Liberal arrogance and opposition mentality fed on and reinforced each other.

With, on the one side, an opposition mentality leading to obstruction and delay, and on the other side, government arrogance treating it with disdain, parliament was not a happy place. The adversarial component of politics was not only maintained but exaggerated even though for the most part elections were not much of a contest. Victory came to the opposition not in elections but in parliament, where success became perversely equated with slowing down proceedings and even preventing the government from getting its legislation through the House.

Thus, opposition strategy became not only the legitimate and necessary function of pointing out the flaws and weaknesses in the government's proposals, but the wilful and often mischievous prevention of decisions by parliament. For its part, the Liberal government, where possible, avoided parliament, in part by introducing omnibus legislation to get as much passed in one bill as possible, or by writing bills in general enabling terms, so that it would not have to return to parliament when its plans changed. It was also very generous in its interpretation of what existing legislation permitted it to do. Procedural problems are inextricably intertwined with the structure of the party system and imbalance between government and opposition. The change of government in 1984 altered this situation, as the Liberal party in particular was so weakened that it had difficulty in being an effective opposition. Once the party does regain its confidence and strength it will, doubtless, pursue adversarial politics in parliament. Mindless obstruction began with the Liberal opposition to Diefenbaker.

Minority Parliaments
With three or more parties represented in the House, parliaments in which the government holds fewer than half the seats are common. Canada's first minority parliament in recent times was elected in 1957, and since then there have been five more. Six out of the eleven elections since 1953 have produced minority parliaments. The arguments are often made that majority government is not only natural and proper, but also the most efficient, and that the lines of responsibility and accountability in minority parliaments are blurred because smaller parties have an undue influence.

Although more than half of recent elections have produced minority parliaments, Canada has had majority government two-thirds of the time. Minority parliaments are not an uncommon election result, but they have a shorter life than majority parliaments. Of the six minority parliaments, three have lasted a year or less, and the longest lasted only three years. And they have been less common in the 1970s and 1980s than in the 1960s.[19]

The six minority parliaments divide neatly into two groups of three: short-lived and longer-lived. The short-lived ones were 1957–8 (9 months), 1962–3 (10 months), and 1979 (9 months). These were all Conservative governments. Two were transient parliaments of change; 1957 marked the first defeat of the Liberals since 1930, and paved the way for Diefenbaker's massive victory (208 seats out of 265) in 1958. This parliament came to an end by the government's choice, without its having been defeated in the House. The collapse of the Diefenbaker government was marked by the return to a minority parliament in 1962. Soon after, the Liberal opposition succeeded in defeating the government in a vote in the House. An election followed, from which a Liberal minority government emerged. The 1957 election was a step towards the Conservatives' ascendancy; that of 1962 a step towards their downfall. The 1979 election, was seen by many Conservatives as comparable to that of 1957, and Prime Minister Clark in particular was prepared for a short parliament and a quick election. But the Clark government was found wanting by both the House and the electorate, and its life ended quickly and ignominiously.

The three longer-lived minority parliaments – in 1963, 1965, and 1972 – all involved Liberal governments. In both 1963 and 1965, the Liberal party was close to a majority (four and two seats short, respectively). In both cases, but in 1965 especially, the Liberals were able to govern as though they had a majority. The opposition parties were not keen for an election. The Conservatives were in disarray, and they and the Social Credit were on a losing streak; the NDP were unenthusiastic about both the costs and the risks of an election. Both parliaments ended when the Liberal government called an election. In both elections, 1965 and 1968, the Liberals increased their support, achieving a large majority under Trudeau in 1968. The absence of only a few opposition members was enough to ensure government success in the House in these parliaments, and this, as much as overt third-party support, allowed the government to maintain power. The parliament of 1972 was different. In it the Liberals had only two more seats than the Conservatives, and the support of a third party, the NDP in particular, was vital. To maintain power, the Liberals made many policy concessions to the NDP – on welfare programmes and in promoting Canadian ownership of industry. Alhough the election of 1974 followed a defeat of the government in the House, it was a defeat on an issue (the budget) at a time (spring) chosen by the government, who in effect engineered the NDP into supporting the Conservatives when the government felt its chances were best. Opposition members who were concerned to stay in parliament until they were eligible for pensions were, also, reluctant to defeat a government quickly. The Liberal government gained the rewards of a majority in the election of 1974, while the NDP dropped from thirty-one MPs to sixteen.

Experience suggests the following conclusions. First, as long as the Canadian electorate votes three or more parties into parliament, minority governments are probable. They will be shorter-lived than majorities. Second, a minority parliament does not alter the structure of power. The government, even though it has fewer than half the seats, and even though it is likely to preserve itself, to be conciliatory and attentive to parliament (the Clark government of 1979 is the aberration here), will still maintain a monopoly over the use of power, and parliament will have no additional influence on administration and executive decision-making. Third, a minority government will make concessions over policy and legislation to gain third-party support (and enable both parties to avoid an election) rather than enter into coalition. Provincial experience, such as the

1985 'agreement' in Ontario between the Liberals and NDP, suggests that the reluctance to enter into coalition is not confined to the federal sphere. Fourth, third parties in minority parliaments can influence the policy direction of government. This fact was especially important in the 1972–4 parliament, when the price of NDP support moved the Trudeau government towards a redistributive, *dirigiste*, mildly anti-business, and nationalist posture. (This posture stood the Liberals in good stead, in giving them two subsequent majority parliaments in 1974 and 1980.) Fifth, the Liberals have been better at managing minority parliaments than the Conservatives, in large part because the Liberals have succeeded in gaining the support of the NDP, while the Conservatives have been hostile, even as a minority, towards the third parties and unable to make the necessary compromises. Sixth, there is no evidence that minority parliaments are less efficient than majorities. The parliaments of 1963, 1965, and 1972 were all productive.

The Parties and the Electorate

Liberal-democratic theory argues that the vote is important because it gives each citizen the opportunity to make a choice between various political candidates and between parties with competing policies and leaders. Early election studies in Britain and the United States found that for most voters the choice had already been made: political parties enjoyed long-term stable support of most of the electorate, and only a small proportion changed their support from one election to the next. The pattern of voter allegiance in these two countries was largely along the bases of cleavages in the society, especially socio-economic class, but also including region, ethnicity, religion, education, and other factors.

Later, when election studies began in Canada, researchers expected to find a similar pattern.[20] They have, however, found an important difference: where in the United States and Britain only 8 per cent and 17 per cent of the electorate, respectively, have changed their party identification, in Canada a much greater proportion, as much as 36 per cent, are reported in voting studies to have made this change. A further large percentage have changed their vote without changing identification. Canada has an unusually large contingent of unstable voters. Any assumption that most Canadians have a party commitment that remains stable over time and that can be easily captured through identification with cleavages is invalid and does not help to understand or predict electoral behaviour. The Canadian electorate has less identification with party, and changes its mind more often, than that of Britain or the United States. This instability makes study and understanding of elections and of the relationships between the electorate and parties very difficult.

A further caveat must be offered. Election studies are based on the claims of a sample of the electorate as to how, and why, they vote or voted. Both methodology and results have been criticized; nevertheless, despite their faults, these studies are an extremely valuable source for understanding some aspects of the relationship between electorate, parliament, and government.

The Canadian electorate, like most other aspects of Canadian politics, is made up of subgroups with regional variations. For most of this century, Quebec has voted Liberal, while more recently the prairies have become predominantly Conservative. The two main parties dominate the Maritimes. The NDP has substantial British Columbia, Saskatchewan, Manitoba, and Ontario representation (although none from Alberta), while Social Credit has been a force in Alberta and British Columbia, as have the Créditistes in Quebec, where the NDP has never gained a seat. Within these regional variations, some correlations between voting behaviour and other factors can be identified. Religion and ethnicity are the most important: Roman Catholics tend to vote Liberal and Protestants Conservative, although in Quebec a higher proportion of Protestants than Roman Catholics vote Liberal; French Canadians tend to vote Liberal, as do those who are neither Anglo-Celtic nor French. In Canada, unlike most western democracies, social class is a very weak indicator of voting behaviour. Both Liberals and Conservatives, but the Liberals in particular, are able to draw support from all occupational groups. Alhough the NDP draws a higher proportion of its votes from skilled and unskilled labour than do the other two parties, it receives its strongest support from persons with at least seventeen years of education.

The electorate usually votes for the party, not for the local candidate. The most important items in affecting a decision are policies and issues on such short-term problems as unemployment and inflation, style and performance, and the leader and leadership. Ideology and long-term policy questions are unimportant. They would have to be, bearing in mind the twists, turns, tergiversations, and prevarications of the parties over time: as has been remarked, no one could be more fickle than one who has followed a party faithfully over the years. Party images and electoral support alike tend to depend on short-term factors that emerge between elections rather than on long-term policies and concerns of the party. The economic condition of the nation and region at election time is crucial. Party leaders are viewed and evaluated in stylistic rather than issue-related terms. But issues are particularly important for the portion of the electorate that is highly interested in politics but is unstable in party choice. Canada is unusual in having many voters with a high interest in politics and at the same time a low commitment to a party. In general, attitudes towards party have more effect on voting than attitudes towards leader, and both are more important than attitudes towards the local candidate.

With this sort of electoral behaviour, the Canadian electorate comes closer to the ideal of independent-minded voters who choose freely in elections than do the electorates in other democracies where voter choice is more stable and predictable. However, at the same time, this voter behaviour produces problems for the parties, parliament, and elected representatives.

The extreme volatility of the electorate in Canada is one of the factors that contribute to the small number of safe seats and the short tenure of office of members of parliament. The voters make their decisions primarily on the basis of party and leader, and with rare exceptions the candidate is dragged along, up or down, with his own performance during office or in the campaign having little effect on outcome. The stability of the Liberals in power has masked considerable movement in the electorate. When this movement is unmasked – as it was in 1984 when the 36 per cent of the electorate who changed their vote moved in the same direction, towards the Conservatives and away from the other parties – the result is a tremendous upheaval in parliament. From the 1980 to the 1984 general elections the Conservatives rose from 33 per cent to 50 per cent of the popular vote, an increase of 51 per cent. Their representation in the House rose from 103 to 211 seats, an increase of more than 100 per cent. The volatility of the Quebec electorate in 1984 was particularly remarkable, with the Conservatives rising from 13 per cent to 50 per cent of the popular vote. Only two of their fifty-eight Quebec MPs had sat in parliament before. In 1984 as in 1958 the Quebec electorate showed that its allegiance to the Liberal party was a relationship of convenience rather than affection, and could easily be discarded when disaffection or the prospect of being on the losing side became likely.[21]

The electorate makes its decisions on the basis of short-term factors, including the economic circumstances, issues, policies, and leadership that combine to create an image of the party. The media are crucial in the creation of this image. At least for the two major parties, there is scarcely any stable base of traditions and ideologies to mould and direct the policies and leadership of the party. The parties can and do change their attitudes: Prime Minister Trudeau ridiculed Stanfield's proposals for a wage and price freeze in 1974, but implemented a severe regimen of controls a year later. The Mulroney government in 1985 made free trade with the United States a cornerstone of its policies, although it had not been an election issue in 1984, with no apparent protest from the party, even though its traditions, going back to Sir John A. Macdonald's National Policy, the 1911 election where the Conservatives defeated Laurier on reciprocity, and John Diefenbaker's 1958 promise to divert a substantial portion of trade from the United States to Britain, were in the opposite direction. The importance of the image, the absence of historic and traditional factors shaping that image, and the importance of short-term factors, all help to make it difficult for the parties to serve as instruments for the formulation of policies.

The links between the electorate and the parties are loose. The parties in parliament are coherent, powerful bodies with an enormous control over the behaviour of elected representatives. They also establish who governs. They are among the most powerful political institutions in Canada and their power ultimately rests on their ability to attract votes. But their organizational linkages with the electorate, constituency associations, and national party organizations are weak, and they have not been able to create long-term, deep-seated allegiance in voters. The identification of the two main parties with policies, regions, or important and stable concerns to the electorate is also weak and fleeting. The high voter turnout in Canada, 76 per cent compared with closer to 50 per cent in U.S. presidential elections, shows that the parties have succeeded in generating a high level of political interest, but this interest has not been translated into allegiance to a given party. Thus, the image the parties project in the short-term through the media becomes all-important.

The stability of the Liberals in office also masks the fact that the electorate has not been kind to governments. Two sanctions can be imposed on a government in a general election: the severe one of a defeat or the milder punishment of reducing a majority government to a minority. In the eleven general elections since 1953, the government has been defeated five times (in 1957, 1963, 1979, 1980, and 1984), and a majority has been changed to a minority twice (in 1962 and 1972). On one occasion (1965), a minority parliament was returned from a previous minority, and a minority was changed three times to a majority (in 1958, 1968, and 1974). Therefore, in seven of the eleven elections the electorate registered mild to severe disapproval, while in only three elections was clear approval registered. Not since 1953 has a majority government been returned with a majority. While this sort of analysis is a gross simplification, not taking into account such factors as whether a government was supported, not because it was good, but because the alternative, the opposition, was worse, nevertheless, it shows that the electorate has made real choices, in its support and disapproval of the government party; although from one perspective much of the recent decades look like a prolonged Liberal reign, in fact there was little security, and governments were more frequently punished than rewarded for their behaviour while in power.

The decisions of the electorate are not only the aggregate of millions of individual decisions but also, for each of those individuals; a decision based on many different impressions and conclusions that have accumulated over the years. Much of the evidence and discussion which affects political opinions in the electorate comes from parliament. The electoral sanction of reduced support can, and does, force a government to change its ways even though it remains in office. Parliament is only one forum among the print and electronic media, the links of pressure groups, and the many other channels of political communication. But it is a central forum. The continuing scrutiny of all aspects of a government's policies and behaviour in parliament is the vital core of the Canadian democratic political processes.

An important question after the 1984 election is: the Conservatives are now the government, but can they become the government party? Diefenbaker was not able to make this change; his government remained an opposition in power. A restructuring of the mentality, practices, attitude towards power, willingness to compromise, capacity to straddle the middle, and willingness to consider collective rather than particular interests will be required for the Mulroney Conservatives to retain office. The negativism of opposition must be replaced by a positive vision. Attempting to harmonize their western wing with the concerns of central Canada could prove to be impossible. Past experience suggests that it is far more likely that an opposition party in power will preserve its attitudes rather than its position; that it will once again become the chronic opposition rather than transform itself into a credible government and government party.

This examination of the electorate does show, however, that support for the Liberal party has not been as deep or as solid as their success at the polls would indicate. Canadian voters are volatile and fickle, and no party has an assured base in power. Majority governments are particularly vulnerable. It would take only a small shift in an already volatile electorate to make the parties much more evenly balanced, reducing the likelihood of a long-lived government party that repeats the past success of the Liberals. The difficulties Conservative governments have in satisfying the electorate are the strongest obstacle preventing this modest shift from occurring.

This chapter has uncovered some of the basic problems in the Canadian parliamentary system. The parliamentary system requires a strong government, and Canadian politics very early on developed a government party to meet this need. However, the parliamentary system does not require a strong opposition, nor has Canada normally had one. The imbalance in parliament between government party and opposition leads to obstruction rather than debate. There is only rarely competition between the parties of visions of what Canada and Canadians might want or become. Political discussion and the possibilities of choice are both debased, and in the absence of vision and sense of direction politics becomes a squabble over the allocation of spoils and other particularisms. The failure of the parties to offer competing visions and senses of direction has led to weak and fickle electoral support, and a politics of the moment, through the media, rather than participation and long-term commitment to a party. Nevertheless, voters have high interest in elections. One party is often rejected for another. The electoral process is by no means meaningless.

In part, the unhappy features emerge from the continuing challenges governments and oppositions face in Canada: the need to assert and create the reality of a nation, and to retain the support from a diverse electorate in a huge country spanning half a continent, containing two major language groups, many regions and sub-economies, and in which there is always a tension of not just east-west national coherence versus regional autonomy, but also of the concept of an east-west nation itself versus the north-south pulls of continentalism. Government parties succeed in finding a mixture of policies that propose some vision of the nation. But the easy route for an opposition is to be negative, and to think and argue about details and particulars rather than to engage in the arduous tasks of proposing some coherent vision of what Canada might become, and then persuading voters to support them in working towards this vision. Taking the easy route enables the chronic opposition to defeat a government and gain power, but it prevents the opposition, once in government, from gaining the kind of support which will enable it to assure the electorate that it is using power wisely. This is not likely to change, because an opposition as divided as the Canadian, and made up of so many groups that have little in common except that they are opposed to the governing consensus, does not find it easy to discover or create a more unified and positive approach. The imbalance is deeply entrenched. The Canadian parliamentary system adequately performs the function of making a government. It also often allows a government to be defeated. What it does not do well is create a strong and credible alternative to the long-standing government party.

4

The Honourable Members

In our parliamentary system the people elect members of parliament to sit in the House of Commons and serve as representatives. This appears straightforward, but the closer one looks, the less obvious and simple the processes of representation become. Between the calling of an election and the decisions and actions of government is a long, involved, complicated, and tortuous route, in which the links between electoral choice and policy outcomes are not only complex, far from clear, and poorly understood, but also of the loosest sort indeed. This chapter focuses on the member of parliament as a representative. After a brief introductory discussion, it examines the electoral system which brings an MP to the House, and the socio-economic and other characteristics of elected members. The political careers of MPs, including pre – and post-parliamentary activities, are then considered. Many of the underlying causes of the weakness of the House of Commons will become apparent in this examination.

Representation can mean many things. N. Ward has pointed out 'that election is not an essential part of representation; the Pope, for instance, represents all Roman Catholics for various purposes, but the rank-and-file members of the Church have no voice in his appointment.'[1] Governments, even when dictatorial or selected through heredity, claim to be representative: 'Caesar was omnicompetent because Caesar was the repository of every citizen's powers; he was the universal agent, the representative of all.'[2] In the early parliaments in England, MPs were chosen by the county courts from those eligible for jury duty to become, in effect, members of the high court of parliament. It was often an unpleasant duty as the MPs' two functions were to authorize increases of taxes demanded by the king, a task distasteful to constituents, and to present grievances of the constituency for redress to a powerful and unsympathetic feudal monarch, a task distasteful to kings. To be a member of parliament was as little liked then as to be a member of a jury often is today. There are records of newly elected MPs fleeing to the continent to avoid service. Representation was an unpleasant incident of feudal service. The popular attitude in the Middle Ages towards parliament, as towards the shire court, was not a question of who was anxious to serve, but of who was obliged to attend.

This situation changed as the importance of parliament grew. An exceptional election of 1807 in Yorkshire is said to have cost the candidates and their supporters more than £250,000 (more than $10 million in today's money).[3] A seat in the House was by then a valuable commodity. Decisions in parliament on authorizing railways and canals, on duties and taxes, and on numerous other aspects of trade and commerce could mean hundreds of thousand of pounds to wealthy land-owners and other magnates. Party lines were weak and many constituencies could be bought, while others were under the direct control of one or a few individuals, and to have one, several, or many MPs under direct influence was not only prestigious but to the advantage of persons of wealth. The unreformed system was defended because it gave influence to those with a stake, or 'interest' in the nation, the land-owning gentry. Nevertheless, the process of reform was under way, and the culmination was the system of full adult suffrage, secret ballot, and single member constituencies which Canada and Britain now enjoy.

The direction of reforms gradually came to be to enable each adult citizen to participate in the process of government through election of a representative in parliament. But the outcome, domination by parties of MPs and the reduction of elections to a choice between two or three teams of party leaders, is not what was intended or expected. On the one hand the MP is now a highly visible public figure, attempting to meet the demands of, and accountable to, a mass electorate. On the other hand he is also lobby fodder to vote as his party bids. Because his success in elections depends more on his leader's image and standing than on his own efforts, his political future is not only insecure but out of his control. Important channels of political communication, the mass media and interest-group lobbying, bypass the member and leave him on the sidelines. Under these stresses, the position of a member of parliament as a legitimate representative is often weak.

The classic statement of a representative's function was Edmund Burke's:

It is his duty to sacrifice his repose, his pleasures, his satisfactions, to theirs [his constituents']; and above all, ever, and in all cases, to prefer their interest to his own. But his unbiased opinion, his mature judgment, his enlightened conscience, he ought not to sacrifice to you, to any man, or to any set of men living. These he does not derive from your pleasure; no, nor from the law and the constitution. They are a trust from Providence, for the abuse of which he is deeply answerable. Your representative owes you, not his industry only, but his judgment; and he betrays, instead of serving you, if he sacrifices it to your opinion ... Parliament is not a congress of ambassadors from different and hostile interests;

which interests each must maintain ... but parliament is a deliberating assembly of one nation, with one interest, that of the whole; where, not local purposes, not local prejudices, ought to guide, but the general good, resulting from the general reason of the whole.[4]

Burke's post-election speech is probably the most widely quoted statement in the English language on the functions of an elected representative. At a later election he claimed: 'I was not only your representative as a body; I was the agent, the solicitor of individuals; I ran about wherever your affairs could call me; and in acting for you I often appeared rather as a shipbroker, than as a member of parliament. There was nothing too laborious or too low for me to undertake.'[5] These different moods of Burke describe two incompatible roles of a representative: on the one hand, the MP is independent and should pursue a general public interest, such as his facilities for reason, system of values, and knowledge of the facts enable him to discern; on the other hand, the MP is agent for his constituents furthering their particular interests and needs. To compound the difficulties there are 'modern ideas of representation' which assume 'that the representative is bound by the will of the represented, but the will of the people is a modern fact which largely partakes of fiction.'[6]

Even this brief analysis is enough to prove that what ought to be and is represented – a national interest, particular interests, or the will of the electorate – and how it is being represented – through individual MPs, the parties, or the party leadership – is far from clear. Concepts such as 'national interest' and 'the will of the represented' are themselves subject to dispute and varying interpretations. The system of representation, like other parts of parliamentary government, is complex and multi-faceted, and embodies trade-offs between many often conflicting objectives. The place of the elected representative is subject to dispute and, as we shall see, is far from satisfactory in Canada at present.

THE ELECTORAL SYSTEM

The members of the Canadian House of Commons are elected in simultaneous nation-wide elections, from single member constituencies covering a particular, discrete, geographical area. All adult citizens, with few exceptions (such as judges, prisoners, and the insane), are eligible to vote. The candidate who gains the most votes in the election wins, even though he has often obtained fewer than half the votes. This winner-take-all system is termed the 'simple plurality' or sometimes the 'first past the post' method. In this system the votes cast for losing candidates count for nothing. This system has been criticized on many grounds. There are many other electoral systems at use in the world and in the theories of political scientists. Most of these include proportional representation, some form of which has in recent years been proposed by many authorities in Canada.

The electoral system, including number and distribution of seats, the franchise, and the election process, is created and regulated by acts of parliament. The system has changed greatly since confederation, the two most important changes being the growth of the House of Commons as the Canadian territory and population expanded, and the gradual extension of the franchise to all adult citizens.[7] The right to vote in federal elections is now entrenched in the Charter of Rights and Freedoms. But this right has to be translated from an abstract concept to an actual, living, House of Commons, and in recent years there have been numerous changes both in the size of the House itself and in the way electoral-district boundaries are determined. The Representation Act, 1974, provided that after each decennial census the membership of the House would be revised upwards. Quebec would be given four additional seats, and the other provinces apportioned seats as their population bore a relationship to Quebec. There were additional provisions which gave the smaller provinces more seats than strict application of proportionality would have warranted. Under this system the House increased from 264 to 282 seats for the election of 1979. The House would have increased to 310 members following the census of 1981, and projections were that it would reach 369 seats after 2001.

The Representation Act, 1985, has drastically curtailed this projected growth. Calculations were simplified. Two seats for the Northwest Territories and one for the Yukon are subtracted from the total of 282, leaving 279 to be divided among the provinces. Canada's population as determined in the decennial census is divided by 279, giving an electoral quotient. The population of each province is divided by this electoral quotient, giving the number of seats in each province. These results are then adjusted by applying 'grandfather' and 'senatorial' clauses, which guarantee that no province will have fewer MPs than it has senators, and no province will have fewer seats than it had in 1976, or had during the 33rd Parliament, when the act was passed.

The results of this process will be a House with 295 members. The electoral quotient as of 1986 was 87,005. The application of the grandfather and senatorial clauses will ensure that while the large provinces will have very close to the number of seats the electoral quotient would predict, the smaller will have more. Prince Edward Island benefits most, with 30,627 citizens per seat; Saskatchewan will have 69,165. The House, if these rules remain in effect, is not likely to grow much larger.

Electoral boundaries are readjusted after each census. Three-member commissions in each province are chaired by a judge designated by the chief justice of the province and include two other members appointed by the speaker of the House of Commons. They devise new electoral districts, and hold public hearings before completing their reports. Each commission's report is sent through the chief electoral officer to the speaker. It is then referred to committee, and the results of this committee's hearings are referred back to the commission. Further adjustment might then be made. The governor in council publicly announces the new boundaries, and one year must then pass before they can be used in an election.

The process of redistribution entails frequent changes of electoral boundaries. The Canadian population is mobile and growing, and stable electoral districts would produce gross inequalities. Even so, the disparities can be great. In 1984 the largest electoral district in Ontario (York-Scarborough) had 127,798 voters; the smallest (Trinity) had 28,867, a ratio of more than four to one. One of every five constituencies in Ontario exceeded the tolerance limits of plus or minus 25 per cent established by the Electoral Boundaries Readjustment Act. Electoral boundaries commissions generally give fewer voters to rural than to urban constituencies, but the disparities in practice are much greater than those permitted in theory.

One reason for the steady expansion of the House has been the reluctance of the smaller provinces, and those whose population has not increased, to lose seats. Readjustments have been easier to make by holding the representation of these provinces (particularly the Maritimes) steady, while increasing the size of the House. There are, then, no apparent losers. A second reason has been that many observers have felt that the House was too small. At slightly more than 260 members, where it had remained since 1949, by the 1970s the House was finding its capacity to accomplish committee work limited by shortages of manpower. Size also limits the number of qualified candidates for the cabinet and opposition frontbenchers. Increasing the size of the House would alleviate these problems.[8] It would also alleviate the problem of excessively large rural constituencies as Canada's population becomes concentrated in large cities. A national assembly with 282 members is still not large. The British House of Commons (which is one of the largest) has 640 members. We shall examine this question of size in more detail in chapter 12.

The arguments against increase were economy and convenience: each additional MP adds a substantial cost to the budget of the House for his salary, staff, and services, and the Houses of Parliament were feeling the strain of space demands. They had been designed for two hundred MPs sharing offices, and now faced the prospect of not only an increase in number of members, but also an expansion of space and budget for each member as the facilities and resources provided by the House were improved. Not the least of the future problems, if the increase continues, will arise when there are too many MPs for each to have a desk on the floor of the House. At that point, either the Canadian tradition of a personal desk for each member may have to be abandoned and a system, like that in the British House, of benches with no assigned seats adopted, or a drastic redesign of the entire chamber will have to be undertaken.

Elections are supervised by the chief electoral officer, an independent official appointed by resolution of the House of Commons under the Canada Elections Act.[9] The date for an election is fixed by the governor general on the advice of the prime minister. The chief electoral officer issues a writ for an election to the returning officer in each constituency, who in turn, after the election, returns the writ with the name of the person elected and other reports on the election to the chief electoral officer. The winning candidate officially becomes a member of parliament when he is sworn in by the Clerk of the House, though he is paid from the day of voting.

Invariably some seats become vacant during the lifetime of a parliament through death, resignation, or some other cause. These are filled through by-elections. The government chooses the dates of by-elections, and seats may remain vacant for many months if the government feels the time is unpropitious. Five seats were vacant at the time of the summer adjournment before the 1984 election. In October 1978, fifteen by-elections were called for the same day by Prime Minister Trudeau. This number of vacancies (more than 5 per cent of the House) had been allowed to accumulate because the government was trailing in opinion polls, and was waiting for a favourable time as part of their pre-election strategy.[10] It did not prove successful, as the Liberals lost six seats. The prime minister's discretion in calling by-elections is a relic of earlier times. It is now misused, and can leave many Canadians unrepresented in the House of Commons for an unreasonably long period. All arguments except expediency to the government favour eliminating this discretion and adopting the British practice of having by-elections called immediately upon a seat becoming vacant.

Electoral Reform
There are many criticisms of the single member constituency, simple plurality system of representation. First, the winning party usually gets more seats than its share of the votes. In the fourteen elections since 1945, only twice has the winning party gained more than 50 per cent of the votes (1958 and 1984); yet eight elections have produced majority governments. Second, measured in terms of the percentage of seats they win compared with percentage of votes, nation-wide third parties such as the NDP are underrepresented, while small regional parties are overrepresented. Third, where one major party has a regional stronghold, the other parties, in particular the other major party, tend to be underrepresented. Thus a characteristic of the House during most of this century has been the virtual exclusion of Conservatives from Quebec, even though they have polled on average close to 20 per cent of the Quebec vote. Similarly, the Liberal party recently has won more than 20 per cent of the vote in the west, but gained few seats. Not for the nation as a whole, and far less for each individual region, is the party composition of members elected an accurate reflection of how the electorate voted.

This, A.C. Cairns in particular has argued, is bad.[11] A substantial number of voters, usually more than half, who have not voted for the winning candidate do not have their views represented in the House. Even aggregating votes on a provincial or regional basis, minority opinions, such as those of the Liberals in the west and the Tories in Quebec, have been grossly underrepresented. For this reason, the House of Commons is not truly representative of the political diversity in the electorate. A further harmful consequence, it is argued, is that the system encourages the regionalization of the major parties. The Conservatives not only have won few seats in Quebec, but have put less effort into winning votes there because they know they will not succeed. The Liberals have acted similarly in the west. The caucuses of the two major parties in parliament also, it was argued, became regionalized. The Liberals, with little representation there, were neither sympathetic nor sensitive to the west, nor were the Conservatives to Quebec. Regionalism, Canada's perennial problem, is consequently made worse by the electoral system. Cairns, in view of all these problems, made a plea for the study of the merits of proportional representation to correct the bad features of the present system.

Most subsequent discussion of representation in Canada has accepted the Cairns analysis, and has centred around alleviating the problems he described. D.V. Smiley proposed that:

Electoral reform would proceed along these lines. Voters would cast their ballots as they now do and the same number of M.P.'s would be elected from single-member districts. But the House of Commons would be enlarged to include one hundred 'provincial' M.P.'s, with Prince Edward Island having one of these and the rest distributed among the other provinces in proportion to their respective populations. The 'provincial' members would have the same standing in the House as their other colleagues and be given services in their respective provincial capitals and travel privileges to and from those capitals.[12]

Others, including the recent royal commission on the economic union, have followed, pursuing much the same approach as Smiley towards some modified form of proportional representation.[13] This, it is claimed, would ensure that the electorate's opinion as expressed in votes would be more accurately reflected in the House, that parties would have MPs from all areas in which they receive votes, and that efforts by a losing party to win votes would still be rewarded. Both parties and voters on the losing side would not, under these systems, have their efforts go for naught. The electoral system would encourage national parties and integration rather than reward sectionalism. Academic discussion of the electoral system in Canada has centred around these sorts of proposals for proportional representation.

Almost alone in questioning this approach was J.A.A. Lovink, who argued that Cairns's propositions 'appear to exaggerate the significance of the electoral system for party policy, to overstate its nationally divisive consequences, and to understate its contribution to the effective functioning of the parliamentary form of government.'[14] Lovink concluded that 'only the direct consequences of the electoral system stand out plainly. Stating these summarily, it has furthered majority and one-party government, quickened the turnover in political leadership, helped regionally based third parties, and hurt the political left.' He also doubted whether the electoral system had been as profound a determining factor on the party system as Cairns had argued.

Most of the public discussion of proportional representation has focused on the inequities of the present system and various ways, similar to Smiley's, of alleviating them. The Task Force on Canadian Unity, for example, proposed an additional sixty seats in the Commons to be filled from provincial lists compiled by federal parties and allotted to the parties in proportion to their share of the popular vote. Apart from Lovink's, there have been few critical voices.[15] The arguments in favour of electoral reform are clear and simple: first, the party composition of the House of Commons would more accurately reflect how the electorate voted; second, greater encouragement would be given to parties concerned with national integration, and there would be fewer advantages for parties with narrow regional concerns. The first of these arguments is a statement of fact, the second largely a matter of opinion. The second argument in particular seems less convincing after the 1984 election, where the Conservatives reversed roles with the Liberals in Quebec, the Liberals became underrepresented compared with the NDP, and the regional support of the two major parties changed substantially.

In comparison, the arguments against proportional representation are neither clear nor simple. They can be reduced to seven. First, the question must be asked of whether we really know why the electorate votes the way it does. Voters can understand the present relatively simple system. Perhaps they are voting for or against a federal leader, a party, or the federal government itself, rather than for a local candidate. Perhaps voters for losing candidates are often satisfied to lose, and are merely protesting, or cautioning a known winner. No convincing evidence has yet been given that the electorate would be happier if some MPs were selected on the basis of proportional representation. If the government party argument is accepted, then voters are making a judgment based more on the performance of the government than on the policy proposals of the opposition. Proportional representation might confuse the issue and make the system more complex.

Second, proportional representation of the type proposed would create two classes of MPs. One class, the traditional one, would continue to be elected from constituencies, would face their constituents in elections, and would continue to have a heavy workload of constituency business. The second class, the proportional representation MPs, would not be elected from constituencies; would, for those high on the list, be guaranteed re-election without being forced to satisfy the electorate; and would not have constituency business. Their position would be more like that of senators than that of members of the House of Commons. The proportional representation seats would be desirable, involve less work, and could become sinecures to reward faithful service much as the Senate has become. To the extent (probably large) that these seats could be used as rewards for loyal MPs by parties, they would strengthen the control of parties over members. As party control is almost iron-tight at present, the desirability of further strengthening party discipline is, to say the least, questionable.

Third, it has not yet been proved that an element of proportional representation would encourage a stronger national orientation in parties. Part of the Canadian reality is that the nation is huge and diverse, and that there are deep-seated differences of interest and viewpoint between regions. Elected representatives in parliament express and reflect regional interests, and regional hostilities. They would not properly represent their constituents if they did not, at least to some extent. The proponents of proportional representation probably exaggerate the degree to which adding a few MPs from regions where a party has low electoral support will alter the behaviour of the party and, in turn, affect the attitudes and behaviour of the electorate. For most of the twentieth century the Liberal party has with great skill succeeded in creating a working coalition to govern Canada. The Conservative party failed to integrate its large Quebec contingent in 1958, and failed to retain power. It now has another chance to forge a governing coalition out of a huge parliamentary majority. It could not have a greater incentive or a better opportunity to adopt a national perspective than at present. Nor could the Liberal party in 1968, when their western representation was greater than that of either the Conservatives or the NDP (27: 25: 16). The Liberals in 1968 failed to take advantage of this large western representation.[16] Much of a party's orientation depends on leadership and personality. Politics is not mechanistic and arithmetical.

Fourth, introducing proportional representation would lead to more minority governments. Is this desirable? The only certain things about minority governments is that they are unstable and that increasing their frequency would lead to more elections.

Fifth, the most important aspects of representation and political behaviour are 'soft,' not 'hard.' They are amorphous and unquantifiable. One reason that the electoral system has received so much attention from reformers is that counting votes involves hard, objective facts, as does analysing changes in party representation from proportional representation. In this technology-obsessed age, a few hard facts are often mistaken for the whole story. An important element of

Canadian political culture that could be affected by the introduction of proportional representation is that it is an adversarial rather than a consensus system. The major public political dialogue is the competition between government and opposition in parliament. Proportional representation is a characteristic of consensus-coalition systems; simple plurality, single member constituencies are a characteristic of majoritarian-conflict ones.[17] The changes to Canadian political culture from the introduction of proportional representation could be unexpected and undesirable.

Sixth, little evidence has been presented to show that the persons who vote for losing candidates are truly unrepresented. It is not only unproved, but probably unlikely that, for the most part, MPs, parties, or even governments make a distinction between supporters and others in the bulk of their interaction with constituents and interests. The difference between winning and losing an election is usually measured in a few percentage points of the vote; a government or an MP who had consistently alienated a large proportion of the electorate would lose support. Essential to the parliamentary system is a sense of fair play. Although the winners in the electorate enjoy some perks, and the losers suffer mildly, these benefits and costs of victory and loss are restrained within narrow limits. For a government to discriminate systematically against a losing minority in any serious way would offend the majority's sense of fair play. The exceptions to this rule in Canadian history are few, but include: French Canadians in Ontario and Manitoba, oriental Canadians in British Columbia, and Japanese Canadians during the Second World War. Some of these wrongs have been later redressed, or are now being addressed through political processes. It is a serious misunderstanding to assume that elected representatives or elected governments are not concerned with the interests and welfare of those who voted against them.

Finally, the Canadian system is already highly decentralized, with the provinces very powerful indeed in relation to the federal government. Federal-provincial conferences, and the constant pressure by the provinces on Ottawa, are at present severe constraints on federal autonomy, and forces to be reckoned with in federal policy-making. There is a likelihood that a system of proportional representation would increase the provincial presence as a concern in the representative processes. This implicitly assumes that the provincial focus ought to have more legitimacy, and more influence, as opposed, for example, to representation of social class, emphasis on philosophical and ideological differences between the parties, or emphasis on national standards, values, and policies. This assumption is, to say the least, highly contestable.

Representation is far more complex than analysis of the factor of votes cast and members returned suggests. An electoral system, like the rest of a political system, is based to a large extent on conventions, and it attempts to meet a multitude of confusing, competing, and often conflicting objectives. Analysed on the basis of only one criterion, an electoral system or any other aspect of a political system is likely to be found wanting. Application of complex and conflicting criteria makes the case for reform less convincing.

THE CHARACTERISTICS OF MPS

It is still true, as N. Ward wrote more than thirty years ago, that 'the House of Commons falls short of being truly representative of the Canadian people.'[18] Many studies have consistently shown that members of parliament, in comparison with the general population, are better educated, have origins in a higher social and economic class, and tend to occupy higher ranks in the social order.[19] The same findings apply in most other countries. Canadian MPs are also likely to come from a background in which other members of their families have been involved in politics, and where there was personal contact with MPs or other active politicians. Approximately one-third of the members are lawyers. MPs tend to be of British or French-Canadian descent. Canadians of other ethnic origins are underrepresented, although incidence of this discrepancy has been diminishing. Nevertheless, members of parliament are more representative of the ethnic and religious than of the socio-economic composition of Canada. Few are women. The parliament elected in 1984 has twenty-five women members, the largest number ever, although this number is still less than 10 per cent of the House. The typical MP is male, of one of the two founding ethnic groups, middle-aged, and a success in a profession or career before entering parliament. MPs from all parties tend to hold higher social and occupational status than their followers and the electorate at large. Table 3 shows some recent figures on the class distribution of MPs and electorate.

Members of the cabinet, and party leaders, usually will be of even higher socio-economic status than the general member of parliament. They are an 'élite within an élite,' which stands in approximately the same relationship to backbenchers as do the latter to the general public. A high proportion of cabinet ministers are likely to be lawyers.

These facts are not in dispute. There is, however, widespread disagreement on how to interpret them. R.M. Dawson argued that 'one of the greatest merits' of the House of Commons 'is derived from the fact that it is not a selection of the ablest or most brilliant men in the country, but rather a sampling of the best of an average run that can survive the electoral system, an assembly of diverse types of varied experience, the members of which are genuinely and actively concerned with the promotion of the national welfare as they see it.'[20] This House was a satisfactory representative assembly, he concluded, because, 'No cabinet which keeps in

TABLE 3
The social background of Canadian members of parliaments

Social class		Per cent of MPS in class	Per cent of Canadian people in class
Upper	I	43	7
Upper middle	II	28	11
Middle	III	26	28
Lower middle	IV	4	38
Lower	V	0	17

SOURCE: Robert Presthus, *Elites in the Policy Process* (Cambridge 1974), 341. The sample included MLAS from Ontario, Quebec, and British Columbia as well as federal MPs.

constant touch with this body can be very far removed from fluctuation in public opinion, for the house is always acting as an interpreter and forcing this opinion on the attention of its leaders; conversely, a cabinet which grows out of touch with the commons is courting disaster.'

J. Porter, in comparison, was highly critical.[21] Though he did not analyse MPS specifically, he concluded that Canadian politics lacked the dynamic quality that came from a polarization of left and right, which, he argued, was evident in both the United States and Great Britain. The two main parties in Canada shared the same conservative values and, because both were closely linked with corporate enterprise, had a dominant focus to the right of the political spectrum. They were brokerage parties, and because they espoused no distinguishable social values, voters had no commitments other than those arising from uncritical family tradition or habits. Porter's conclusion was that the political processes in Canada suffered as a result. Implicit in his analysis is the view that Canadian politics would be improved by the creation of a major, ideologically oriented party of the left, based in the working classes. He wanted for Canada the same sort of political polarization as has existed in Britain and the European democracies. A social democrat party of the left such as Porter envisages would mean more working-class participation and representation in parliament. Many modern observers from a Marxist perspective have made criticisms similar to Porter's.[22]

Within the mainstream liberal-democratic literature there is no real agreement on the significance of the biases in representation in Canada. R.M. Dawson, in noting that 'there is little or no correlation between the occupations of the members and the number and importance of these occupations in the country,' concluded:

This should not be unduly emphasized, for it is not desirable that members should look upon themselves as the exclusive representatives of any special economic or social group. Yet this occupational distribution of members cannot be ignored. The fact that approximately one-third of the total number are lawyers, and that agriculture, business, manufacturing, finance and insurance, and teaching come next in about that order will have its effect on the House and will influence the general approach of the members to many public questions; the House rarely contains a carpenter, a truck driver, or a railway porter or indeed anybody from the non-professional wage-earning segments of society. It is difficult to believe that a distribution which corresponded more closely with the occupational census of the nation would not furnish a more useful Parliament for most purposes.[23]

R.J. Jackson and M.M. Atkinson state flatly that 'no one in Canada ... has demonstrated how differences between representatives and the represented affect the pattern of legislative behaviour or the pattern of public policy.'[24] They argue that a representative's behaviour is influenced by many factors, including external ones such as social origin, constituency, and profession, and ones internal to the legislature such as institutional norms, the hierarchy of offices, and organizational resources. Because an MP acts under these multiple and conflicting influences, no single factor such as class can adequately explain legislative behaviour.

U.S. studies of this question have the record of a congressman or senator's votes in Congress as a measure of both his behaviour and the legislative output. Representatives in the United States have few sanctions of party to direct their votes, and are measurably responsive to a wide range of external and internal influences. Students of Canadian legislative behaviour have no such easily measurable dependent variables. The Canadian MP votes as his party directs. Party is such an overwhelming control over behaviour that all other observable variables pale in comparison. It might be argued that this makes the class origins of MPs irrelevant, and the only question worth examining is how parties make their choices. This is the implicit proposition behind Porter's and others' concentration on the cabinet and exclusion of backbenchers in their analyses of political élites. Members of parliament are, in their view, simply lobby fodder, and of little importance to the determination of policies.

One useful study, in contrast, argues both that parliament is important and that the personal characteristics of MPs matter. P.A. Hall and R.P. Washburn argue that MPs stand at the centre of the political system. Traditionally, they are representatives of the people, presenting the views of the latter to government. This role remains an important one; the government still relies on members' views, more than on polls, to judge the viability of projected legislation and the opinions of the electorate. Second, MPs are representatives of the regime, interpreting the actions of the executive to the electorate and mobilizing their consent or opposition of the people to government policies.[25] On the basis of responses by MPs to a questionnaire Hall and Washburn uncovered interesting data on the attitudes and perceptions of members.

They first compared the attitudes of members of parliament towards redistributive welfare policies with the attitudes of the public at large and party supporters in particular. They found that members of parliament appear more hostile to welfare redistribution than members of the electorate. When their sample was broken down by party affiliation they found that MPs in every party except the NDP were more conservative on social policies than their own partisans in the electorate. The views of the majority of the electorate were clustered towards the centre of their scale, while the NDP MPs were well to the left of this and the Progressive Conservative MPs far to the right. The Liberal MPs were closest to the middle position of the electorate, but even they were to the right of their supporters and the electorate. The divergence of views between parties in the House was more extreme than between their partisan supporters, and no party accurately reflected the public at large.

Next, the two researchers examined the cabinet, and discovered that its members appeared to be even more conservative than any of the parties in the House.

Finally, they studied the perceptions MPs had of the economic well-being of Canadians. Here they found:

That most Members are somewhat out of touch with the economic situation of average Canadians ... 95 percent of all MP's overestimated the economic well-being of Canadians. And 65 percent did so by substantial margins ... on such matters as how many married women work, how much the average family pays in income taxes, and where the poverty line now stands for a family of four, over 80 percent of all MPs considerably underestimated the real figure, that is overestimated how well- off Canadians are. The *extent*, that is the number of MP's overestimating, the *scope*, that is the number of perception areas overestimated, and the *intensity*, that is the degree of overestimation, are all substantial among our sample of MP's. This provides some evidence that misperceptions of the distribution of income and economic well-being of Canadians may be partially responsible for the unrepresentative conservative attitudes of MP's to redistributive social policies.[26]

This last supposition was supported by evidence that MPs who overestimated the economic well-being of Canadians were more likely to be opposed to redistributive measures than MPs who made a lower estimate of well-being.

Hall and Washburn attempted to uncover the factors which contributed to these distorted perceptions. They found that the older the MP, the more likely he was to overestimate the economic well-being of Canadians. This relationship of age and perception did not appear, however, in their sample of the electorate. MPs who had held senior management positions in business or law tended towards greater overestimation than other MPs. The more upwardly mobile the MP, the greater the tendency he seemed to have to generalize his success to all Canadians, and hence to overestimate well-being. Age, former occupation, and social origins were the most influential factors in determining perceptions. Members from poorer constituencies and regions tended to overestimate less often than those from affluent areas.

The conclusions of the Hall-Washburn study were: first, that the monolithically middle-aged and middle-class character of the House may be adversely affecting the representativeness of the policy preferences articulated there; and second, that the failure of MPs to pierce the myths of affluence and to estimate accurately the well-being of Canadians is cause for concern, especially since it seems to be associated with unrepresentatively conservative attitudes on social policy. MPs, the study found, occupy a kind of political twilight zone where they play a role of linking the executive and electorate which no other group is prepared to perform. Their distorted perceptions of the electorate weakened their capacity to perform this role. This study reinforces analyses of the socio-economic characteristics of members by showing that not only in composition, but in attitudes and perceptions as well, MPs are unrepresentative and have an élite perspective.

There are several conclusions to be drawn from this look at the characteristics of members. First, it proves that the concerns social scientists have shown over the possible consequences of the economic and social (although not the regional) unrepresentativeness of the membership of the House of Commons have some grounding in fact.

Second, the question of why the House of Commons is not representative has been answered only by conjecture. Porter's view was that the cause is the absence of a mass-based party of the left, but the NDP in parliament, a party of the left, does not appear to be much more representative of the socio-economic composition of the general population than the two major parties. Ward asserts that the dominant single factor making the electoral system highly selective, even though theoretically it is open to all qualified citizens, 'is almost certainly money.'[27] Others have suggested that the hazards of the political career, or its structure of rewards, make it peculiarly attractive to lawyers in particular.[28] A further conjecture is that Canada is still, in Bagehot's term, a 'deferential' society, and that the average Canadian wants to be represented by his 'betters.'[29] These conjectures are, however, only hypotheses which are desperately in need of closer study. But it should be emphasized that Canada is not alone in having an elected legislature whose composition is drawn from the higher levels of society. This situation is more the norm than the exception in democracies.

Third, the illusions uncovered by Hall and Washburn are not only common property of the class to which MPs belong, but part of the mythology of the major parties. The absence of a major party of the left is probably more important for political attitudes in the House than are the social origins of members of parliament. The existence of the NDP nevertheless provides an important means of expression of left-wing views which broadens the political discourse in parliament.

Fourth, Canadians for the most part do not think of policies and issues in terms of socio-economic classes. Nor do MPs. R. Presthus discovered that 'almost 60 percent of Canadian MP's, in effect, deny the existence of the class phenomenon by maintaining that they never think in those terms.'[30] Religion, region, language, and ethnic origins are all more important as determinants of voting behaviour than is class. Political issues are not, for the most part, defined in class terms, nor are the politically important cleavages those of socio-economic class. As a result, analysts such as Porter, Panitch, and Clement, among others, who have looked at these aspects of representation, have made little impact on Canadian politics. There is, consequently, a cleavage between the terms and perceptions of academic discourse on representation and the popular discourse of the media and everyday political discussion.

Not only Marxists argue that it is to the advantage of a ruling élite for political discussion to be carried on in terms that mask and conceal its domination. False consciousness of both masses and élites has a function in supporting the social structure. An important part of political activism is the expression of different perceptions of reality, and of what is important, and the attempts to persuade the electorate towards a different view. Those in Canada who would argue for a class-based perception and orientation for Canadian politics have not won many converts. The argument over the importance of the socio-economic composition of the House of Commons is an argument over values and interpretation. The facts are not in dispute.

Representation is not a neutral process. The representatives elected contribute their own colour both to the demands and needs that they transmit to government and to the arguments and explanations they offer the public. To the extent that the attitudes and perceptions of members are out of step with those of the majority of the electorate, and the evidence suggests that they are so, especially for the Progressive Conservatives, a government faces the problem that programmes and policies which satisfy the House and the government's backbenchers will diverge from those which the electorate would want. In some areas, such as redistributive welfare measures, the House will be to the right; in others, such as capital punishment, it will be to the left. Neither the House of Commons as a body nor the elected member simply transmits views one way or the other. Rather, they actively influence both perceptions and choices.

The Political Careers of MPs

The political career of a member of parliament has three stages: the pre-parliamentary career; the career in parliament; and the post-parliamentary career. What happens in each of these stages influences what happens in the others. The general pattern of political careers of Canadian MPs can be summarized as follows: one, they generally have little pre-parliamentary experience in elected office; two, their careers as parliamentarians tend to be brief; and three, many, especially former cabinet ministers, receive some sort of patronage appointment after they leave parliament. The typical Canadian MP, consequently, is an amateur politician, for whom election to parliament is a short-term interlude or break in a career outside politics. Since competent, experienced personnel are the strength and backbone of any organization, these characteristics of the political careers of MPs are cause for some concern.

N. Ward found that approximately one-third of the members of the House go there directly from local politics. The number of MPs proceeding from provincial legislatures to the federal House was lower, and was steadily declining. It had been over 20 per cent in all parliaments before 1917, but was only 9 per cent in 1945. In comparison, the percentage of MPs with no known political experience had risen, reaching 59 per cent in 1945.[31] A later study by D. Hoffman and N. Ward found that these trends were continuing. In 1964–5, slightly more than 25 per cent of MPs interviewed had previous municipal government experience, and only 4 per cent previous provincial experience. The most striking conclusion to emerge from their data was the small previous political experience of their respondents in general: '30 per cent of the back-benchers interviewed said that they had no previous political experience either in government or the party; 26 per cent had been members of their local party executive at one time or another; another 24 per cent had been members of their party's provincial or federal executive; and 30 per cent had received other previous political experience as constituency organizers, youth organizers, or within university political groups.'[32]

A high proportion of MPs have had their interest in politics kindled by relatives and a further large proportion by friends. There is, however, a difference between political interest and political participation. The interested and the only slightly interested must still be recruited to political roles. The political party plays the role of recruiter, which can involve press gang tactics in attempting to persuade a respected citizen to run for parliament. Competition for nomination is often absent or minimal in Canada, unlike Britain where the normal rule is ten or more, and often a hundred candidates for the party's nomination in a constituency, and where the winning candidate will likely have proved his mettle by running in losing ridings before being nominated in a safe, winnable constituency.

Hoffman and Ward found 25 per cent of their MPs to be self-selected, 37 per cent to be conscripted, 29 per cent co-opted, and 9 per cent uncertain. Their conclusion was that the most interesting feature of members was the low level of commitment to a political career.[33] There appears to be an unspoken folkway of the House that members should not appear to have been too eager to be candidates; nevertheless, more than the blushing bride syndrome is at work here, and a high proportion of Canadian MPs have, it appears, reached parliament without, before becoming a candidate, having seriously wanted or even considered a career in federal politics.

A. Kornberg found in 1962 that 62 per cent of NDP and 56 per cent of Conservative, as opposed to 34 per cent of Liberal MPs, had held other elected office. More Conservative than Liberal, and all NDP members, had held party office.[34] These findings are in line with earlier ones: the government party recruits candidates with the least previous political experience; the NDP those with the most; and the official opposition falls somewhere in between.

As N. Ward had before, in 1976 V.P. Harder found that 'the most noteworthy feature of the Canadian data on previous elected experience is the overwhelming lack of any.'[35] Two-thirds of the MPs he studied had no previous elected experience, and of those who had, it was almost exclusively at the local level. Only the NDP, with 16.2 per cent of its MPs having previously sat in provincial chambers, provided an exception. In Canada there were separate career systems for local, provincial, and federal elected office, with little overlap or integration, particularly between federal and provincial legislatures. This exclusivist feature of the Canadian political system Harder found to be the direct opposite of the U.S. system. It confirmed the observation that the Canadian system is confederal in nature, characterized by party careerists fulfilling their ambition through serving only at one level of government. In the United States, there was a clear ladder through which members of Congress had progressed: local government; state elected office; and, finally, as culmination of a long political career, election to the national assembly.

The data on pre-parliamentary experience suggest the conclusion that Canadian MPs are political amateurs. Data on length of their stay in parliament confirm it. Historically, the number of new members in the House of Commons after an election has ranged from a low of 20 per cent in 1926 and 1962 to a high of 60 per cent in 1921 and 1935.[36] The norm in recent years has been around 40 per cent, although in 1984 it climbed to 52 per cent. An analysis by region would show even greater volatility. For example, Quebec has often been treated as a safe Liberal stronghold, but in 1957–8 and 1962–3 the turnover there was 62 per cent, while in 1984 it exceeded 80 per cent. New members do not appear to be any more vulnerable than those in their second or subsequent terms; the percentage of experienced members not returning to the House is similar to the percentage of first term members.[37] Consequently there is a steady and large attrition from parliament, and the bulk of members (roughly 80 per cent) is likely to have served fewer than seven years at the beginning of a new parliament, and only on rare occasions will more than 10 per cent of the House have served longer than twelve to fifteen years.

The rapid turnover in the Canadian House of Commons is unusual amongst western legislatures. A more common pattern is that of Britain, where 70 per cent of the elected assembly is likely to have served ten years or more, and the proportion of new members after an election is rarely greater than 20 per cent. U.S. senators serve at least as long as British MPs. U.S. congressmen have a more rapid turnover, though about 90 per cent choose to run again, and of those 90 per cent are returned. The majority of the losers are relatively new congressmen, serving their first or second term. As a result, there is a substantial core of long-term congressmen in the United States.[38] The average length of time members serve in the Canadian House of Commons is half that of British members. Canadian MPs are short-term amateurs, where their British MPs and U.S. counterparts are long-term professionals. Not only in comparison, but in absolute terms, the average five-to-seven–year stint that a Canadian MP serves in the House is a brief interlude in his career.

The length of stay in parliament varies from region to region, with the longest-serving members coming from regions where party support is strong and stable: Conservatives in the west and, until 1984, Liberals in Quebec. Electoral defeat is the cause of most MPs leaving parliament, averaging 20 per cent of the membership at each election. The percentage of members who do not run for other reasons (such as retirement, appointment to the Senate, a judgeship or other patronage post, or death) is nearly as large at 16 per cent, and is greater in some periods, such as 1968–72, when 16.7 per cent of MPs were defeated and 23.1 per cent retired for other reasons. Nevertheless, either electoral defeat or resignation, taken singly, produces a turnover in the Canadian House of Commons comparable to what both together produce in the United States and Great Britain. The House of Commons elected in 1984 shows these characteristics in the extreme: more than half the members are new, as is a much higher proportion of the Conservative caucus, including fifty-six of their fifty-eight MPs from Quebec.

As in many demanding jobs, there is a roughly four-year period of learning before a new MP can perform his job effectively. On average, close to half the House is in this learning period, and not fully functioning as MPs. The regular attrition of experienced as well as new members (unlike Britain and the United States) means that there are few experienced members in the House. The very small proportion with fifteen or more years' experience creates an absence of a sense of history and tradition. There is a lack of continuity and contact with the past, whether the rules and procedures of the House, the great occasions of debate and parliamentary government, the role of the House in times of crisis, the previous attitudes of members, parties, and committees, or in continuity of relationships with civil servants, interest groups, the media, and the electorate.

An MP must, when he reflects about it, justifiably feel insecure. Because of the amateurism of Canadian politics, few MPs before they reach the House are aware of what the job entails, or how brief their tenure is likely to be. Once they are there and begin to appreciate some of these facts of life for an MP, the likelihood of their imminent departure must affect their attitudes, wants, and expectations. In short, a high proportion of Canadian MPs are learning their job, and an equally large proportion are planning to leave, expecting to leave, going to leave, or all three.

The two facts of a high percentage of MPs defeated at election and a high percentage retiring for other reasons are causally related, although the relationships are difficult to disentangle. The high risk of electoral defeat and consequent insecurity of MPs doubtless make the prospect of a comfortable secure post, whether a patronage appointment or post in the private sector, very appealing, although, quite understandably, few MPs will admit to the expectation that their service will be so rewarded.

Prime Minister Trudeau in 1984 appointed, or arranged for his successor, John Turner, to appoint, nearly 20 per cent of the Liberal caucus to patronage positions, enough to change the government from a majority to a minority. More, and possibly most, would doubtless have accepted positions if they had been offered. The likelihood or even the possibility of defeat influences the behaviour of MPs, and encourages many to jump from the House to greater security before the defeat happens.

However, it is possible that some MPs, because they know that they want to leave the House, are defeated in elections because they do not perform the work necessary for victory before or during the election campaign. This factor is even more obscure and difficult to uncover than the previous one. Studies of voting behaviour strongly indicate that how well an MP or candidate performs his role has little effect on election outcome.[39] The party leader, economic issues, and other factors outside their control are far more important in determining how an individual votes.

One way of measuring an MP's prospects is by whether his seat is 'safe' or not. A safe seat is one which his party is certain to win, regardless of candidate or opposition. Both Britain and the United States have a large number of safe seats. In Britain it is not unusual for an MP's parliamentary career to begin with candidacy in a riding which is safe for the other party, and after he has proved his mettle there to move to a marginal seat which he might win, and after some time in parliament to gain candidacy in a safe seat and hence be assured of a long and secure career in parliament. In Canada the number of safe seats is much smaller. Lovink found that 23.6 per cent of the seats in the Canadian House of Commons were 'no change' safe seats, as compared with 78.2 per cent in the U.S. House of Representatives and 77.0 per cent in the British House of Commons.[40] The upheaval of the 1984 election and its aftermath will probably make this figure even smaller for Canada. Few seats in Quebec can now be regarded as safe for the Liberals, and the Conservative domination of the west is likely to weaken as the Conservative government accommodates the interests of central Canada. The reasons for the small number of safe seats have not been studied adequately. Electoral volatility is an important cause, as is demographic change.[41] Whatever the cause, the fact remains that only 20 per cent of Canadian MPs at most can reasonably feel assured they, and their party, will hold their seat in the next election, whereas nearly 80 per cent of British and U.S. members can have this confidence.

The small number of safe seats is the greatest single factor contributing to the high turnover in the Canadian House of Commons. Another important factor, which contributes to the high number who retire, is that many MPs, once they reach Ottawa, discover that they do not like the job. Among the reasons for their dislike are the disruption of family life because of residence in Ottawa, the demands on the time of an MP and the lack of privacy, the financial costs of being an MP, and disillusionment because there is little a backbench MP can accomplish.[42] According to one MP: 'This has to be one of the most demanding jobs in Canada. The responsibilities are enormous; the hours punishing; and the sacrifices of your wife and family unrealistic. You know this – in a vague sort of way – before you run, but the full impact of the job has to be experienced personally before you truly understand it.' Another, more bitterly, reflected that, 'Unless you are willing to divorce your family, a family man should not become a Member of Parliament. Families suffer emotionally, sociologically, and economically. Even with subsidy from personal equity, which is rapidly depleting, my family lives at a lower standard than we did before I came to Ottawa and my net worth is 30 per cent lower. I will not divorce my family and therefore I will probably not run again and instead return to the community to rebuild my equities. Parliament is structured for the very young, the very old, and independently wealthy people.'[43]

Less is known about what happens to MPs after they leave parliament than about their tenure and pre-parliamentary experience. Ward found that between the years 1911 and 1930 (12th to 17th parliaments, inclusive), 10.3 per cent of MPs had died while in office, 30.7 per cent had been defeated and retired, and 6.2 per cent had left to enter provincial politics; 23.9 per cent had left to take a patronage appointment: 5.9 per cent on the bench, 11.9 per cent in the Senate, 1 per cent as lieutenant-governor, and 5.1 per cent in the public service;[44] 28.7 per cent had retired undefeated, and a proportion of these would, doubtless, be the beneficiaries of government patronage. Leaving out those who die while in office, close to 30 per cent of MPs appear to retire to a patronage post. There are more boards, corporations, and commissions now, and probably more MPs win this sort of reward. A high proportion of MPs are independently wealthy. Many return to business, or gain employment in the private sphere because of their experience as MPs. Lawyers who have served on the government side can benefit from lucrative government contracts. A generous pension plan now gives MPs some assurance of reasonable prosperity, and a career in parliament, precarious though electoral fortune might be, is by no means lacking in rosy future prospects.

Ward also found that the correlation between years of service as an MP and reward received was not nearly as great as might be expected. The proportion of MPs who left unrewarded decreased with years of service, but a high percentage, and frequently a majority, of those who received prizes did so after one or two terms in parliament.[45]

Porter discovered that a political career has its peculiar exits as well as its entrances.[46] From his examination of cabinet ministers between 1940 and 1960, he found that of sixty-eight who had left office, 11.8 per cent had died while in office, 29.4 per cent had been defeated and retired, and 4.4 per cent had entered provincial politics. 27.9 per cent had left to take a patronage appointment: 14.7 per cent on the bench, 10.3 per cent in the Senate, and 2.9 per cent as lieutenant-governors. Of those who were defeated or resigned from the cabinet, three (4.4 per cent) later went to the federal bureaucracy, and four (5.8 per cent) later were appointed to the Senate. These figures do not differ greatly from Ward's for the House of Commons as a whole. They show that the patronage system was as alive and well in 1960 as in 1930. Patronage of this sort helps a party, particularly a government party, lure able persons to the House, and in part makes up for the paucity of safe seats. Losing opposition members, in comparison, often have a very difficult time adjusting to defeat and finding satisfactory employment.

Both Ward's and Porter's studies underestimated the significance of post-parliamentary patronage plums, because of the many hidden forms of patronage, including providing posts within sympathetic non-government organizations, posts within provincial governments of their party, and the support of lawyers, accountants, consultants, and other professionals by government contracts. There have been no recent comparably detailed studies. A. Kornberg and W. Mishler found that 37 per cent of the members they interviewed would like to hold another public office at some time, 35 per cent said they would not, while the remaining 28 per cent would not reply;[47] 12 per cent were interested in judgeships and appointments to the Senate. These proportions of MPs expressing interest in future positions are not far out of line with realistic expectations based on the Ward and Porter data.

It is clear that many MPs, especially on the government side, brief and unsettling though their tenure in the House might be, do not leave it to go out into the cold. It is also clear that the party serves as a comfortable guardian angel to a very high proportion of ex-MPs. Nevertheless, for many ex-MPs defeat is a traumatic experience, and service in the House a severe disruption of career, family life, and emotional equilibrium.

The House of Commons, like any other organization, is only as strong as its manpower. This examination of the career patterns of MPs has shown that they are, for the most part, not professional politicians, nor do they stay in parliament long. In both these characteristics they are unlike their British or U.S. counterparts. Many of them will depend on their party to ensure their well-being after they leave parliament. The conclusions to be drawn from this are: first, that parliament is not composed of an experienced long-term cadre of professionals skilled in the work of the House; and second, that future prospects for many MPs depend upon how well they please and serve their party, rather than how they serve the House, or their constituents.

The Canadian political system is built up from many sub-systems. Three of the most important are the federal bureaucracy, private interest groups, and political parties. These groups, particularly the first two, are strong, stable, and led and controlled by powerful, long-term members. The system of representation in the House, by contrast, throws up short-term amateurs. These amateurs are frequently dependent on the other sub-systems – especially those of party and government – for their future well-being. This factor of manpower alone is enough to make parliament, regardless of its constitutional or legal position, weak in the face of the other sub-systems.

To make service in the House of Commons longer would be the greatest single change that would strengthen parliament. An obvious route to doing so would be to install a system of proportional representation. But this system would strengthen the control of parties over MPs, and create two classes of MPs. Bearing in mind the rigid control which parties already exert over MPs, and their peculiar élitist unrepresentative nature, this cure could well be worse than the disease. A second route would be to increase the number of safe seats. Whether a seat is safe or not depends, however, more on the electorate than on the actions of MPs. What makes a seat safe is sufficient stable commitment from the electorate to guarantee the return of a party's candidate in the riding. So far there are few places in Canada where parties have earned this sort of assurance. A large proportion of the breakdown in the system of representation caused by the rapid turnover of MPs is directly attributable to this feature of the electorate and party system. A third way of reducing turnover would be to reduce the desires of MPs to leave parliament. The percentage of MPs who leave the Canadian parliament through voluntary resignation is often higher than turnover from all causes, including election defeat, of members of the British House of Commons, or of congressmen and senators in the United States. Efforts to improve the work conditions of MPs in parliament will be examined in the next chapter. But as long as the problem of high turnover exists, and it shows no signs of disappearing or even diminishing, the prospects for stronger control over government by elected representatives are not great.

The honourable member is the basis of the system of representation, but in comparison with the prominence of party leaders, and the clarity of the contest between the parties, his role is confused and obscure. The prime minister and party are the central, stable elements of representation. Most members are transient and inexperienced, which makes the House of Commons a relatively weak recruiting and training ground for political leaders. The Progressive Conservative party often selects as leader someone with little or no experience in parliament, and the Liberal party as well on occasion goes outside parliament, or selects a leader with only a few years of service in the House. Because of these same factors of transiency and amateurism, a prime minister in selecting his cabinet is likely to have difficulty in finding candidates of the desired experience and quality. A leader of the opposition, particularly when his party is a sadly depleted rump like the Liberal caucus after the 1984 election, can have equally severe problems, and this makes the contest between the parties less interesting and useful than a more balanced and experienced House would permit.

5

The Workworld of Parliament

In 1957, Senator C.G. (Chubby) Power, a long-time member of parliament and holder of several cabinet portfolios between 1935 and 1944, wrote that 'not only has the position of the member of parliament altered in the last half century but he is being metamorphosed into another species'.[1] From confederation down into the first decade of this century, Senator Power stated, 'the representative of the people achieved his position, as such, because he was a distinguished citizen of his locality upon whom his fellow-citizens wished to confer an honour or distinction. In rural parts, he was often a country merchant or a well-to-do farmer. In urban ridings, he had usually been through the municipal mill as an alderman, and perhaps as mayor; or he was taken from the industrial or mercantile classes, a president of a Board of Trade, a manufacturer, or a merchant. Again, he had usually reached a certain age and was looked up to by his constituents. He was a solid man who represented them with dignity and decorum.' This type of man was favoured by the leaders of political parties because he had money and could be counted upon to finance his own election, an important matter because party election funds were scarce.

In those days the workworld of parliament was comfortable and prestigious. An elected MP was an important man. His wife was the envy of her peers in his constituency because she moved in the highest circles in Ottawa, meeting titled lords and ladies – even princesses of the blood royal – at Rideau Hall. In their work as members these men were rarely good debaters or orators, but they did know the sentiments of their community and conveyed these to their leaders. Sessions lasted two or three months. The member had an established business which did not suffer in his absence and to which he could return if he was defeated. When he left parliament he suffered no financial disaster. He simply lost the privileges of a first-class and very interesting club. The issues in politics were not complicated, and a member through his own knowledge and experience could usefully argue for or against policies.

This, Senator Power thought, had all changed. Government activities had increased so that expert and detailed knowledge was now needed to comment on policies. Citizens now needed a full-time representative, an efficient professional, rather than the dilettante in politics, the distinguished local amateur. By 1957, persons sought the position of MP because of a desire to embark on a political career and to obtain rewards such as a cabinet portfolio, a judgeship, or an appointment to a commission. The new member, because he had actively sought the position rather than having it conferred on him because of his personal qualities, was under an obligation to his constituents, and having become, in effect, their employee, received far less consideration than had his predecessors. The experiences of wartime had also harmed the role of members because then and since members were rarely consulted about policies and often learned about decisions in their seats, sometimes long after action had been taken. MPs felt impotent. The prestige of cabinet and government had increased, while that of parliament had declined.

MPs must now, Senator Power concluded, be professional and committed full time. Public opinion had not, however, come around to this view. Politics remained one of the few professions where the applicant was better advised to boast of his ignorance of the job he was seeking to obtain. In sport the cult of the gentleman-amateur had been abandoned long ago because the well-paid professional gave a better return for the money; the same now should be true in politics. But the role and position of the MP would have to be improved to ensure that the professionals were competent and provided full value:

The leaders of parties, particularly those in office, must understand that, however convenient it may be to have at their disposal a docile and disciplined party, they owe it to the country, their supporters and themselves to provide an army which will be composed not only of generals and desk thumping privates, but will have trained replacements for the higher ranks ... The greatest threat to party success, and indeed the direct way to national political ineptitude, is to allow bright, ambitious, young men to become politically atrophied by neglect and consequent indolence and frustration.

There is nothing more disheartening to the devotee of Parliamentary institutions than to observe, as he frequently must, the slackening in zeal and enthusiasm of men of great inherent worth who ... allow their legitimate ambitions to be stifled, and their natural political aptitudes to go to seed.

A problem had emerged because, despite the change to a year-long job for an MP, the position itself was becoming less important, partly because of the declining role of the MP in the constituency, and partly because of the shift in power to the executive. The member himself had less prestige in both constituency and Ottawa.

Nearly thirty years have passed since Senator Power wrote, and the problems in the role and position of MP he described have grown far worse. The House sat for 125 days per year in the early 1950s; now it sits for 170 to 175 days, in effect, an addition of ten weeks to a schedule Senator Power already considered to be full time. Despite this change in position to one that is demanding and full time, the MP is, as we have seen, for the most part a short-term amateur. A high proportion of members still leave because they are defeated by the system, not by the electorate. They are dissatisfied with the job, and find the role engenders, as Senator Power observed, frustration and slackening of zeal. With this mixture of amateurism and professionalism in the role it is not surprising that the salaries and pensions of MPs remain in dispute. The modern member is well equipped with secretarial, office, and research facilities, but he is still a party man who votes as his party decides. He has been given many of the tools to permit him to make an independent informed judgment, but he does not have the freedom to exercise this independence in public. It is in the curious combination of the job's importance and benefits, on the one hand, and its frustrations and limitations, on the other, that many of the roots of the dissatisfaction of members of parliament and problems in the parliamentary system are to be found.

PAY AND BENEFITS FOR THE MP

No other single question about parliament attracts so much media attention as the pay and benefits of members. Prime Minister Mulroney doubtless had this fact in mind when his government made, as one of their budget cuts in November 1984, a 15 per cent reduction in his special salary as prime minister, and a 10 per cent reduction in the salaries of his cabinet. A similar reduction in the pay of senior public servants would have had more effect on expenditures, but would be impossible to institute because of the complex nature and ramifications of public-service salaries and wage scales. The cuts made to their own pay by the Mulroney cabinet were, because they were limited to only a few people, of purely symbolic importance. An implication was made that the members of the House should also re-examine their pay scales; for his part, John Turner, the leader of the opposition, refused to make a similar reduction, saying that he had not been consulted beforehand by the government and did not feel that this was the right approach to reducing government expenditures. In 1984, as in 1979 and 1980, the government, under section 34(7) of the Senate and House of Commons Act, created a commission to review the salaries and allowances of members of parliament and senators.[2]

In 1986, the basic salary (sessional indemnity) of MPs was $56,100 per year. In addition, most members received a tax-free expense allowance of $18,700 per year, while members from remote communities and the Northwest Territories received slightly more. The 'special salary' over and above this amount received by the prime minister was, with the reduction, $52,955; the reduced special salary of cabinet ministers was $37,530. The speaker and leader of the opposition received a special salary of $42,800. Other officers, such as party leaders, whips, the deputy speaker, received somewhat smaller special salaries. Members contributed 10 per cent of their salaries for pensions; in return, after six years of service they would receive a pension based on the best six consecutive years' earnings of 5 per cent for each year of service up to a maximum of 75 per cent after fifteen years.

In addition, an MP has an ample travel allowance. He is allowed fifty-two return trips by air to his constituency each year, and up to ten of these can be to other points in Canada. An MP's spouse, family, and staff may use some of these trips. Local travel and use of a car in the constituency are paid for. Unlimited free rail travel is provided for the member, spouse, and children. Moving expenses from the constituency to Ottawa, and back, are covered once per parliament. Travel expenses within the constituency are allowed on a graduated scale, with members from urban constituencies permitted the least, rural more, and remote large northern areas the most. There are also ample budgets for telephone, mail, and Ottawa and constituency offices.

To many Canadians, both salary and pension seem excessive. The MP's salary is far more than that earned by the average Canadian, and the pension benefits are very generous, giving a maximum pension in fifteen years instead of the more usual twenty-five to thirty years, and offering pension benefits after only six years. The tax-free allowances are criticized as being further salary, since they do not need to be accounted for. The 1980 commission which reviewed members' salaries received many comments like: 'Many people feel that if Government salaries were fixed, they would do a far better job of controlling inflation' and: 'It is the opinion of this writer that Senators and M.P.'s, with a very few exceptions, are grossly overpaid both as to salaries and allowances; that their constantly self-increased incomes in recent years have no justification and have been a bad example in an economy suffering from inflation.'[3] It was doubtless in response to sentiments such as these that Prime Minister Mulroney and his cabinet reduced their special salaries.

The commissions which examined members' salaries and allowances came to different conclusions, however. They have asserted that 'the country can no longer tolerate a system that seems likely to attract mainly the independently wealthy to seek public office,'[4] and 'improvement must be made to salaries and allowances so that finances do not continue as a deterrent to candidates seeking public office.'[5] The McIsaac Commission found that there were thousands of people in Canada in the private sector and at all levels of government earning much larger salaries than

MPS. In most cases those earning more logged shorter hours in positions less vital to the welfare of Canadians.[6] They felt that 'because of the uniqueness and importance of this high elected office, a strong argument can be made that Members of the House of Commons should be paid considerably more than decision-makers in the private and public service sectors,' but because of the need for restraint in the economic circumstances of the times, recommended an indemnity which, it could be argued, was 'still below a fair and adequate level relative to other positions of responsibility.'[7] Further, the commission recommended an annual adjustment to maintain members' salaries in line with those of professional and managerial personnel elsewhere.

The McIsaac Commission also examined the pensions paid to MPs and their surviving spouses and dependants. They found the widely held public view that all former MPs received handsome pensions to be a fallacy: the median pension was between $3,000 and $3,999, and 70 per cent of those examined received less than $5,000.8 They concluded that the majority of men and women who had served Canada as elected members were not receiving adequate pensions, and suggested that adjustments ought to be made to those with very low pensions. Pensions are an especially important problem since persons usually serve in parliament at a central point in their careers and such service often means loss of a job, or at best failure to advance, and has very uncertain and usually short tenure. Following the McIsaac Commission's report, MPs' salaries and pensions were improved. Severance pay for MPs who are not re-elected, whatever the reason, was also introduced.

The Clarke Commission, established in 1984, reported in 1985. It recommended that member's salary be set at $69,000 or three times the average annual earnings of Canadians. This, they felt, should subsequently be adjusted yearly. The commission further proposed that the tax-free allowance be replaced by $100 per diem living expenses for members while in Ottawa. Senator's salaries, they proposed, should be set at 60 per cent of those of MPs. The Progressive Conservative government stated that this report did not reflect its policy. In 1986 Prime Minister Mulroney and his cabinet again reduced their special pay.

The two sides in the battle over the remuneration of members are clearly drawn. On the side opposed to increases are those who feel that a person ought not to profit from public service, and that to make the position of MP as rewarding as comparable positions elsewhere would make the position attractive as a source of financial gain and early, generous pensions. This reasoning is partly traceable to the British tradition of the gentleman-amateur, where the MP receives small financial reward, and his role is one of service, rather than of salaried employment. Others object to improvements in members' pay and pensions because they dislike politics and politicians. On the side favouring increases are those, such as the commissions that have examined members' pay and benefits, who feel that adequate remuneration is necessary to attract good MPs; that MPs should not suffer financially from service in parliament; and that there is conclusive evidence that inadequate remuneration causes hardship.

Incomes policy, wages, and salaries are among the most contested and changing aspects of the modern economy and society. MPs are far from being in the best-rewarded category, but their pay and benefits are among the most visible and as such are subjected to extended public discussion. MPs are in the difficult position of having to decide on and defend their own pay raises, unlike most other wage-earners. The arguments of the two sides are irreconcilable, and as long as the discussions are reintroduced after each election through examination by commission as legislation now requires, will continue to engender much public discussion. Some of the important issues, such as the appropriate size of the tax-free allowance and redressing the inequalities caused because some constituencies are remote from Ottawa and others close, tend to get lost in the process. A useful resolution to the issue of salaries might be to have them automatically mirror those in government, tied perhaps to those of judges or, as the Clarke Commission proposed, to the average income of Canadians. Discussion could then focus on the details of allowances and other benefits, the principle having been established that MPs are holding positions of the highest responsibility and should be rewarded at the same level as other senior executives and high public servants.

Offices and Other Facilities
The House of Commons, as of September 1986, provided a budget of $100,400 to each MP for his constituency and Parliament Hill offices. Of this 20 per cent, or $20,100, had to be committed for salaries and office expenses in Ottawa. Most office expenses on Parliament Hill, apart from salaries, are paid for by the House of Commons, including space (a suite of three rooms is standard), furnishings, telephone and long-distance calls, word processor, electronic-memory typewriter, dictaphone, calculators, and stationery and office supplies. A further allowance of $11,450 per year was supplied to cover office expenses in the constituency. Most of the budget goes for salaries in Ottawa, where the member's staff may include a legislative assistant, a special assistant, and any number of other assistants. The salaries for these senior positions compare well with public-service, university, or business salaries for similar research workers and administrators.[9]

These comfortable provisions for constituency and Ottawa offices are relatively recent. Until the 1960s two MPs would share an office and the services of one secretary. Since then there has been gradual but great improvement made in an attempt to upgrade the position of the MP, and to give members resources commensurate with their responsibilities. Facilities are not lavish in comparison with those for congressmen in the United States, but compare very favourably with Britain, where:

MPs, when they arrive at the House of Commons, find facilities available to them which seem designed to ensure that they encounter the greatest possible difficulty in performing their duties. All now have a desk, although most still share a room. But it was only fifteen years ago that a new Member's only accommodation might be a small locker in a corridor, or a filing cabinet in the gentlemen's cloakroom – and consequently off-limits to secretaries who, incidentally, had to be paid for from the MP's own resources. Since 1969 MPs have received an allowance towards the cost of employing a secretary, although until recently the amount paid did not come close to meeting the full cost, and no allowances are made towards the cost of employing a research assistant in addition to a secretary.[10]

The intention in improving the facilities available to the Canadian MP was to give him the ability to keep in touch with his constituency and to enable him to conduct independent research and investigations into issues of policy and administration. The political parties perform much of these functions in Britain.

Because of the large space requirements for their offices, MPs in Canada are now spread through several buildings. At the same time the central parliament buildings are increasingly being filled by offices of ministers and the cabinet. This expansion, necessary though it may be, has, some have argued, helped to reduce the cohesiveness of and close contact between MPs. Whether the home of parliament ought to be so stuffed with government offices is doubtful.

In 1969 the government began to make funds available to the opposition parties to hire research staff.[11] In 1970 this funding was extended to the governing party as well. The allocation is made according to a sliding scale: parties of from twelve to thirty MPs receive a basic $200,000; for each additional MP, up to fifty, this sum is augmented by $8,000, and from there on by $1,000 for each further MP. This budget covers the costs of salaries and contracts for research staff. The House absorbs the costs of employee benefits including severance pay and bilingualism bonuses. Office space, supplies, and services are also provided for the research groups. These groups assist the caucus, party leaders, and individual members in analysing legislation, preparing for committee investigations, and marshalling the material for debates and questions in parliament. They are of low visibility, but are of great assistance to the parties in parliament. There is nothing comparable in Britain, where many of their functions are performed by the parties themselves. The research capacity of the parties in Canada is much weaker than in Britain.

The Library of Parliament also provides research services for MPs and senators. The Information and Reference Branch will provide source material for use in speeches, prepare bibliographies and abstracts, and answer factual inquiries. However, the most important group for aiding MPs in intensive investigations is the Research Branch of the library, which is staffed by many specialists in various areas of public policy. They provide research papers and reports and summaries to members and committees. Often research officers are assigned to committees to aid in a particular investigation, where they will brief committee members on specific issues, prepare questions to ask witnesses, provide research studies, and draft reports. The work of the branch is not partisan. It is carried out in a strictly objective and impartial manner, but will stress a particular viewpoint if an MP so desires. Reports prepared for members or committees are confidential and are not released without permission, but this is often granted.

The Clerk of the House and the other table officers assist individual members in procedural questions, including interpreting standing orders and parliamentary practice in the House, speaker's rulings, and drafting motions. The Table Research Branch will also research specific points of procedure, practice, and precedent. The law clerk advises members on legal questions that are not procedural in nature. His office will also assist members in drafting bills they wish to present to the House, and provide legal advice to members.

THE JOB OF THE MP

The member of parliament represents his constituency through service in the House of Commons. This does not mean, however, that he spends most of his time sitting in the House, or even that attendance there is the most important part of his work. An MP spends far more of his working life outside the House than in it. 'Most MPs are activist, talkative and run from meeting to meeting' is one former MP's description of the job.[12] Only a few of these meetings are of committees of parliament; the others are with constituents, groups wanting to bend his ear on some matter of policy or administration, other MPs, journalists, civil servants, groups from foreign countries, or any of the innumerable groups and individuals whose interests and concerns are affected by government and politics. The job is people-oriented, involving talking about and listening to ideas, proposals, and complaints, reconciling opposing viewpoints, explaining party or government policy to citizens and citizens' views to party and government, getting action out of the government on problems of constituents, and examining how the government uses or abuses the power it exercises on behalf of the people of Canada.

The relationships of an MP with the enormous variety of people with whom he comes into contact are the core of his workworld. Of these relationships the four key sets are: first, relationships with constituency; second, relationships with interest groups; third, relationships with the public service; and fourth, relationships with party. In handling these relationships an MP decides how to balance local with national interests, with whom and on what he will spend his time and energy, and, except when he is motivated by a prior concern of conscience or philosophy, what his attitude will be on the issues of public policy that come before parliament.

Two studies made in the 1960s examined the roles of MPs through interviews and surveys of serving members.[13] It was found that MPs for the most part view their task as being constituency-rather than nation-focused, and somewhat more concerned with liaison and constituency matters than with policy – and law-making. The NDP and Social Credit members, as would be expected from ideologically oriented parties, had somewhat more of a national orientation than the two major parties. There was, however, little difference between French – and English-speaking members. In short, a typical MP 'would see his job as involving a mixed type representational role, a constituency-dominant areal role, and a liaison officer purposive role.'[14] Mixture and complexity were the key characteristics of the MP's job.

These surveys were useful steps towards understanding the role of the MP. They have, however, some limitations. Based as they were on surveys and interviews, they relied very heavily on the MPs' subjective sense, at a specific time, of what they thought to be most important, and on their subjective sense of what the interviewer or survey was asking. Some questionnaires were filled out by secretaries and research assistants. The results of the studies also relied on the interviewers' and data analysts' interpretation and coding of what an MP's answer meant, introducing another element of subjectivity. Both studies were also based on a role-analysis approach to the behaviour of legislators developed in the United States, where the structure of government is quite different and the representative, because he is not controlled by party discipline, must analyse and choose very carefully on policy issues because of the direct and immediate impact of such decisions on his chances of re-election.[15]

In Canada, unlike the United States, a representative's claim to be oriented towards constituency or provincial rather than national concerns, or vice versa, is an expression of subjective sentiment with little real effect or meaning in his behaviour towards legislation, apart from how it helps shape his party's policy. Further, this sort of sentiment is something that will change between issues and over time. An MP who represents a prairie farm riding would be committing political suicide if he did not overtly and strongly defend the interests of grain farmers; his could be termed a constituency, provincial, regional, or even national focus, depending on how it was expressed. However, the same MP might also, against his constituents' opinions, be a supporter of the abolition of capital punishment, while he might have a strong commitment to issues of little interest to his constituents, such as military spending or north-south relations. Depending on which of these issues he was thinking about, he could give virtually any answer to a question on role orientation and be speaking the truth. Thus, while these surveys of the opinions of MPs add to our understanding, it must be recognized that little is known about many aspects of the job of MP, let alone what the determinants are of legislative behaviour.

The Constituency

Modern MPs find, as Senator Power did, that the MP lives in two worlds. Douglas Roche described his thoughts while flying from Ottawa home to Edmonton: 'Living and working in two different locations two thousand miles apart produces a sort of schizophrenic effect. It's two different kinds of existences. Different people. Different problems. Different wardrobes. Different lifestyles. People, especially constituents, seem to depend on one more in Edmonton than they do in Ottawa.'[16] Another former MP, Gordon Aiken, discovered that:

When a person is elected to Parliament, he gets much more than a new job; ... His place of business moves two hundred or two thousand miles away. His own community and his own home are no longer havens from the world outside. He is on call 24 hours a day. There are compensations, but these only make the change more positive. He is a local celebrity, a person of influence when home. He travels continually, in his riding, to Ottawa, throughout Canada and occasionally abroad. He is constantly busy.[17]

Ottawa and the constituency are geographically separated, for many MPs, by thousands of miles, several time zones, and at least a half-day of travel; in the constituency the MP is constantly in demand for public occasions and constantly being sought by constituents with problems; in Ottawa he mixes with different people, performing quite different functions.

One of the first issues that new MPs must face is whether to move their families to Ottawa. For members from the Montreal-Toronto axis this decision is not of great importance. The distance from the constituency to Ottawa is not great in either time or miles, and public transportation is frequent and easy to use. But the farther an MP's constituency is from Ottawa, the greater the problem becomes. D. Hoffman and N. Ward found that French-speaking MPs were much more inclined than the others to leave their families at home, stay in Ottawa during the week, and return to their constituencies for the weekend.[18] This inclination can doubtless partly be explained by the great ease of travel from Ottawa to Montreal and Quebec City. The families of about a third of MPs move to Ottawa. Such a relocation causes some loss of contact with the constituency, not the least of which is that provided by the services of the spouse: 'A wife at home actually becomes something of an assistant Member. That is both good and bad. It's good for the public and for the Member. It keeps him in touch with his riding. But it's bad for her. Answering the telephone and the door, taking messages, guessing when he'll be home and what he will do, fitting in at public events and wedding anniversaries keeps a woman with a family pretty busy.'[19] 'Politics is best suited for two kinds of people.' Gordon Aiken quotes former MP Paul St Pierre as saying, 'Young, unmarried, intelligent men in their twenties, or men near retirement but still active. In between it's no good.' The vast majority, however, are in between, in their forties and fifties and with families. Paul St Pierre himself faced the problem: after being elected in 1968 he lived alone in Ottawa for two years. His family then moved to Ottawa, but returned to British Columbia after a year because, even while living in Ottawa, they saw so little of him. 'They were reconsidering at the time the 1972 election was called, but no further decision was necessary because he was defeated.' Especially because of the short tenure of most MPs, this problem of where to live causes severe disruption and difficulties for members and their families.

Regardless of where his family is, an MP must keep close contact with his constituency. The office in his constituency provided by parliament is an important link, as is his staff in Ottawa. There are, however, many other points of contact. Many MPs have office hours in their constituencies on a regular basis. Most make use of local radio and television, a high proportion write columns for local newspapers, many make regular mailings of newsletters and other material, and virtually all attend meetings and social gatherings in their constituencies. In addition Douglas Roche said that he tried to telephone the twenty or thirty people closest to him in his political organization:

at least once every two or three weeks. These are the people who worked hard to put me in Parliament and they appreciate a phone call from Ottawa. For my part I like to chat with them and pick up local news and opinions. These conversations are not meant to be profound analyses of events, though often they prompt a lot of horse-sense reaction from my friends. Rather they keep me close to the group around me and prevent me from sliding off into my own dream world, which would be my natural inclination and certainly the trap for those who begin to think that Parliament Hill is the world.[20]

Much of MPs' contact with their constituency, and even more of their office staff's, is involved with helping constituents with problems. The bulk of the work of the office staff of most MPs is, in fact, involved in constituency case work.[21] This 'ombudsman' and 'social worker' activity ranks very high in importance to the electorate. A poll, according to Aiken, 'asked Canadians to list the principal duties of an MP as they understand them. No hint whatever was given as to the type of answer expected. No sample replies nor choices were offered. And over half said, in one way or another, that looking after the problems of his constituents should be a Member's first priority. This was far ahead of any other suggestion.'[21] Hoffman and Ward found that:

There seem to be three aspects of the perception of the job of M.P. among constituents which can be distinguished. The first is the tendency for constituents to be ignorant of the scope of the job of the Canadian M.P., that is the tendency to press upon the M.P. tasks which are more properly those of municipal or provincial representatives (a fact especially apparent to French Canadian M.P.s). The second is the assumption on the part of some constituents that M.P.s have access to a great deal more patronage than they actually control (a matter mentioned especially by M.P.s from the Atlantic provinces and Quebec M.P.s). The third is the indifference of constituents to the legislative aspects of the job of M.P. It was this latter complaint that ranked especially high with French-speaking Liberals, and also with M.P.s from the Atlantic provinces.[23]

Canadian members of parliament have always been concerned with government activities which could directly benefit their ridings and constituents. For many years before confederation, in the Canadas and perhaps elsewhere, members were responsible for the allocation of the public works budget in their constituencies – what roads, bridges, and wharfs were built or repaired, who got the contracts – and this municipal council sort of activity became, with the development of centralized cabinet government, an important part of the patronage function. The activities of MPs in getting government jobs for constituents which Senator Power referred to were not only a way of rewarding supporters but also a means of alleviating hardship. The rationalization of government administration has reduced though not eliminated these patronage activities. There are still many nooks and crannies in the bureaucracy where the recommendation of the MP is helpful in getting a summer job or some other plum. But at the same time, government has become actively involved in welfare programmes, unemployment insurance, old-age pensions, job-creation programmes, support for citizen groups, neighbourhood-improvement programmes, and countless other programmes which offer, or promise, the citizen at the least some help and often much more. The administration of these programmes always involves elements of discretion and choice, and some citizens inevitably feel that they have been hard done by.

The member of parliament has become an important avenue for reaching government with complaints, and the growth of office facilities enables MPs to handle more of them. This ombudsman function is relatively new.[24] The public ranks this role very highly, more important even than the MP's role as legislator. Here the public perhaps shows more realism than MPs: Hoffman and Ward found that while virtually all members of parliament stressed the role of liaison officer between constituency and government, less than a third felt the ombudsman role to be important, while fully two-thirds rated the law-maker role highly.

One area that has not been examined closely is how this burgeoning ombudsman activity by MPs affects the administrative practices of government. Some government offices in response established two kinds of resource teams for handling complaints: the first, composed of experienced and skilled workers, gave quick, efficient service to complaints passed on by MPs and other notables; the second, composed of the less-qualified staff, gave slower and less personal attention to the complaints of ordinary citizens. The extent of practices such as these, and the real nature of the relationship of the MP to constituents – whether only select portions of the electorate, or all of it, use this channel and whether other biases knowingly or not enter into the process – would have to be examined before any final judgment is made on the effectiveness and impartiality of the complaint-handling procedures of various government welfare and benefit programmes. Until then, Gordon Aiken's judgment stands:

For some years, there have been proposals to appoint an ombudsman in Canada. This is an officer who investigates and reports on complaints against the public service. At the moment we have 264 people doing this job, in his or her particular way. Until someone decides that they can be more usefully occupied, one more isn't going to help very much. Furthermore, some Members like being an ombudsman. It gives them a feeling of satisfaction and importance to right wrongs and give the public a break. It compensates a little for the discouragement of House business. And it helps them to get elected again.[25]

The member of parliament still enjoys high prestige in his constituency. 'Prime Minister Trudeau's famous phrase that twenty minutes from Parliament Hill MPs are nobodies is incorrect,' according to J. Gillies and J. Pigott, both former MPs. 'The reality is that twenty minutes from Parliament Hill MPs are somebodies. It is on Parliament Hill, when assessed in terms of impact on policy formation, that MPs are nobodies.'[26] Gordon Aiken agreed: 'The fact is that when most members leave Parliament Hill and return home they become somebodies. Not lumped with 263 others in the chamber, each member is the federal presence in his own riding. He is a political authority, socially acceptable and the only one of his kind in the area. He goes to a lot of social events, wedding anniversaries, official openings, annual meetings and turkey dinners with no obligations except to "say a few words", these are the happiest parts of many members' lives.'[27] Some people like the rubber-turkey circuit and being on call twenty-four hours a day more than others; those who do have definite assets in getting elected to and enjoying life as a member of the Canadian House of Commons.

The member of parliament also interacts with his constituency on many matters of policy. On some of these, including capital punishment and bilingualism, most MPs are to the left of their constituents. Gordon Fairweather, later chairman of the Canadian Human Rights Commission, frequently found himself at odds with his constituency of Fundy Royal. Gordon Aiken relates:

Now, a dissenter is fairly safe if he agrees with the party in parliament, though that may be out of tune with his riding. And he is safe if he disagrees with the parliamentary group, but has the feel of his riding. When he is in disagreement with both, trouble awaits; and it often awaits Gordon Fairweather.

'They have always grudgingly let me go along on those issues I care about,' he says of his constituents. He also knows that his constituents are just a bit smarter than they get credit for. And they put a high value on honesty. 'Though an honest answer was unpopular,' he says of a grilling he once got on bilingualism, 'I had to give it.'[28]

Interest Groups

The member of parliament is expected to serve as a link between citizens and government, and as we have seen, contact with constituents and helping them resolve their problems with government are large and valuable parts of the workload of an MP. But in modern society many of the most important links between citizens and government are not direct and personal. Rather they are indirect through interest and pressure groups to which citizens belong in some capacity – workers, business owners, church-goers, consumers. These linkages are at least as important in the formation of policies as are political parties, the press, or the public service.[29] To operate efficiently, to be aware of how its policies and proposals do or might affect business, industry, labour, agriculture, education, and all the other myriad interests in society and the economy, government must keep in touch with these groups, hear their complaints, get their reactions, listen to their proposals, and respond to their concerns.

For the most part these relationships between interest groups and government bypass MPs and parliament. Interests tend to begin their lobbying activity well down in the system and to appeal upwards when they lose. Their first efforts are directed at departments and the public service so that memoranda submitted to cabinet will reflect their concerns while policy is being formed. If this fails, they will meet with senior public servants, perhaps the deputy minister, or even the minister. 'If these efforts are unsuccessful and legislation is proposed to which it is opposed, the group may then decide to lobby members of Parliament and eventually appear at the hearings on the bill before a committee of the House of Commons or the Senate. Parliament, in other words, is the last line of defence.'[30] One senior civil servant has been quoted as saying:

People who really want to guide and influence government policy are wasting their time dealing with members of Parliament, senators and, usually, even ministers. If you want results – rather than just the satisfaction of talking to the prominent – you deal with us, and at various levels ... To produce results you need to see the key planners, who may be way down in the system, and you see them early enough to push for changes in policy before it is politically embarrassing to make them.[31]

This was not always so. The origin of the House of Commons in the calling of two knights from every shire and two burgesses from every town to attend parliament was a way of ensuring that the important property-owning groups of commoners were represented, as the House of Lords ensured that the hereditary aristocracy and powerful religious orders were. In those days interest groups and representation in parliament were the same. The patron-client relationship of MPs and wealthy interests in the unreformed Whig parliaments also meant that parliament represented powerful interests. The Labour and Conservative parties of the twentieth-century British parliament have also included substantial representation and influence by interest groups within the parties, and even though much of the linkage of interest groups in government in Britain as in Canada is outside parliament, influence can be exerted on party leadership through parliamentary representation. Early–twentieth-century MPs in Canada were influential, according to Senator Power. The peculiar character of the modern major political parties in Canada – without mass membership, without articulated ideologies that identify them with some interests and oppose them to others, without specific platforms and proposals that affect interests, and without open public support and participation by interest groups in the formation of these non-existent programmatic platforms – means that MPs, through party, do not have the same formal and informal links with interests as their British counterparts.

But, even though the influence of individual MPs on legislation and policy is usually small, this does not mean that they are totally neglected by interest groups. Jean Pigott recalled that as a parliamentarian she found herself overwhelmed by group petitions and representations: 'Preparing a speech for an association of executive directors of associations, she decided to keep tally of the materials crossing her desk in one week. She brought to the speech a pile of some two hundred papers – briefs, magazine articles, letters – from groups wanting to inform an opposition backbench MP of their point of view, or to get her on their side.'[32] She concluded that perhaps members are flooded with information from pressure groups this way because while the lobbyist finds that there are many places where influence may be exerted and access is not difficult, access to MPs is the easiest, hence groups appear to have their greatest legitimacy with MPs.

In spite of this inundation, both interest groups and MPs find that when a piece of business is before parliament, and especially a parliamentary committee, the MPs are all too often lacking in knowledge and that they have not been adequately briefed.[33] Some MPs specialize in a policy area and become expert enough in it to be respected by both interest groups and government, but most do not. Many are not in parliament long enough to do so. MPs have tremendous demands on their time, and they and their staff are often hard pressed to keep up with constituency and caucus work and the regular routine of parliament, let alone delve into complex and abstruse areas of policy. Many an MP's office staff is loaded down with constituency work. However, David MacDonald, as opposition critic for cultural affairs, found that his assistant was able to develop quite a bit of expertise: 'People who got to know how I operated felt that it was almost more worthwhile to talk to him. That's an unusual situation. But if you give your staff an opportunity to develop their expertise, it does become known. I could do this more easily than some MPs because I had such a small constituency [in PEI] and my caseload was probably smaller.'34 Some of the blame for inadequate briefing of MPs also rests with interest groups. Many members feel that the private sector does not make enough effort to establish long-term rapport with MPs. Then, when an issue comes up, they haven't laid 'the groundwork so that MPs will have a means of grabbing onto their case.'35

This lack of interest in parliament on the part of pressure groups arises because the nature or intent of legislation is not normally changed during its passage through parliament. As Gillies and Pigott concluded: 'Representation to members of Parliament and to a committee may lead to the rewriting of particular clauses in a bill but such changes will always be minor; certainly no changes of any significance will or can result from special interest groups working with the legislature.'36 This is not always true. Interest-group representation added to strong press opinion has on numerous occasions persuaded the government to alter or drop legislation during its parliamentary stages. In addition, it is to the advantage of most interest groups to ensure that at least some influential members of parliament on both sides of the House have some knowledge of their activities and concerns. Then, when issues come up, it is easier to alert members. The question can perhaps be raised and resolved in caucus before it reaches the floor of the House. Such educational and general-information lobbying with members is an investment in the future. The backbencher of today may tomorrow be a cabinet minister, and the contacts that special-interest groups make with the opposition and government backbenchers may some day pay rich dividends.

The strengthening of the privy council office and the prime minister's office during the Trudeau era created problems for interest groups. The influence of their traditional links with departments weakened, while the new power centres tended to be self-sufficient and closed to interactions with the interest groups. As a result, Gillies and Pigott argued, policy was being made in Canada without adequate input from those affected by it. This situation could only be remedied, they concluded, if policy-making powers were shifted from the executive to the legislature, so that the individual MP would have more power and be free from party discipline. Then the role of interest groups would change from influencing the bureaucracy to influencing members of parliament.

But even without such a dramatic remodelling of parliamentary institutions much could be done to alleviate the present problems, where MPs are woefully inadequately informed and briefed on the business they must deal with, and most interest groups look on lobbying members as a last resort. Well-informed MPs can be influential in caucus, public meetings, the press, debates, committees, and other public forums; one of the tasks interest groups perform least well is ensuring that there are well-informed MPs in parliament. Along these lines, A.P. Pross argues that there has indeed been a change in recent years and that parliament's role has increased because the diffusion of power has placed a premium on its legitimating capacity. The legislature's ability to focus public debate now makes direct appeals to MPs (which produce results in debates and question period), and the presentation of briefs to parliamentary committees, highly desirable to interest groups.[37]

On free votes in the House, where an MP can choose as his conscience or good sense of the pressures on him dictate rather than as party demands, there is some likelihood that interest groups will try to persuade members. These occasions are, however, rare. The most important in recent years was the abolition of capital punishment. It, and other similar issues, such as abortion, which are matters of moral values, where there is wide disagreement that cuts across party lines, and where there are few or no financial implications or impacts on other programmes, are possible candidates for free votes in the future. They will doubtless arouse even more intense involvement by interest groups in the future than they have in the past. The MP can be left in a very vulnerable position in his constituency on issues like these because a small group in the electorate with very strong feelings could cost an MP a great many votes if he were to choose a position with which they disagreed. Strong party discipline has the often unrecognized advantage of protecting the individual MP from this sort of pressure; and curiously enough a free vote on these and other issues, such as the decriminalization of marijuana, could have the effect of making MPs more vulnerable to strongly felt minority opinions and less able to follow the dictates of conscience. This point can be made more general: unless the mix of interest groups concerned with an issue is varied and sensitive enough to express adequately the variety and strength of opinion and interests among the public on complex issues, the result of more free votes is likely to skew severely the pressures on members and therefore bias outcomes. The lack of party discipline in the United States makes congressmen and senators very vulnerable to this sort of pressure by single-interest groups such as the moral majority or those opposed to gun control.

The Public Service
MPs interact with the public service at several levels. First, in handling constituency casework, the member, or more accurately most of the time his staff,

is in constant touch with local offices and senior levels about particular problems of individual constituents. This kind of interaction is concerned with the detailed handling of specific cases by the public service. As an ombudsman activity it is involved with monitoring and ensuring a high quality of service delivery from government.

Second, there are opportunities for contact in dealing with larger issues of service in the constituency. Harbours and wharfs are a federal-government responsibility, and the MP can usefully discuss and investigate problems in these areas in conjunction with both headquarters and field staff.[38] The member can similarly interest himself in other government facilities, such as research, military, or parks, in his riding.

Third is the question of the formation of policy and legislation. Here the member of parliament is virtually excluded from the process. Any serious effort to involve parliament more closely in law-making and policy-formation would have to be based on much more and closer interaction between MPs and the public service, but there are enormous and perhaps insuperable obstacles in the path towards this goal.

The fundamental principle of responsible parliamentary government is that the minister is responsible for administration and policy-making and accountable to parliament for his handling of this responsibility. The public service is anonymous and faceless. It acts only on the minister's behalf and in his name. Nowhere is this anonymity and principle of ministerial or cabinet responsibility more jealously guarded than in policy-making. And no group is more systematically excluded from the process than are MPs. Despite the reduction in interaction between government and interest groups caused by the centralization of policy-making, there is still frequent and close contact between the two, but most of this is a private, behind-the-scene, secret process which is rarely the subject of public discussion. There is also some contact with the media when, for example, the government wants to float a trial balloon to discover public and press reaction before publicly committing itself to a policy. But members of parliament have neither the strength of knowledge and power that interest groups have nor the capacity for engendering public discussion that the media possess.

As a result, the informal interactions of the public service and MPs while policies are being formed are very few. This is not to say that parliament and parliamentarians have no role in policy-making. We shall examine policy-making later and discover that there are many points of contact. But it is to say that there are two separate political worlds in Ottawa: the public world of parliament and the media; and the private world of the public service, cabinet, central agencies, and their contacts with interest groups. The linkages between the two worlds are weak and unsatisfactory, and this problem remains a crucial one in policy-making and the mobilization of consent. Although there are good reasons of constitutional principle to support the practice, it is still notable that the elected representatives are so markedly excluded from policy-making, and that this vital process, which affects the welfare and prospects of all citizens and interests, should remain private and, in effect, the personal property of the ruling cabinet to do with as they choose.

A recent study has discovered that senior public servants in Canada tend to relegate MPs to the periphery of the policy-making world more so than those in Italy, Germany, the United States, or the United Kingdom. Canada is more like France than the other democracies in this regard.[39] The study also concluded that the cause of this remoteness was more a matter of attitude than necessity. Nevertheless, this tradition is deeply ingrained in Canada and has its roots in historical efforts to eliminate patronage in the public service, in the longevity and dominance of the Liberal government, in the weakness of parties outside parliament, in the brief tenure of MPs, and in the close connections between powerful business and financial interests and the government party.

Here is where the true meaning of Trudeau's comment that MPs are 'nobodies' can be found. As we have seen, they are far from being nobodies in their constituencies. Similarly, they are personages with privileges and influence on the floor of the House and in committees. But in relation to the small closed circle of power-wielders within the executive – cabinet ministers, central agencies, senior public servants, and a few others – MPs, like the vast majority of Canadians, are indeed 'nobodies.'

When government was smaller the civil service was unabashedly partisan. Sir John A. Macdonald defended patronage appointments by arguing: 'I think that in the distribution of governmental patronage we carry out the true constitutional principle. Whenever an office is vacant it belongs to the party supporting the Government; if within that party there is to be found a person competent to perform the duties. Responsible Government cannot be carried on on any other principle.'[40] The member of parliament had a more prominent position in Ottawa society, and could mingle socially with civil servants, because they, like MPs, wore their political colours openly; but now, when the public service is in theory neutral and to be kept innocent of party bias, informal contact between MPs and public servants is frowned upon and suspect. And the opportunities for formal contact in parliament are precious and few.

As a result there are strong formal and informal barriers separating the member of parliament from the other most active political group, the public servants engaged in planning, policy-making, programme-evaluation, the preparation of delegated legislation, and the exercise of discretionary powers. Not a small part of the contact is the surreptitious leakage of documents by disgruntled civil servants, perhaps those who were on the losing side in some battle hidden within the bureaucracy. Gordon Aiken's comments are very apt:

If there is validity to my theory that Members are trained seals, I don't know what I would call the individual public servant. His freedom of independent expression is just nil. Yet he gets his revenge in his own way. Over the past couple of years, a lot of so-called secret documents and information have leaked out. In most cases, it happens when the government is saying or inferring something inaccurate. It only takes a minute for someone to photostat a document and put it in the mail.[41]

An MP with this sort of private source often has a great deal of power, at the least to embarrass the government. But what is leaked is only part, and often a biased part, of the full story. Leaks are usually made to opposition members and are not a good way to keep members of parliament informed of what goes on within government.

Party
Gordon Aiken claims that George Drew, then leader of the Progressive Conservative opposition, was the first to describe members of parliament as 'trained seals' because they complied without question to the orders of their leaders.[42] The occasion was the pipeline debate, perhaps the most important debate in parliament's history, which inaugurated the modern parliamentary age of both obstruction and reform. The term has been used by many later commentators. It has nothing to do with the member's constituency work, which, as we have seen, is not only an extremely important part of the workload but is also normally carried out in a non-partisan manner. Rather it refers to the more visible part of the member's activities, partly in committee but especially on the floor of the House, where party, party lines, and party discipline count for everything and the autonomy of the individual MP is negligible. Although George Drew was referring specifically to government backbenchers, 'trained seals' now, as then, are to be found on both sides of the House.

For most of this century a British political party, like one in Canada, has been assured that its members would vote according to party lines. This now has changed. In the years 1974–9 some members of the British House of Commons dissented from party on 28 per cent of recorded divisions; and the government, between 1970 and 1979, was defeated by the defection of members twenty-nine times, on some issues which were very important.[43] Dissension, defection from party discipline, and defeats of government business have been even more numerous and important in committees. In comparison, a Canadian political party still has almost certain assurance that on the floor of the House or in committee its members will adhere to the party line. The defection rate is now (although not from 1867 to 1872) of negligible proportions and has no effect whatever on outcomes. Defections are not of such proportion as to cause problems but rather are limited to sporadic occasions when a member, or a few members, defects from party line on the basis of conscience but where that defection will not, at least for the government, cause serious damage. When members break rank in Canada, unlike in Britain, it has only a symbolic importance.[44] The public dialogue in parliament is not the exchange of views between informed individuals representing different constituencies and viewpoints, but the confrontation of highly disciplined party teams expressing a party viewpoint, and following strategies and tactics dictated by the parties.

The political party is the dominant control over how a Canadian MP argues, questions, and votes in the House and its committees. It is an easy enough trait to condemn, and most would-be reformers of parliament propose that party discipline be weakened. To Gillies and Pigott reform should ensure that 'the government and the opposition loosen the rules of discipline with respect to voting by individual members on committees,' and T. d'Aquino and G.B. Doern similarly recommend 'that the leaders of both the government and opposition parties recognize and adopt in practice a less stringent approach to the question of party discipline and rules governing confidence.'[45] The 1985 Special Committee on Reform of the House strongly recommended that the rules on confidence be relaxed. They felt a change in attitude by government and opposition was the essential first step.[46] Yet the blandishments of these many critics have persuaded no one, and party discipline remains firm. Party discipline must be supported by powerful forces of persuasion to remain so pervasive while at the same time it is so often criticized and is reason that members are ridiculed and belittled as being 'trained seals.'

Within the parties there are three possible loci for the instruments for maintaining discipline: the central organization of the party outside parliament, the constituency association, and the parliamentary party. Of these the first is the weakest. The party organizations outside of parliament function in part as adjuncts of the parliamentary party, as means for organizing and financing elections rather than as autonomous bodies. In part, also, the central offices are reservoirs of advisers for the leaders. They have little or no ability to compel an MP to vote one way or another, or to prevent him from doing so. One exception has been the Liberal party in Quebec, which traditionally retained the power to nominate candidates, leaving the constituency associations with little real power. The other exception is that the Canada Elections Act grants funds to the national party organization for election expenses. The party leader therefore has a measure of control over who will bear the party's name in an election, and can withhold funds if the local candidate is not acceptable. This power was used by the Conservative party when Leonard Jones, who was ardently opposed to bilingualism, was chosen as candidate by the local constituency association in Moncton.

In most of Canada the constituency organization not only has more power than the party organization, but also can be very influential over election outcome. One very right-wing Conservative sitting member, John Gamble, although he succeeded in being renominated by his constituency associations, was defeated in the 1984 election because both the Progressive Conservative and Liberal constituency organizations put their efforts behind an independent candidate who was duly elected to become the only independent member in parliament. William Yurko, the MP for Edmonton East, left the Conservative caucus in 1982 after disagreeing with his party over its position on patriating the constitution. Until the 1984 election he sat as an independent, resisting the blandishments of all parties. He was not renominated by the Conservative constituency association. He ran as an independent in the election, and was soundly defeated, coming fourth after the winning Progressive Conservative and the candidates of both the Liberals and the NDP. In spite of these isolated events, most sitting MPs, if they want it, obtain the nomination and support of their constituency associations. Support by the constituency association and party identification are normally powerful determinants of electoral success. And the constituencies, as the Yurko incident shows, are unlikely to support an independent candidate unless, as in the case of Gamble, some other unusual factors are at work. Constituency associations in Canada do not have a strong record of supporting maverick MPs who are at odds with their parliamentary parties.

The sources of the party discipline that determines MPs' behaviour are, however, largely within parliament itself, in the structure, values, and processes of the parties in parliament, and in parliamentary procedure and practice, to the large extent that these are controlled by the parliamentary parties. These parties are highly disciplined and organized teams. The basic unit of organization is the party caucus, to which all MPs and senators of the party belong. The party caucuses are complex and multi-functional institutions which have a pervasive influence on individual members, front benches, and parliament generally.[47] The structure and activities of caucus vary from party to party, and also change when a party moves from opposition to power or back. They have in common the features of meeting in private, of being the most important forum for interchange between front and back benches, of being the forum in which dissenting members are heard, and, particularly for the opposition, of establishing party policy on business before parliament. In many other respects, they differ.

In Britain, caucus officials are elected by backbenchers. The caucus of the Conservative party (the 1922 Committee) meets without cabinet ministers unless they are invited. In Canada the caucus officials of the two major parties are normally appointed by the leadership (although the chairman of the Liberal caucus was elected under Prime Minister Trudeau) and the caucus has much less autonomy and independence of leadership than its British counterpart. In part this difference is a reflection of the stronger and more secure position of British MPs. In part, also, it is a reflection of the larger size of the British House. It would make no sense, for example, for the current Liberal House of Commons membership of forty MPs to divide into front – and back-benchers, with less than half its membership in the latter group.

The party caucuses meet on Wednesday mornings. For the Liberal government these meetings were preceded by meetings of four regional caucus committees. In addition, the party had a number of ad hoc legislative committees which examined bills before, and during, their consideration by parliament. For the most part, ministers presented legislative proposals to caucus for discussion and explanation rather than for alteration, but on a few occasions caucus rejected or demanded amendments to the draft bills put before it. The function of the caucus was not, and has never been, to make policy and formulate legislation; rather it was a means of communication where ministers sought and found support for their proposals. Reports to caucus were oral, an agenda was not circulated, and no votes were taken or minutes recorded. Six or more items would be discussed during a two-hour meeting, and an individual MP would not have more than five minutes to present his views.

Brief though these caucus discussions are, members consider them and the once-weekly caucus meetings very important. Liberal MPs during the Trudeau era expressed such sentiments as:

Caucus is not a place where we ceremoniously endorse government policy; it's the place where we get in the elbows and knees.

We have frank exchanges behind closed doors, and it's like a family-type reunion.

The ministers are there with the Prime Minister and MPs have an opportunity to question them on any of their portfolios. Our caucus is run by the backbenchers (the executive is all backbenchers) and we chose our own subjects. If parliament is going to work, you need strong discipline within the party and caucus is one of the great escape vents for our feelings, particularly if we have some negative attitudes to bring across.

Caucus gives ... the backbenchers a chance to vigorously protect things the government is doing without washing our dirty linen in public.

Caucus can be not only a way of developing policy and of making sure that there is discussion, consensus reached and subsequently policy brought forward, but it can also be a way for a Member of Parliament to seek solutions to problems in his own region.

Some of the better debates that I have heard have taken place right in caucus along with significant changes in legislation.[48]

The Progressive Conservative party has a similar organization and schedule of meetings. It has had much greater problems with cohesion and conflict than the Liberal party. These problems, coupled with the greater freedom of the opposition side (because it did not hold power it did not have to be as rigorous and consistent as government), meant both that the caucus had to cope with more dissension and that there was more opportunity for diversity of expression in public. Both Robert Stanfield and Joe Clark faced difficult problems in gaining full support of caucus. Brian Mulroney as opposition leader was more fortunate. The party could sense the majority victory that had eluded them in 1979 and was united in the electoral combat, and as a result there was little internal party strife. A committee chaired by Mr Frank Oberle, MP, was established by Mr Clark to examine caucus organization and procedure. Its report (submitted after Mr Mulroney became leader) recommended democratization through the election of caucus officers and the use of caucus committees to develop policy. Nevertheless, Prime Minister Mulroney appointed the first chairman of caucus for his new government. Neither his government nor his caucus has had the experience and tradition of unity and internal resolution of conflict of the Liberal party, and sorting out caucus-cabinet relations could become one of the major challenges his government faces, as could be preventing the disorder and strife which damaged the parliamentary party under Diefenbaker, Stanfield, and Clark.

The NDP has the smallest of the caucuses (the Liberals after the 1984 election had only forty MPs compared with the NDP's thirty, but the addition of senators brought the Liberal caucus to more than a hundred). Its size as well as the party's traditions affect its structure and procedures. Outsiders, including the federal secretary of the party, the leader's staff, some members of the caucus research staff, and a liaison person from the Canadian Labour Congress, regularly attend (in the Progressive Conservative caucus one member of the leader's staff also attends). All caucuses on occasion are, however, addressed by outsiders, such as the chairman of the CBC. The officers of the NDP caucus are elected. The caucus does not normally formulate policy. This task is done by the party itself, which is more powerful than is the case for the other two parties. Dissent from party position is more frequent for the NDP than the others, and the caucus tolerates dissent on matters of moral and religious principle, providing the objections have been raised in caucus ahead of time.

Secrecy is a fundamental guiding principle for all three caucuses because caucus is the one forum within parliament where interchanges between leaders and followers are frank, open, and often critical. According to a member of the Conservative opposition, 'there are some very harsh exchanges in a caucus and members must bear in mind that these exchanges are not meant to belittle or to attack individuals; we are really debating issues. But it can be very damaging and harmful for leakages in caucus to get out ... There is always the danger of misrepresentation and misinterpretation and taking statements out of context. There are some very hot and sometimes very bitter debates in caucus.'[49] A member of the Liberal-government caucus concurred: 'If caucus becomes too leaky, members won't really speak their minds, the ministers will stop telling the caucus what they are doing and the prime minister will say "to hell with caucus". The guidelines say they must discuss certain proposals when they are at the proposal stage and not finalized and if it is all out in the press they will stop levelling with us.' This rigorously observed rule makes caucus 'the one place where you take off the gloves and fight for everything you're worth because that's the forum, the spot where decisions are ultimately made and you win or lose usually in caucus. It is probably the most serious debating forum in parliament.' Caucuses do, however, have their leaks.

One reason caucus is so highly regarded by MPs is that it is the only place they are free from party discipline, and can openly speak their minds and vent their feelings. The price paid is that in the public parliamentary occasions of debate and question period the MPs cannot be open and frank, and discussion is constrained and artificial because of the need to adhere to the party line and to reduce all shadings of viewpoint to two or three highly selective and biased positions. The role and influence of the press and media is crucial in shaping these traits. Crucial to the influence of caucus is whether a party is government or opposition.[50] Within the Liberal government's caucus there were strong motivations for conformity and discipline. Power resided in the cabinet, and the caucus occupied a consultative role and was consulted only infrequently on legislative priorities. The Conservative caucus in opposition had more influence over the policies and attitudes of the parliamentary party. There was a much smaller gap between front and back benches, and much more room for inconsistency and idiosyncrasy.

The structures and procedures of both caucuses alter with a change of sides in the House. If the Liberal party were to become the chronic opposition, it would undoubtedly face the same divisive tendencies as the Progressive Conservatives during their long sojourn in the wilderness. The Tories as government face a greater need for discipline and reining in disagreement and minorities within the caucus. Both parties could find it hard to maintain discipline in these reversed positions. Perhaps under these stresses the convention that party discipline must be constant and rigorous will be relaxed.

There are, however, other instruments besides caucus which encourage discipline. The most important of these are the party whips. The party whips of the Liberals and Progressive Conservatives are appointed by the respective party leaders. The NDP whip is elected by caucus. The whips have four functions: party discipline, communication and liaison between party leadership and caucus, management of the party's participation in debates and other activities of parliament (including ensuring enough are there for debates), and negotiation between parties.[51] The house leaders share some of these functions.

Party discipline is the most important of the whips' functions and is performed effectively with the powerful instruments at the whips' disposal. First, they allocate offices and office space, and a member out of favour with the whip is likely to find himself in a remote, second-best, location. Second, they decide who participates in question period, on committees, and often in debate as well. The speaker, during both question period and debate, recognizes members from lists submitted to him by the whips, and whips, to discipline members, have gone so far as to advise the chair not to recognize a member in question period. Similarly, an unruly member could find himself unable to participate in a debate on which he disagrees with his party's policy, or he can be punished by being left off a committee which he cares about.

Third, one of the most desirable rewards for MPs is to travel abroad with parliamentary delegations and associations. These trips, Aiken says, are 'a real prize. And party representatives decide who will go on the party's allotment. This isn't overlooked when a Member adds up the cost of becoming an internal nuisance.' One thing the member knows is that 'he would like to travel again. So would his wife. If he minds his business and works hard, fortune may smile on him once more.'[52] Promises of trips abroad, or the threat of withholding them, can be used as carrots or sticks to dissuade ordinary contrariness in members.

The threat of an election, which many textbooks make out to be an important instrument in the hands of the prime minister for ensuring discipline in his caucus, is not in fact very powerful. Prime ministers are as aware as other members of the costs and risks of elections, and a time when a prime minister's party is so divided that he is facing serious revolt by backbenchers is not likely to be an auspicious one for electoral success. Elections are not called to discipline renegades in parliament.

But sometimes a member refuses to obey the whips on what he regards as a matter of principle. On these more serious issues the whip would ask the recalcitrant member to stay out of the House rather than stay in his seat, vote contrary to party, and perhaps persuade other members to do likewise. The party leadership tolerates this sort of behaviour, with the additional concern on the government side that there must be enough members in the House to win a vote. A whip must be sensitive in his use of sanctions, and know when and when not to get tough.

The speaker has become an accomplice of the parties in enforcing discipline, for without the chair's consent these instruments associated with debate, question period, and committee could not be used.[53] To this extent, the speaker has now become a perhaps unwitting instrument for keeping the individual member under the discipline of party, rather than what the speaker's role in England originally was, a safeguard to ensure that the individual representative could without penalty exercise his abilities and follow his conscience in speaking freely in parliament and questioning the ministers of the Crown about their handling of the business of government.

In order to rally support for a vote or marshal members for an important committee meeting, a whip must keep track of the whereabouts of all members of his caucus. The whips must also know how members feel about issues, who the likely dissenters are, and what particular problems are likely to arise to make discipline difficult. They and their staff are, consequently, in constant touch with members to find out their views. The whips keep records of attendance of members in House, caucus, and committee, and how they vote. Not the least of their jobs is to ensure that enough members are around to enable sittings or committees to proceed. This task is not always easy. A chief government whip noted: 'I think it's the same in any party caucus – one third of the members are where they're supposed to be, one third are travelling or where they're not supposed to be, and one-third just don't care ... It seems as though it's a lot harder than it used to be to keep track of where members are and what they're doing. What with riding activities and trips and travelling committees, they may not even be in Ottawa, let alone on the Hill and where they're supposed to be.'[54]

The whips perform an extremely important function, although one that is normally hidden, that is, they ensure that party discipline is maintained, and that enough members are present for winning, or putting on a good show, at votes. They are sensitive to the currents of opinion and feeling in parliament. They encourage, cajole, threaten, and punish MPs. They are paid extra allowances, like cabinet ministers, the leaders of opposition parties, and the speaker. Their function is mainly to ensure that individual MPs do as party leadership and caucus want. Their role in telling party leaders or cabinet what the members will tolerate or not, and when they are likely to have a revolt on their hands, is much smaller. They also have only a small role in negotiations between the parties on parliamentary business. The whips are not a channel for communicating grievances and dissent. That role belongs largely to caucus.

Two opposing principles are at work in the functioning of caucus and the whips. One is the need for members to work together and cohere in groups so there can be identifiable government and opposition sides, and some integrity and consistency of viewpoints within parties. The other is that each MP is unique, both in terms of the constituency he represents and in terms of his own understanding and moral principles, and his function is to express this individuality and commitment to the best of his ability.

The present structure and processes of the Canadian House of Commons mean that the first principle guides most public activities of debate, question period, and committee work while individuality is suppressed and recognized only in the private spheres of caucus and constituency work. The discipline of party is essential to our system of responsible cabinet government. The compromises and trade-offs which are involved in interest articulation and aggregation take place within caucus. The freedom of discussion there, and the discipline enforced by the whips, are essential for the parties to function as united teams. Don Mazankowski of the Conservative party expressed it well:

Caucus serves a vital role in arriving at a consensus. A Member comes to the House of Commons with a particular point of view which is basically reflected by the location and background from which he or she comes. After the first immersion in caucus, Members quickly realize that the country is very complicated and that what they perceive to be in the best interests of their own particular region may not necessarily be the best for another region or for the country at large. As a result, caucus brings the various viewpoints into focus and then attempts to narrow that divergence and come up with a consensus that can be supported by the party.

Frank Oberle, also a Conservative MP, was less enthusiastic:

In the Canadian setting, caucus is nothing more than 'bitch sessions'. Caucus is one of the first things to seriously reform before reforming the House of Commons. The question is 'Where does the Member exercise his mandate? Does he do it in caucus or in the House?' If we want to continue the casual collegial system that we have in caucus, then the Members must have greater freedom to exercise their mandate in the House ...

Members of caucus generally feel that they are accountable to a constituency larger than just the party or the caucus. Members, particularly those who are not in high profile positions in caucus, are often very frustrated because they don't feel that they have sufficient power or opportunity to hold the officers of the party accountable to the larger constituency. That creates a lot of frustration, anxiety, controversy and discord.[55]

Even more severely critical was M. Juneau, a parliamentary intern, who concluded that the rigid application of party discipline and the requirement of obedience on the part of the member lead to the defence of ritualism and cause a general dissatisfaction among members. 'The paralysis of the institutions strikes the eyes of anyone able to observe regularly the work of the House of Commons and its various committees.'[56] The Canadian Study of Parliament Group was concerned about how little it takes to encourage MPs to conform. The difficulty with the discussion of sanctions at its seminar was that if those described constitute an accurate and complete list, then MPs are conforming to the party line for what appears to be very little in exchange. 'Can they really be bought for so little?'[57] their report wondered. The answer appeared to be yes.

But the price is not really so little. The powers of the whips are not trivial. Without the support of the whip, an MP would find it hard to get the opportunity to speak in debate, ask questions, or participate in committee work. He would have very few opportunities in parliament to express the concerns that had made it impossible for him to accept the discipline of a party caucus. He would have no access to the research funds granted to party caucuses. Likely he would also lose the support of his constituency association, and with it the chance for re-election. He would get none of the post-parliamentary patronage plums so important to many MPs. The political parties dominate and control virtually every significant aspect of parliamentary existence – apart from constituency work and the unimportant private members' time – and without the facilities and support of a party an elected representative is treated as a second-class member of parliament. Mr Yurko, after he became an independent, found that he had to fight for every chance to speak. He had, however, been an MP long enough to know enough about procedure to bargain for speaking time in the Commons by, for example, threatening to deny unanimous consent to routine procedural motions. 'I simply made it clear if I was not treated properly I could be miserable.'[58]

The emphasis on the first principle of party cohesion means that the second principle, that of respect for the individuality of the MP, gets little recognition. This lack of respect is what makes MPs into 'trained seals,' or 'lobby fodder,' and 'nobodies.' The frustrations of this blinkered role are also what makes the carrot of the trip abroad, which to an outsider seems to imply that MPs are prepared to sell their birthright for a very small mess of pottage, so important. Gordon Aiken's experience was: 'Conferences abroad turn the pale luminaries of parliament into shining lights. Some members become leader or deputy leader of the delegation, a real diplomatic honour. Others are Canadian delegate to one of the committees, spokesman in effect for his 22 million countrymen. At receptions and dinners, the formal old world courtesies make the delegate feel exalted. It is stimulating, but temporary.'[59] And he must soon return to a position without much honour in his own land.

Less well examined than the pressures for conformity on MPs are the reasons why political parties want this conformity. The assumption that solidarity and discipline are necessary seems to be so firmly embedded in the myths and folklore of parliament that neither the outside observers nor the parties themselves know why it is so desirable, or what the gains and losses would be from more relaxed discipline. Many interrelated factors appear to encourage the party leadership to demand such rigid discipline. The most important factor is that party discipline like everything else in politics is about power – who has it and how it is used. Discipline puts power into the hands of party leadership at the expense of followers. On the government side it also puts power into the hands of the government at the expense of the opposition. A weakening of discipline to an extent that would allow MPs to ignore party lines and vote as their consciences and constituency interests dictated would result in a loss of power for party leadership and the government. It would mean that a cabinet would not only be uncertain as to how the House would vote on government business, but would have further problems because timetabling of legislation, already extremely difficult and unsatisfactory, would become even more anarchic.

There are additional factors. Both participants and observers view parliamentary politics as a team sport. The essence of a good sports team is discipline, coherence, and co-ordination, and the parties are criticized if they fail to exhibit these characteristics. Deviance and dissent are perceived by both insiders and outsiders as weakness. As Elmer MacKay, MP, noted: 'If you depart from the official party line you are looked upon as being disloyal to the party.'[60] The media in particular are quick to jump on any presumed disagreement within a party as evidence of failure of leadership and proof of incapacity and incompetence within the party. Such bad press harms a party's image and weakens electoral support.

A further complication is that both major parties often face situations where the leaders want to go one way and the backbenchers another. The normal regional skewing of the parliamentary representation and the recruitment of MPs from upper economic and social levels mean often that what the rank-and-file members of parliament see as good policy conflicts with what the front bench sees as necessary for good government or electoral success. Bilingualism caused this sort of problem for the Conservatives under Stanfield, tax reform caused it in 1971, and again with MacEachen's budget of 1981, for the Trudeau government. The leadership must exert strong discipline over backbenchers in these circumstances, and must have powerful instruments to exert it. Once in place and in use, these instruments are used more often than is perhaps necessary. In the NDP parliamentary caucus there is less of this sort of pressure because much party policy is determined outside parliament and MPs have accepted these policies before they are elected. Nevertheless, the caucus can still run into problems like those caused by Mr Broadbent's whole-hearted support of Prime Minister Trudeau's constitutional proposals, which he gave before the party itself had made a decision on the issue. The NDP is also more tolerant of dissent on moral principle than the other parties – a tradition going back at least as far as J.S. Woodsworth's vote against Canada's declaration of war against Germany in 1939.

A party can suffer from a genuine rift. Dissension tore the Diefenbaker cabinet apart, and the aftermath of these disputes continued to plague the Conservative party for many years. Mr Stanfield and Mr Clark, as leaders of the party, even with all the powerful instruments of discipline and control at their disposal, were unable to prevent dissension becoming public and harming the party's electoral chances. Party leadership will try to prevent large-scale damage by extinguishing revolt and dissension while they are still small. Clearly media and public reaction to dissent is a large factor in making the parties view discipline as so essential, and also, perhaps the instruments for discipline are not always as great as they might seem. Much of the obedience to party comes willingly from MPs, who are loyal, and owe their election success to their parties.

Finally, the present attitude of government, opposition front bench, and many outsiders is that virtually all items of government business are considered to be matters of confidence which the government must win. The standing orders even make some motions, by definition, votes of confidence. As long as these constraints prevail, the government is not going to be prepared to go very far in relaxing discipline or accepting dissent from its backbenchers. The Special Committee on Reform in 1985 argued for change to the confidence conventions, and hoped for a change in attitude of members, government, and press to lead to a reduction in party discipline.

Why Party Discipline Hasn't Weakened

Disciplined parties are necessary for responsible government, but it is difficult to escape the conclusion that discipline is excessive at present. A terribly high price is paid both in terms of bringing parliament into disrepute and in terms of restricting the contribution individual members can make in parliament.

For most of this century, party discipline in the British parliament, was as rigid as in Canada. Recently it has loosened. An examination of the reasons that British MPs are both motivated to dissent from their party and are able to do so with impunity shows the complexity and deep roots of the factors that affect this crucial aspect of MPs' behaviour.

The first difference is that, as we have seen, most of the seats in the British House of Commons are 'safe,' held securely from election to election by one of the two major parties. Once elected in these constituencies, a member will continue to be re-elected until he retires. In post-war Britain, MPs who voluntarily retire normally have served for more than sixteen years in the House, and not infrequently for as many as thirty or forty years. At elections, on average only 7 per cent of MPs lose their seats through defeat.[61] With this sort of security, the vast majority of members need only be renominated to be assured of remaining in parliament. Patronage plums for retiring MPs are less common, and the stay in parliament longer than in Canada. A higher percentage of MPs retired to patronage positions in Canada in 1984 than are normally defeated in a British general election. Service in the British House of Commons is more of a career than is service in the Canadian House, and it is more independent of party rewards.

Second, nominations in Britain are in the hands of constituency associations, and those associations are prepared to renominate members who do not obey the whips in parliament, or who have fallen out of favour with the national party executive or the leadership of the parliamentary parties. The local constituency associations in Britain, particularly for the Conservative party, are more independent of the national party than is often appreciated. The national party cannot insist that a candidate by adopted; however, disapproval is very rare. When a seat becomes vacant, a constituency association selects a candidate from would-be MPs who submit their names. There can be more than a hundred of these, especially for a good safe seat. The executive of the local party association normally makes the selection in private, unlike the Canadian practice of selection by ballot at open meetings. Constituency associations jealously preserve their independence. Once elected to parliament, the member's prime controlling relationship is with the local party association. Since 1942 no British Conservative MP has been denied the party whip, and the position of members who have resigned the whip or failed to support the party in parliament has been looked on as a matter not for national interference but for local discretion. Local parties are quite prepared to defy the national and parliamentary leadership of the Tory party, particularly when the MP has erred to the right rather than left. At the time of the Suez crisis in 1956, four of the seven left-wing rebels failed to secure readoption by their constituencies, while all eight of the right-wing rebels were readopted, and without criticism.[62] The national leadership of the Labour party has exerted slightly more influence in candidate selection and renomination, but the difference is only marginal, and the final word rests with the constituency association and not in the central party. Labour constituency associations, like those of the Conservatives, are quite prepared to defy the national party and parliamentary leaders in reselecting or (less frequently) rejecting a sitting member. Consequently, to be assured of remaining in parliament, the British MP need only retain the support of his constituency-association executive. He does not need the support of the party's general membership in the constituency, because they do not participate directly in his nomination, nor does he need the support of the national party as long as (and this is the normal rule) his constituency executive is prepared to defy it, and most, once elected, are in safe seats untroubled by electoral swings. In comparison with the Canadian MP, the British member is very secure in his seat indeed.

Third, there are 650 MPs in Britain compared with 282 in Canada. This in itself makes for greater variety, and makes it more difficult to maintain discipline. The whips in Britain have more responsibility than those in Canada for finding out what backbenchers think and feel, and advising the party leaders as to what the rank and file will or won't stand for. It is for this reason that the chief government whip is a junior minister.

Canadian observers often mistakenly assume that because the timetabling of parliamentary business is much more rigorous in Britain than in Canada, and because debate on government business, especially second reading of bills, is much shorter (rarely more than one day), the British government is certain to get anything it wants through parliament. This is far from true. Some pieces of government business are rejected by the House in Britain. Other legislative proposals are abandoned by the government because the whips discover that the parliamentary party will not support them. These hidden failures mean the true failure rate is higher than the parliamentary record indicates.

When it was first asking the British government to have the Canadian constitution amended in 1981, the Trudeau government did not appear to appreciate this power of the British backbenchers to reject their government's proposals. The objections of the eight provinces and their lobbying in Britain had made approval of the Trudeau government's proposals by the British parliament very doubtful even before the Canadian Supreme Court ruled on the issue. After the ruling, in which the Court decided that constitutional convention required substantial support of the provinces, there was no chance that the original Trudeau proposals – even if they had passed the Canadian parliament – would be accepted by the British parliament. The British government would have provided time for their debate if the Canadian government had insisted, but it could not guarantee passage. The reports of the whips showed that the backbenchers would not accept the Canadian package without more support by the provinces. This was a very important influence in persuading the Trudeau government to accept the final constitutional proposals supported by nine provinces, even though they included many features the government did not like. With such substantial provincial support, the new package had no problem getting through the British House.

Fourth, a British MP can have a satisfactory life as a member even if he does defy the whips. The number of sittings in a year of the British parliament is the same in Canada, but since there are more than twice the number of MPs, there are fewer, and briefer, occasions for debate and question available to each MP. There are not enough seats in the House of Commons for all members. Even if they wanted to, they could not all attend question period or debate. There are also fewer, and smaller specialist committees; where the Canadian MP will sit on one, or even two, specialist committees, many British MPs will sit on none. Office space is limited and unsatisfactory at Westminster. The British member of parliament, as a result, has less opportunity and less incentive to be in the House or the Palace of Westminster (Parliament Buildings) than his Canadian counterpart. Also London, unlike Ottawa, offers many of the attractions of a big city, and many opportunities for an MP to have a part – or even a full-time job and still fulfil his duties as member. As a result, for most British MPs, the House itself is a less important part of their activities and interests than it is for Canadian MPs. This fact has perforce made the British whips increasingly tolerant of dissent and disagreement among backbenchers. At the same time, more backbenchers are finding that they want to pursue a career as a parliamentarian outside the lines of advancement controlled by the whip. Some do not particularly want to become ministers or frontbench spokesmen, and post-parliamentary patronage positions are much less of a carrot than in Canada.

Fifth, the differences between the parties in many policy areas have narrowed with the weakening of ideologies. Rigid discipline arrived in the British House with the coming of the division into two parties, each representing different, and supposedly hostile, class interests and proposing conflicting policies. In recent decades there is less satisfaction with this simplified view of policy issues. There are wider shades of opinion within each party, and disagreement is more and more coming to cut across both parties. MPs consequently more often find themselves in agreement with some members of the other party, and in disagreement with their own.

Sixth, the British members of parliament have always had more independence from party than the Canadian MPs, and more of parliamentary procedure is outside the control of parties. Unlike Canada, Britain has a long tradition of non-partisan parliamentary committees, chaired by either government or opposition members, and outside the control of the government. Committee membership is not controlled by whips, and committees choose their own chairmen. The speaker is more independent, and the parties have little role in deciding who shall perform in question period and debate. On the government side in particular, party leaders change more frequently than in Canada, and the prime minister dominates his parliamentary party less, and for a shorter period. Competition between disciplined teams is still an important element in the British parliament, but it is less all-pervasive, and an MP can be a team player part of the time and ignore or defy party discipline part of the time, and still be respected by party. The press and media are also less alarmist about this sort of behaviour. Much of this difference is one of attitude in both participants and observers, but attitudes, when they are held long enough, and are considered important enough, become conventions and ultimately rules of behaviour. Far more than in Britain, in Canada parliamentary politics have congealed and hardened into a team sport that dominates all aspects of structure and proceedings.

Seventh, the conventions on confidence in Britain have been relaxed in recent years. Between 1970 and 1979 British governments suffered sixty-five defeats on division in the House. Twenty-nine of these were caused by dissent within the party, and thirty-six were the product of opposition parties combining against the government in a minority parliament. Only one of these, in 1979, was considered a vote of confidence and led to an election. On the rest, the government accepted its lumps and remained in power without the uproar from press or parliament which the very rare defeats of government business provoke in Canada. Many of these government defeats in Britain were on three-line (the most insistent) whips. Governments have been defeated on important issues, including major policy issues (the Conservative government on immigration legislation, the Labour government on devolution of power to Scotland and Wales), on matters of expenditure, and even on matters of parliamentary procedure. In Britain 'the Government knows that it cannot take its backbenchers for granted; unthinking loyalty is no longer a feature of British politics in any party these days.'[63]

Obstacles to Change

The workworld of parliament of earlier times portrayed by Chubby Power was one of amateur members and amateur government. The MP's position was one of honour and prestige, with few serious responsibilities. Not many important items of policy came before the House, and few of those that did required detailed professional knowledge to discuss. Being a member of parliament was a part-time task, requiring only a few months of the year. A member's pay was then accurately referred to as an indemnity (according to the *Oxford English Dictionary*, 'compensation for loss incurred; sum exacted by victorious belligerent as one condition for peace'), rather than as salary.

The Canadian party system developed in those days as a means for controlling the immense centralized power of parliamentary cabinet government. The instrument of control was rigid party discipline supported by the carrot of patronage to ensure support of both members of parliament and the electorate. The two major parties did not emerge from the electorate as a means of expressing ideology or interest, later to seek power through representation in parliament. Rather they evolved as creations of the parliamentary leadership, especially the prime ministers, as leader-centred instruments for getting, keeping, and using power. In order to do this in a country which was still emerging from colonial status and had yet to develop the foundations of a national economy, culture, or identity, the parliamentary leadership needed very strong instruments of coercion and control over parliament, the source of power and authority. This need was the source of rigid party discipline. Policy could not be trusted to amateur, short-term, part-time MPs who served in parliament as a matter of prestige and perhaps had no strong views or concerns apart from local interests. The government had an important job of nation-building to do, and to accomplish it needed to brow-beat, cajole, coerce, persuade, and compel uninterested and often unwilling representatives in parliament.

Present-day Canadian politics are very different. The member of parliament now has a demanding full-time, year-long job. He is paid a good salary, and has ample office and staff resources in both Ottawa and his constituency. The MP performs an enormous amount of casework on behalf of his constituents. Government is huge, and in every year there are many important issues with which parliament must deal. Parliamentary committees occupy themselves with examination of policy and administration. Other factors have not changed, however. The member is still short-term, and as a result most remain amateurs. The major parties still remain centred around their parliamentary leadership. Party discipline in parliament remains rigid. To party leaders, the function of the MP, like the function of the party outside, is to support. Though MPs find their party a source of strength and influence, they also submerge their identity within party. Party and party discipline have moulded the structure and processes of parliament, and the attitudes of MPs, the press, government, and opposition leaders. It is the most dominant and pervasive force in parliament and the workworld of MPs.

Many MPs chafe under this extreme discipline and control. But reform will not be easy. The parliamentary committees which looked at this question discussed reform in terms of changing attitudes. They failed to note that in Britain the change of attitude of leaders came second, following the change of attitude of private members. Party leadership was forced to accept the change to survive. The comparison with Britain shows that many of the factors that permitted private members to change their attitudes and behaviour are lacking in Canada. We do not have a large number of safe seats, strong independent constituency associations, or members able or prepared to pursue a career in parliament outside the channels controlled by whips. Party control is reinforced by the legislation governing election financing, and by many rules and conventions of procedure. What has been discussed in Canada is not real reform, but simply a loosening of discipline at the discretion of the cabinet. This situation is a world apart from the British experience, where independent-minded members forced the party leadership, against its wishes, to accept more relaxed discipline. The obstacles to reform in Canada lie far outside the ability of parliamentary committees to change, in the electorate, the constituency associations, the media, public perceptions of the role of the MP and the forces that make most MPs short-term amateurs. To make the workworld of parliament more attractive, and to encourage MPs to make service in the House more of a career, is the greatest single challenge facing the Canadian parliamentary system.

6

Procedure

Procedure, like most other aspects of parliament, is about power and about the terms and conditions of discussion of its uses. Procedure is a means of reaching decisions on when and how power shall be used, and a process for considering and evaluating proposals for its future use and for criticizing and defending the present use. Procedure ensures that the parliamentary processes create a continuous dialogue between government and populace as represented by members of parliament. At some point the discussion of government proposals ends and parliament grants government the necessary legislative authority and funds; at a later stage discussion begins again on how the government has used these powers. In both stages procedure sets the rules and conditions of the discourse between government and parliament.

In setting these rules and conditions parliamentary procedure is not just a part of, but one of the most important parts of, the constitution. Procedure establishes some of the fundamental decision rules of the political system – the terms by which proposals for the use of power are reviewed and by which authoritative decisions are made and ratified. Democracy is not only a system of majority rule; it is also a system in which minorities are listened to and taken into account. Parliamentary procedure, because it sets the conditions of discussion and decision-taking, determines the relationships between majority and minorities, government and opposition parties, government and the individual member. Procedure creates not only the opportunities for the minorities to have their say, but the mechanism by which discussion ends and the majority gets its way.

Parliamentary procedure tries to ensure that there is adequate opportunity for varieties of opinion to be expressed and listened to. It provides opportunities for the government to be interrogated, examined, and forced to explain and defend itself. It recognizes the need for a time limit on both expression and interrogation, so that decisions are taken and discussions on one issue terminated in order for discussion of another to begin.

These three goals are not entirely compatible. Ministers of government cannot spend all their time in the House of Commons listening to other members, explaining their programmes and proposals, and answering questions, nor can discussion be allowed to proceed until everything that can be said has not only been said, but said many times over with no end in sight. Governance is the exercise of power, and this exercise requires, at times, that a discussion is ended before some would like, and that decisions are taken which go against the interests of, and even harm, some individuals or groups. The purpose of parliamentary procedure is not to ensure that every member can say as much as he wants on every topic, or that groups or individuals can prevent decisions which they do not support from being taken, but to ensure that there is a balance in discussion between the holders of power and citizens, that on the one hand the majority does not have the power to prevent discussion, reconsideration, and change, while on the other hand a minority cannot immobilize the whole system.

Because the principles are not compatible there is no static point of rest in this balancing act. And there is no overriding principle to establish when discussion ought to end. In reality, the decision to end discussion is one of the most important acts in the exercise of power. It establishes the relationship between rulers and ruled. It is quite natural, even inescapable, therefore that parliamentary procedure will often be a source of argument and discontent. Procedure is intended to ensure fair play, but what to a government looks like a reasonable and fair time to end a prolonged and no longer productive debate can look to the opposition like an unreasonable trampling of their rights of expression and interrogation.

Parliamentary procedure, like many other aspects of the Canadian polity, is still evolving. Some issues, such as the timetabling of government business and the use of closure, which create almost intractable problems in Canada, were resolved many decades ago in Britain. But what is appropriate in Britain is often not appropriate here: Britain does not have Canada's features of two major language groups and a strong federal system. The imbalance between government and opposition in Canada creates special problems, as does the lack of identity of either of the two major parties with an established ideological position and the inability of the parties to generate political discussion and create viable, coherent, policy proposals.

Only within this decade has the Canadian polity been able to arrive at the crucial decision rule of an amending formula for its constitution. Constitutional amending procedures are at least as fundamental and essential as parliamentary procedure. Yet even here, after a century of discussion, the amending formula finally agreed upon is less a rule for creating a decision binding upon all parties than a means by which dissenting minorities (provincial governments) can opt out. The Canadian polity, because its elements are so disparate, shows great tolerance for dissent and variety, and correspondingly less tolerance for the imposition of the will of the majority on the minority. Because it has been created and is viewed within this framework of values and attitudes, parliamentary procedure in Canada is far from satisfactory. Procedural problems cannot be cured by a technical fix. They involve disagreement and uncertainty over power and how it ought legitimately to be used. Little wonder therefore that parliamentary processes and procedure often seem cumbersome, frustrating, and ill-adapted to their purposes.

Like other structured situations where human beings have to reconcile conflicting values and interests, the rules of parliamentary procedure tend to become detailed and complex. In this way parliament is comparable to sport, where football, for example, requires numerous referees and linesmen, has a written rule book, and involves a special language of signs, signals, terminology, concepts, and actions which are unintelligible to the outsider. The judicial processes and the law courts similarly involve enormously sophisticated, refined, and complicated rules and procedures which require specially trained experts (lawyers) to use and decode them, and which seem like unintelligible mumbo-jumbo to the outsider. Like the rules of procedure in both these areas, and innumerable other aspects of life, parliamentary procedure tends to become complex and esoteric. Also, in practice, as is true of decisions of referees, judges, and juries, it has an arbitrary element, involving the use of human judgment, and is not an exact science.

The first basic principle of procedure is that discussion in the House should lead to a decision. Most of the time of the Commons is occupied with debate, and debate is always centred on a motion. There are many sorts of motions, including the three readings of bills, resolutions to go into committee of the whole, motions to adjourn under Standing Order 29 to discuss a matter of urgent public importance, substantive motions to elicit a statement of opinion or determine the will of the House (such as a specific motion of want of confidence and the motion on the speech from the throne), motions to amend other motions, and motions for clauses and timetabling.[1]

Debate is often adjourned, and is sometimes not taken up again, and as a result the House does not always make its decision immediately if at all; however, as long as debate is under way it must focus on a motion. Thus, the House, in theory, is not spending its time in idle, aimless discussion, but members are arguing for or against a specific proposal; for example, that a bill ought now to be read a second time, that the House does not have confidence in the government, that the House ought to go into committee of the whole to consider taxation legislation, that the

House ought to adopt an amendment to a bill. An MP's speech, to be in order, must be relevant to the motion. This rule does not preclude repetition and tedium. A member can and often does say what many other members have said before in the same way, and can say it in a dull and repetitious way, but his words must be directed to the motion.

The rules of procedure determine which motions are admissible, which are not, how they should be worded, who can make them, what sort of notice must be given (the House is not normally caught by surprise), when they will be debated, whether they are voted on or not, which are of confidence, what amendments are in order, who (speaker, government, opposition, or private member) makes the selection of the motion to be debated, and so on. These rules form an intricate framework for the major business of the House. They establish the agenda for parliament's business.

Motions, and the business of the House, divide into three categories. The first, government business, is the most important and occupies the most time. It includes most legislative proposals, the throne speech debate, budget and other financial debates, and various other motions (such as the time-consuming business involved in constitutional amendment in 1981–2). The second category, private-members' business, occupies only a small part of the time of the House, and whether it is in the form of motions relating to bills or other motions it rarely receives more than a brief debate, and even more rarely is voted upon. The third is opposition motions. These include amendments to the motion on the throne speech, and to budget proposals, amendments to legislation, or motions to adjourn for emergency debates. The amendments would be dealt with under government business. Opposition motions are also made on supply days – twenty-five days during each year when the opposition selects topics for debate on the floor of the House as an adjunct to the normal consideration of appropriations by standing committee.

The end of the process of debate on a motion is the taking of a vote. Many motions, particularly routine ones, are voted on without dissent; most voting is made by voice, that is, the speaker asks for the ayes and then the nayes, and declares which side has won. On some motions, however, there is a recorded division and each member present individually indicates his choice. This process is time consuming, and is used on only a few of the many motions before the House. A motion is approved as long as a majority of the members present vote to support it, majority normally being fewer than half the full membership of the House. The quorum is twenty members. But regardless of how many members were present and voted for or against, once approved a motion is a decision of the House, and one made with the support of 11 members has the same power and force as one made with the support of 250. Many motions, of course, do not reach the stage of having a decision taken upon them. Opposition obstruction has as its purpose not the defeat of the government, but the prevention of a vote being taken, and over recent decades there has been a progressive slowing down of the parliamentary processes as obstruction has become more entrenched and systematic. The government often leaves debate on a motion adjourned because it does not want to pay the price of overcoming obstruction. Most private-members' business is talked out (discussed for an hour and then adjourned with little likelihood of being resumed) and does not come to a vote.

Sittings of the House begin at 11:00 am on all days except Wednesday, when they begin at 2:00 pm. At 2:00 pm on all days except Friday (when it commences at 11:00 am), a period of house business begins which is an exception to the principle that the House must have a motion before it. For fifteen minutes members other than ministers make brief statements on subjects they consider important. This procedure replaced, in 1982, the activity of proposing motions under old Standing Order 43, which permitted motions to be made without previous notice with the unanimous consent of the House. After the rule changes of 1968–9 members gradually began to use Standing Order 43 to propose numerous motions to draw attention to issues. Leave was almost never given for these motions to be debated. This procedure was confusing, and its purpose was not to propose serious debate, but to make a statement. Present practice recognizes this purpose. Immediately following the statements comes question period, so the statements in practice serve as a warm-up to it. Question period continues for forty-five minutes. At 3:00 pm (12:00 pm on Fridays), the ordinary daily routine of the House begins. This includes the presentation of reports from committees, the tabling of documents, statements by ministers, introduction of bills, first reading of Senate public bills, and government notice of motions. On Wednesday and Friday, these items are followed by questions on the order paper (written questions) and on some days there is also provision for notice of motions, including motions for the production of papers.

Slightly more than an hour of each daily sitting is taken up with these events. Debate on motions (usually government business) occupies the bulk of the rest of the time. Since the House sits from 11:00 am to 1:00 pm and from 2:00 pm to 6:00 pm on all days (except Wednesday, when there is no morning sitting, and Friday when it adjourns at 5:00 pm), there are roughly five hours of debate on motions for each hour devoted to other business.

The second basic principle of procedure is that the speaker presides over the House and its proceedings. The speaker is the principal officer of the House of Commons, the guardian of its privileges, and the protector of the rights of all members. As presiding officer the speaker ensures that debate is in accordance with the rules and practices of the House, decides points of order, and interprets rules. The speaker's job is to ensure that all proceedings of the House are conducted with fairness and impartiality, and he protects the freedom of speech of members:

The Speaker belongs to the House, not to the Government or the Opposition. Although the servant of the House, the Speaker is expected to show leadership in promoting and safeguarding the interests of the House and its members. Decisions of the Chair may not be appealed except by way of substantive motion. The Speaker thus enjoys the full trust and confidence of the House without which no incumbent would be able to discharge the onerous duties. Thanks to the successive speakers who have occupied the Chair of the House of Commons, the Canadian speakership has developed a tradition of impartiality and devotion to duty of which we can all be proud.[2]

The speaker is also the head of the administration of the Commons, and in that position fulfils a role similar to that of a cabinet minister in relation to a government department. The staff of the House of Commons, including that of members' offices, now exceeds 3,000, and the demands and complexities of the administrative side are no small part of the speaker's job.

There are several problems with the position and role of the speaker in Canada. One has to do with the method of selection. The practice has been that although the House elects its own speaker, the prime minister has controlled selection by controlling nominations. In the past the position was often regarded either as a stepping stone towards becoming a cabinet minister, or as a consolation prize for failing to become one. This, not unnaturally, made it possible for the opposition to charge that the chair was biased in favour of the government, and these charges appeared to have some credibility in the important pipeline debates of 1956.

Subsequently efforts have been made to assert the independence of the speakership. Prime Minister Diefenbaker in 1957 asked Mr Stanley Knowles of the opposition CCF to accept the nomination. Although Mr Knowles declined, the gesture does show the depth of Mr Diefenbaker's concern with the well-being of parliament. Mr Speaker Lamoureux, an outstanding speaker, resigned from the Liberal party in 1968, was re-elected as an independent in the general election of 1972, and in toto served three terms as speaker. Mr Speaker Jerome, who succeeded him, was retained in the position by the Conservative government of Mr Clark after the election of 1979, becoming the first speaker to survive a change of government since Speaker Lemieux in 1926, when Meighen's government briefly replaced Mackenzie King's.[3]

No recent speaker has subsequently entered the cabinet. They have, however, left parliament after stepping down from the chair. Two, Mr Roland Michener (who was defeated in the election of 1962) and Mme Jeanne Sauvé, subsequently became governors general; two, Mr Lamoureux and Mr Lloyd Francis, became ambassadors; Mr Jerome was made a judge. They were thus rewarded for their service. Nor have speakers, for the most part, remained in the position long. The three terms of Mr Lamoureux are the exception. Most serve only one term.

Unlike the British House of Commons, the Canadian House does not have a large reserve of experienced parliamentarians, well-versed in procedure and familiar with both the rules and the moods and idiosyncracies of the House and its members, from which a speaker can be selected. A new speaker – such as Mr John Bosley – might have served only one term in the House before election to the chair. This, coupled with the brief length of tenure, means that the speaker often does not have the wisdom and authority of experience behind him. This problem has been exacerbated when the speaker nominated by the prime minister does not have a great love or understanding of the House and the traditions of parliamentary government. Mme Sauvé, who was outstandingly successful as administrative head of the Commons, and did an enormous amount behind the scenes not only to make the House more efficient but also to protect it from the intrusion of an aggressive government (in which she had previously been a cabinet minister), was not a 'House of Commons person' and was not sensitive to the nuances of moods and procedure. As a result her effectiveness as presiding officer and impartial arbiter was reduced. Her successor, John Bosley, had even greater difficulties and resigned in the summer of 1986, after only two years in the chair.[4]

The Special Committee on Standing Orders and Procedure of 1982 and the Special Committee on Reform in 1985 both recommended that the speaker should cease to be nominated by the prime minister and should be elected by secret ballot (much the way the pope is elected), with members voting for whomever among themselves they choose on successive ballots until one candidate finally has a majority. This they felt would enhance the authority and independence of the chair, and would also make it likely that a successful and effective speaker could retain the chair for a long period.

This procedure was adopted for the election of Bosley's successor, John Fraser. Though Mr Fraser was not the apparent choice of the government, and though he had resigned as minister of fisheries only a year before because of a mini-scandal involving tainted tuna, he was an experienced, able, and dedicated member of parliament. His selection was supported by both government and opposition members. Mr Fraser proved himself far more successful in managing and disciplining an often unruly House than his two most recent predecessors in the chair. Partly this is attributable to his personal qualities, partly to his method of selection, which for the first time in Canadian history gave the House a speaker whom the members themselves had selected rather than one in effect chosen by the prime minister, whose concerns have often not reflected those of the average members. The new procedure for election proved to be a great improvement.

The quality of advice the speaker receives on procedure and other matters is crucial. The speaker's adviser on procedure is the Clerk of the House of Commons. This officer of the House, whose position is somewhat analogous to that of deputy minister of a department, is aided by other clerks at the table and a staff of committee clerks and other officers. Until very recently, the structure, training, and promotion and selection processes for this procedural staff were crude and did not develop the skilled experienced advisers the chair needed. This is not to imply that procedural advice was always bad or unsound, for some senior officers of the House were very able, but nevertheless, the staff of the table lacked depth, and the retirement of a senior officer sometimes left a gap which was extremely difficult to fill. The senior officers of the House were often recruited from outside. Recently a determined effort has been made to create a professional procedural staff capable of ensuring that adequate potential table officers are trained and available, and that promotion to senior positions will normally be from within. The benefits of these extremely important reforms are already being harvested.

The senior officers of the House – the clerk, the clerk assistants, the law clerk, the sergeant at arms – are appointed by order in council. In effect, therefore, they, like the speaker used to be, are the choice of the prime minister. In the past these positions have often been used for patronage purposes, and some of the early clerks unquestionably considered it one of their functions to help the government keep out of trouble on procedural matters. Many officers of both the Commons and Senate appointed by the government have had previous affiliation with the governing party. Regardless of the merits of these officers (and some have been very good indeed) there is still something distasteful in the government having the power to choose the senior officers of parliament, the elected assembly to which it is accountable. The government also controls the salaries and merit increases of the senior officers. Responsible government would be better served, and the House would be more independent, if the speaker, rather than the government, were in control of these matters.[5]

All these problems, added together, unquestionably damage the authority and prestige of the speakership in Canada. During the 1960s this was manifested in continual appeals of speaker's rulings which occupied much of the time of the House. Speaker Lucien Lamoureux succeeded in controlling proceedings in a fair and impressive manner. James Jerome was also highly regarded. In general, however, the Canadian House is not noted for either its respect for the chair or its knowledge of rules and parliamentary procedures. The imbalance between government and opposition, the emphasis on the adversarial aspects of parliament, and the inexperience of members all contribute to discontent, general churlishness, and propensity for bickering. Question period in particular, as we shall see in the next chapter, which has become the most important daily occasion in the House, is an exceptionally difficult challenge to any speaker.[6] Speaker John Bosley's difficulties with question period contributed to his decision to resign.

Both government and opposition, mistrustful of the chair, lacking confidence in the speaker's wisdom, and desiring to pursue their own objectives in proceedings, have been unwilling to allow the speaker much discretion or authority. More responsibility was given to the speaker in the reforms of 1986. The chair can now select and combine motions for discussion at report stage, and can discipline a member by 'naming' him (in effect expelling him for a day) without requiring a vote of the House. The position is still not strong, however, especially in comparison with Britain, and many procedural issues are still the victims of unpleasant partisan wrangling.

With a long-lived government facing a perpetual opposition, there has been little mutual understanding and sympathy. The government's concern is to get its business through, not to do what it would consider fair if it were in opposition; while the opposition's concern is to delay and oppose, not to accept what it would consider reasonable if it were government. The speaker in Britain, where the two sides are more evenly balanced, has a much easier time not only because the members on either side have experience of being on the other, but also because they have a reasonable expectation of changing positions again within the foreseeable future. This is a powerful persuader for moderation, accommodation, and acceptance of the speaker's authority. Mr Speaker Bosley, new to the job and with only one parliament's experience behind him, somewhat enviously described the authority of the speaker in Britain:

I stood and watched the [speaker's] parade with one very senior member of the House and he didn't just nod at the Speaker, he bowed. I asked him why and his answer was, 'Because if I didn't I wouldn't get to speak in the House, let alone ask a question or be involved in Question Period, for six months.' And he meant it. The British Speaker has quite a different set of powers – for example, the power to decide who's going to speak in debate – because the House has decided that he should have this power. It is effectively his small-political decision when a debate has gone on long enough. It ends. Matters come to a halt. A member will rise in his place and move that the question be put, which is not a debatable motion and the Speaker either accepts it or doesn't. The bells are eight minutes and that's that, its over ... The Canadian Speaker certainly does not have those powers.[7]

The third principle is that proceedings in the House of Commons are conducted in terms of a free and civil discourse. Civil in this usage means that the participants recognize and accept that they are members of the same society and have interests in common; and that the discourse is polite, and not rude or offensive. The rules on parliamentary language, such as the prohibition against stating that another member has lied to the House, and the tradition of referring to MPs as 'honourable members' embody this principle of civility. As a civil discourse, parliamentary proceedings can be contrasted with some other forms of political discourse, such as a violent riot, the imposition of order through the use of force by police, or the arousing of mass emotions through inflamed oratory. The usual tone of delivery in parliament is moderate and conversational – 'civil' as opposed to 'uncivil'. Each member, regardless of his political opinion or the wealth or poverty of the people whom he represents, is entitled to his fair share of time and the opportunity to speak, be listened to, and be queried; each is accepted and recognized as an equal member of the same community, and has the same rights, privileges, and immunities.

As a free discourse, parliamentary proceedings are protected from laws of libel and slander. A member cannot be charged in court for what he says in debates. This freedom ensures that members can say what they feel or believe, even if others find it offensive or harmful. But it also places a responsibility on members to ensure that they recognize the principles of civility. In the fall of 1984 Mr Svend Robinson, MP of the NDP, accused two executive officers of Petro Canada of being agents of the CIA, in effect spying on the Canadian government on behalf of the United States. These would have been damning accusations if they had been true. However, no evidence was presented to justify them, and they were obviously harmful. Strong pressures were placed on Mr Robinson by other members and the public to withdraw his comments. His own party was among the most insistent. Mr Robinson in the end made a complete apology and withdrew his comments. Undoubtedly they had done damage, not the least of which was to Mr Robinson's own credibility and the respect in which he was held by other members. Because the statements had been made in parliament Mr Robinson was immune from prosecution in the courts. The House has rarely accepted the responsibility of reining in its wilder members.

Exaggerated statements are often made in parliament, and members on one side accuse those on the other of every sort of peccadillo, knavishness, and self-interest short of actual thievery or lying. Politics involves basic human emotions of greed, lust for power, envy, domination, compassion, and aggression. It is not reasonable to expect political discussion always to be carried out in the calm reflective style of a Quaker meeting. Among the basic principles of the parliamentary system are, however, that these emotions are: first, expressed in words rather than acted out; second, expressed freely without fear of punishment; and third, expressed in terms which even at their worst are within the limits of civility. One of the most important functions of the speaker is to ensure that these three principles are met, and in so doing he needs all the tolerance and firmness of a good judge, schoolmaster, or sheepherder.

One of the ugliest incidents in modern parliamentary experience came when the Liberal government, on 23 October 1980, after eleven days of debate, moved closure on their proposal for the creation of a special joint committee on constitutional reform. When the time came for a vote, several Progressive Conservative members demanded that the chair allow debate to continue. Mr Francis, in the chair as deputy speaker, following the rules, refused. These members then stormed the chair with threatening gestures. Mr Francis managed to impose discipline. Parliamentary consideration begins and ends with words. There is no place for intimidation or violent gestures.

Some first-time viewers of the House are surprised and dismayed by the rowdiness of proceedings. They wonder whether this is the proper atmosphere in which to consider grave business. The viewer should bear four factors in mind: first, that there are powerful emotions at work, and exuberance and some unruliness are to be expected; second, that much of the rowdiness is theatrics for the consumption of the media, the consternation of opponents, and the delight of supporters; third, that viewer reaction to seeing the House on television has encouraged members to moderate their behaviour (it was worse in the past); and, fourth, that in comparison with other legislatures around the world the Canadian House of Commons is relatively decorous. Warren Allmand, in defending the House, pointed out that only 25 of the 150 countries in the United Nations have functioning legislatures, where elected representatives 'can come together and fight out issues on the floor of the house in a very moving and passionate way. Once these issues are voted on and resolved here we accept them. We do not resort to terrorism, bombing or shooting it out in the streets.' This, he argued, is a rare and valuable achievement: 'Canadians should understand that no matter how good our rules are ... there will always be partisan debate and strongly held differences.'[8]

Civility involves listening as well as speaking. It requires paying attention, taking the other person's views into account, and responding to them: it is in effect an acknowledgment of the basic humanity and equality of the other person. Most criticisms of incivility in parliament refer to the expression and gestures of the members speaking but there can be an equally uncivil manner in listening, one which is unfortunately all too prevalent in a government too long and secure in power. The government often doesn't listen. The very real inequality between parties has taken its toll here as elsewhere. Of course, debate is often so repetitious and boring that nobody listens. This is one of the worst features of the House.

The fourth principle is that there must be a balance between the government's need to get its business through parliament and the opposition's right to discuss it. This principle is at the very heart of parliamentary government. The structure of relations between the ministers of the Crown and parliament is not simply one of, as Bagehot argued, the cabinet, as the executive committee of parliament, doing parliament's bidding as set forth in legislation and appropriations. In many ways the Crown controls and sets the terms of discourse for parliament. The speech from the throne sets the agenda for most parliamentary business. Money bills (entailing demands on public funds) and taxation legislation can be introduced only by ministers of the Crown. The cabinet is far more than a committee of the House.

Historically, parliaments were called into session when the Crown needed money or an extension of authority through a change in law. A parliament in those days was in effect the opposition, and demanded a price for its support of the Crown's request. This price was that the Crown listen to parliament, and take action upon the complaints and problems of the populace as expressed through their representatives. Parliament demanded, and obtained, the right to set its own agenda, and it placed the expression of grievance before the King's business. Only in this way could the Commons be assured of a sympathetic and attentive ear. 'Grievance before supply' became one of the key principles of parliamentary government. The Commons also insisted that it could discuss the King's business as long and in such manner as it wished. From this comes the principle that the House is alone responsible for its own proceedings, and its own rules and procedures. These are not the King's business, but the Commons'. This relationship between parliament and the Crown is expressed in the old adage: 'The Government proposes; Parliament disposes.'

A delicate balancing act is required to make this principle work. A government cannot be so insistent that it rushes business through parliament without an adequate opportunity for discussion, consideration of the issues, exposure of faults as well as virtues, and the formation of an informed opinion in parliament and the country; however, parliament cannot be so wilful and reluctant that it denies the Crown the resources and powers necessary for good government.

The development of responsible cabinet government, in which the Crown's ministers sit in parliament and enjoy the support of a majority of members, is the constitutional adaptation which ensures that the government's programme will be supported by parliament. The price for this support must still be paid, however, and it now falls to the opposition to express grievances and disclose the flaws and weaknesses in the Crown's proposals. To do this effectively the opposition must have the freedom to choose which items it wants to discuss at length and which it is prepared to accept with little comment; it must have enough time available for citizens and interest groups to learn about, evaluate, and make their views known on legislative proposals; and it must be able, when it feels there is need, to delay government business long enough to exact a price for passage, either in terms of the formation of a hostile public opinion, or in terms of concessions, changes, and amendments. For its part, however, the government must also be assured that this price is not exorbitant blackmail or ransom, and that its proposals will be discussed and approved within a reasonable length of time.

Inability to resolve these conflicting demands is the fundamental problem in the procedure of the Canadian House of Commons. The importance of party as shaper of the attitudes and actions of members means that business is almost invariably treated as a conflict between government and opposition; the strength of this one feature is so great that it dominates even those aspects of procedure and business which are not necessarily by nature partisan – such as private-members' business or investigations by committees. The right of parliament to examine and discuss parliamentary business is twisted by the opposition into the right to delay and obstruct, while the government deforms its right to get business through parliament into a desire to control all aspects of business and procedure. The House has not yet been able to resolve these issues. In fact, they have become worse in recent decades: parliament takes more time to discuss government business; a greater proportion of legislation fails to get through the House; and the government increasingly tries to avoid parliament. Timetabling is not just a technical issue of tinkering with procedural rules. It is a vital question of the relationships between the wielder of political powers and the subjects, between government and governed; it sets the terms and conditions by which the people's representatives in the House of Commons debate, examine, and approve or reject proposals for the use of power and authority.

TIMETABLING THE BUSINESS OF THE COMMONS

Until 1960 there was no serious problem of fitting the business of parliament into yearly sessions. Between 1950 and 1959 parliament sat an average of 127 days each year, and since the reasonable number of sittings that can conveniently be fitted into a year is approximately 175 (assuming recesses at Christmas, Easter, and in the summer, and other breaks so that MPs can renew their contacts with constituencies), there was little difficulty in allowing the House to discuss business as long as it wanted. But after 1960 this changed. The pressure of business became greater and the sessions longer until, by the mid-1960s, timetabling was a major procedural and tactical problem facing the government. In 1964 parliament sat 214 days. Several factors combined to create these pressures on parliament's time. Parliament had more business before it. The government was becoming more activist, and programme innovations such as Medicare and the Canada Pension Plan were not only complex, but aroused strong feelings. Because the federal government increasingly engaged in joint programmes with the provinces, the number of subjects expanded on which legislation was required. The position of member of parliament became a full-time occupation. Previously, parliament had sat for only part of the year, with extended breaks at Christmas, Easter, and in the summer. But pressure of business, improvements to salary, and changing public attitudes gradually led members to look at it as a year-round task, and as the need for MPs to finish parliament's business so they could get home to their own affairs diminished, their willingness to discuss at length in the House increased.

But more important than either of these two factors was the change in the attitudes of the opposition to government business. Obstruction and delay became habitual tactics. This change has deep and powerful roots. John Diefenbaker became prime minister in 1957 as a champion of the rights of parliament. The crucial debates in parliament which had won press and public opinion to the side of the Conservatives were the 1954 debate where the opposition had fought at length the government's plan to extend wartime controls over the economy, and the pipeline debate of 1956, where the opposition, particularly George Drew and Davie Fulton of the Conservatives and Stanley Knowles of the CCF, had fought, on the basis that the rights of parliament were being trampled on, a government proposal to ensure that legislation was passed by a given day to enable construction of a pipeline.[9] The lessons the opposition learned from these experiences were that it took a lot of time for a hostile public opinion to be created, and this required many weeks of debate in parliament, and that the rights of parliament meant a lot to Canadians. J.W. Pickersgill concludes that 'most of the difficulty the government had in the pipeline debate resulted from the failure of the speaker to enforce the rules, but there is no denying the government had lost the battle for public support even before the debate started.'[10]

As the bloom came off the rose for the Diefenbaker government the Liberal opposition found that it could use delay and obstruction as effective weapons to expose the confusion and indecisiveness of the cabinet. Prime Minister John G. Diefenbaker, because of his belief in the rights of parliament, would not use closure to limit debate. Taking advantage of this, and the lax rules of the times, the Liberals delayed passage of appropriations, discussed legislation at excessive length, and used an ingenious and varied grab-bag of other tricks such as prolonging question period, appealing the speaker's rulings, and proposing many emergency debates, to make the government look foolish and incompetent. When the Liberals regained power in 1963 the Progressive Conservatives proved to be good learners, and used the same sort of tactics to obstruct the Pearson government. The pettiness of the bickering in the House, and the animosity between the two leaders, brought parliament into a disrepute from which it has not yet fully recovered.

Since the mid-1960s the rules of the House have been tightened in an attempt to limit obstruction. Appeals to the House from the speaker's rulings have been abolished. Debate on the speech from the throne was limited to ten days in 1955 and eight days in 1962, the budget debate to eight days in 1955 and six days in 1962, and debate on supply is now limited to twenty-five days. Nevertheless, pressures of time still remain. They are particularly evident in the consideration of government business, where, if anything, the problem has grown worse. In 1969–70, thirty-four out of sixty-five government bills, or 52 per cent, were debated for less than two hours at second reading. By 1974 this proportion had dropped to only three out of fifteen, or 20 per cent, and it is still at this low level. Between 1950 and 1955 the House passed one public bill in every 1.8 sittings; by 1970–4 this rate had dropped to one for every 3.3 sittings.[11] Even routine business is taking longer than it has in the past, and more important issues occupy unreasonably large amounts of parliament's time.

There are approximately 125 days for the consideration of government business during a session, assuming a session of 175 days, 14 days for throne and budget speeches, 25 allotted supply days, and perhaps 12 days more in an average year for emergency debates, debates on committee reports, and other such matters. The government's legislative programme normally includes about fifty bills, of which half are routine, and many others of such minor importance that they would not require more than a day's debate. While 125 days would appear adequate to consider this amount of legislation, it has not proved to be so. Not only has parliament sat for more than 175 days in the year, but sessions themselves have not fitted into a yearly cycle: the 1974–6 session lasted from 30 September 1974 until 12 October 1976 and included 343 sittings; the 32nd Parliament began its first session on 14 April 1980 and prorogued on 30 November 1983, after a total of 591 sittings.

This situation is not a satisfactory one. Debate in the House is not only interminable, but dull and repetitious. It makes the House and parliamentarians appear aimless and inefficient. The government, knowing that the House will drag its feet, and also knowing that there is, despite the lengthy sessions, a chance that it will not get its legislation passed (success rate for government bills in Canada is slightly over 70 per cent, compared with closer to 90 per cent in Britain), tries to avoid the House whenever possible. Legislation is couched in broad vague terms so that the need for future amendments is reduced, much legislation is by order in council rather than by parliament, the meaning of existing legislation is stretched and bent so that the government can avoid asking the House for amendments on new legislation, and complex legislation is presented to the House in the form of omnibus bills embodying several distinct acts, so that debate and votes on one bill in effect authorize several. These practices weaken the effectiveness of statute law as a control over government, and harm the ability of parliament to examine and discuss the government's policies. Mr Ged Baldwin, a senior member in the Conservative opposition, stated in 1975 that: 'debate has got out of hand in this house. And there are reasons for it: it is too long, it is too repetitive, it is too virulent, it does not do the job.'[12] Since then it has got worse.

Parliament must have the right to choose how it uses its time, and the opposition must have the opportunity to examine legislation, expose weakness, and allow opinion to form, but these tasks must be balanced with the need for parliament to be an effective legislative body. Legitimate dissent becomes obstruction when it has no other purpose than to delay, when it is not exposing weakness or moulding opinion, but simply preventing legislation from being passed. This sort of obstruction has become common in the Canadian parliament. Curiously enough, it does not do the opposition much good: its effective points get lost in the verbiage; excessively long debates conceal the sparseness of government legislation on the order-paper; too much freedom leads the opposition to sloppiness and they are not inclined to separate what they fundamentally object to from what ought to be supported or opposed only on minor points and let through without delay; and the opposition gets caught up in a bad habit of mindless and irresponsible opposition to virtually every piece of government business without being forced to consider whether, if they were in power, they would be proposing the same legislation. This 'opposition mentality' – of being against everything and in favour of nothing – reduces their credibility as an alternative government. It enables any small group within the opposition to express its hostility without the party as a whole being forced to decide where it stands on an issue.

The problems of timetabling and debate have ramifications far beyond competition between government and opposition. The fundamental issues involved are the accountability and responsiveness of the government. The most important weapon the opposition has is its ability to prolong debate and delay a decision in parliament until the government is forced to listen to critical voices. No reforms to timetabling should take away the opposition's freedom to pick and choose among issues that it wants to discuss at length. Parliament must not be deprived of the ability to serve as a sounding board for both government proposals and public opinion. The problems arise because this picking and choosing is not done well. The House is not selective enough in distinguishing between the important issues and the routine ones.

The government has two weapons available to force an end to debate. The first is closure under Standing Order 57 (old SO 33). Closure has several faults as a timetabling device. It adds a day to debate and requires at least two days of debate on each motion for which it is used, making it unsuitable for the report stage where it would have to be used repeatedly. It cannot be applied to bills being considered by legislative committee. The second weapon, which was introduced in 1969, is timetabling under standing orders 115, 116, 117 (old SO 75A, B, C), which give the government the ability to allot time in advance for all stages of a public bill.

Standing Order 75A permitted timetabling in advance when all parties were in agreement, 75B when a majority of parties agreed, and 75C when there was no agreement. It was hoped that 75A would be the main timetabling device, but it turned out that co-operation and agreement were not forthcoming, and 75A was used only five times, 75B never, and 75C the most used of all. Both Progressive Conservative and Liberal governments have used it. In all, by the time parliament was dissolved in 1984, Standing Order 75C had been used a total of forty-one times. The Progressive Conservative government used it nine times between 1984 and the end of the session in July 1986.

Curtailment of debate through closure or timetabling in advance no longer arouses the revulsion incurred during the pipeline debates. Nevertheless, it is an unpleasant and awkward method of timetabling, involving as it does coercion of the opposition by a government majority and at least one day of debate. It would be far better if the parties were able to agree more often, especially on routine legislation where much time is unnecessarily wasted. But the attitudes of the parties congealed during the period of 1954–64, where intense hostility and obstruction became the norm, and nothing since then has been able to encourage more co-operation. No reform has yet made co-operation more appealing than obstruction to an opposition which feels it has some chance of embarrassing a government or winning public support by delay and criticism.

THE PROCESS OF PROCEDURAL REFORM

Between 1964 and 1968 the House adopted many rules on a trial basis. These lapsed with the dissolution of parliament, and the newly elected Trudeau government was faced with an immediate problem of what to do to improve an institution with archaic rules and procedures. A special committee on procedure was accordingly immediately set up after the parliamentary session began. The reforms made on the recommendations of that committee succeeded in imposing the present limits on supply debates, in introducing standing orders 75A, B, and C, and shifted much of the discussion of government legislation from the floor of the House to standing committee by having them rather than committee of the whole undertake the committee stage of legislation. Of these changes, Standing Order 75, not surprisingly, received the most attention. The government at first had proposed timetabling of many pieces of legislation at one time, which would have deprived the opposition of its ability to select and reconsider where it wanted to devote its attention; after backing down on this extreme proposal the government used closure to have the less severe Standing Order 75 accepted. These reforms inaugurated the modern era of parliamentary government. The committees, which had for the most part not been effective, were revitalized; the government was given a more effective means of timetabling; and the supply procedures were brought under control.

Nevertheless, serious problems still remained. The committee system still had many faults, and the time that had been saved through supply and committee reform was being consumed in the second-reading debates before the committee stage, and the debates on amendments at the subsequent report and third-reading stages. Although there were discussions on further reforms within the government, not until after the election of 1974 did the Standing Committee on Procedure and Organization begin investigation. Some minor reforms were made on this committee's recommendation, and it prepared draft reports on many important questions, including the use of time by the House, the way private-members' business was considered, and standing committees. But Mr Mitchell Sharp, who as government House leader had been the driving force for reform, resigned from the ministry in 1976 before the committee reported. His successor, Mr Allan MacEachen, did not reactivate the committee. He was unable to get his ministerial colleagues to accept the proposals for reform, and the enterprise was abandoned.

The Clark government proposed minor changes to improve the likelihood of private-members' business coming to a vote, and to enable standing committees to initiate investigations, but it left office before action could be taken on these proposals. Not until 1982 was procedural reform to be considered again by the House. In effect there had been no important changes since 1969, and the Standing Committee on Procedure and Organization had been inactive except for the aborted work of 1975–6.

In February 1982 the Trudeau government introduced Bill C-94, an enormous, wide-ranging omnibus bill covering many aspects of the government's energy programme. Relationships between government and opposition were strained at the time: the Conservatives were still angry because of their loss in 1980; the government had low standing in opinion polls; the Conservatives had been impressive in forcing the government to bend and seek compromise on constitutional reform; and the new Conservative House leader, Mr Erik Neilsen, was much more hostile and more of a scrapper than his predecessor, Mr Baker. Mr André for the Conservatives asked that the speaker rule Bill C-94 out of order because of its form, but Madame Sauvé refused in a ruling made on 2 March. Mr André then moved that the House adjourn, and when the bells began to ring for a division, the Conservatives left the House. They did not return for over two weeks. The procedure on recorded division is that the bells stop ringing and the vote is taken when the government and opposition whips approach the Chair to tell the speaker that their parties are ready. Because the Conservative whip did not appear, the bells continued to ring.[13] The speaker (or a deputy) sat in the chair day and night. A clerk sat at the table. Apart from these two lonely figures the chamber was deserted.

Not surprisingly a huge amount of press and public discussion was aroused by this unhappy spectacle. As the bells continued to ring, both government and opposition faced pressure to reach a compromise. In the event, the government agreed to break C-94 into eight separate bills, and the Conservatives agreed to a time limit for their consideration. On 17 March the House resumed its sitting of 2 March and the bells stopped ringing. The government came out somewhat the better on this occasion. It had expected the Conservatives to fight the energy programme as vigorously as they had the constitutional proposals, but the total time for consideration of the bills, even including the more than two weeks of bell-ringing, was probably less than it would have been without the procedural confrontation.

The most important consequence of the bell-ringing episode was the creation of a special committee on procedure and organization in May 1982, which made the first productive review of procedure in thirteen years. The committee was composed for the most part of backbenchers from all parties. The House leaders were not members, nor were the whips. The recommendations of the committee reflected this membership. They did not deal with the question of timetabling, considering it too contentious and politically loaded. Nor, for the same reason, did the committee consider the problem of omnibus bills. Nevertheless, it produced wide-ranging and influential reports, and succeeded in having several important reforms made. The impetus for reform caused by the bell-ringing bore useful fruit.

The main successes of the special committee were contained in its third report, tabled in the House on 5 November 1982. With only a brief debate, this report was accepted and changes to procedure were adopted on a provisional basis (lasting until about 30 May 1985). The main changes were:

1 An annual calendar of fixed sittings and recesses was established which enables the House to sit for about 175 days of the year. This was intended to make it easier for MPs to plan their lives.

2 Most night sittings were eliminated, and morning sittings were instituted. The hours of House sittings now approximate the working hours of a business, another indication of the changing attitudes of MPs.

3 The maximum length of most speeches was reduced to twenty minutes from forty, and provision was made for a ten-minute give-and-take period of questions and comments following each speech. This was intended to improve the liveliness of debate in the House. Speeches after the first eight hours of debate on second reading, and on motions at report stage, were reduced to ten minutes, with no question-and-comment period.

4 The use of Standing Order 43 for raising subjects before question period was replaced by a period, provided under a new rule (SO 21), for brief statements by private members on matters of interest.

5 The handling of private-members' business was streamlined.

6 The standing committees were reduced in size, and the procedure for substituting members became more controlled and restrictive. In addition, reports, returns, and other papers laid before the House by a minister in accordance with a statutory provision are now automatically referred to the committees.

7 A new procedure was adopted to guard against lack of a quorum, and other procedures were changed to permit the House more easily to extend a sitting beyond the usual hours of adjournment.

By the time of its termination, the committee had made a total of ten reports, of which seven, including the third, contained substantive, wide-ranging proposals for change. These changes included: establishing a new way of electing the speaker; giving committees more independence; creating of ad hoc legislative committees for bills with chairmen chosen from either side of the House; creating of new committees to improve review of government finances; giving all committees the power to retain whatever staff they needed; creating a new board of internal economy composed of the speaker and members of all parties to replace the existing Commission of Internal Economy, composed of the speaker and four cabinet ministers; resumption by the government of the practice of making ministerial statements in the House; a reduction in the number of motions considered votes of confidence; and a continuing mandate for the Standing Committee on Procedure and Organization.

A theme running through these reports was the desire to restrain the control the cabinet exerted over the House and the need to enhance the role and authority of the private members. The committee felt there was a common interest among members on both sides, although it was often neglected, in asserting independence from the government. In all, the committee found that interpersonal relations within parliament were as important as if not more important than the rules. The breakdown in these relationships had caused many of the problems in Canada.

The most important procedural issue the special committee did not deal with was the problem of timetabling. This issue remained contentious and unsatisfactory until the end of the 32nd parliament. The tactic of letting the bells ring before a division was used subsequently to delay proceedings on eight occasions. Seven of these were instigated by the opposition, and one by the government, when it delayed the vote for twenty-two hours to allow its members, who had been detained by bad weather, to return to Ottawa after the weekend.[14] The speaker, Mr Francis, told the House in 1984 that there was a serious problem in refusing to vote. The chair had decided to declare dilatory motions to have lapsed if not voted on by the hour of automatic adjournment, but when the question before the House was a substantive one, the bells were allowed to ring. In making this decision, the chair was influenced by the need to maintain the dignity of the House: 'The spectacle of a lone occupant of the chair and a gowned clerk, during the fullness of the night in an otherwise empty House, the prisoners of a theoretical assumption that the house might be ready to vote at any time appeared to the Chair to be absurd.' On substantive motions, therefore, the bells were suspended overnight, to resume the next day. The problem was a very serious and urgent one, according to the speaker: 'Let us consider the implications of allowing the bells to ring indefinitely. When taken to an extreme, the practice can paralyse Parliament completely. We have seen in Manitoba how the Government was forced into proroguing the legislature because an indefinite bell was used by the opposition to prevent a vote on an important government measure. We can imagine a government in a minority situation using the indefinite bell to avoid facing defeat on an issue of confidence.'[15] He wondered: 'Do we in this house really want to enshrine this device permanently in our practice?'

Mr Neilsen, then House leader of the Progressive Conservatives, replied that the problem of obstruction had begun with the Liberal opposition to the Diefenbaker government. When the Liberals subsequently took power, they changed the standing orders to prevent this sort of obstruction, and:

In the process the effectiveness of the Opposition was weakened. The tools it had hitherto possessed in order to discharge its responsible function as an Opposition were taken away. In doing that, the Opposition was left with precious few tools with which to oppose when it believes that opposition is warranted. All it is left with are the tactics that we have used that focus on ringing the bells or moving dilatory motions ... That is all the Government has left any opposition as tools with which to perform its functions.[16]

With this sort of bitterness and hostility colouring negotiations, the problems were not going to be resolved in that parliament. The new Liberal opposition, after the 1984 election, showed no less willingness to impede parliamentary business, and let the bells ring on several occasions.

The Mulroney government in 1984 set up a committee of seven backbench members chaired by James A. McGrath to examine all aspects of procedural and other reforms of parliament. Its first report recommended that the House adopt changes proposed by the previous committee including the new method of electing the speaker, the creation of special legislative committees, more power to standing committees and the Board of Internal Economy. Its second report recommended that the House adopt an electronic voting system to save time, and that the precincts of parliament be placed under the authority of a new officer, the intendant of parliament. The committee felt that ministers' offices and staff should be moved out of the centre block, which would then be designated primarily a legislative building. The committee's final report, submitted in June 1985, they claimed was the most ambitious attempt to pursue major and comprehensive reform in the history of the House.[17] The various reports of the McGrath Committee covered many important areas. Its proposals for reform were debated in December 1985, and again in February 1986. Some of its proposals were adopted. On others it was less successful.

Among the important successes was the adoption of the new method of electing the speaker, first used in the fall of 1986 after Speaker Bosley's resignation. The chair was also strengthened through the enhanced disciplinary powers. The possibilities for prolonged bell-ringing were curtailed. The committee system was overhauled, and committees were given new powers, including the power to review senior apppointments. (We shall examine these changes more closely below, in chapter 8.) Some opposition members were appointed to the Board of Internal Economy. Numerous other smaller changes were made. Pleas for the removal of government offices from the centre block, however, fell on deaf ears. And on two important issues, reform was not successful. These were private-members' business, and the question of confidence.

To improve the position of the individual MP, the special committee proposed making private-members' business more influential. Although private members propose hundreds of bills each session, few of these are debated, and even fewer are voted upon. Only a few hours each week are devoted to private-members' business, and most items are 'talked out' and lapse at the end of the hour. The items that do pass have been of such small importance as changing the name of the national holiday from 'Dominion Day' to 'Canada Day.' Private-members' business has, however, been important because many substantial issues, such as divorce-legislation reform and the abolition of capital punishment, have first been discussed in parliament through this means. As we saw in chapter 10, a problem can be remedied through a private-members' bill that is not even debated. Influence can be great, although indirect.

The special committee proposed making influence more direct. One proposal (which was not accepted) was to enable a wider range of topics to be raised in private-members' bills by allowing bills containing financial provisions (which are the responsibility of the Crown) to be introduced and debated, although they would not become law without the government's approval. The committee also proposed that there be a draw for twenty bills or motions which would come first and be debated, and out of these six would make the selection. In this way at least some items would have the possibility of becoming law, and the occasion would become less of a toothless ritual. These changes were accepted by the government.

The new committee began to make its choices. The twenty pieces of business selected included one from a Conservative backbencher that would restore the death penalty for premeditated murder, treason, and sedition. Reconsideration of abolition of capital punishment had also been part of the election platform of the Progressive Conservative party. The House of Commons contains many strong abolitionists as well, and one of them, the Liberal whip, was the proposer of the first bill drawn by the committee. He threatened to paralyse the work of the committee to prevent the bill restoring the death penalty from going forward. 'If there's going to be a free vote on the death penalty during this parliament, as Mr Mulroney promised during the 1984 election campaign, then it's going to have to be introduced by the government. It won't be a private bill from Bill Domm – no sir,' Mr Gauthier was quoted as saying. 'Mulroney won't get out of his promise that easy.'[18] In the event, the committee decided not to accept Mr Domm's bill on the curious basis that to debate capital punishment was government policy and hence not appropriate for private-members' time. In effect, this ruling suggests that private-members' business cannot be used for the most important issue facing parliament, which completely negates the intention of reform.

The process of passing government legislation (as we shall see in chapter 7) includes many checks and balances. The main weapon in the opposition's hand is to delay, and delay has the essential purpose of allowing public opinion to be formed. Not all the legislation a government introduces into the House actually gets enacted. Many of the failures are caused by the development of hostile opinion through prolonged discussion in parliament. The new rules on private-members' business, by insisting that some items would come to a vote after seven hours of debate, to a large measure circumvented this safeguard of delay. The special committee doubtless did not intend its proposals to permit important issues to be voted upon with less consideration and fewer safeguards of delay simply because they were in the form of private-members' rather than government business, but that was the unintended and unanticipated outcome. There is a tension between the traditional assumption that important items of business are the responsibility of the government to introduce and defend, and the desire to give more power to private members. The problems faced by the committee and the House in making private-members' business more influential are not trivial. They are closely related to the basic procedures by which majority and minority opinions are heard and balanced in parliament. Curiously enough, the safeguard that private-members' business will not be voted on permits it to be used to raise a wider range of issues, and more important ones. Drawing attention to a problem, and ventilating opinions, are the real sources of influence.

The conventions on confidence determine when a government has lost the support of the House and must either resign or ask the governor general to call an election. The special committee felt that too many issues are now considered questions of confidence, and that it would be healthy for parliamentary democracy if the government could be defeated on more issues without these defeats being construed as a loss of confidence and all that that entails. This change, the special committee felt, could come about by a change in attitude on the part of the government, opposition, and public.[19]

The committee noted that the minority government of Prime Minister Trudeau lost eight of eighty-one recorded votes between 1972 and 1974, and only asked for a dissolution when it had been defeated on an important issue relating to the budget. The minority governments of Prime Minister Pearson lost three votes without resigning or asking for an election. One of these defeats was on a budget matter, but had been the unexpected result of some wily opposition manoeuvring, and Pearson had counterattacked by asking, and getting, the support of a majority vote of the House for a motion explicitly stating that his government enjoyed the confidence of the House. The minority Conservative governments of John Diefenbaker in 1963 and Joe Clark in 1979 had both asked for elections after being defeated in the House. Nevertheless, there were precedents for governments to continue in office after defeats on their business.

The special committee claimed:

In a parliament with a government in command of a majority, the matter of confidence has really been settled by the electorate. Short of a reversal of allegiance or some cataclysmic political event, the question of confidence is really a fait accompli. The government and other parties should therefore have the wisdom to permit members to decide many matters in their own deliberative judgement. Overuse of party whips and confidence motions devalue both these important institutions.[20]

The arguments the committee offered for this change were
a   that historically Canadian MPs had had this autonomy, but that 'in recent years the influence of the private member in the legislative process has been seriously reduced,'
b   that British MPs now had this sort of freedom, and
c   that it was self-evidently good 'private members must again become instruments through which citizens can contribute to shaping the laws under which they live.'[21]

The committee ignored the obvious non sequitur in the quotation cited above: that if the electorate has settled the question of confidence by giving a government power, then it is the government that ought to make the decisions and take the responsibility; it, not the individual MPs, was chosen to make the decisions. This objection is more than a quibble about details. It is a questioning of the basic reasoning of the committee over which element, party or individual MP, is the more authentic representative voice. The committee did not, apart from the arguments mentioned above, come to grips with this issue.

By October 1986 nothing had been done to change the confidence conventions. Nor is that change likely to occur. The change from tight discipline to free votes would mean a substantial shift of power from parties to the individual MPs. At first glance this might not appear attractive to party leadership as it would involve their giving up something for nothing. But on some issues, where the government is either indifferent over outcome or is sure that the outcome of a free vote would be in line with what it wanted, it might be to the government's advantage to release its members from the whips and say it accepts no responsibility for the outcome. The opposition parties might well refuse to follow along, and instead argue that the government was abdicating its duty. Especially if strong public opinions were involved – as, for example, on moral questions of pornography, abortion, capital punishment, or drugs – relaxation of discipline could well be expensive to a government.

These problems are not only theoretical, but very real possibilities. They were ignored by the special committee because it ignored the fundamental difference between the British and Canadian examples. As we have seen, in Britain party discipline has loosened in recent years because MPs on both sides of the House refused to accept the whips. They defied party and won. The party leadership, both government and opposition, accepted defeat with the best grace they could muster, and the confidence conventions changed. A shift in power from parties to MPs caused a change in attitude. What the special committee proposed for Canada was the reverse. The committee wanted a change in attitude to come first and cause a shift in power. In effect, it was asking for a grace-and-favour gift from the parties, not for the recognition of the reality of a new, enhanced authenticity and power base for Canadian MPs – for which there is no evidence, and which in fact does not exist.

What the special committee did not do was to examine why British MPs have been able to display such independence, and why in comparison Canadian MPs have not. There is a clear answer to this question. In the British House of Commons, which has 650 members, two paths for career advancement have emerged: first, the traditional path controlled by the whips from backbencher to frontbencher and ministry; and, second, one outside the control of the whips, of a satisfied backbencher who is secure in his seat, who perhaps participates in committee activity, but has no overriding ambition to reach the front bench. In Canada, only the first path exists. There is no body of backbenchers in Canada secure in seats and satisfied with a long-term career in the back benches. Canadian MPs are most unlikely to get re-elected if they defy the whips and fall out of favour with party leadership. In other words, the committee's proposals, and the reality of parliamentary life, would enable Canadian MPs to play at being independent when the party leadership so permitted, but when the crunch came on important issues, the pressures of party discipline would be as strong and irresistible as ever. There is a vast difference between an MP, as he would in Britain, voting as his judgment dictates with the support of his constituency association and those who voted for him, and in so doing defying party whips, and an MP in Canada, as the committee proposed, being permitted by his party to vote independently on a few selected issues.

A basic question pervading all procedure and most other aspects of an MP's work, is the locus of final authority. There are two possible loci: the parties or the speaker. In Britain it is the speaker; in Canada, the parties. For the private member to be truly independent in Canada, much of the power now wielded by whips and House leaders would have to be shifted to the speaker, including some measure of the decisions on accommodation; participation in question period, debates, and committees; and visits abroad. Decisions on the use of closure and the guillotine might also usefully involve more participation by the speaker. The present Canadian practice of giving parties the final authority usually means giving it to the government. An independent and strong speaker is at least as important to an influential and effective House as is relaxation of rules of confidence.

The realities of parliamentary government in Canada make fundamental reform difficult. High turnover means that there are few members with a knowledge of the rules. Procedure does not interest many members in the Canadian parliament. Few MPs, academics, or journalists have the time or the inclination to become knowledgeable in the workings of the House. The House leaders, and to a lesser extent the whips, along with the occupants of the chair, are the only members who, because of their position, need to know the intricacies of rules and procedures. The day-to-day workings of the institution are left to political professionals and officials. The members feel little proprietorship towards rules and procedure.

The pervasive dominance of parties over all aspects of an MP's career, and all aspects of parliamentary life, is an overwhelming obstacle to real reform. It is easy to say that there ought to be fewer votes of confidence, or that private members ought to have more freedom, but almost impossible to make the change. The iron discipline of party is a consequence, caused by factors outside the ability of procedural and even attitudinal changes to reform. In particular, the electorate is an essential determining factor. It votes on the basis of party and leadership, not on the merits of individual MP or candidate.

There are many different interests to be accommodated in reform; to a government reform means getting its programme through without problems; to an opposition it means the opportunity to criticize, embarrass, and prove fault. The interests of the front benches are in partisan warfare, those of the back benches in questions of autonomy and greater influence. Until backbench members are able to regard their careers in parliament as long-term ones, and until many backbench members choose a career as a parliamentarian outside the channels controlled by the whips, the interests of the parties will continue to dominate. Mr McGrath himself chose to resign his seat in parliament to become lieutenant-governor of Newfoundland soon after the reforms were adopted in 1986. The parties are interested in confrontation and drama, not in parliament as a legislature, or the back benches as an influence on government. The Canadian House of Commons is locked into an all-consuming ritual of adversarial combat whose end is its beginning: the complete domination by the parliamentary parties of every important aspect of representation, participation, and procedure. No alternative locus of power, either in the constituencies, the speakership, or the individual members, has yet emerged that poses the slightest threat to this domination.

The committee's approach and concerns were very much those of back-benchers. The concerns of the government in reform received no attention. Nor did those of opposition front benches. The committee made no recommendations on the fundamental question of timetabling. Problems in timetabling are of crucial concern to the government, and to parliament. Perhaps more than anything else the difficulties in getting business through the House and the unseemly practices of obstruction have brought parliament much criticism. There is no excuse for a committee concerned with reform of the House to ignore this issue.

The committee assumed that the need for the sort of parliament-centred reform they proposed was self-evident or justified by historical precedent. This approach meant that the committee did not argue for the changes on their own merits, nor did they consider what would happen to the influence and power of the various participants in the legislative process, or to the practice of responsible government. As adopted, and this is still short of what the committee wanted, these recent reforms are likely to make the system more permeable to particular interests and to make it more difficult for the government to assert a more general, collective, public interest. The result could well be greater conflicts between parliament and government, more paralysis in the system, and more, not fewer, problems of ungovernability.

7

Debate and Question Period

Regardless of whether politics is 'the authoritative allocation of value,' or 'who gets what, when and how,' the process of reaching a decision in a democracy involves an enormous amount of talk. The success of a political system, in truth, can be roughly measured by the degree to which conclusions are reached through talk rather than force or other instruments of coercion. The central forum for political discussion and arguments in a liberal democracy is the elected representative assembly, Congress in the United States, parliament, and more particularly the House of Commons, in Britain and Canada. The main modes of discussion in a parliamentary system are debates and question period. In theory, a debate is an argument between two sides in which one side wins because its arguments are more persuasive – such, for example, are the famous arguments in Thucydides, or Burke's speeches in the great age of parliament. In theory, also, the purpose of a question is to ask something in the expectation of obtaining an answer. But in the Canadian House of Commons, practice belies the theory. Debates rarely persuade, and the answers to questions are less important than the questions themselves. As George Hees noted, 'the unwritten rule is never to ask a question unless you know the answer.'[1] John Reid argued that 'the purpose of most debates in the House of Commons is not to enlighten but to beat one's opponents to death by dullness.'[2]

Debates and questions occupy most of the time of the Canadian House of Commons. But they do not perform their stated functions. They must have value, or even the slow processes of changing parliamentary procedure would have modified them, but these values are not the obvious ones. This chapter explores these functions and their utility.

The setting for both debate and question period in the Canadian House of Commons is adversarial. The chamber is rectangular. On one side, the speaker's right, sit the government members, with the prime minister and cabinet ministers occupying the front rows. To the speaker's left sit the opposition, with their chief spokesmen and the leader of the opposition at the front. The third and, on occasion fourth, parties occupy positions beyond the official opposition at the far end of the chamber. At the centre, at the end away from the formal entrance, sits the speaker, in an elaborately carved chair, wearing a black gown. At a table below him, between the two sides, sits the clerk of the House and the clerk assistants.

Each of the members, except the speaker, has a desk on the floor of the House. Members, while the House is in session, often sit at their desks reading correspondence, writing, or performing other chores. This physical setting of the Canadian House of Commons is quite different from its British equivalent. The British House is much smaller, has benches instead of desks, and has not enough room for the 650 members to sit at one time.

Although this setting in Britain was originally an accident of history, it was perpetuated by choice. The old chamber of the British House of Commons was destroyed by bombing during the Second World War. When reconstruction was being planned, the possibility of seating all members was rejected. Sir Winston Churchill, the greatest parliamentarian of this century, explained as follows:

If the House is big enough to contain all its Members, nine-tenths of its Debates will be conducted in the depressing atmosphere of an almost empty or half-empty Chamber. The essence of good House of Commons speaking is the conversational style, the facility for quick, informal interruptions and interchanges ... But the conversational style requires a fairly small space, and there should be on great occasions a sense of crowd and urgency. There should be a sense of the importance of much that is said and a sense that great matters are being decided, there and then, by the House.

Further, Churchill argued,

Its shape should be oblong and not semi-circular. Here is a very potent factor in our political life. The semi-circular assembly, which appeals to political theorists, enables every individual or every group to move round the centre, adopting various shades of pink according as the weather changes. I am a convinced supporter of the party system in preference to the group system ... The party system is much favoured by the oblong form of Chamber. It is easy for an individual to move through those insensible gradations from Left to Right but the act of crossing the Floor is one which requires serious consideration. I am well informed on this matter, for I have accomplished that difficult process, not only once but twice. Logic is a poor guide compared with custom.[3]

The division into government and opposition is a great simplifier. There are only two sides to every issue. A member is either for a motion or against. All different shades of opinion are forced into these two aggregations. There is no room for single-issue politics in the parliamentary system. The parties, and the members, win or lose on the basis of their total choices, policies, and decisions; the individual member is protected by party discipline from single-issue pressure groups. But he must also pay the price of conforming to that discipline. The physical setting of the House reflects that discipline and simplifying aggregation. 'We shape our buildings,' Churchill said, 'and afterwards our buildings shape us.'

The Canadian House lacks this intimate atmosphere. Although it is full for question period, for most of the time it is nearly deserted. A member speaks from his place, at his desk, and before him stretches a vast wasteland of empty desks, with a few inattentive colleagues doing their own reading, letter-signing, or other business. This physical setting, by itself, is enough to make speaking in the House a difficult matter, with no sense of closeness, audience, contact, or excitement. Since 1977 the House has been televised. At first, the picture the television audience saw was quite different from that seen by a spectator in the gallery. The other members in the party of a colleague who was speaking crowded into the desks around him, so the narrow frame of the television camera gave the illusion that the House itself was crowded. There is less tendency to do this now. Except on grand or urgent occasions the chamber is an intimidating and depressing place in which to speak, and this in itself contributes to the dulness of debate.

Question period occurs five times each week while parliament is sitting. From Monday to Thursday it occupies forty-five minutes between 2:15 pm and 3:00 pm; on Friday it occurs in the morning. Unlike debates, question period is a time of excitement. Most members are at their places, the press gallery is full, as is the visitors' gallery. The Canadian question period is unique. For forty-five minutes opposition members attack the government. Most questions are of the 'have you stopped beating your wife yet' variety. They are, in effect, miniature speeches, in which the questioner claims that some problem or desperate situation exists and asks the government what it is going to do, or stop doing, to solve it. The opposition parties have in recent years organized themselves to make a systematic choice of which ministers, policies, and problems to attack. They also decide who shall be questioners, and the speaker, for most of question period, follows lists of questioners given him by the opposition parties. Each question is normally followed by supplementaries, in which the initial questioners or a colleague try to elicit further confessions from the minister, who in turn tries to give as good as he gets.

Questions are in order as long as they are, in fact, questions (although this rule is often bent, if not broken), are asked about something for which the minister is responsible and answerable, and are phrased in parliamentary language. Answers by the minister are acceptable as long as they are relevant, in order, and delivered in parliamentary language. A minister can choose not to reply and simply sit and ignore a question.

Question period is a free-wheeling affair, with tremendous spontaneity and vitality. The main topics raised are often those on the front pages of the major newspapers, or ones raised on national television news the previous evening. No notice is usually given for questions. However, the ministers' staff are at least as diligent in spotting possible questions and briefing their ministers with answers as opposition members and research staff are in preparing questions and supplementaries. The speaker's role in question period is to ensure that the rules of order and procedure are respected. He is not responsible for ensuring that topics are adequately covered, or that ministers give useful answers, and his role in ensuring that all opposition members have the opportunity to participate has been severely curtailed since the parties themselves began to choose their own batting order.

The bulk of the television and newspaper coverage of parliament comes from question period. After it is over there is a remarkable exodus: where there were 280 members there are now 25; where the press gallery was packed, three, two, or even no reporters remain; the public galleries empty.

In Britain, most questions are written and there is usually notice of at least a week during which ministers and their staff can prepare answers. Although supplementaries introduce an element of spontaneity, much of the British question period is a ponderous dance, in which in effect the ministers give carefully phrased replies to questions at least a week old. Question period in Britain is sophisticated, and frequently clever, but it is rarely as spontaneous or dynamic as it is in Canada.

Question period is in essence a contest between two cohesive and disciplined teams, the government and the opposition. Question period is a means of discrediting individual ministers and government alike, so that the public will be persuaded that the opposition would be the better choice at the next election. Neither the prime minister nor any other government official has any control over whether question period will occur, or what will be asked in it. It is a gruelling occasion, regularly taking place approximately 175 days of the year, during which the rulers of the country are forced to listen and respond to the complaints and grievances of the nation, as expressed by the opposition and in the spotlight of intensive coverage by the media. There is no counterpart to question period in the United States. Neither presidential press conferences, where questions are limited, pre-selected, and orchestrated, nor presidential state-of-the-union addresses to Congress, where there are no questions, compare with the Canadian question period.

Most of the rest of the House of Commons' time is occupied with debate. In a given year, 15 or 16 days will be taken up with opening the session and the throne speech and budget debates. After deducting the 25 opposition supply days, there will be about 110 days left for government business, or about 400 hours. This, the majority of the time of the House of Commons, is spent primarily on bills.[4] But a few times each year the normal routine will be interrupted by debate on a motion under Standing Order 29 (formerly so 26), to discuss a matter of urgent public importance.

We have already noted that debate is protracted and dull. A study in the mid-1970s found that even though the House spends far more time debating bills than on question period, newspaper coverage of question period exceeded coverage of debate on government bills by a ratio of thirty-five to one.[5] This ratio would be even more lopsided now after the introduction of television. The normal speech is wordy, unnecessarily long and repetitious, and, in the British House, would be drowned out and terminated by the shuffling of feet and catcalls. Only because nobody is listening does this not happen in Canada. Similarly, debates themselves are overly long and repetitious. Virtually every interesting point to be made in a debate can be found in the first three and the last speeches – those of the leading party spokesmen. The dozens of speeches and hours of time in between are chaff, best lost in the winds of time. So far, the recent reduction in length of speeches, and the brief question-and-answer period, appear to have had moderate success, but the problem of length and dulness of debate still remains. The reason for this lingering malaise is that the function of much debate is not to state, convince, prove, persuade, rally, or support, but simply to occupy time. Timetabling, as we have seen, has become one of the major problems of the House.

The sources of the problem of timetabling are complex and tangled. Some are obvious, such as: members like to speak and do not want their opportunities to do so to be limited; or the opposition likes to embarrass the government. Some, however, have deeper roots. Before examining them, and before coming to an assessment of the more general functions of debate and question period, it is useful to look at examples of them in action.

Example 1. The creation of a Committee of Inquiry to examine the security service of the RCMP. The government reversed itself on the issue of setting up an inquiry to investigate alleged illegal acts of the RCMP, and parliamentary questions and debates were the major weapons in this battle. This issue was first raised in parliament on 31 March 1976, when the solicitor general was asked if he was aware of alleged RCMP involvement in a break-in at the Agence de Presse Libre du Québec in 1972. On 2 April, M. Matte proposed that a committee of the House, or a commission of inquiry, be established to investigate. Sporadic questioning on this and related issues continued for well over a year, until in May 1977, a trial began in Montreal of police officers involved in the break-in. The RCMP officers involved entered a plea of guilty. In the House, the solicitor general was vigorously questioned, as before, on whether headquarters had authorized the break-in, the extent to which the minister and headquarters had subsequently known about it, whether it was an isolated incident of law-breaking, and whether the government would set up an independent inquiry. After the Government of Quebec announced that it would establish an inquiry into the affair, Mr Clark, the leader of the Progressive Conservatives, and Mr Broadbent, of the NDP, demanded similar action by the federal government. On 17 June, Mr Francis Fox, the solicitor general, made a lengthy statement to the House in which he said that a year earlier, when the issue had first been raised, the government had considered establishing a commission of inquiry, but had received 'repeated and unequivocal assurances from the RCMP that the APLQ incident was exceptional and isolated and that the directives of the RCMP to its members clearly require that all of their actions take place within the law.'[7] They had therefore decided against establishing a commission.

The opposition was not satisfied with this response, however, and continued to demand an inquiry. Several other instances of possible illegal or improper activities by the RCMP had emerged – the Praxis break-in in Toronto; an investigation of Royal American Road Shows in Edmonton – and question period on the Monday following Mr Fox's Friday statement was completely taken up by the issue, and continued until 3:45 pm, taking nearly twice its usual time. The next day there was only one question, but a discussion of question of privilege over the accountability to parliament of former ministers occupied nearly two hours, and a debate under SO 26 (for the purpose of discussing a specific and important matter requiring urgent consideration) in which both Mr Broadbent and Mr Clark demanded a public inquiry occupied a further four hours. Much of question period the next day was also on the same topic, and similarly for the remainder of the week. Monday, 27 June, saw renewed attacks. By this time, the opposition was supported by major newspapers across Canada, and outside the House many allegations were made of further RCMP wrongdoings. On 6 July, the solicitor general told the House:

These allegations received our immediate attention. At my request, the deputy solicitor general of Canada and the assistant attorney general, criminal law, personally met with some of the individuals who made these allegations. In addition, I asked the Commissioner of the RCMP to undertake the investigations which were warranted. He later informed me, after having made preliminary inquiries, that some of these allegations might well have some basis in fact. According to the commissioner, it would appear that some members of the RCMP in the discharge of their responsibility to protect national security could well have used methods or could have been involved in actions which were neither authorized not provided for by law. As a result, the commissioner has modified his position and has recommended that the government establish a commission of inquiry into the operations and the policies of the RCMP security service, on a national basis.

[Translation]
In the circumstances, Mr. Speaker, and considering these new developments, the government has decided to establish an inquiry commission composed of three members who will be responsible for determining the scope and frequency of inquiry practices and other activities which are not permitted or provided for in the law, involving members of the RCMP, and for examining the policies and procedures regulating RCMP activities in their task, which consists in protecting the country and ensuring its security.[8]

With this capitulation, a new chapter began.

It would be an exaggeration to claim that questions in the House caused the government to capitulate. A political system is complex and multi-channelled, and each institution overlaps in function and activity with many others. Also involved in this issue were the courts in Quebec, the Government of Quebec, the mass media, civil-rights groups, individuals, personal contacts of ministers, and many other interested bodies. Parliamentary debates played their part. Nevertheless, question period was the forum in which the government was forced to face, day after day, incessant nagging on the issue. It could not prevent questions from being asked, nor could it, because of the importance of the issue, ignore them. It took well over a year from the time an inquiry was first requested, but in the end the opposition had its way. The constant nag of question period, and the attendant media exposure, had no small part in the decision.

Example 2. The debate on the constitution, 1980–1. After the Clark government was defeated in the election of February 1980, the Trudeau government, and many other groups, including the opposition parties in parliament, fought the separatist Parti Québécois government of Quebec on the issue of sovereignty-association for Quebec. The anti-separatist forces won the referendum on 20 May 1980 and the Trudeau government then attempted to implement the promise it had made during the referendum campaign that it would renew the Canadian constitution. The story of how these efforts reached fruition is long and complicated. In it the House of Commons played a crucial role.[9]

The referendum was held in May 1980. During the following summer, Prime Minister Trudeau and the provincial premiers attempted to create a new constitution which would, for the first time, give Canadians full control over their constitution and its amendments. Up until then, because the basic constitutional document, the British North America Act of 1867, was an act of the British parliament, the final authority for change remained with the British parliament, and not in Canada.

The summer discussions failed. On 2 October, Prime Minister Trudeau announced on nation-wide television his intention to introduce a motion into the federal parliament, asking the British parliament to 'patriate' the constitution, create an amending formula, and entrench a charter of human rights. Unilateral federal action went against the principles and traditions of the Canadian federal state. Opposition leader Joe Clark, who immediately followed Trudeau on television, said that his party could not support unilateral federal action. However, Ed Broadbent, the leader of the NDP, committed his party to supporting the government. Soon after, the motion was introduced into the House. Although the government at first proposed that the motion be passed quickly, without examination by committee, it backed down after several weeks of debate, and referred the issue to a special joint Senate–House of Commons committee. This decision was, apparently, still within the government's game plan. However, the Progressive Conservatives then seized the initiative. Through protracted procedural wrangling they delayed business in the House of Commons until the government agreed, first, to televise the proceedings of the joint committee and, second, to extend the deadline for the committee's report until well beyond the limit in the government's private schedule.

The committee was a huge success and mobilized support for the federal government's position to a point where the support for the provincial governments' opposition was severely damaged. In the meantime, however, three provincial governments had appealed the legality of the federal government's unilateral action in the courts. Two supported the federal government's position, but to say the least there was no overwhelming support for unilateral federal action.

The Supreme Court of Canada, in the fall of 1981, ruled that substantial support of the provinces for constitutional change was necessary to be in accord with conventions of the constitution. After more prolonged and difficult discussions, nine provinces and the federal government agreed on the final wording of the new constitution. Quebec was alone in disagreeing. A motion embodying this agreement was passed easily in the Canadian parliament, and then quickly approved by the British parliament. It became part of the constitution of Canada on 17 April 1982.

Parliament was enormously influential in determining the final outcome. The prolonged processes of debate, particularly the concessions made by the government in face of opposition intransigence and obstruction, and the proceedings of the special committee, gave the final product extraordinary legitimacy and support in most of Canada, but not in Quebec. Obstruction by the opposition was essential in forcing a stubborn, wilful government to adhere to what the Supreme Court determined to be the constitutional conventions. The struggle and drama itself also helped to mobilize support and consent. Both the strategy and the tactics of the Progressive Conservatives during the confederation debates had a great deal to do with internal party politics. Joe Clark's position of leader was precarious after his embarrassing, unnecessary loss of office in 1979–80. The party itself was confused and uncertain about reforming the constitution. The approach they took, of insisting that the role of the provinces be recognized and that due process and constitutional convention be observed, was a safe one which enabled them to stand on a matter of principle without committing themselves to a matter of substance. Their use of the tactics of parliamentary opposition and obstruction to achieve their ends was competent and impressive. Both Clark and the party emerged from the fray with renewed strength, although Clark's was not enough to enable him to retain the leadership for much more than a year. The NDP, however, found the process divisive. Broadbent had committed his party without consulting his caucus or party outside of parliament. Many MPs and supporters, particularly in the west, were outraged at this whole-hearted support of a questionable Liberal initiative. A weakening in popular support for the NDP began as the dust settled from the constitutional fracas.

Example 3. The Crow's Nest rates debate. One of the most enduring beliefs in Canadian politics is that the west is 'hard done by' and exploited by the east. Since 1897 western prairie grain farming had been supported by a guarantee of cheap rail transportation through the 'Crow's Nest Pass' rates. But where in 1897 these guaranteed rates had covered the full cost of transportation, by 1980 they covered less than a fifth.10 The railways, because of this uneconomic traffic, had not developed the western railway network to its optimum. By 1983, after many years of discussion, the Liberal government proposed legislation to change the rates. Only a Liberal government could do this with impunity: they had only one seat in the west.

Opposition within parliament was immediate and strident. The NDP delayed introduction of the bill (usually a mere formality) for several days. Passage of the legislation took up most of the time of parliament from spring until Christmas. Not only was debate at each stage prolonged and acrimonious, but the opposition parties as well tried many new and not so new delaying tactics. Irrelevant points of order were raised to delay normal business. Innumerable petitions were submitted to take up parliament's time. The opposition on several occasions boycotted votes.

By the fall, the bill was out of committee, and several hundred amendments awaited consideration. The Progressive Conservatives appeared weary of the battle. Opinion polls showed they were almost certain to win the next election, and it was to their advantage to let the Liberals take the blame for the change, and to have it well in place by election time. Their fight was by then only enough to show their opposition, but not enough to prevent passage. The NDP, however, remained adamant. Saskatchewan wheat farmers, the main opponents to the bill, were a big source of support to the NDP Opinion polls ever since the confederation debate had shown the NDP to be slipping, and a passionate fight against changing the Crow's Nest rates was a means of regaining lost support in the west. But though the NDP fought a good fight, the bill became law in November.

It was not, however, a good bill. Many of the proposed amendments would have been useful and constructive, but the way the bill was opposed prevented their adoption. For some this was because of lack of time, for others because they were ruled out of order by the speaker and the unanimous agreement needed for their introduction was not forthcoming. The bill was substantially changed in its passage through parliament, partly because flaws in it were exposed through debate, and partly because the government compromised some of its original intentions in order to get at least passive support from the Progressive Conservatives. By the end, a newly drafted bill would better have reflected the intentions and compromises that had emerged, but obstructionism in the House would have meant a replay of the entire exhausting performance, something the government was not prepared to endure. As a result the bill became law in its patchwork amended form, flawed though it was.

Example 4. The Department of National Revenue. In the fall of 1983, the Progressive Conservative opposition raised in question period the issue of whether the Department of National Revenue, which collects business and income taxes, had adopted a 'quota system' which meant that tax auditors were judged by how much revenue they extracted. The minister, Pierre Bussières, denied these charges. Nevertheless, the opposition continued to hound him. They produced documentary evidence which appeared to prove that the minister was not aware of what was going on in his department. Not only quotas, but an aggressive and hostile attitude towards taxpayers was, it seemed, being adopted by the department. For days on end, Bussières was the object of hostile attention for the bulk of question period.

The minister did not concede that there were grounds for these allegations. He did, however, establish a task force of management consultants to examine the tax-collection administration and procedures, and the deputy minister (permanent, civil servant, head of the department) was relieved of his job by the prime minister. The Progressive Conservatives, in the meantime, having been rebuffed by the government in their demand for an investigation by a parliamentary committee, set up their own task force of MPs which toured the country, found substantial support for their allegations, and published a report including recommendations.

The government in this instance refused to accede to the demands of the opposition. They were wounded, as their actions showed, but they denied culpability. They did not follow the tradition of ministerial responsibility because it was the civil servant, not the minister, who was punished. The opposition, nevertheless, scored substantial points, and succeeded in uncovering, at a relatively early stage, a problem which needed action. Problems in ministerial responsibility became obvious during these exchanges. The department has not been considered a politically important one, and has had low-level ministers, and many of them. The average stay of a minister in recent years has been less than a year. The government responded to the attack, and doubtless some improvement will result, but noticeably absent from the response was an acceptance of blame by minister or government. The new Conservative government in 1984 appointed Mr Perrin Beatty, who had chaired the party's task force, as minister of revenue. Some changes already have occurred, and others have been promised.

THE USES OF DEBATE AND QUESTION PERIOD

Question period and debate, it can be seen, fulfil many functions, although these do not include, most of the time, changing the minds of listeners or eliciting information. One function, as performed in the creation of the commission of inquiry into the RCMP and the national revenue problems, of question period in particular, is to draw attention to an issue and force a response from the government. A second function, as shown in the constitutional debate and the Crow's Nest rates debate, involves obstructionism used to force compromises from an unwilling government. A third, as shown in the constitution debate, is to delay a headstrong government until other forces and events make their influence felt, and to exert some control over the government. A fourth, performed by both debate and question period, is to prove that the government has faults. A fifth function, often the point of a parliamentary battle, is to rally the troops within an opposition party itself and is only remotely directed towards forcing change on the government. Finally, as can be seen in all four examples above, the gamesmanship and strategies involved in parliamentary processes function to create elements of excitement and drama. The fact that it is a battle, and is hard fought and won, in itself provided a symbolic and emotional, as well as a legislative, legitimacy to the government's proposals in both the constitution and Crow's Nest examples. Both question period and debate mobilize consent, partly through the trial-by-battle aspect of the legislative process (the fact of perseverance and willingness to suffer proves virtue and commitment), and partly through the visible evidence that the government is not only being called to account, but is also responding to these calls.

There are obviously weaknesses in the process. It is immensely selective. Only a few items can be given the sort of treatment described in the examples. Others are neglected, or dealt with only partially. The Progressive Conservatives, after upholding civil liberties so splendidly in the 1977–8 revelations of misdeeds in the RCMP, havered when legislation embodying the recommendations for improvement made by the commission were put before the House. Their nostalgic love for the RCMP led them to forget the faults which had initiated the process. Parliamentary attention, and the use of question period and debate, like puppy love, are exuberant, fickle, sporadic, and spotty. They do not ensure that everything gets discussed, or that what is discussed is covered thoroughly or in depth. Legislation is not always in as good a form as it should be, because of obstruction. Obstruction also makes the government try to avoid parliament wherever possible, either by stretching the meaning of existing legislation, or by phrasing bills in very general terms. More effective timetabling would produce more, and better, legislation and in this way improve parliamentary and judicial control and review of government. Nevertheless, debate and question period ensure that no issue is inviolate, that all are eligible to be examined, and some certainly will be, in the glare of the most embarrassing public spotlight. To institutionalize this type of accountability in a political system is no mean feat.

Party lines (except on rare occasions such as during the debate on capital punishment) are rigid, and members of a side must support their leaders in both debate and voting. The struggle in the House is not to change the minds and votes of members of parliament, but to woo and win the voters in the next election. This aspect of parliamentary politics is in large part a game, and its livelier moments, like question period, have all the excitement and aggression of a contact sport. There is a close similarity, even a resonance, between the two-sided competitive structure of parliament and team sports, even to the speaker as referee and procedure as the rules of the game. Parliamentary politics is fun, good entertainment, and a spectator sport. The mixture of serious business and sporting elements is part of the British heritage and political culture.

The audience for debate and question period is, for the most part, outside the House. While this is particularly true for debates, question period, although it is an exciting and enjoyable time in the House, finds the justification for its format and style in the audience outside. The present type of parliamentary question, with its ponderous preamble, statement of the problem, and the response as well are designed to fit into television news, and to become an effective thirty-second clip. They are very successful in doing this. Televising the House has put its proceedings back into the news, though thirty seconds of audio-visual coverage has replaced the extended newspaper attention accorded debates in the nineteenth century. The present question period is in part a child of the television age.

Its adversarial nature makes parliamentary politics a simplifier. Issues, by the time parliament looks at them, are reduced to party viewpoints. This reduction is an artificial one, but it has the virtue of making issues understandable and forcing parties and MPs to show where they stand. In this simplification, the processes also aggregate. The government in particular becomes the owner of, and is responsible for, a collection of policies, viewpoints, and ideas. This aggregation forces some (though frequently not much) intellectual and ideological discipline on the government. It also protects the individual MPs and parties from single-issue pressure groups, so that both are free to respond to a collective general interest rather than a small but vocal group. The discipline imposed on the opposition is less demanding than that on the government, but none the less an effective and credible opposition will also select and choose. (Below, in chapter 10, we shall examine in more depth the impact of these adversarial features on policy-making.)

DEBATE AND QUESTION PERIOD AND THE MEDIA

Apart from question period and other rare occasions, parliament is not good theatre. The action is slow, the dialogue is ponderous and interminable, the scene is sparsely populated, and the wit has all the subtlety but none of the force of a Mack truck. The problem of the scene has its origins in the historic need for all members to have desks, and an opportunity to remedy it will come when the House has to cope with more MPs than can be accommodated at desks. The problem of dulness and poor use of language arises because the purpose of debate is to fill time, not to enlighten or entertain, and will only be remedied when this purpose disappears. Question period serves the opposition and to a lesser extent the government well in its present form and is not likely to be changed substantially. It is not subtle or clever but it is effective in making points – for both sides.

This sort of analysis does not, however, exhaust consideration of debate and question period. They have both, particularly question period, now taken their place in the television age, partly integrated into news and other current-events programming, partly as a broadcast of the House itself, watched by several hundred thousand Canadians. To appreciate their significance as part of television and the other means of mass communication, it is necessary to take a step back and look more broadly at what is happening in both television and parliament.

Debate and question period embody scepticism. Their essence is one side making claims, the other side proving these claims false or misguided. Neither parliamentary occasion is fully choreographed, nor are their plots always predetermined. As the examples of the RCMP security service, the Crow's Nest rates, and Revenue Canada show, they can be both open-ended and unpredictable.

The scepticism of the opposition in parliament (and of the government when it is criticizing the opposition) is directed towards the statements the other side is making. Statements by politicians in parliament, like most political statements, are mixtures of fact, value, and fantasy. The three are often difficult to disentangle, as in such statements as 'the Canadian economy is in good shape,' or 'income tax reform will lead to social justice,' or 'Canadianization of the oil industry is vital for our future.' They are claims for the importance of an issue: the correctness of the facts as stated; the worthwhileness of the values asserted or implicit in the statement; and the causal relationships embodied in the proposition. Question period and the protracted debates on government business are extended, formal dialogues on the claims and statements of the government.

Question period and debate institutionalize doubt and scepticism in the political system. Plato was correct in arguing that some of the myths of government and the state are 'noble lies.' Debate and question period serve, within their limits, to expose these lies. In this age we cannot afford to test, with reality, many of our myths, such as the nuclear deterrent. The challenging of the 'noble lies' of the state through the institutionalization of doubt in question period and debate is one of the unusual and underappreciated virtues of the parliamentary system. There is no counterpart to them in the congressional system, and the myths of politics (some of which are dangerously simplified and naively optimistic) are less consistently and systematically subjected to a thorough debunking in the United States. The arduous task set the leader and cabinet in parliament by question period and debate ensures that the fallacies of many romantic political myths of the heroic leader and the marvellous policy are exposed, that the political leaders who survive must endure and triumph in a challenging and exacting combat, and that no leader for long retains his mythic heroic grandeur.[11] President Reagan would not last long in the parliamentary bear pit. A prime minister who avoids parliament is likely to lose support.

The process has its limits as has all political dialogue. In Canada it operates within the broader system of political parties and discourse. It accepts the desirability of private property, the market economy, and the resulting inequities of society although these are tempered by the argument for a strong role for government in reducing disparities and alleviating hardship. Many myths are not debunked. Doubts in parliament in October 1970 over the need for the imposition of the War Measures Act were drowned out by the pressure of public opinion; Medicare reforms in 1984 had an easier time passing through parliament than in being put into effect. There is no expression in parliament of the Marxist perspective so pervasive in academic political analysis nor is there much questioning of the general liberal-democratic perspective. The extreme right is also less audible in parliament than it is in parts of society. Debate and question period do not alter the imbalance between a strong stable government and a weak parliament. Nevertheless, they do far more than is generally appreciated to ensure good government and good leadership in Canada.

Although for question period the House is at the centre of attention and fulfils its functions as the prime political forum, for most of its time, which is spent in debate, the House is sadly irrelevant and lives up to one member's description of it as 'underdeveloped, immature, retarded and defective.'[12] Parliament is a place of words, and politics is a war of words. These words only have value and meaning when they are communicated to the world outside. The essential links in these connections are the media. And the media ignore debates. As a result, debate, for the most part, is a failure.

This failure takes its toll of members. Many report a feeling of despair that when they speak in the House, they are 'speaking to nobody ... absolutely no hope of changing anybody's mind.'[13] Mr Cooper, a member of the Special Committee on Reform, related that once he was so bored and depressed that he sat down and stopped in the middle of his own speech. He wasn't excited by the material, nobody was listening, nobody gave a hoot.[14] Some do not participate in debates because 'Members are simply repeating what has been said by others. It is part of a game that is played between both sides of the house.'[15]

Media interest in debates has declined. As recently as twenty years ago an MP rarely took part in a debate without having at least one paragraph in a Canadian Press story. These were translated into the other official language. The maiden speech of an MP received even better coverage. Newspapers, however, have lost interest in this coverage, and the Canadian Press has dropped it. The dulness and lack of newsworthiness of debates caused the press to lose interest. To some extent, poor coverage has been exacerbated by the growth of newspaper chains. Southam newspapers, for example, cover areas represented by seventy newspapers. According to Charles Lynch, a very senior member of the press gallery, not one of the MPs from a region covered by a chain newspaper 'has the slightest chance of his or her speech ever being reported in those newspapers.' It was different when there were more independent, locally based papers.[16]

One factor which has made debate less newsworthy is that they are less meaty and interesting than they used to be. The media focus on the party leaders, and party leaders take less part in debate than in the past. Both Prime Minister Trudeau and Prime Minister Mulroney have records of very infrequent participation – often a year will pass without the prime minister entering into debate. With the prime minister not participating, other leaders stay out as well. Also, during the Trudeau years the practice of ministers making important statements in the House, with brief responses from frontbench spokesmen of the other parties, was largely dropped. Policy statements were made elsewhere. This helped to make the House irrelevant. Recently attempts have been made to change this, but there is a strong temptation for the government to make important announcements in speeches outside the House where they are not subject to criticisms and the opposition does not get equal billing.

Another factor is the format of the House. The time has long since passed when MPs needed desks on the floor, and benches like the British would make the entire operation more intimate and exciting. The recent Conservative government decision to slow the growth of the House will postpone the time when this reform must be dealt with. Television coverage of the House does not, at present, permit reaction shots. It focuses solely on the member speaking. This makes for dull coverage. The Special Committee on Reform of 1985 noted that television had caused few changes: members now applaud rather than thump their desks, and they tend to move around to sit behind the person speaking. But attempts to counter the impression that a member is talking to an empty house are not successful. 'No one is really fooled; the game of musical chairs simply adds an artificial element.'[17] They proposed that the guidelines for televising be revised. An alternative would be to recognize that moving members around is a poor and artificial substitute for the needed drastic reduction in the physical size of the chamber. There is no good reason to expect most MPs to be in the House during debates; the format of the House should reflect its real function and use, not some spurious ideal of 100 per cent attendance.

Most media coverage is distressingly superficial, in large part not because the press gallery is incompetent (though many members of it are inexperienced and ignorant of political history and parliamentary tradition and deficient in substantive knowledge of policies and administration), but because the demands of the media are restricting. There are exceptions in several excellent columnists, and the weekly CBC television and radio shows in both English and French. But for most journalists, the constraints of the media lead to poor journalism. Douglas Fisher told the special committee:

We have something like 10 or 12 camera crews wandering around the Hill. There are basically seven networks ... and most of these people are chasing the same thing. Because of tape, for radio you do not have a story, if you can help it, longer than 50 seconds. For television you do not have a story longer than 75 or 80 seconds. So right away you have all these people tending to look for the same thing. They do not want to get beat, and those are the kind of limitations of radio and television. This means that you look for the simplest thing to present. The simplest thing to present is Warren Allmand saying it is a shell game and Flora saying it is a magnificent challenge; or you have your MP: My God, here is one of those Tory cruds from the back benches in Quebec and he has a mind of his own. This is news. You know, look at the system.[18]

A CBC reporter told the committee:

Question Period is really the only part of the Commons where there is an exchange of ideas and a clash of personalities ... the question-and-answer period after the speeches now does provide some exchange of ideas, but by and large, once the lead-off speaker [of] each party has spoken, you know what every other speaker is going to say and, let us face it, you do not even go to hear them yourselves. You keep enough people there to keep the House going, but MPs do not go to hear what other MPs are going to say because they know darn well what they are going to say.[19]

As a result, reporters look elsewhere. According to Fisher:

Most of us – and this is not putting us down – look pretty coldly at what is going on. If you are a radio reporter who has to put in two or three items a day, the Question Period and the scrum [outside the House after question period] are the handiest things to get. You sort of feel around: What is the big news today; God, what is it? Today, is it abortion? Is it trade? Has Joe Clark goofed again? It tends to become sort of stylized in manner. We had thousands of little items on Trudeau over the years. He was always good for something.[20]

What gets covered by the media are the times when debate fails: when the bells ring, a member has a tantrum, or a party objects to a ruling by the speaker. This encourages the worst aspects of parliamentary behaviour.

The coverage of politics and parliament by the media tends to accent the negative. The items that are considered news are the failures, the faults and the weaknesses, not the successes and achievements. The destruction of heroes and heroic myths has its concomitant, making politics smaller than life. This is doubtless not entirely the media's fault, for it is an often–remarked-upon Canadian characteristic that we do not have national myths and heroes. Canadian politics are human rather than heroic in scale. But the process can go beyond legitimate criticism, and many good persons have had their careers and lives savaged in parliament and the media. There is a danger that the parts of parliamentary politics that reach the public are not those that explain and defend, but those that oversimplify and attack. This undoubtedly explains in part the low esteem the public has for politicians, and the difficulty the government finds in mobilizing consent for programmes and policies. Nevertheless, media attention is essential to politics and politicians. Parliament's communication functions are at their most visible in debate and quesion period. Question period in particular informs the government of how the populace, through the opposition, views the behaviour of the government and the state of the nation. In turn, debate and question period give the government a chance to present its case and to educate the nation. The superficiality of media coverage is the greatest single obsacle to making these highly visible and influential occasions more useful in terms of content and depth of discussion.

8

Committees

Committees are near the top on any short list of reforms to parliament. Not the least of the reasons for this emphasis is the inescapable example of the United States, where committees of Congress are active and highly visible and give elected senators and representatives a strong voice in the management of the nation's affairs. Committees offer the beguiling prospect of a stronger, more independent role for parliament. Committees can do things which the House itself cannot. They can make investigations, during which they interrogate ministers and public servants, call expert witnesses, travel, and hire research staff; they can prepare reports which consider and accommodate the various interests and viewpoints of members and the public; they have the possibility of being non-partisan in a way the House rarely is. Committees can be a means by which members of parliament can integrate their viewpoints into policy proposals, or act together to call the executive to account for its use of funds and authority. In almost every respect, the ideal of the committee stands in contrast to the reality of the House: they can be small and personal where the House is big and cold; the individual MP can be important in committee instead of being effaced by party discipline; the outcome of committee deliberations can be creative and exciting; committees can be non-partisan, sensitive, and subtle where the House is partisan, crude, and blunt; and above all, committees might, like those of the U.S. Congress be powerful and efficient, where the House appears ineffective and cumbersome.

To the government, parliamentary committees offer the prospect of more channels for processing legislation and reducing in the demands on the time of the House, and consequently the promise of getting more business through parliament. To opposition members and government backbenchers, committees promise opportunities to question ministers and public servants and to examine important issues. To pressure groups, committees offer a point of access to the system of power, and a public platform which they can use to pursue their interests. For reformers, committees offer a chance for MPs to get beyond rhetoric and posturing to effective non-partisan participation in the processes of governance.

With all this promise it is little wonder that committees rank so high on agendas for reform. And over the past decades a great deal has been done to improve the committee system. But the results of reform have, by and large, been disappointing and have not realized the hopes of reformers. Success at best has been moderate. The reasons for this are complex and embedded in the way the parliamentary system of representative government works in Canada. This chapter will examine both the efforts to reform committees and the reasons for the limited success of those efforts. The primary focus will be the involvement of committees in the function of making a government work, in the discussion and examination of policy and programme issues. The role of committees in making a government behave, especially the very important public accounts committee, will be considered later, in chapter 11.

THE COMMITTEE SYSTEM

The Canadian House of Commons has had a system of specialist standing committees since confederation. In this it has been quite different from the British House, where the committee system has been slow to develop, and where until recently there have been no small specialist committees covering the departments as the Canadians have. In practice, however, although committees were regularly established at the beginning of each session of parliament, for the most part this was the end as well as the beginning of their existence. Many never met, and remained moribund from one session to the next.[1] Exceptions were the committees which considered private legislation, although even these committees became less active as, over the years, private bills became a far less important part of parliamentary business.

From time to time other committees were active. The public accounts committee on occasion investigated abuses in spending, especially when there had been a change of government and the new cabinet wanted to use the committee to expose the sins of its predecessor.[2] The agriculture committee, because of its many able, knowledgeable members, often performed useful investigations. The veteran's affairs committee was influential in establishing the scheme of benefits for veterans after the Second World War. On three occasions during the first two post-war decades the Canadian nuclear-energy programme was examined by committees. These were a valuable means of making public basic information on a programme which was then still mysterious and cloaked by military secrecy. But in spite of these and other exceptions, the committees were generally not active, nor were they an important part of parliament.

Prime Minister John Diefenbaker made the first important reform when, in 1958, he ensured that, for the first time, a member of the opposition was appointed as chairman of the public accounts committee. This committee, which considers the report of the auditor general and, through its examination, attempts to ensure propriety and economy in government spending, is an essential part of parliament's control over government finances. A chairman selected from the opposition has a strong interest in pursuing possible government wrong-doing, while a chairman from the government side is more likely to be protective. The modern era of efforts to improve the financial accountability of government to parliament can properly be said to date from this reform. Diefenbaker, because of his huge majority, also encouraged activity in other committees as a means of keeping his backbenchers busy. He, however, did not consider committees to be an important part of parliament, and never sat on one himself. Under Prime Minister Pearson there were also noticeable increases in committee activity. Nevertheless the committee system remained substantially as it had been.

Under the new Trudeau government, in December 1968 the committee system received its most drastic overhaul since confederation. Although the names and number of committees were not changed, most other aspects were. The maximum size of most committees was reduced to twenty members. Committees were given the right to sit while the House was sitting and during adjournment, and the right to delegate all their powers, except reporting to the House, to subcommittees. Change in membership was made easier by making it through notice to the Clerk of the House instead of, as before, by order of the House. But more important than all of these were the new functions given the committees. The estimates were now to be referred automatically to the appropriate specialist standing committee. Most government legislation after second reading was to go to the standing committees instead of committee of the whole. The committees were also, upon order from the House, to make investigations into issues of policy or administration. The Canadian House of Commons now had not only its comprehensive system of specialist committees covering the programmes of government, but a new assignment of responsibilities which ensured that they would meet frequently and occupy much of the time and energy of members of parliament.

Canada was unusual among parliamentary legislatures in adopting this sort of committee system. The influence of parliament over the executive normally comes not so much through the rejection, alteration, or approval of bills by parliament as through the deterrent effect of bad publicity from parliamentary scrutiny and debate. An argument against strong parliamentary committees is that they submerge the distinctions between parties and give power to 'irresponsible' committees rather than a 'responsible' government. The Trudeau government in its reforms to the committees had no intention of moving away from this structure of responsible parliamentary government. Its main concern was to reduce the pressure on time available on the floor of the House. It also had a concern for improving parliament, and the report of the Special Committee on Procedure in the fall of 1968 expressed the views of many members of both government and opposition when it hoped that the reports of the committees would now 'assume a critical significance related more closely to the national interest as a whole than to simple political differences,' and for 'debate in the Standing Committees to be well-informed and pertinent; their members to become influential in the areas of their specialised experience.'[3] In suggesting that the committees should be less partisan, and that members of parliament should be specialized experts, the committee was proposing revolutionary changes in the highly partisan, amateur, and non-expert Canadian House of Commons.

In fact, the committees were doomed to have a strongly partisan component by the nature of the tasks assigned them. Their function of handling government bills, estimates, and other inquiries gave the committee two sorts of functions: one on bills and estimates, of handling the government's programmes, which is a highly partisan endeavour and which the government, under the conventions of responsible parliamentary government, must control to ensure that its legislation gets passed in an acceptable form; and a second supposedly non-partisan function of making independent investigations on behalf of the House as a whole. The government, to ensure that its needs were met by the committees, had by necessity to exert a strong control over the committees so that it could control its legislative programme. The reality of this problem meant that instruments by which the government could control the committees were always there, even when they were making non-partisan investigations. This prevented the committees from developing a strong independent corporate spirit. These and other factors combined to make the committees unsatisfactory. The most important problem areas were chairmanship, membership, work procedures, and staff.[4]

Apart from the special case of the public accounts committee (which does not consider estimates or legislation) the chairmen of the committees were selected from the government side. Chairmen in effect wore three hats: one, they were to ensure that the committee proceedings were orderly and fair, the same sort of impartial role as the speaker plays for the House; two, they had some responsibility for the effectiveness of the committees and the quality of this work, and helped to organize and lead investigations; and three, they had a function of protecting the government's interests when these were under attack by opposition members of the committee. Some committee chairmen were able to balance these roles better than others, but regardless of the personal abilities of the chairman, conflicts were created by the incompatibility between the role of the chairman as a member of the governing party and his role as chairman of an independent committee scrutinizing the government and calling it to account.

There were problems in the tenure and promotion patterns of the chairmen.[5]

The government, through its House leader, had the dominant hand in selecting them. Since 1972, there has been a slight loosening up, and the government members of the committee have exercised more independence in choosing chairmen, although they are still chosen from their own side. Once appointed, committee chairmen do not usually last long in their positions. In the 1974–9 parliament more than 65 per cent of the chairmen left their position after serving less than two years, and only 16 per cent served for more than two years. More than half (55 per cent) left to become parliamentary secretaries, and an additional 12 per cent left for a post higher than parliamentary secretary. The position of committee chairman became, in effect, the proving and recruiting ground for advancement of government backbenchers:

The government succeeded in recruiting parliamentary secretaries in this fashion by maintaining inequities between committee leadership and parliamentary secretary positions. Committee leaders were more than anxious to abandon their committee assignments for the more prestigious and financially rewarding job of parliamentary secretary. Parliamentary secretaries enjoy the privilege of occasionally attending cabinet meetings, the opportunity to answer questions during Question Period, and an annual indemnity of $5,400.[6]

Parliamentary secretaries were obviously higher up the pecking order than committee chairmen. They also sat on the appropriate committee, acted as go-betweens between government and committee, and made certain that the committees did not deviate from the government's wishes. Maxwell Henderson, the former auditor general, claimed that the government enticed the opposition chairman away on an official delegation to Japan so that the deputy speaker, a government supporter, would be able to ensure the government's viewpoint prevailed at a crucial meeting.[7]

There is little possibility that the standing committees will become powerful independent bodies as long as they suffer from this kind of leadership. A committee cannot be better than its chairman. In Canada the position has low prestige, it is used by the government as a stepping stone to unabashedly partisan positions, and its incumbents view the position as short term. Whatever hat the chairman wears in his role, he will have an eye cocked to pleasing the government: the rewards system of the House demands this.

At first glance an obvious solution to the problem would be to give the position of chairman more prestige. Chairmen might, for example, be appointed for the life of a parliament, and be paid at a better level than the parliamentary secretary, perhaps even as high as a minister. But this reform has an overwhelming disadvantage: as long as the chairmen are appointed exclusively from the government side, additional rewards and prestige for the position would favour government members at the expense of the opposition. Bearing in mind the way the other rewards in parliament are handled, it would be almost inevitable that committee chairmanships would become, even more than they are at present, another form of patronage controlled by the whips. Members of the government caucus, in seeking to get and keep the positions, would be more aware than at present of what would please the government. This would make the committees even weaker as an independent control over the government. If some equal sharing of chairmanships could be ensured, and committees were free to choose their own chairmen, this change could, however, lead to a new sort of career path for MPs outside the front benches.

Membership of committees also had problems. With more than 440 committee places to be filled, there were approximately two committee positions for every eligible member of parliament (ministers, the speaker, the leaders of the opposition parties, and some others do not sit on committees). This contrasts with the British House, where positions on investigative committees are available for fewer than half the members. The competing demands on MPs' time in Canada, coupled with the lack of appeal of committee work, meant that there were problems in attendance of members, and frequent substitutions. Average attendance of eligible members in the 28th Parliament was little over 60 per cent.[8] Liberal backbenchers attended an average of 56.5 committee meetings per session, or 70 per cent more than the Conservatives, who averaged 39.4. Attendance of the NDP members was as high as that of the Liberals, while the Ralliement des Créditistes averaged less than half that of the Conservatives. Government members obviously had more interest than opposition, perhaps only because the government whips insisted that they be there to maintain the government majority on the committee, and the NDP, with their national focus and concerns over policies, more interest than the other opposition parties. The Créditistes, with their local orientation towards constituency and Quebec, had little interest in the committees. Within the parties there was also a marked variation between individuals. A few members attended more than a hundred committee sittings per session, and the top quarter was responsible for more than half of attendance, while the bottom third was responsible for only a tenth. These figures suggest that a small proportion of members was keenly interested in committee work, but that the bulk of the members treated it quite casually.

Membership substitution shows a similar trait. During the 30th Parliament (1974–9) there were 8,380 membership substitutions, averaging between two and three per committee meeting.[9] Some of these substitutions were made because a committee member would be away from Ottawa, perhaps on a trip with another committee. Others were made because a member would want to get onto a committee while a particular bill or issue of interest to himself or importance to his constituency was being considered. The whips would take a member who disagreed with party line off a committee. The Liberal government was particularly concerned to ensure that it had adequate attendance when the committees were considering reports and during clause-by-clause consideration of bills, and would fill up places at these times. One opposition member complained of 'roving squads of [government] members whose chief ability is to sit in on committees, read newspapers, sign letters and at the same time raise their right hands in approval of matters on which they have had no previous experience. These members have not participated in the committee discussions, and are merely present to fill a seat or fill out a quorum.'[10]

With this frequent substitution committee membership was very unstable. Some committees had so many changes during the 30th Parliament that only four of the original twenty members remained on the committee by the end. In this same period the Standing Committee on Broadcasting, Films, and Assistance to the Arts not only had this instability in membership but also had four chairmen and four vice-chairmen, with only one of the new chairmen being promoted from vice-chairman. The Standing Committee on Veteran's Affairs had greater stability in membership, with eleven of the original members remaining at the end of the parliament, but there were three changes in the chair and four vice-chairmen. Each of the new chairmen had, however, previously been vice-chairmen, giving some continuity to leadership.[11]

The instability in both leadership and membership, coupled with low attendance, shows that for the most part the committees were not cohesive, autonomous bodies working together towards a common purpose. Rather they had a large component of ritualistic and symbolic activity which they performed so there would be the appearance of a committee study of legislation and estimates. This suited the government's purposes more than it did the opposition, as is shown by the attendance figures.

Another element of rigidity entered into the system because of the large number and size of the committees. They were scheduled in a 'block system,' limited to five ninety-minute meetings in every two-week period.

The basic work procedure of the standing committees is the questioning of witnesses. When estimates are being considered, the main witnesses are the appropriate minister and his senior civil servants. Both committee members and witnesses have felt that the review of estimates is not very useful – hence the low attendance. The civil servant and minister were interested only in defending the estimates, and questions and answers alike tended to be desultory and unfocused. Members and witnesses knew that the estimates would be passed regardless of what the committee did. The rules of the House were interpreted so as to prevent committees from making substantive reports on the estimates, and when they had the audacity to defy this stricture, the substantive report would not be accepted by the speaker.[12]

For inquiries into policy issues, and for consideration of bills, outsiders may join ministers and civil servants as witnesses. On occasion, there can be a problem of too many voices clamouring to be heard. The finance committee, in its examination of tax reform in 1970–1, was faced with over a thousand submissions from which it could hear only a small fraction. The Special Joint Committee on the Constitution had a similar problem.

The chairman of the committee does little if any questioning himself, and usually also does little to guide proceedings. To ensure fairness, he normally allows all members an equal amount of the time available for questioning. Members ask questions for their allotted five or ten minutes, to be followed by the next questioner. Each member has his own interests and will often have prepared his questions before a meeting without regard to what other members have asked. The interests of members are often unrelated and members are often halted in questioning before they have concluded or reached the point they wish to make. This creates sessions which are disjointed and without direction.

This situation has been quite dissatisfying to members. It is, perhaps not so unsatisfactory to ministers, who are usually able to find an opportunity to make the points they want, and are otherwise concerned with defending themselves from opposition attack. Nor is it unsatisfactory to civil servants, whose role is to protect the minister and defend government policy. It can be, however, often a frustrating and unpleasant experience for outside witnesses. 'The committee system as it exists today is probably one of the most degrading performances I have ever participated in,' according to a former chairman of Imperial Oil Limited. 'There is no continuous attendance, people come and go out of the room and members obviously aren't familiar with the subjects. We arrive with a presentation that has involved a great deal of work and preparation and nobody knows what we are talking about. That's what I think of house committees.'[13] The president of the Canadian Bankers' Association was equally scathing:

The format is unsuitable to achieving the purposes because the chairman has no more authority than that of a glorified time-keeper. He has little authority to intervene to keep committee Members relevant and he has no control over the discussions because the Members are each allotted 10-minute intervals, the result of which is a mechanical transfer of time from one Member to another. Therefore, you can't possibly keep focused on a given issue until you are finished with it. The next Member will revert to some other clause or section. It's very repetitive and wasteful of time and, on top of that, committee Members have never been well served by staff.[14]

In contrast, witnesses find committees of the Senate more pleasant. The senators are more knowledgeable and more familiar with their subjects and the potential impact of legislation. The Senate committees are more deliberative and willing to take time. In addition, questioning in the Senate is by issue rather than by an allotted ten minutes per member. This allows them to focus the discussion, and give priority to a lead questioner.

Not the least of the recurring complaints about Commons committees has been that members are inadequately prepared and briefed. They do not have enough background knowledge, nor do they have a sense of direction in their questions. This problem arises in part because MPs are busy people with many demands on their time. The pressures of caucus and constituency force them to move from one subject to another, and one task to another, in a way that prevents them from becoming specialists in one area of government or putting much effort into one committee study. This problem has been aggravated by the frequent substitutions, which meant that at most committee meetings several members would not be familiar with what had gone before, and in questioning would either be ignorant of the subject matter and asking for basic background information or repeat the questions asked at an earlier meeting. The chairman's role has been so limited that he could not ensure directed, productive questioning. The opposition members of committees tried, for some investigations, to co-ordinate their questioning so as to pursue selected issues, but the impact of this preparation was blunted because unrelated questioning by members of other parties would intervene, or because a substituted member, unaware of these preparations, would wander astray in his questions. The inability of the standing committees to develop effective work procedures shows the small importance the committees held in the eyes of both government and individual members of parliament.

Staffing the committees has also been an area with continual problems. The staff of the House provides a clerk for each committee, whose duties are to arrange meetings, call witnesses, make travel arrangements, and perform the paperwork associated with the committee. Although they sometimes help committees to prepare reports and advise on questions of parliamentary practice and procedure, the committee clerks do not normally assist investigations by suggesting lines of inquiry, evaluating evidence, or drafting committee reports.[15] This resource is obviously inadequate to permit the committees to make anything but a rudimentary study.

There are, however, other sources of staff. The committees often hire temporary professional assistance. The Standing Committee on Finance, Trade, and Economic Affairs in 1969–70 utilized nearly twenty outside consultants in its mammoth investigation of the White Paper on Tax Reform. Temporary staff of this sort was hired by the committee itself, but the government kept close control over the numbers, and on occasion even who is appointed. An innovation has been the use of the Parliamentary Centre for Foreign Affairs and Foreign Trade, a non-profit organization financed by parliament, outside groups, and by revenues from its services. Its founder was Peter Dobell, a former foreign-service officer. It advises on sources of information, witnesses, written material, and the organization of investigations; prepares bibliographies; suggests lines of inquiry to members; and assists with the drafting of reports. It provides many other forms of assistance, such as research staff to many committees, including the special committee on procedure and the very important joint committee on the constitution. The centre has served a useful function within parliament in spite of its anomalous position as a private organization providing essential services to the central representative institution of government.

The parliamentary library and the political parties also have research staffs. The library has proved to be a major resource to committees, providing, for example, the assistance that enabled the public accounts committee to produce a useful report after its chaotic investigation of nuclear–power-station export contracts in 1977.[16]

Nevertheless, members of committees constantly complain that they have inadequate staff resources. This weakness in staff is one of the many factors contributing to poor questioning of witnesses. It is also one of the ways that government control, though invisible, strongly limits the capacity of parliament to investigate policy proposals and to hold the government accountable.[17]

In 1977 the finance committee investigated the subject matter of proposed amendments to the Combines Investigation Act and related statutes. The committee retained its own legal counsel and had briefing sessions with appropriate government officials and its counsel. In this way, before its public meetings began, the committee became familiar with the subject matter of its investigation. Then, when it received testimony from interested individuals and parties, it was better able to test the merits and inclinations of the views put forward. The committee completed its work and submitted its report within four and a half months. In terms of speed and preparation, this was a model of how a committee should operate. The limitations of time and other resources prevented the committee from commissioning its own independent research, but a large resource of relevant studies and experts was available outside parliament. It should be noted that in such an ideologically charged area the biases of both staff and MPs will have a noticeable impact on outcomes.

The Successes and Failures of the Committees
Regardless of the hopes reformers might have had, standing committees have not noticeably reduced the pressures of time in the House. Debate at both second-reading and report stages is still prolonged, repetitive, and unproductive. Whatever the satisfaction committee members might have found in the examination of legislation in the standing committees, this had little impact in the House

itself. Although members from all parties might be happy with a piece of legislation in committee, other members of the opposition caucus might be less happy when it reaches the House and would insist on having their say then. The committees are a much more private forum than the floor of the House itself, and fulfil a different function. As long as the opposition has nothing to gain by expediting business, and the government is unable to impose some discipline on the parliamentary timetable, this problem will remain regardless of improvements made to the committees.

The consideration of estimates by committees was, as we have noted, not good. Members tended to get drawn into discussions of trivia. Ministers were asked leading questions and replied with long and tortuous answers which consumed the available time. Meetings on estimates have been highly partisan. The process has had a large element of futility because everyone present – chairman, witness, and members – knew that the government would not permit estimates to be changed. And regardless of what the committee did, the estimates were automatically reported out of committee and passed by the House. The Lambert Commission in 1979 concluded that 'the key to the House of Commons assuming a more effective and influential role in financial management and accountability lies in its committee system.'[18] They recommended a drastic overhauling of the system, and many of the reforms they proposed have now been adopted. Nevertheless, the problem of parliamentary consideration of spending proposals is nowhere near being satisfactorily resolved.

Many proponents of improvement to committees see them operating as calm, wise, impartial investigators into policy and administration. These would-be reformers often seem unaware of the intensely partisan, goldfish-bowl reality of the parliamentary workworld. Discussion in committees as much as in the House can miss many important issues of substance and deep significance because the opposition members, who are the driving force behind criticism of the government, have a strong tendency to pick on the superficial and possibly scandalous. J.R. Mallory noted with some concern that in 1974, on what was probably the first opportunity in twenty years for a parliamentary committee to examine the workings of the modern cabinet system, the Standing Committee on Miscellaneous Estimates failed to elicit much that was useful on the working of the executive. The confrontation was adversarial, and psychological issues were more important than substantive ones. Questioning concentrated on trivial questions of chandeliers, swimming pools, and the prime minister's personal relations with his senior advisers. 'Parliamentary politics is a game played by hardened professionals who like to win,' Mallory concluded. 'If they can get away with the equivalent of the bean-ball and the butt-end in the corners they will do so. And few votes are likely to be garnered by discussing the machinery of government.'[19]

In contrast, a good example of an effective, independent committee in recent years was the Standing Committee on Justice and Legal Affairs under the chairmanship of Mark MacGuigan (who left this position to join the cabinet, and later was appointed to the judiciary). This committee had the experience of a useful subcommittee investigation into prisons behind it when, in 1978, it was assigned consideration of Bill C-26, which was to authorize the opening of mail by the RCMP security service (which previously it had been doing illegally). The committee showed no haste in considering the bill, and doubtless some reluctance was emerging within the Liberal caucus against such an impulsive, Draconian response to the discovered breach of civil liberties. The press and opposition were strongly hostile to the bill. The chairman followed his own inclination and that of members in dragging his feet. The solicitor general also in all likelihood had second thoughts. The bill was not reported from the committee, and died with the end of the session. Here the chairman, the members, the various caucuses, and the government, all had some influence over how the committee operated, with the chairman having a key role in balancing interests, directing inquiries, and ensuring fair play. The outcome was that the government changed its intentions.

Two contrasting examples of influence on policies and legislation are the committees on external affairs and on finance. The external affairs committee has been a non-partisan forum for investigation, and has made general examinations of policy areas with little expectation of immediate implementation of recommendations. In contrast the finance committee in its very important investigation of tax reform worked on a policy area which quickly led to legislation. Where the external affairs committee was able to operate independent of government and government policy, the finance committee and government were inextricably intermeshed. The former committee became autonomous and bipartisan to the point of being ignored; the latter relevant to the point of becoming an instrument to aid the government. Both were useful within the limits of the roles they accepted. Contributing to their success was the fact that their membership was composed of urban middle-class professionals, well educated, affluent, and interested and informed on world and financial affairs. The Liberal party had this sort of backbencher in abundance. In comparison, the Committee on Agriculture during the Trudeau era had a large number of knowledgeable opposition members, but few from the government side because of liberal weakness in rural ridings. This imbalance handicapped its work, although the Conservative members, because of their great knowledge and experience, made this an influential committee, and one which refutes the general argument of the amateurism of members.[20]

Successful committee work in both finance and external affairs in the Trudeau era came from the support of government members. The finance committee in 1969–70 heard in its study of the 211 briefs and 820 individuals (it received a total of 524 briefs and 1,093 letters and other submissions), held 146 meetings, and digested a bookshelf full of information on the way to producing its hundred-page report. It performed a valuable service to the government by hearing criticisms and crystallizing them into recommendations. The extent to which its recommendations were adopted, however, reflected a prior understanding between Liberal committee members and Mr Benson, then minister of finance, during the investigation. The inequality between government and opposition members weakened opposition interest in the committee's work, and only one, Mr Marcel Lambert, in fact participated to any great extent. When the report was finally being considered in the committee the Conservative members did not vote on it, while the NDP voted against. (Since committees cannot, under the rules of the House, present minority reports, the NDP submitted their own critical report to the press.) The extent to which this sort of investigation serves the interests of parliament as a whole rather than government is questionable.

Other committees as well, like justice, and legal affairs in its consideration of C-26, showed this inequality between government and opposition members. For example, Liberal backbenchers regarded amendments dealing with breathalyzer tests to the omnibus justice bill as an instance where backbench pressure changed the government's policy. Yet this bill was discussed at least five times by the Liberal caucus, and the battle in the committee was an extension of the battle in the caucus. Opposition Conservative and NDP members had only the route of the committee through which to confront the government, and did not have the advantage the Liberals had of discussing the legislation in caucus before it reached parliament. In an imbalanced parliament like the one elected in 1984, the gap between opposition and government in committees becomes even greater.

A further question must be asked about the capacity of a parliamentary committee to represent the interests of all Canadians. The finance committee pointed out that proposals for tax reform only came before it after a long process of discussion, consultation, and negotiation:

The process of public participation did not of course begin with the referral of the government's tax reform proposals to your Committee. It began with the appointment of a Royal Commission on Taxation in 1962. The Commission's Report and the reports of several provincial tax commissions, notably those of Ontario, Quebec, and Saskatchewan, formed the basis of widespread debates and discussions of the principles upon which Canada's tax laws should be based. Following its assessment of these reports and taxpayer's submissions with respect to them, the Government of Canada issued its White Paper, containing numerous proposals for tax reform.[21]

Examination by the finance committee came at the end of this long process. There is a serious question on an issue like this of whether a parliamentary committee which contains only a few members from a selected social stratum, which can hear only a few witnesses, and whose members are not only likely to stay in parliament only a short while but will serve on the committee for an even briefer period can adequately represent the people of Canada or reflect the public interest.

This problem was compounded for the finance committee because it was deluged with briefs from the powerful interests which stood to lose from the proposed reforms, while those who would benefit – the poor and the unorganized – were scarcely heard from. The committee, whose Liberal and Progressive Conservative members were mainly small 'c' conservatives, recommended changes away from the equity and neutrality in the taxation system that had been proposed by the Carter Commission and adopted in the White Paper. As a result, the committee investigation made it more difficult for the government to reform taxation.

This experience shows a fundamental problem of parliamentary committees. In their investigation they are inevitably going to hear more from the organized, advantaged segments of society than from the disorganized and poor. The orientation of the major parties towards the upper social and economic levels exacerbates this problem. A royal commission can recognize and counterbalance this bias through commissioned research, or subsidies to disadvantaged groups to enable them to make their case before the commission. Governments can also ensure some measure of adequate representation in this selection of commissioners. Committees of the House of Commons work under more severe constraints of time, staff, and other resources than commissions. They are consequently particularly vulnerable to the risk of their hearings providing a well-publicized forum for a narrow range of advantaged interests, and the attendant one-sided media reports. The government, which must be sensitive to the electorate as a whole, can find itself at odds with a committee and with the media presentation of its study. In fact the experience of the Trudeau government with the finance committee's investigation of tax reform so soured them against this sort of 'participatory democracy' that they did not subsequently use committees for the study of a major financial issue.

The processes of consultation, investigation, and public discussion must be carefully balanced in policy-making. The imbalance of the finance committee's study of taxation showed flaws in the attempts to use parliament. An unhappy experience with inadequately prepared and considered tax reform in the budget of November 1981 showed that the Trudeau government's centralizing of policy-making within the executive was also prone to error. Policy-making processes have not yet resolved the problem of balancing the need for consultation with the need to avoid bias in the groups listened to, and of ensuring fair and adequate publicity for all sides.[22]

As parliament and interest groups have become more familiar with the committee system some of these problems have been better recognized, if not resolved. The finance committee reviewed the Bank Act in 1978–9. This review was a departure from the previous practice, when the influential stage was private consultations between the government and the interested parties who, for the most part, were the small number of powerful chartered banks. The finance committee in its review of the Bank Act heard from many different groups, including cattlemen, auto dealers, trust companies, and consumer groups. Even though groups representing such concerns as consumer, environmental, and human-rights interests lacked expertise and financial resources, or even legitimacy, the MPs on the committee recognized that these groups should be included in the consultation process if they wanted to find a balanced long-term perspective. The élite groups, especially the chartered banks, were less influential in these revisions because of the increased influence of the parliamentary committee. The recent problems in the Canadian banking system, incuding the failure of two banks, suggests that perhaps the committee, despite its good intentions, did not produce good policies.

But in spite of these advances, assessments of the success of the committees is mixed. Two experienced observers concluded with a strong negative that 'while it is quite true that since the reform of Parliament in 1968 and 1969 all legislation must go to a parliamentary committee, no committee can change the intent of legislation and only the most naive believe that parliamentary committees, when they are considering legislation, will ever change or modify the legislation against the express desire of the government.'[23] More positively, the Canadian Tax Foundation regarded the examination of the Combines Investigation Act by the finance committee as a model which provided the fullest possible guarantee that all relevant points were brought to the minister's attention, and gave the public a better understanding of the background to changes. Thus, there was more likelihood that the public would accept change. MPs also became better informed. However, the Tax Foundation, itself an élite organization, did not discuss the question of bias in favour of élite groups.[24] As noted, the appearance of success by a committee may occur because the committee's report reflects the government's intentions so clearly that any claim that the committee is influencing government policy is illusory. Or the recommendations in a report may point in the direction the government is already leaning. However, while a report that attacks the government is not likely to be accepted, a unanimous all-party consensus in a well-publicized report is difficult to ignore, even though it may be critical.[25] A study of the review by the finance committee of the Bank Act concluded that the committee did, for better or worse, have clout and counted in the final outcome.[26]

Variations

If the records of the standing committees were the only measure of the usefulness of parliamentary committees, the conclusion that must be drawn would be almost wholly pessimistic, suggesting that not only have the committees been of limited usefulness, but also that there are only limited prospects for reform. There have been, however, numerous experiments with the committee system to find a format which would be more effective than the standing committees, particularly in the function of making investigations. These variations include subcommittees, task forces, special committees, and joint Senate-Commons committees.

As the standing committees found problems with their size, partisan functions, work procedures, and problems of substitution, they tended to use subcommittees for making inquiries. The very useful investigation of the subcommittee of the Standing Committee on Justice and Legal Affairs into penitentiaries was a model for this sort of activity. The subcommittee has the advantages over a standing committee in making investigations of being, first, smaller; second, able to eliminate substitution; third, composed of members interested in a problem; fourth, able to be more flexible in work procedures; fifth, likely to be less partisan; and sixth, working on a specific problem, with a time limit and some sense of need and urgency in the investigation. However, subcommittees can detract from the time and energy members have for the full committee, and they run the risk of reflecting narrow and unrepresentative preoccupation, as happened with the subcommittee on maritime forces in 1970 which recommended nuclear submarines for Canada, a recommendation which was later revised by the full committee.[27] In addition, they divide members of the standing committee into two categories, those privileged to serve on the subcommittee, and the rest. But in spite of these problems, the subcommittees proved to be successful enough that they pointed the way towards task forces, the next approach to improving the quality of committee inquiries.

In the spring of 1980, after extensive negotiations with the opposition, the re-elected Trudeau government announced the creation of six parliamentary task forces, each of which had a mandate to investigate a topical policy issue and to make recommendations before government policy was established.[28] Each task force was composed of seven members, and unlike the standing committees, there could be no change of membership unless it was agreed to by the committee. In addition to the usual powers given to parliamentary committees, each task force was given the authority to hire supplementary staff, to travel inside or outside Canada, and to release and make public reports even though the House was not sitting. The topics assigned to the task forces were: government regulation; alternative energy supplies; relationships between developed and developing countries; employment opportunities in the 1980s; programmes for the disabled and handicapped; and a national trading corporation. In none of these areas had the government committed itself to a policy, and the process of consultation between parties before the task forces were created determined that there were no strong party divisions on the topics, and that both opposition and government, as well as many members, were interested in the inquiries.

These task forces had more freedom in their work procedures than normal committees. They could sit for longer sessions than the standard ninety minutes, and the small number of members meant that questioning could be more flexible and directed. They were not subject to the usual restrictions of five meetings every two weeks. The small membership of the task force gave each member the opportunity to explore a line of questioning, while the elimination of substitution enhanced the non-partisan nature of their work and got rid of the need for new members to catch up. Work did not suffer when all members could not attend meetings or hearings, and it was found that permitting even one member to hear evidence proved useful.

The task forces emphasized public hearings and stressed the role of public participation in the policy-making process. For the most part, they decided not to undertake extensive research but to bring together existing information and knowledge. Their short-term nature did not lend itself to exhaustive original studies; rather they could consolidate other research from sources in both government and the private sector and bring it together in a coherent analysis. The short deadline focused the task forces' time and energy.

The task forces had the advantage that, being mission oriented, members, staff, and witnesses alike had a sense of commitment and direction. The subjects of investigation were of importance and ones on which a parliamentary committee could make a useful contribution. A disadvantage of the task-force format was that once the study had been completed and reported on, the group was disbanded. Thus, the task force did not remain alive as an instrument for ensuring that the report was acted upon or for monitoring the government's activity in the field. Like those of royal commissions, the task force's mission ended with the report, not with action. A further problem is that only a few areas of policy are amenable to this sort of non-partisan, consultative investigation.

The task-force format was used subsequently. The committee established in 1985 to examine reform of the House of Commons was structured as a task force. It supplanted the Standing Committee on Procedure and Organization, as had the study of procedure by special committee in 1982–3. Despite their limitations, the task forces had pointed towards an important line of reform to the committees of the House.

Special committees have frequently been used to examine important and contentious political issues. Such was the joint Senate-House committee created to consider the government's proposals for constitutional reforms in 1980–1. The creation of the committee was preceded by a break-down in federal-provincial negotiations on the subject, and by a prolonged bitter debate between government and opposition in parliament. The creation of the committee, although it was done with a show of some reluctance, was within the government's game plan. The committee soon developed a strong, independent corporate spirit. Its life was longer, its sittings more useful, and its media coverage more comprehensive than the government had intended. Its investigation succeeded in drawing attention away from provincial viewpoints, and it mobilized support for changes including an entrenched charter of human rights which, in the end, made it impossible for the provinces to resist reform. The strong support created by this committee was an important factor in causing the provinces to back down in their opposition to entrenchment of women's and native rights, and the committee turned out to be a valuable weapon in the federal government's arsenal, strengthening its hand in dealing with the provinces.

Special joint committees have also been used to examine complex bills. The very important legislation which introduced a comprehensive system of collective bargaining in the public service was preceded by an effective study by such a committee.[29] The presence of senators on both this committee and the committee which examined the constitution helped to reduce partisanship and added experience and a sense of direction to the investigations. The Standing Joint Committee on Regulations and Other Statutory Instruments, which was created in 1974, is another example of a committee where senators have made an important contribution.[30]

THE PATH TOWARDS REFORM

The special committee on reform of 1982–3 proposed the first important changes to the system of standing committees after the reforms of 1968–9. In their deliberations they had the example of the task forces in mind. Important as well was the model of the British House of Commons, where there is a very different, but successful, system of committees for handling legislation, and a long history of effective small investigative committees.

In their third report, the special committee recommended several changes: first, that the size of the standing committees be reduced from twenty to between ten and fifteen members; second, that substitution be made more difficult by limiting alternates to one for each member, the lists of both members and alternates to be established at the beginning of each session; third, that the order of reference be expanded through the automatic referral of annual reports of departments and Crown corporations to the committees; fourth, that the government be required, if so requested by a committee, to table a comprehensive response to a committee's report within 120 days of its being tabled; and fifth, that the practice of using task forces be continued.

These changes were adopted by the House, but the force of the reforms was tempered by several qualifications. The size of the committees was disputed between the parties, and the friction generated by this came close to shutting down the special committee. In the event, a standard size of fourteen was adopted. The problem was largely in the concerns of the opposition and smaller parties to ensure that they had adequate representation on the committees. The strength of the limiting of substitution was nullified by the addition of a change to standing orders (recommended by the committee) permitting the whips to make substitutions at pleasure with twenty-four hours' notice. The recommendation for automatic referral of reports did not have the force the committee hoped for because it had been construed narrowly to mean that investigations were limited to an examination of reports rather than to broad studies, and because some departments and agencies were found not to be required to submit reports to the House. This problem was resolved in 1984–5, with a new interpretation and revision to the standing orders.

In its fifth report the committee recommended that the Clerk of the House act as convening agent to call committees to their initial meeting so they could elect a chairman and begin their work. This was to eliminate a practice which governments had used for preventing committee activity by not allowing them to begin work. The Standing Committee on Procedure and Organization was kept inactive for many years through this practice. Without an order of reference there was no need for a meeting; without a meeting there was no pressure for an order of reference. Meetings of a committee, it was proposed, must also be called by the chairman if any four members of the committee so demanded.

In its sixth report the special committee recommended that an ad hoc committee be established for each bill. The standing committees would no longer consider legislation. These ad hoc committees were to be of no more than twenty members, and perhaps smaller, depending on the importance and interest of the bills. The committees were to be presided over by chairmen chosen from a panel representing both sides of the House and appointed by the speaker. In part, this proposal had emerged from the special committee's appreciation of the problem that the load of government legislation sent to the standing committees was uneven and creating bottlenecks and problems of overload. More important, however, was the committee's appreciation of the British techniques for handling the committee stage of legislation.[31]

British standing committees are in effect miniature parliaments which, like the House, clearly divide into two sides along party lines. The chairman functions much like the Speaker of the House. He is not responsible for the quality of discussion or ensuring that the committee does its work well. That is the responsibility of the government side in the committee. The chairman ensures that order is maintained, and parliamentary procedure is observed. The chairman can be chosen from either government or opposition side because he is not an instrument of government control, nor does he lead an investigation which might harm the government. In Canada the deputy speaker and chairman of committee of the whole is sometimes, in minority parliament, an opposition member; the chairman of British standing committees fills an analogous role. This practice makes it clear that the government is in control and responsible for the work of the committee in considering legislation, and it gives members of both sides the opportunity to serve as chairman. The speaker's panel of chairmen serves as a proving ground for future speakers.

The British structure of standing committees assumes that the committee stage of legislation is a debate, not an investigation. The recommendation of the special committees was not for an emulation of British practice, but for a possible partisan forum where witnesses could be interrogated, maintaining the practice of Canadian standing committees.

The special committee did not report on another recent development in the British House: the creation of a system of small specialist committees. Although Britain was ten years behind Canada in creating such a system, the British committees have already proved to be more independent of the government, less partisan, more purposeful, and more satisfying to members.[32] Fourteen new committees were appointed in Britain in 1979, added to the pre-existing ones, making a total of twenty-five committees concerned with overseeing policy, administration, and expenditure of departments and other public bodies. Unlike in Canada, the members of British committees are chosen by backbenchers rather than by the whips. The committees choose their own chairmen, and half are from the opposition side. In their first three years, the committees produced 172 major reports, including the important one on Canadian constitutional amendment.[33] The value of this work is not just in the reports but in the improvement of the quality of debate in the House because so much more basic information is available for members. 'No one who heard the sensitive debates here on the Canada bill,' a senior clerk in the House reported, 'could deny how improved they were by the work done on the bill by the foreign affairs committee; and that is only one example.'[34] The committees, which act independently and without government control, give backbenchers direct access to the civil service and to issues of policy and administration. They have been so useful that a popular weekly half-hour radio programme covers their work.

In short, the British House of Commons has not only succeeded in creating a system of independent specialist investigatory committees, but has also made them a useful part of parliament in which many backbenchers find great satisfaction. Britain, although it started later, has been more successful than Canada. It has succeeded in creating two types of committees in which opposition backbenchers participate equally both as members and as chairmen. This equality is especially and notably true for the chairmanship: in one type, the standing committees, opposition members can hold the chair because their qualities as impartial presiding officers are important, not their leadership of investigation; in the second, the specialist select committees, opposition members can hold the chair because the committees are free of government control, and the quality needed in a chairman is the ability to lead an investigation and not loyalty to party.

The Canadian House has had great difficulty in creating non-partisan committees. The key problem is the lack of a resource of experienced, independent-minded members. One knowledgeable estimate is that not more than sixty-five members contribute strongly to keeping the committee system going. The Lambert commission discovered that half of all committee attendance was accounted for by only forty-two MPs.[35] Unlike the British House the Canadian House does not have a wealth of backbenchers, secure, comfortable, and experienced in safe seats, who are interested in pursuing a career in parliament outside those controlled by the whips and party leaders. Partisanship dominates parliamentary life, including appointment to and chairmanship of many committee activities, and a member who frequently defies party will have little opportunity to serve on committees.

The committee on reform of the House in 1985 again recommended the creation of ad hoc legislative committees. This time the change was accepted, and a panel of chairmen composed of members from all parties was created, from which the speaker would select the chairman for a given study. To increase the authority of the standing committees, it recommended that:

each standing committee have before it the full departmental policy array to review and to report on, including, but not restricted to the following: the reasons for a department's statutes; the statutues themselves; a department's objectives in relation to its statutory mandate; the activities carried out in pursuit of these objectives; a department's immediate and long-term expenditure plans for these activities; and the achievements of the department measured against its objectives.[36]

Thus, a committee would be able to make intensive investigations into an aspect of government activity without awaiting a special order from the House.

The 1985 committee also recommended that the size of most committees be reduced to seven, and that parliamentary secretaries no longer be members of standing committees. The system of alternate members should be abolished, the committee concluded, because the practice had developed that alternates attended meetings in addition to, not in place of, regular members, and therefore the size of committees had not in reality been reduced. Also, the list of alternates was constantly changing. Further proposals included giving committees stronger powers to compel witnesses to attend, wider use of parliamentary committees to review draft legislation, an opportunity for members tabling reports to give the House a short description of their recommendations, the creation of a liaison committee composed of the chairmen of the standing committees, and increased autonomy to committees in hiring staff and making expenditures. It also recommended that the standing committees be permitted to question appointees to the positions of deputy minister and order-in-council appointments to Crown corporations. Nominees to the major regulatory boards and commissions would also be reviewed by the committees. Committee proceedings should be televised according to network preference. The special committee proposed that the review of delegated legislation should be improved by referring it to the standing committees as well as the joint committee on statutory instruments, and by giving the House much greater power to disallow delegated legislation. In short, the committee system envisaged, with the exception of the review of senior appointments, was in structure and functions to be much like that established the British.

The Mulroney government announced its intention to accept most of these recommendations, but this was far from the end of problems. When the legislative committees were set up in 1985 the relevant standing order was drafted so that a new committee was struck for each bill that had passed first reading. As a result, where the Special Committee on Reform had envisaged at the most eight legislative committees, by December 1985 there were seventeen, and the system was proving very difficult to man, to arrange meetings for, and to administer. At the same time there were thirty other committees, either standing or special. Consequently each MP was, on average, a member of four committees, an impossible and totally unnecessary burden. Warren Allmand, a long-standing Liberal member, expressed a general dissatisfaction: 'There have been days in the last few weeks when at nine o'clock in the morning we have had standing committees; at eleven o'clock we went to legislative committees that went on until five or six in the afternoon, and then we went back to standing committees again' until late at night.[37] The opposition in particular found it difficult to man the committees because of their small numbers. The government also proposed that parliamentary secretaries remain on the standing committees.

When reform was debated in December 1985 members from all parties criticized the heavy demands of the committee system, and the intention to keep

parliamentary secretaries on the standing committee. The government consequently took the parliamentary secretaries off. The size of committees was also
reduced. There is now a series of small standing committees with overview of
governmental activities, the public accounts, statutory instruments, etc. As of
March 1986, several special committees had also been created to examine such
questions as acid rain, Canada's international relations, and child care. In all, there
were nearly thirty investigatory and standing committees. Most had seven
members, although several had eleven or more. There were 340 positions to be
filled on them. A typical seven-member committee had a government backbencher
as chairman (although the chairmen of the public accounts and statutory
instruments committees are chosen from the opposition), four other Conservative
members, and one member each from the Liberals and NDP.

There were also forty-four legislative committees. Twenty had twenty
members and twenty-four (the more recently established) had seven members.
Twenty-nine of the legislative committees had been created to handle private-
members' bills, and were in effect pro forma creations to comply with the
requirements of the badly drafted standing order. They would never meet. All but
one were nominally chaired by Marcel Danis, the deputy speaker. Fifteen serious
legislative committees were established to consider government legislation. They
would become active once a bill passed second reading.

The system now provides something over two committee positions for every
eligible member, one on the standing committees and another on the legislative
committees. The scheduling of meetings has become even more difficult with the
multiplicity of committees, overlapping memberships, shortages of meeting
rooms, members absent with travelling committees, etc. Many of these problems
require only minor changes to resolve. For example, the number of legislative
committees would be reduced, and their management simplified, if they were to be
established after second reading rather than before. This could be accomplished
through an amendment to standing orders. Their management would also be
simplified if they were to meet at regular times and places, with some sort of
queuing order of committees and bills so that scheduling would be more
predictable and orderly. This, also, would be easy to achieve.

The review of order-in-council appointments proposed by the special committee was accepted by the government. It is still too early to determine how effective
this reform will be.

Many observers, including the Lambert commission on financial management and accountability and the Clarke commission on members' pay, have
recommended that committee chairmen receive additional pay. This proposal has
very great merit in recognizing the additional work and prestige of committee
chairmanships. It is a practice adopted by all provincial legislatures. It would

begin to provide a recognized and rewarded channel for advancement outside the partisan positions of parliamentary secretary, minister or opposition leader and whip. It could only be done equitably, however, if committee chairmanships were distributed in a balanced way between parties. They are, now, for the chairmanship of legislative committees, but they are not for the standing committees. And additional remuneration for chairmen would only achieve the desired effect of enhancing the autonomy and prestige of the position and of backbencher if the selection of chairmen were outside the control of the whips, as it is in Britain. This change also has to some extent been achieved with the creation of a panel of chairmen for the legislative committees, but much of the influence over selection of the chairmen of standing committees in Canada still rests with the government whips.

Further problems are created for committees in a parliament as lop-sided as that elected in 1984. Opposition members in particular have exteme demands placed on their time and energy by the committee system, and are unable to perform the research, or give the steady attention needed to be influential and effective. With such a preponderance of government members, committee proceedings more often give the appearance of being a public continuation of private discussions and negotiations in caucus between Canada and government backbenchers than of backbenchers of all parties united to confront and challenge the government. Some recent committees have been so dominated by Conservative backbenchers that the opposition parties have dissociated themselves from reports, and in effect prepare their own, unofficial, minority reports. This sort of committee is not what reformers wanted; the intention was to create committees where backbenchers would work together, and partisanship would be reduced. Instead, some have become even more partisan, and rather than uniting backbenchers of all parties, have been instruments of divisiveness. The committees also, from the government's point of view, are potentially dangerous and irresponsible threats from an inexperienced and unruly caucus, which is right-wing, parochial, and unconcerned with the larger questions of governance. The expression of an opinion is not policy-making. Accommodation of conflicting interests, the balance of competing needs is, and that is what overly partisan committees cannot do.

An additional question is whether committees with seven members are large enough to do the job. Committees must educate the public and the caucus, they must represent the variety of opinion and interests in the House, and they must ensure that the government is informed of viewpoints and issues. One member each from the two opposition parties is a very small level of participation, for a very large degree of responsibility. Especially on important government legislation seven is too small, and a committee of eleven or even fifteen would be preferable. The House of Commons is not, however, large enough at present to allow committees of this size to function effectively without extreme pressures on their members. Membership of the House would have to be increased quite significantly to permit a committee system as comprehensive and thorough as that envisaged by reformers, or even in operation at present, to work effectively.

More and better research staff can do little to alleviate the deficiencies of committees as long as the problem of the limitations of time, experience, and energy of MPs is not resolved. As we shall see in chapter eleven, the public accounts committee, which has in the auditor general and his office the largest staff of any parliamentary committee, is much the weaker partner in the accountability processes, and the auditor general the stronger. It would not help the democratic and representative processes to have parliamentary committees more generally subordinate to their staff. Permanent staff conjoined with transient members of parliament in committees would create a very real danger of this happening.

Committees serve a useful function, and on rare occasions can be astoundingly valuable and influential, as was the special joint Senate-House committee on the constitution in 1981–2. But committees do not often reach these heights. Committees only help parliament perform functions of examining legislation, scrutinizing estimates, and making investigations. They do not create a new role for parliament, nor do they alter in any substantial way the relationship between government and parliament. Competition between political parties is the driving force in the Canadian parliamentary system. Committees, when they are successful, subordinate partisanship in the efforts to reach all-party consensus. Therefore, they can fill only a secondary place in parliament and the concerns of MPs. The responsibility still remains with the government to devise policies and administer the executive branch. For the most part the committee's excursions into policy-making are only into minor areas where there are no strong partisan feelings, but they can be of great value to the government in ventilating issues and working towards consensus. Among the most important constraints working against more effective committees is the limitation of manpower. The working procedures of the standing committees have not been satisfactory and have made many committee proceedings into a formalistic, empty exercise with little commitment on the part of chairmen or members and little importance to government and public. Committees are now stronger and more influential than they ever have been in the past. But they are not ever going to have the influence of their U.S. counterparts, nor should they.

9

The Senate and Its Reform

The Canadian Senate is a frustrating puzzle. It is the most criticized institution of government in Canada and proposals for its reform, including its abolition, abound and have been part of political analysis and discussion for at least sixty years.[1] Its outstanding characteristic is not what it does, for that is not impressive, but that it has survived, and despite continuous criticism has been substantially unchanged since confederation. Proposals for Senate reform divide into two distinct groups. The first, smaller group consists of those concerned with improving the existing Senate. The second consists of reforms tied in with questions of the federal system in Canada and its weaknesses. These have little relevance to the composition, functions, activities, or achievements of the present Senate, but have a life of their own as part of the ongoing discussion of national unity and federal-provincial relations. In effect, they propose a totally new second chamber.

THE PRESENT SENATE

Confederation would not have happened without the creation of the Senate. Quebec in particular was concerned that its unique characteristics be recognized in the new parliament, and accepted representation of the provinces proportional to population in the House of Commons only on the condition that this be counterbalanced by representation on a regional basis in the upper chamber. The BNA Act as a result provided for a senate of seventy-two members, with twenty-four from each of Ontario, Quebec, and the Maritimes. With the geographical expansion of Canada and the creation of new provinces, Senate membership has now been increased to 104, with the addition of six senators from each of the western provinces and Newfoundland and one each from the Yukon and the Northwest Territories. Not only was the Senate intended to represent regions and cultural diversity, but it was also to be a conservative body and a counterbalance to radical tendencies of the elected Commons. Senators had to be at least thirty years of age. A property qualification of $4,000, considered large for the time, restricted membership to persons of some wealth. Senators were to be appointed for life, until they resigned, or until they were disqualified by such reasons as failing to attend parliament for two consecutive sessions, becoming bankrupt, or being convicted of treason, felony, or any 'infamous crime.'

The fathers of confederation saw the Senate as a minor legislative body, with a role of revising legislation emanating from the House of Commons and of restraining and delaying its more dangerous impulses. Although there were no restrictions placed on the legislative powers of the Senate, money bills could be introduced only in the lower chamber. The cabinet was understood to be responsible to the House of Commons rather than the Senate. The Senate would have less legitimacy than the House because its members would be appointed rather than elected. In Macdonald's first cabinet, five ministers out of thirteen were senators. Most important cabinet posts, including the prime-ministership, but not the minister of finance, have been held by senators at some time. But now it is rare for the Senate to have more than one cabinet minister, or for that minister to be the head of a spending department. A prime minister wanting to bring a person from outside into his cabinet is more likely to have him seek a seat in a by-election than to appoint him to the Senate. Prime Minister Trudeau once elevated a sitting member, Peter Stollery, from the House to the Senate so that Jim Coutts could run in a by-election in what seemed a safe Liberal seat. (The electorate, however, was unsympathetic with this manoeuvre and Coutts lost the election.)

This incident illustrates both the usefulness and the weakness of the Senate. Senate seats are among the most sought after patronage plums. The position is well-paid, prestigious, secure, and undemanding. Senators are appointed by the prime minister through 'instrument of advice,' and since the time of Sir John A. Macdonald successive prime ministers have used the Senate to reward loyal supporters and politicians deserving a dignified retirement. Appointment has gone almost exclusively to adherents of the party in power, although Prime Minister Trudeau made several notable exceptions, including the redoubtable Eugene Forsey. The reason for appointment generally has not been what they could contribute to the welfare of Canada through service in the second chamber, but what they have already contributed to party and prime minister. Whatever lack of legitimacy the Senate has because its members are appointed is compounded by this partisan and often unimpressive motivation in appointment.

In 1985 the Senate had 101 members. The average age was over sixty-two, with five senators younger than forty-five, and nine older than seventy-five, having been appointed before 1965, when the compulsory retirement age of seventy-five was introduced.[2] The oldest, Senator Florence Inman (now deceased), was born in

1890. Eliminating senators over seventy-five, the average age is now sixty-one, compared with an average of sixty-six in 1945 or sixty-four in 1969. Thus compulsory retirement has done little to lower the average age of senators, and it is still largely true, as R.M. Dawson remarked thirty years ago, that 'no one goes to the Senate with an eye to a future career, but always with the sense of opening up the last chapter.' It is 'a shelter for those whose active life is almost over and who are primarily concerned with a pleasant, secure, and not very strenuous old age.'[3]

Of the 101 senators in 1985, seventeen had sat in provincial legislatures, including several provincial premiers. Twenty-six had sat in the House of Commons. Two had held seats in both the federal and provincial legislatures. Eight had been candidates in federal or provincial elections but had failed to gain seats. More than half (fifty-two) had neither been elected to a legislature nor been a candidate, although many of these had been ardent workers in support of a party. Seventy-two senators were supporters of the Liberal party, twenty-seven of the Progressive Conservatives, and three declared themselves as independents. None was a supporter of the NDP, Social Credit, or other small parties. Twelve of the 101 were female. Twenty-seven had been appointed by the Trudeau government between 1980 and 1984, eight by the Clark government in 1979, forty-eight by the Liberal government between 1963 and 1979, eight by the Diefenbaker government, and five by the previous Liberal administration.

The end result of the appointment procedure is a Senate that is: old; composed of many wealthy people; unduly biased in favour of the long-lived government party; totally unrepresentative of minor parties; male-dominated, though less so than the Commons; and composed of members with, on average, more political experience than those in the House of Commons.

Senators, while they are not paid as highly as members of the House of Commons, nevertheless have comfortable salaries. The Senate rarely sits more than three days a week, whereas the Commons sits for five. Its sittings are brief, its holidays long, although its committees often work during holidays. Some senators attend only rarely. Senators usually have none of the arduous constituency chores of MPs, although the Liberal senators from the west in recent years have had to perform this sort of work to make up for lack of party regional representation in the Commons. Senators enjoy the use of the parliamentary library, restaurant, and other facilities on Parliament Hill. In short, the Senate is a comfortable, easy-going, and rewarding club to belong to.

WHAT THE SENATE DOES

Many roles have been discovered or proposed for the Senate, including investigations, revision of legislation, representation of the regions, representation of special interests, and protection of individual rights. Of these, only investigations and revision of legislation are important.[4]

Since the late 1950s numerous Senate committees have investigated different social and policy questions. For example, a special committee on land use in Canada was created in January 1957. By the time the committee's third and final report was completed in 1963, it had heard 109 witnesses and held 56 meetings. Its main concern was the agricultural use of land, the quality of rural life, and forestry. Many of the thirty recommendations of the committee found their way subsequently into legislation, including the important Agricultural and Rural Development Act (ARDA), the Farm Improvement Loans Act, the Farm Credit Act, and the legislation creating the department of forestry. Soon after, another Senate committee studied manpower and employment, the result again being many innovations in policies and legislation.

The influential Special Committee on Science Policy (the Lamontagne Committee) was established in 1967. The hearings of the committee provided a public forum and launched a national debate on science issues. Its conclusion that the central machinery for the formulation of science policy needed to be strengthened was acted upon with the rejuvenation of the Science Council and creation of the Ministry of State for Science and Technology. The first stage of this committee's work was completed in 1973, but it continued to perform a watchdog function, and in 1975, after concluding that hoped-for progress had not taken place, the committee began a second investigation, which again stimulated action.

Other important studies by Senate committees include the inquiry into the mass media chaired by Senator Keith Davey, which was concerned with the concentration of ownership in the media. The Standing Committee on Agriculture in 1984 examined the issue of soil degradation, which it concluded was a more pressing problem to the environment and agricultural interests than was acid rain. In 1982 a committee chaired by Senator G. van Roggen examined the question of free trade between Canada and the United States. It supported the proposal, but did not anticipate that the government would have enough fortitude to implement its recommendations. The Senate Committee on Banking, Trade, and Commerce has been very influential over the years both in its examination of the banking and financial industries and government legislation controlling them, and also in other areas such as its 1975 study of the textile industry. Other important and useful studies include those on poverty and aging.

These investigations are usually of a higher standard than those by committees of the House of Commons. Reasons for the differences include: first, many extremely able and experienced Canadians sit in the Senate and contribute to this investigative work; second, investigations by the Senate are usually non-partisan; third, Senate investigations do not suffer from excessive exposure in the media;

fourth, senators have the time and leisure to conduct diligent research and exhaustive analysis; and fifth, investigators can work on for many years, immune from the vagaries and demands of the electoral process. The work procedures of Senate committees are far better than those of the House, and ensure that witnesses are given the time to present their case, and are questioned carefully. Competence, freedom from competing demands on energy, low partisanship, and an absence of pressures of time and fears about re-election, are the keys to successful Senate investigations.

Although the Senate has virtually the same legislative powers as the Commons, the actual legislative tasks it performs are only a small and not very visible part of the parliamentary legislative process. Not for it is the partisan battle and media visibility of the great debates in the House of Commons. The Senate considers legislation before or after these battles and has the function of tidying up the details and defects in bills which were neglected by the lower chamber. Besides this role of revising legislation it also has important functions in the handling of private bills and the review of statutory instruments.

Bills passed by the Commons often still require technical changes such as drafting corrections, and last-minute changes requested by the government – sometimes to fulfil a commitment made to the opposition to ensure passage. These revisions do not usually introduce new principles or modify the original intentions of the bill. Once passed by the Senate they must be approved by the Commons, but this is usually an easy process. While this revisory role is somewhat less important now than it was in the past when the legislative drafting skills of the government were less adequate, drafting is still by no means perfect, and this is still a very useful function of the Senate.

Often it has been of less use than it might be because legislation is passed by the Commons late in the session, and must be rushed through the Senate without much debate or examination. In 1971 the Senate inaugurated a new way of coping with this problem by adopting the practice of studying the subject matter of a bill while it is still being considered by the Commons. The bill in question in 1971 was the mammoth tax-reform legislation. The Senate Banking Trade and Commerce Committee spent:

three months examining the preliminary White Paper, received some 443 briefs, heard 118 witnesses and suggested over 40 changes in the proposals. The government embodied most of these changes in the bill introduced in the House of Commons (they were able to do this through the Senate's advance study.) The Senate Committee then subjected the bill itself to the same meticulous scrutiny for another three months, and recommended another nine amendments, all of which were adopted by the House of Commons. When the bill came to the Senate, therefore, that body had already, in effect, put in six months work on it, and secured most of the changes it thought necessary and was able to dispose of the matter in a few days. The press noting only those few days, attacked the Senate and its committee for shirking their duty on one of the longest, most complex and most important bills in the history of the country.[5]

The same committee made a detailed study of the government's legislation on bankruptcy a few years later, and produced a report with 139 suggestions for amendments. Although the particular bill in question was not passed, most of the amendments suggested by the Senate later found their way into legislation in the form of amending bills.

Sometimes, however, even a Liberal government will not listen to the Senate despite its Liberal majority. The Senate Committee on Banking, Trade, and Commerce was not happy with many aspects of the Canada Oil and Gas Act which set conditions on exploration for oil and gas as part of the Trudeau government's National Energy Program. But the Liberal majority in the Senate followed the government's wishes and refused to accept the amendments proposed by the committee. At times, as in the consideration of legislation on magazines and broadcasting in 1976, the Senate can disagree strongly with the government and ultimately win on at least some points.

In any given year there is far more legislation enacted by the cabinet through statutory instruments under powers granted by parliament, or, rarely, by royal prerogative, than there is actual statutory legislation passed by parliament itself. The review and control of delegated legislation has long been a concern to parliamentarians, lawyers, and others concerned with ensuring a proper role for parliament in the legislative process, and a proper balance in the relationship between the individual and the state. In 1972, the Joint Committee on Regulation and other Statutory Instruments was created to review this delegated legislation in order to ensure its validity, necessity, and effectiveness and to ensure that it does not represent abuse of powers. Although this is a joint Senate-Commons committee, it is the work of the senators that makes the committee valuable. As J.R. Mallory noted: 'The senators not only have more time at their disposal, but are likely to be on the committee for longer periods of time and thus are more familiar with the work. Furthermore senators are likely to be more dispassionate and less partisan in their work on the committee.'[6]

A private bill is one that confers special powers or rights on a person, a body of persons, or a corporation and is not related to general public policy. Most of these bills deal with the incorporation of private companies or charitable or religious organizations, or the amendment of existing acts of incorporation. Unlike a public bill, which is either presented directly in the Senate or introduced on motion in the House of Commons, a private bill is solicited by the parties who are seeking to have it adopted and is founded upon a petition to parliament. Private bills may be introduced in either house, but because the majority of public bills are introduced in the House of Commons, the practice has developed of encouraging, through lower fees, the introduction of private bills in the Senate in order to balance the workload between the two houses.

The need for these bills has been drastically reduced in recent years by changes in Canadian law that enable most incorporations and amendments to acts of incorporation to be made through administrative action that does not require the intervention of parliament. The Senate examines private bills carefully, listening to both petitioners and adverse parties in committee, and taking care that the public interest is protected. Until 1963, the most prolific source of private bills was petitions for divorce from Quebec and Newfoundland, which did not have divorce courts. Legislation has now eliminated this function by requiring divorce petitions to be heard by the courts in all provinces.

There are other functions that the Senate performs. The less partisan atmosphere of the Senate and the greater expertise of its members can be of use to the government in dealing with difficult problems in legislation. In 1983 the Trudeau government introduced in the Commons Bill C-157, An Act to Establish the Canadian Security Intelligence Service, its response to the earlier McDonald Commission's report into the security service. This bill aroused widespread opposition among civil-liberties groups and other concerned members of the public. It was not debated by the Commons. Instead the government created a special committee of the Senate, chaired by senator Michael Pitfield who earlier, as Clerk of the Privy Council, had had a substantial internal government role in security matters. The report of this committee proposed important changes which went a long way towards correcting the flaws in Bill C-157. These changes were ultimately adopted by the government and passed by parliament as part of a new bill.[7] It is no tribute to the House of Commons that the government felt it necessary to use the Senate rather than the elected chamber to review this vital legislation, but it was important for the protection of civil liberties in Canada that it be reviewed by a parliamentary committee, and the Senate enabled this task to be performed.

In 1961 the Diefenbaker government introduced in the Commons a bill composed of three lines and twenty-five words. It stated that 'the office of the Governor of the Bank of Canada shall be deemed to have become vacant immediately upon the coming into force of this Act.' This bill was the means Prime Minister Diefenbaker chose to assert the government's power over the bank, whose governor, James E. Coyne, had made many public statements outside his proper sphere of monetary policy that were highly critical of the government's fiscal policy. The Diefenbaker government had also found it impossible to get the bank to follow the government's wishes in monetary policy. Coyne refused to resign when asked to by the government.[8]

This bill was quickly passed by the House of Commons. It then went to the Liberal-dominated Senate which, unlike the Commons, allowed Coyne to testify before a committee. In the Senate the governor had ample opportunity to present his case, which was what he really wanted, and after he had promised to resign immediately (making the intent of the bill meaningless) the Senate committee voted against proceeding further with the bill. The Senate gained strong press and public support for its anti–Diefenbaker-government stand on this issue, which came to be seen as a question of the rights of a senior official who was being harassed by politicians, and whose sole protector was the Senate.

The situation the government had been in was untenable. Relations between the government and the governor of the Bank of Canada were in an unpleasant state and were harming the country. There was no provision in the legislation to allow the government to overrule the bank when there was disagreement on key policy matters. Something had to change. But Coyne had only six months of his term left to serve, and at worst a few months' wait would have seen an end to the problem. As it was, the government chose a course of action which left it open to serious criticism and enabled the Senate to put it in a bad light. The subsequent Liberal government changed the legislation so that, when there are disagreements on policy, the bank must follow the government's orders.

A Liberal-dominated Senate again came into conflict with a new Conservative government in the 1984–5 session when the upper chamber delayed Bill C-11, a $19.3 billion borrowing bill which had been passed unanimously by the House of Commons. The lower chamber had passed it, with some opposition, but the Liberal senators, led by Allan MacEachen, formerly a very senior cabinet minister with a reputation as a cunning political tactician, claimed that the Senate should not pass the bill until the government's spending estimates were tabled in parliament. Advocacy of this correct constitutional principle caused a delay that forced the government to borrow money without parliament's approval. The bill was finally passed by the Senate after the tabling of the 1985–6 estimates and was given royal assent on 27 February 1985, but not before the press had strongly criticized the senators' actions. The defence that the Senate was constitutionally entitled to act independently on legislation, even money bills, was given less weight than the argument that this was properly the Commons' business, and the Senate's action was seen as mischievous partisan meddling. The Mulroney government in response threatened to reform the Senate by drastically reducing its powers to delay legislation.

The activities of the Senate in its investigative studies and in its revision of legislation are a useful complement to the work of the House of Commons. In both of these spheres of activity the experience and competence of the senators and the freedom they enjoy from the partisan and other pressures of the Commons add a valuable dimension to their work. The Senate has been criticized for being a lobby within government for big business,[9] but it would be more accurate to describe it as a defender of the rights of property, a function which it was intended to perform by the fathers of confederation. Nevertheless, in other areas where it was expected to be useful, especially in defending the interests of the provinces and regions, minorities, and human rights, its record has not been impressive. It is difficult to disagree with Dawson's long-standing conclusion: 'It would be idle to deny that the Senate has not fulfilled the hopes of its founders; and it is well also to remember that the hopes of its founders were not excessively high.'[10]

Improving the Present Senate

Among the criticisms which have been levelled at the Senate are that members are subservient and too partisan because of the method of appointment, that it does little, that it is not accountable, that the imbalance between parties reduces its effectiveness, that it is given insufficient work, and that it has no legitimacy or secure political foundation because of the method of appointment of senators, and its unimpressive record.

The list of proposals for improving the present Senate includes change in the method of appointment, with some senators being appointed by the provinces, fixed and limited terms of office, retirement at a definite age (accomplished in 1965), and curtailment of the Senate's power so that it could only suspend but not block ordinary legislation from the Commons and would have no control over money bills. Most of these proposals were included in the Trudeau government's 1969 recommendations for constitutional reform.[11] The last, curtailment of the Senate's powers, emerged again in 1985 in the Mulroney government's reaction to the Senate's obstruction of Bill C-11. The most interesting thing about these proposals is that they have not changed for several generations: like the weather, everybody talks about Senate reform but nobody does anything about it. The Senate has undergone fewer reforms than the Commons. For a body with such obvious faults this stability is somewhat surprising. The Senate continues unchanged in part because there is no agreement on the direction which reform should take: possibilities range from abolition to enhancement of its powers and the election of senators. Perhaps also it has more uses than are recognized, including the function of a dignified pasture for superannuated political war horses. If it were agreed that the revisory, investigative, and representative functions of the Senate were justification enough for its continued existence, it could certainly be made more useful and lively. The time-honoured list of changes is too timid.

A good starting point would be to question whether membership in the Senate ought to be remunerated (as it now is) as a full-time job. The relatively small number of days the Senate sits each session, the short hours of sittings, and the infrequent attendance of some senators suggests that it is a full-time job only to those who make it so. To the rest it is a comfortable club, a well-paid source of prestige, and a means to make occasional contributions to discussion of public issues. Perhaps appointment to the Senate should be treated as part time. Senators would be remunerated only for the days on which they actually attend parliament. If this reform were accepted, most senators would no longer need offices and there would be room for more senators. The method of appointment could be improved and the base for selection expanded. Clear limitations on the Senate's legislative powers would ensure that the will of the House of Commons would not be frustrated by the upper chamber, while at the same time senators who wanted to could contribute to the investigative and revisory work of the Senate to the same extent that they are now able to.

A truly improved version of the present Senate might look like this:

1 It would be much bigger, with, for example, double the present membership (208).
2 A senatorship would be recognized as an honorific position, but at the same time provision would be made for those senators who so wish, to contribute to its activities. To this end, they would not receive an annual salary. Instead, they would be paid on a per-diem basis for their actual attendance at sittings of the Senate or its committees. They would not be paid if they did not attend. Each senator could choose how much parliamentary service he would want to perform.
3 The per-diem payment would be related to the sums paid members of the House of Commons. A full-time senator's salary could nominally be the same as that of members of the House of Commons. This sum would then be divided by the number of days in the year that the Commons sits to arrive at the appropriate per diem for senators.
4 Half the senators (the same number as at present) would be appointed by the federal government.
5 One-quarter of the senators would be appointed by the opposition parties in the House of Commons.
6 One-quarter of the senators would be appointed by provincial governments or legislatures.
7 Senators would serve for a fixed term of six years, with the possibility of reappointment.
8 In legislative powers the Senate would more clearly be made subordinate to the Commons. It would be able to delay ordinary legislation, but would have no control over money bills.
9 Present senators would be equitably pensioned off if they chose not to serve in the reformed Sendate.

These reforms would make the Senate a much more varied, lively, and interesting place. They would not greatly increase its costs, and might reduce them. In reducing its financial attractiveness, and broadening the base for recruitment, the worst abuses of patronage appointments would be eliminated. The Senate would be less of what Grattan O'Leary (who later became a senator and raised his estimation of it considerably) described when he commented: 'A senatorship isn't a job ... it's a title. Also it's a blessing, a stroke of good fate; something like drawing a royal straight flush in the biggest pot of the evening, or winning the Calcutta Sweep. That's why we think it wrong to think of a senatorship as a job; and wrong to think of the Senate as a place where people are supposed to work. Pensions aren't given for work.'[12] And it would help to eliminate the complacent cynicism noted by one senator, who claimed that senators are not prepared to go along with arguments of new senators that they should work five days a week: 'A lot of Senators didn't come here on that kind of contractual basis at all – they were recruited for three days a week on the understanding that it's not really a full time job, as Prime Minister Trudeau in effect told me.'[13]

Reforms like these would give the Senate better tools to perform and expand its useful functions, and would permit many more senior and experienced Canadians from all regions and all political parties to contribute to governing the country.

Improvement to the existing Senate is not, however, the direction which recent discussion of Senate reform has taken.

SOLVING THE PROBLEMS OF CONFEDERATION: A DIFFERENT UPPER CHAMBER

Virtually every problem of government has a federal-provincial aspect, and the federal-provincial struggle often seems to dominate politics.[14] Whether federal-provincial discussions are with one or a few provincial governments, as occurs with energy policy, or with all, as occurs with constitutional reform, the process involves meetings and negotiations between the two levels of government. The process is determined by the executives, particularly the cabinet ministers of the respective governments. Underlying the importance of federal-provincial relations is the geographic and cultural reality that Canada covers a huge area and contains many different sub-economies and cultural groups, particularly French Canada. Regional interests often conflict with one another and with the federal government's perception of the national interest. Provincial governments, some with a colonial history pre-dating confederation, are the powerful spokesmen for regional and other interests. There are profound inequalities in the distribution of population, wealth, and language in Canada.

Federal-provincial relations can be looked at in two opposing but not necessarily mutually exclusive ways. On the one hand they are a means whereby regional and cultural diversity find expression, and where the rights and interests of the groups that make up the Canadian mosaic are recognized in the policy-making processes. In this view, federal-provincial relations are important because they are a natural and proper expression of the organic base of the complex Canadian polity. On the other hand federal-provincial relations are a claim for identity and autonomy of the various governments, particularly the provincial ones. Viewed in this way, federal-provincial relations are arguments over who should have power and resources rather than over the uses to which power should be put. Federal-provincial relations, viewed either way, are executive-dominated. They are also divisive as they pit government against government and area against area. In recent years this divisiveness has been especially noticeable: under the Pearson and Trudeau governments they tended to be conflict-oriented and, particularly under Trudeau, confrontationalist in nature.

Underlying any discussion on the reform of federal-provincial relations and amelioration of their divisive and unproductive aspects lies some assumption about which of the two approaches is the right one. Most political scientists and others concerned with institutional reform have tended to adopt the first approach, and to assume that the fundamental causes of federal-provincial conflicts are rooted in the inescapable organic realities of the Canadian confederation. Following from this, the challenge in reform is to find institutional structures and processes that will permit accommodation of regional interests and diversities within the federal framework. Electoral reform to ensure better representation of all regions within the major parties and Senate reform to create a new institution which will allow stronger regional influence in the federal parliament have been the two most-discussed proposals.

But the existence of the second source of federal-provincial conflict poses questions of the utility of reforms which emphasize accommodation and reasonableness. A presumption behind proposals for institutional reform is that provincial governments are the legitimate expression of regional concerns. A pronounced characteristic of provincial governments, however, is that they are even more executive-dominated than the federal government, and that their legislatures are comparably weak. The provinces tend to have long-lived governments and oppositions of low visibility and ephemeral leadership and representation. The governments are the permanent and stable elements, and the legislatures part-time and unimportant – more like nineteenth-century than late–twentieth-century Canadian parliaments. From the early years of confederation provincial governments have found in confrontation with the federal government a convenient and easy route to legitimacy, and the federal government a convenient scapegoat for problems in the province. Since the Second World War, tax-sharing, joint programmes, and overlapping concerns have meant that virtually every aspect of government has a federal or provincial dimension. To a provincial government, confrontation with the federal government often has the added advantage of forcing provincial opposition parties into line, so that disagreement within the provincial legislature is obscured by the need for loyalty and support in the government's federal-provincial battle. Provincial governments as a result present a very biased view of regional concerns.

These tendencies are so pronounced in federal systems – and not just in Canada – that some analysts have concluded that federal states have an inherent unstabilizing 'gaming' element in them of tensions and rivalry between the two levels of government. The lower level barters threats of secession for concessions of fiscal and other resources.[15] To the extent that this divisive, gaming element exists, reforms which are intended to mute and accommodate conflict are not likely to work. They simply do not deal with the real problems, which are endemic to the federal system and more related to the continuing political needs of provincial premiers and their cabinets than to resolvable issues of policy.

In the 1970s, with the increasing importance and acrimony of federal-provincial relations, the growth of Quebec separatism and western alienation, and the accelerating regionalism of the major parties so that the Liberals appeared to represent mainly Quebec and Ontario and the Progressive Conservatives the west, the focus of discussion of Senate reform shifted from improvement of the existing Senate to ways that the Senate could be transformed so that it could fulfil its function as a body representative of the regions, provinces, and various minorities. For many reformers, a new Senate would replace the unsatisfactory forums in which federal-provincial negotiations are now held with a better functioning, more formal part of the political structure. Senate reform was an important aspect of constitutional proposals put forward by, among others, the Government of Canada in white papers of 1969 and 1978, and Bill c-60 of 1978; the Special Joint Committee of the Senate and House of Commons on the constitution in 1972; the governments of British Columbia (1978) and Alberta (1982); the Ontario advisory committee on confederation (1978); the Progressive Conservative Party of Canada (1978); the Canada West Foundation (1978, 1981); the Canadian Bar Association (1978), the Pepin-Robarts Task Force on Canadian Unity (1979); La Féderation des Francophones hors Québec (1979); the Quebec Liberal party (1980); and the Senate Standing Committee on Legal and Constitutional Affairs (1980). This list of distinguished participants and serious proposals is much larger than the comparable list of proposals for reform of the House of Commons over the same period.

Many of these proposals envisaged giving provincial governments direct representation in the Senate as a means of accommodating regional and provincial interests. For example, the Canada West Foundation (1978) recommended that the

Senate be made up of provincial delegations composed of cabinet ministers, members of the legislative assembly, and civil servants. The federal Bill c-60 proposed that half the members be selected by the House of Commons, half by provincial legislatures. The Canadian Bar Association, the governments of Ontario and British Columbia, and the Quebec Liberal party also leaned in the same direction in varying degrees. These proposals drew on one another, and on the example of other federal states, particularly West Germany.

Combined with this new membership were various proposals to give new powers to the Senate (to be renamed the 'House of the Provinces'). These included such items as an absolute veto over appointment of heads of Crown corporations, regulatory agencies, and the judges of the Supreme Court of Canada; an absolute veto over legislation which was of direct provincial interest, that included the use of the declaratory, spending, and emergency powers, or that affected areas of concurrent jurisdiction; and the ratification of treaties. Also proposed were varying sorts of powers to suspend or block legislation coming from the Commons, particularly legislation affecting language rights and areas of provincial jurisdiction. Almost all proposed reforms would have increased the powers of the upper chamber, and given to provincial governments or legislatures some measure of direct participation in the federal parliament.

There are fashions in parliamentary reform as much as in clothes, pop music, and architecture, and the idea of a 'House of the Provinces' has now lost favour. Many of the proposals were highly asymmetrical, giving the provincial governments ways of influencing the federal government's use of its powers, but giving Ottawa virtually no power to influence the provinces when they challenged important federal interests.[16] Also, the ability of the federal government to discharge its responsibilities would have been restricted by the proposed new second chamber. There was no guarantee that provincial particularism would have been alleviated by substituting a 'House of the Provinces' for federal-provincial conferences; quite the contrary, the new chamber could well have given each province more freedom to act in its own individual interests, leading to an unregulated, harmful, grab for power.

In the 1980s proposals for reform have leaned more towards an elected second chamber. In 1985 a committee of the Alberta legislature, for example, proposed that senators be elected on the basis of province-wide constituencies;[17] in the previous year a joint committee of the federal parliament also had recommended an elected Senate.[18] More recently, the proposal for a 'Triple E' Senate (elected, effective, equal) has been ardently pushed by the government of Alberta. The royal commission on the economic union similarly proposed an elected Senate, though one with quite limited powers. The commission's report, however, was more enthusiastic about what Senate reform might accomplish than the cautious studies made for it.[19]

Much of the discussion of Senate reform is simplistic. Behind proposals is the example of the United States, where the Senate is very powerful indeed, and uses its power over legislation, treaties, and appointments to influence other decisions which formally are not within its purview. A new Canadian Senate similarly could have far more influence than its powers imply. Discussion of Senate reform has not considered whether a more powerful second chamber, with more direct influences in it by provinces, might lead to unwanted biases. Reforms might well give the groups that influence provincial governments more power, and these usually represent particular, advantaged, economic interests.[20] The American Senate is a far more effective lobby for already powerful interests than the present Canadian Senate. It has also, in effect, replaced state governments as the articulater of regional interests.

Proposals for an elected Senate argue, or assume, that party discipline would not be strong in the new chamber. No evidence or arguments are presented to support this contention, and it is highly doubtful that it is correct. Why party discipline is so bad is not made clear, and is apparently assumed to be self-evident.

Reformers also assume that election would give the Senate greater legitimacy. But this might not be so. Voter participation is likely to be very low in Senate elections, especially if they were to be held at times other than general elections for the House of Commons. Voter participation in off-year elections in the United States is only 37 per cent. It might well be even less for a relatively impotent Canadian Upper Chamber. Because of voter indifference an elected Senate might well have very little legitimacy in confrontation with a Commons elected through the participation of more than 75 per cent of the electorate.

Finally, it must be asked whether a reformed Senate would alleviate federal-provincial conflict. The short answer is that it will not. Five reasons can be postulated for the importance of federal-provincial relations in Canada: first, with only ten provinces, each individual province is prominent; second, the provincial level of government has large and increasing responsibilities and functions and these inescapably overlap with federal activities; third, the French fact in Canada and the representation of French Canada by Quebec, a province with more than a quarter of the people of Canada, gives an emphasis to provincial autonomy of which other provinces take advantage; fourth, the dominance of the cabinet in the parliamentary system, and the importance of issues such as tax-sharing, make interaction between governments rather than conflict resolution within the federal parliament an appropriate mode of action; and fifth, the political leaders at both levels gain prestige and media attention from confrontation.

None of these five factors is likely to be resolved by Senate reform: one, a reformed Senate will not increase the number of provinces; two, the provincial level will not lose responsibilities in reform – if anything it will gain; three, it will not change the French fact or the special characteristics of Quebec; four, it will not reduce the dominance of cabinet at the federal or provincial level, or at least will not do so without creating extraordinary tensions between the Senate and the federal government; and five, political leaders will still gain as much from confrontation. A strong case can be made that a reformed new upper chamber would become an enhanced forum for confrontation and impasse. This does not leave much ground for optimism about a new upper chamber. Probably the reason that Senate reform has been such a popular topic is not that it would make things better, but that it is a displacement activity, a pleasant diversion into the realm of political fantasy, an escape from grappling with complex and difficult issues where reality imposes more constraints. The problems and the asymmetries of the Canadian confederation are not going to be resolved by the technical fix of a new upper chamber.

The constitutional accord reached between the provinces and the federal government in April 1987 included entrenching Senate reform on the agenda for future discussion. The federal government also agreed to appoint senators from lists provided by the provinces. This, bearing in mind the present powers of the Senate, gives provincial governments the potential for far more influence in the federal parliament than do most proposals for a new upper chamber. This change will, however, be slow to make its impact felt. A new upper chamber is now possible.

Of the two discussions of Senate reform, the one dealing with improvement to the present Senate, the other with an entirely new upper chamber concerned with federal-provincial issues, the second is by far the more extensive. But it is the less likely to have useful results. The present Senate does valuable work and could do a great deal more with some improvements. However, no change to the second chamber is likely to do much to ease federal-provincial tensions, and the creation of an elected upper chamber that competed with the elected House of Commons could cause a great deal of harm. Comparisons with Australia, where the upper chamber is elected, do not often take into consideration the comparative weakness of the Australian lower House. Nor do comparisons with the United States recognize the weakness of state governments. The problem with the kind of new upper chamber being proposed for Canada is not just that it is not likely to be created, but that it will not produce the results proponents hope for. It will not reduce federal-provincial conflicts, and could quite possibly be as unruly and ineffective a decision-maker as present federal-provincial conferences. It could make Canada more, not less, ungovernable.

A prime minister and a House of Commons are not likely to want a strong upper chamber. Nor would provincial premiers be happy with a truly effective and elected upper chamber, like the American, which would mean a substantial shift of power from provincial governments to the new upper chamber. An improved Senate might, however, be attractive to all. Abolition would be preferable to some of the recent, ill-considered, proposals.

Refer to role that trade played by provinces replaces function of US senate.

10

Parliament and Policy-Making

Nowhere else do all the contradictions and problems of Canadian parliamentary government come together so powerfully as they do in policy-making. The parliament-centred rhetoric of reform demands a strong role for the House of Commons, while the executive-centred reality puts parliament on the sidelines. The transformation during the last century from laissez-faire to the positive state has caused a huge growth in the public service, so that there are now more than a thousand civil servants for every member of parliament. Government now intrudes into most nooks and crannies of the economy, culture, and society. Rapid changes in the economy, technology, and the international sphere put additional stress on government. The growth of government has created a deep division between discussions on the inside, within government and between government and pressure groups, and discussion on the outside, in parliament and the press. The links between the two spheres are weak and create difficulties in the mobilization of consent.

We have seen how limitations of manpower severely restrict what parliament can do, and how the work of the House of Commons is further conditioned by the realities of partisanship, adversarial conflict, and party discipline. While these enable parliament to fulfil the necessary requirements of responsible government – clear assignment of responsibility to a government, debate between two sides, formation of an alternative to the government in the official opposition – they also reduce parliament's capacity to serve as an effective investigating and policy-creating body. Its weakness in this function of making a government work is among the most criticized features of the Canadian Parliament.

Parliament has two modes of action. One is adversarial, in debates and question period, where the parties compete with each other. The government proposes, the opposition criticizes. The second is the consensual, seen most often in committees, where the partisan strife is muted and members from all parties work together towards a common objective. Proposals for the reform of parliament's role in policy-making for the most part advocate reducing partisanship and strengthening the non-partisan consensual elements. Efforts over the past twenty years to reform committees have had this as a prime objective. But the process has been frustrating and the results less satisfactory than reformers have hoped. This chapter will explore some of these questions in policy-making – why it has become so much of a problem in the era of big government, the kind of influence parliament exerts, and the balance between, and strengths and weaknesses of, the consensual and adversarial elements.

THE PROBLEMS OF POLICY-MAKING

When A.V. Dicey examined the relationship between law and public opinion in nineteenth-century Britain, he could describe with accuracy and clarity each step from the time an idea began to be discussed in public until it was embodied in legislation.[1] A long period, often decades, elapsed between the birth of an idea and an act of parliament, and there were few enough important policy innovations that each could be identified and savoured as a unique event. The 'public' that was actively involved in politics was small. There was, in this nineteenth-century British society, a direct, visible, and linked policy-making process in which both actors and events could be identified. Parliament was the representative public body in which much of the discussion took place, and which gave final form in legislation to new policies.

The liberal, parliament-centred conception of parliamentary government, with its key role for parliament in policy-making, emerged in this small, élitist, and leisurely political environment. Perhaps also much of the present desire for active involvement by parliament in policy-making finds its source in nostalgia for those simpler and more manageable times. Robert Stanfield certainly had the past in mind when he remarked that 'there is, I believe, only one choice. We can accept the loss of parliamentary responsible government or we must accept a more limited role for our federal government.'[2] But in political as in personal life it is an inescapable truth that we cannot go back. We must go forward, and present and future realities are that we will live with both big government and the parliamentary system. And we will also have a mass public. Modern problems of policy-making are in large part a product of the transformation from the small government and small public of Victorian times to the modern reality of big government and mass public.

Government is now so big and such an important part of society and the economy that people need to pay attention to it because, like it or not, it affects all of us much of the time. Arguments over policies are arguments over what we want and get as individuals and as a society. The rapid rate of change in society, technology, and the economy creates a corresponding need for policy adaptation and innovation. Government is expected to mitigate the hardships and dislocations caused by change. Modern theories of politics make policy-making a duty of both politicians and administrators. Various economic theories (such as Keynesianism), political ideologies (such as collectivism), and management theories dictate an active and constantly changing set of policies for government. In short, there are more policies, they are more important, and they need more attention than ever before. Policy-making has become such a large area of study in itself that it sometimes appears to be ready to overwhelm public administration and even political science. Or it threatens to break out and become a separate discipline. Reintegrating policy-making with politics and with the traditions of ministerial responsibility and parliamentary government is a difficult challenge.

As part of the same changes that increased the importance of policy-making, parliament became less important. In theory it remained the central forum for the discussion, legislation, and review of policies. But the growth of the administrative organs of government, and the growing complexity of the political system and its relationships with the economic and social spheres, meant that many links and channels of communication between government and public developed which bypass parliament. Caught between big bureaucracy on one side and a mass public and a complex system of interest and pressure groups on the other, parliament, far from serving as the joining link, has all too often been regarded as an irrelevant sideshow. Policy-making has remained firmly within the hands of the government, even though the government once elected might have no idea of what it wants to do apart from uttering vague motherhood statements like those in the 1984 speech from the throne of creating a 'national consensus,' ensuring 'social justice,' and facilitating 'economic renewal.'

In the immediate post-Second World War period wartime structures and processes were continued into peacetime. The federal government had led the country during the war with massive public support but without public participation in policy-making. At the war's end, Canada was accustomed to big government, and the Keynesian programme of management of the economy and redistribution through welfare programmes promised, through continuing guidance and executive-centred policy-making, to ensure, unlike in the post-1918 era, the preservation of prosperity into peacetime. Keynesian and collectivist policies also promised to avert the traumas of depression and unemployment suffered before the war. They were proposed and adopted within the centralized structure of decision-making and the overwhelming consensus of wartime.[3] Unlike Britain, there was no immediate repudiation of wartime leadership in Canada. The same government continued to develop and extend the policy framework established in the war, and was confirmed in office in successive elections for more than a decade.

The Diefenbaker government of 1957–63 represented a change not only of party but of attitude, and its problems mark the end of the previous consensus and sense of direction. Policy-making in the Diefenbaker era had two aspects: first, it was a 'balkanized' system relying on individual ministerial and departmental power rather than on collective cabinet decision-making; and second, there was a pronounced dependence on royal commissions for policy development. Within the government, departments were like feudal fiefdoms jousting for power. It was a period of strong pluralist politics, as departments and ministers did not, and could not, act in isolation, but formed coalitions with their clientele and powerful interest groups to exert both internal and external pressures on government. Widespread use of royal commissions was in large part an attempt to find a mechanism to integrate the conflicting wants of various interests, and to find a way to assert a general public interest above and beyond those of departments and groups. These tendencies became, if anything, more pronounced in the Pearson era. The reports of commissions on energy, medical care, taxation, bilingualism, and government organization, to mention only some, are significant landmarks in the evolution of federal policies, and many did in fact become important counterweights to the particularism of the system. Not the least of the reasons that these counterweights were needed was the absence of other strong collective voices in policy-creating, in either political parties or non-élite pressure groups. Parliament had a negligible role in policy-making in this period.

Keynesian economic and redistributive policies were adopted within the consensus that had emerged through the depression and wartime. By the late 1960s the momentum of these policy thrusts was exhausted; the consensus was dissolving.

The Trudeau government attempted to transform policy-making.[4] It criticized the then-existing process as failing because it 'relied so heavily on the initiatives and frailties of personalities. The structure was inadequate and personal energy was insufficient to cope with broad, multi-departmental problems.'[5] The emphasis on individual ministerial and departmental responsibilities discouraged collective policy-making. The new government adopted a 'systems approach' in which structure and process became major determinants of public policy. Emphasis was placed on designing structures which would enable the best policies to emerge. As part of these reforms, the central agencies of government, especially the prime minister's office and privy council office, were strengthened; policy and planning branches were created within departments; and persons with skills in policy analysis were recruited. Methods to stress technical efficiency and competence were introduced to aid central resource allocation. These included planning, programming and budgeting, efficiency and effectiveness evaluation studies, an operational performance-measurement system, and the introduction of techniques such as management by objectives. The repercussions of these reforms still reverberate through the federal government. Though much of the zeal for a rational, systems approach has abated, its terminology and concepts are still used and have force.

Like any other technology, this new approach to policy-making had its own specialized language and body of skills and knowledge. These were the property of trained technicians. These technicians, and their discussions of policies, formed a sub-system and esoteric language distinct from the more general public and governmental discussion of policies.[6] Thus, a gap was created between the insiders, the adepts and experts who performed and evaluated the rational analyses, and the others involved in the policy process – the administrators responsible for implementing policies, the public affected by them, and the politicians who must, as cabinet ministers, choose them, or as members of parliament, discuss, evaluate, and criticize them. This situation was a source of hostility with the Trudeau reforms. Parliament, pressure groups, and the line administrators of government found themselves left out of the charmed inner circle of policy adepts. The Trudeau government recognized the possibility that this sort of problem might arise, and attempted to compensate through various approaches to 'participatory democracy,' such as the creation of departmental advisory committees, consultation with interest groups, and the use of green and white papers to encourage and focus public discussion. But these did not solve the problem.

Changes in policy-making meant a shift of power. The Trudeau reforms were intended to break down the strength of departments and the close ties between departments and interest groups which had dominated much of previous policy-making. Power shifted to those who talked the language of rational policy-making, and to the central agencies which designed, created, and ran the system.

The system of policy-making had implicit within it a particular view of how politics ought to operate. Based upon a 'scientific' means-ends approach, it assumed that ends can be identified and agreed upon, and that a rational choice can be made between options on the basis of how well and at what cost they achieve defined ends and resolve stated problems. Real-world politics pose difficult challenges to this rationalist approach. The ends of policies often are not defined or agreed upon. Much of politics is argument over values, and what is good to one person can be bad to another. The values held by individuals and society change, and much political argument, such as in family law, abortion, censorship, pollution, and the non-medical use of drugs, is about how fast and in what direction change ought to take place. A key issue in policy-making is not to achieve defined ends, but to discover some acceptable mix of values. Only to a limited extent is this a rational process. Federal-provincial relations are a constant proof and reminder of this.

Political discourse is not like the natural sciences, where the more abstract and general laws are the most powerful and comprehensive. The challenge in politics is not to make abstract statements of values, but to translate them into living, useful programmes. Only when rationality connects, through hard work, wants and needs to the cold facts of reality does it become useful. The Trudeau government turned its attention inward and prevented dialogue, public argument, compromise, and negotiation between rulers and citizens. And the policy-making process became so exaggeratedly executive-centred it left public and parliament dissatisfied, with negligible and frustrating roles.

By the end of the 1970s the enthusiasm for rational policy-making had abated. Factors that were not amenable to rational analysis, or that were outside the control of policy-makers, beset federal governments. French-English relations and Quebec separatism raised questions about the continued existence of the country, and forced a political and legal definition of linguistic and cultural national characteristics. Unequal economic development in various regions led to disaffection and alienation. With its reliance on international trade for economic development, Canada is particularly vulnerable to such problems as the energy crisis and the world market for agricultural products and other raw materials, problems that originate beyond our boundaries and over which our governments have no control. The increasing importance of the United States in trade, defence, culture, and other areas raised questions of the real autonomy and capacity for independent action of Canada. Canada is still in a stage of nation-building. It is also only semi-autonomous, and much policy-making must by its nature be reactive rather than independent. Even within Canada the autonomy of the federal government is severely restricted. Executive federalism makes many important aspects of policy-making into a form of negotiation and treaty-making between semi-sovereign governments.[7] All of these affect the role of parliament.

Two other forms of policy-making have also weakened the force of rational policy-making and pose further threats to parliamentary government. The first, and less important, is the expanded use of opinion-polling and survey research. The second, and the more important, is the continuing growth of bureaucratic pluralism along with expansion of government.

Opinion-polling has added further complexities to policy-making, and weakened the role of parliament. In 1969 two social scientists proposed that governments should make more use of surveys of public opinion and attitudes. 'The decision-making system at the federal level is changing,' they claimed, 'with policy innovation now shifting back to the cabinet and particularly to a strengthened office of the prime minister. This modernized, dynamic institution is in a particularly advantageous position to use survey research.'[8] The office of the prime minister, armed with such an array of information, would be in a very strong position not only for evaluating policy proposals emanating from the departments in the usual fashion but for the planning and initiating of policy alternatives. Opinion surveys would allow the privy council and the prime minister's offices to bring the opinions of ordinary citizens directly into the process of policy-formulation, and would give the cabinet a new independence from the bureaucracy. This, the social scientists argued, would lead to a more participatory democracy, and integrate public concerns with government policy-making.

They were correct in predicting the growing importance of polling, but wrong in assuming it would lead to greater participation. Opinion surveys by now have become immensely sophisticated and go well beyond simple collection and tabulation of data. Pollsters such as Allan Gregg for the Progressive Conservatives or Martin Goldfarb for the Liberals are more than technicians taking simple measurements of public opinion. They are like skilled and experienced doctors who not only measure temperature and blood pressure but use the accumulated art and knowledge of many years of practice to evaluate and diagnose the condition of a patient before prescribing a remedy. This sort of advice – up to date, based on accurate sampling, and filtered through the trained intelligence of an expert pollster – is not only valuable but necessary to a modern government or opposition.

The data and analyses prepared by analysts like Gregg and Goldfarb are private, and are the property of the client who commissioned the studies. They are also expensive to prepare, and only clients such as governments, big business, and major political parties can afford frequent, current, and detailed survey research. The two social scientists optimistically thought that nobody would have a corner on survey techniques, but the costs are prohibitive, and parliamentary committees and groups without large financial resources do not have access to survey research. As a result there is a vast gap in the timeliness, depth, and quality of the knowledge of public opinion between the insiders in government, business, and parties and outsiders in the public and parliament. Increased use of survey techniques has shifted power to the executive and party leadership, and made the media and the member of parliament less important. This problem has been partially corrected as the media pay for their own surveys and make them widely accessible, but a severe imbalance still remains.

Polling can make policy-making a reactive process in which policies are chosen not so much because of their anticipated benefits as because they are in line with measured public opinion. The Conservative government of Ontario followed opinion like a hound a scent, without lifting nose or eyes from the ground. This response impeded long-term planning, education of the public, and policy innovation. A government with vision can use polling to assess changes in opinion so that they can plan, adapt, and time a campaign for important innovations. But there is a strong risk that excessive reliance on survey research will reduce the creative element in policy-making. Polling gives the government a way of directly assessing public reaction to policies and proposals that bypasses the traditional link of parliament. Survey research treats the populace as an anonymous mass public, a passive vessel being subjected to an opinion poll. The government certainly becomes more aware of moods and views of the public, but neither the public nor parliament actively participates in discussing and influencing the decision that affects them.

Bureaucratic pluralism makes government departments and agencies, and the interest groups with which they interact, into key players in policy-making. The executive is now a large and complex system. It, like much of the private sector, is composed of large organizations. These large organizations are 'bureaucracies,' based on legal rationality, with a formal structure, a career pattern based on the technical competence of employers (rather than, for example, kinship or patronage), and systematic and impersonal administration and activities. Bureaucracies are immensely stable, and do not alter much in composition (or personnel), work procedures, or attitudes except under strong and prolonged pressures. They have an innate tendency to increase their power and the resources at their disposal. They have a desire for security, and to achieve this they attempt to control and regulate their environment so that outside forces will support rather than harm them.

Government and private bureaucracies inevitably affect and interact with one another. Many government bureaucracies have been created to regulate the private sector. Others are there to aid it. Interdependence and mutual support of the public and private sectors has become a fact of modern political life. Among the most important questions a modern society faces is how the bureaucratic organizations of the public and private sectors interact. If the government bureaucracies dominate there is a strong risk that the private sector will be stifled. If, however, the private bureaucracies dominate, there is a risk that big business will be unduly favoured by government to the neglect of small business, the individual citizen, and the non-bureaucratic sectors of society and the economy. David Lewis's and the NDP's criticism of big business as 'corporate welfare bums' in the 1970s was based on this sort of concern. For government administrative agencies and private business to be at war is not healthy, but for them to be too co-operative and cosy together also has its dangers.

The vast and extensive interrelationships between government and business exist at many levels. Most departments of government have advisory committees composed of members from outside government. There are other formal and informal processes for the solicitation and exchange of views between departmental officials and their 'clients' or affected interest groups in the private sector. The release of green papers (which raise issues and indicate how the government is thinking on an issue) and white papers (which describe what the government intends to do) encourages discussion and interaction. Where the government is actively involved in regulating a sector of the economy, formal, quasi-judicial processes of hearings are often used. This is true, for example, for the CRTC in its regulation of the communications industry, and the NEB in its regulation of the petroleum industry.

Most of the interactions between government and interest groups take place in these interchanges between bureaucratic organizations, although private consultation also occurs at the ministerial level, such as between the minister of finance and senior business and labour leaders when tax changes are being considered during budget preparation. The kinds of questions considered in the ongoing, day-to-day interchange at the lower levels include the implementation of policies agreed upon by parliament and cabinet, in effect the translation of often vague instructions into a programme of action; the formulation of regulations and other types of subordinate legislation which affect the private sector; the alteration of regulations and programmes when economic and social changes so require; proposals for changes in policies and programmes coming from the private sector; and the reactions of contacts in the private sector to ideas for change coming from the government side.

Quite possibly more of the real issues in policies are sorted out, and more real impact is made on who gets what when and how, in these interrelationships than at the parliamentary and ministerial levels. Most policies established by parliament in legislation or by cabinet ministers are vague and capable of many different interpretations. They need to be defined and fleshed out to become living, workable programmes. These government–interest-group relationships have a powerful stabilizing influence on both public and private sectors. They make government agencies and their client organizations interdependent, and give them a common interest in maintaining each other's well-being.

These relationships create a strong, stable environment which limits the range of policy options. By their nature they have a pronounced element of autonomy and independence. They are an important forum for policy-making which for the most part operates below the purview of parliamentary discussion. Parliament and members of parliament serve as a last resort for interest groups when they have failed to get their way with the government bureaucracy or with ministers. While parliament is alerted to problems in this way, it also becomes a squawk box for voicing complaints, often to the neglect of the happier parts of the story.

As long as Canada has a large private sector, and as long as big government is with us, there is no possibility that either cabinet or parliament can set up its own structures to control and direct all aspects of government bureaucracies and their relationships with the private sector. The best that either can do is to specify intention in adequate detail, and ensure through proper administrative and accounting procedures that their wishes are being respected, and that problems and issues are identified before they become serious. The administrative branch of government is not monolithic, nor is it a neutral instrument which responds automatically to the directives of its political master. In reality parliament and cabinet both know very little about what goes on within government, and at best have only a loose control over administrative activities and bureaucracy–interest-group interaction.

There is a danger in creating a large political 'bureaucracy' within central agencies, particularly the prime minister's office and the privy council office, to enable prime minister and cabinet to control bureaucracies. A powerful non-elected and non-accountable partisan element is introduced into administration. This element can, and undoubtedly did, under both Trudeau and Mulroney, help weaken ministerial control over departments. It also helped to politicize much of administration, such as senior appointments in the bureaucracy, and appointments to boards, commissions, and Crown corporations.

A.P. Pross has recently argued that the system of bureaucratic pluralism makes the centre, the prime minister and cabinet, mere symbols. Power is diffused through the administrative arm, leaving the political and administrative executive with a much reduced capacity to control policy development: 'In essence the diffusion of power represents the loss of control of the machinery of government on the part of the political executive and the senior public service. In many respects the decline of the executive has had disastrous effects on the efficiency and effectiveness of modern Canadian government.'[9] This diffusion of power has, however, Pross argues, strengthened parliament. Administrative agencies increasingly use parliament as a vehicle for exploring policy issues and for securing the support of public opinion. Further, as the control of the political executive has weakened, parliament has retained its status as the pre-eminent legitimating institution, and both government and private bureaucracies seek to win legitimacy by gaining the support of parliament. There is not likely to be, however, a dramatic improvement: 'When observing the enhancement of parliament's role in the policy process, we are talking of a modest amelioration of a situation that has een described as "intolerable."'[10] It is curious that after sixteen years of rule by a powerful prime minister intent on making policy-making more systematic, controlled by the centre, and rational, the end result is criticized for being diffuse and unsystematic, with greatly weakened central control. It would be unwise, however, to take much comfort out of the trends Pross identifies. Parliament's capacity to handle policy-making is (as we have seen in the consideration of committees) severely limited.

Pross is far from being alone in perceiving these sorts of problems in policy-making, and in looking towards parliament for at least a partial remedy. The recent Royal Commission on the Economic Union and Development Prospects for Canada expressed similar concerns about the power of the bureaucracy and asserted that responsible government:

requires that the legislature have a greater capacity to represent openly the multiplicity of interests which exist in an advanced industrial society such as Canada. It also requires the legislature to serve as an arena in which organized interests bring their expertise to policy discussions and, in turn, are challenged to represent their particular interests in the context of the competing interests of others and the larger interests of the nation.[11]

These sorts of proposals ask a great deal of parliament. They also raise questions of the role of the political executive, and whether stronger parliamentary committees and more independent members are likely to strengthen or weaken political control of the bureaucracy. The arguments of the royal commission, like many others, fit comfortably within the parliament-centred rhetoric of reform. In so doing they ignore some of the constraints and virtues of the present system, and present a rosier picture than is warranted of what parliament might reasonably be expected to do. They also ignore the central feature of responsible parliamentary government: that the prime minister and cabinet have the responsibility of governing, not the individual members of parliament or the opposition parties.

PARLIAMENT'S ROLE IN POLICY-MAKING

Among the most important attempts to use a parliamentary committee to consider major policy proposals was the work on tax reform of the Standing Committee on Finance 1970–1. By any standards this investigation was extensive, assisted by many man-years of research and other staff resources, hundreds of briefs and other submissions, and more than a hundred committee meetings. The intervention of the committee skewed the outcome away from fundamental change that would have promoted neutrality and equity in the tax system. Powerful, particular interests had their voices strengthened through the legitimacy they gained in the committee's hearings; the less powerful voices of more diffuse and general interests which stood to gain from reform were heard scarcely at all. As a consequence, the taxation system remained riddled with tax expenditures which benefit already advantaged groups. These tax expenditures create a substantial proportion of the federal government's deficit and they also mean that the levels of taxation for the unprivileged remainder of society and the economy – the average taxpayer – must be higher.

Much of the reluctance of the Trudeau government to strengthen parliamentary committees stemmed from this unhappy experience. This committee's investigation of tax reform was the first major attempt by the Trudeau government to use a parliamentary committee as part of a process of 'participatory democracy.' It did not produce the desired results, and quite the contrary, soured the government on parliamentary committees as an effective means of discovering or moulding public opinions.

There are examples of parliamentary committees participating in policy-making with better results. Committees of the House of Commons have, over the years, done much to change the federal government's policies and administration towards native Canadians. One of the most influential of these studies was that performed in 1981–2 by the Special Committee on Indian Self-Government. Its report, *Indian Self-Government in Canada*,[12] has to a large extent set the agenda for the movement towards aboriginal self-government, which is likely to be the major thrust in policies of the government towards native people for several decades to come. This special committee and the Standing Committee on Indian Affairs have done a great deal to change government policy. There are several able and experienced MPs interested in native issues who contribute to the committee's work. Strong native organizations use the committee and MPs as means to reach the media and influence government.

We have seen how debates and question period can have a powerful influence over government intentions and policies. Parliament forced the government to create a royal commission to investigate the security service, and the end result of this, several years later (and with the strong help of a committee of the Senate), was a much-improved system of control over the service, a security service separated from the RCMP, a legislative mandate for the service, and the assurance of future review by parliament.[13] Parliament had tremendous influence in the debates on the new constitution. It is not likely that the constitution would have been accepted without the public support created by the debates and by the work of the joint Senate-House committee. Legislation on the Crow's Nest rates was changed in important ways during its passage through parliament.[14] Opposition complaints about the collection of taxes alerted the government to a serious problem. Parliament was neither irrelevant nor unimportant in all these issues. Senate committees, as we have seen, are also often very useful parts of the policy-making process.

Private members can be more influential than is generally recognized. John

Reid, an able and experienced backbench Liberal member, noted in 1978 that he had many avenues through which to contribute to policy-making.[15] After some negotiation with all parties the House approved a motion of his, seconded by James McGrath, a Conservative, to refer six private-members' bills dealing with obscenity to the justice committee for hearings and examinations. He also was able to get amendments to the regulations of the Ontario Pension Commission which ameliorated a problem in adjusting disabled persons' pensions for increases in the cost of living. He achieved this through the introduction of a private-member's bill which, although it was never debated, stimulated other bodies to action. With the improvements to committees, the opportunities available in debate, and the additional resources available to MPs, Mr Reid concluded that 'For those members with a legislative bent (we do not all share that impulse), the opportunities are more readily available now than they have been in the past.'[16]

These examples show that in some instances parliament, its committees, and private members can be, and have been, very influential. Influence can be wielded at different stages, and in many different ways. In the issue of the security service parliament served as a problem-identifier and helped set the political agenda. Investigations by committees of the Senate have also identified problem areas and subjected them to thorough examination and public discussion. Private-members' bills can be influential even though they are not debated. Lobbying in caucus and behind the scenes can have results, even though these are not visible.

There is no consistent pattern to parliamentary influence and concern. Topics come and go, and yesterday's cause can soon be forgotten. Nor is consistency of attitude a notable feature. The Conservative party had two different and opposing approaches to security matters: one, critical of the RCMP when problems were being exposed; the other, supportive of the RCMP, when legislation creating a separate security service was being considered. Very few areas receive consistent strong attention over a period of years. Native questions are an exception here, partly because of the interest and concern of a few long-term MPs, and partly because of the effectiveness of determined native pressure groups which have found a sympathetic and useful ear in parliamentary committees. Parliamentary attention and parliamentary influence depend on many factors, including the interests and concern of individual MPs (such as John Reid's concern with a particular pension question), the structure and attitudes of pressure groups, and the items on the national and regional political agendas. Equally important, the opportunities for debate, question period, and private-members' bills and for examination in committee are limited, and a rigorous selection procedure excludes all but a few of the potential issues. Those selected vary with changing political, personal, and party concerns.

The topics on which parliament is influential are rarely the great matters of state. The exception to this is the constitution, where the joint committee made a stunning contribution in generating support for change and for an entrenched charter of human rights. Parliament tends to be most effective in handling specific questions relating to identifiable interests, as is clear from the Crow's Nest rates and native-issues legislation. Veteran-affairs committees, after the Second World War, were particularly useful in ensuring that veteran's rights were recognized, and often, in effect, seemed the spokesmen for the Canadian Legion. Noticeably absent from the list of issues in which parliament has exerted influence are those concerned with budgetary matters and fiscal policy (apart from unhappy experience with taxation legislation), or general questions of economic and social policy.

On balance John Reid was right in his assertion that MPS have more opportunities to influence policies and legislation now than in the past. These opportunities have increased since he wrote in 1978. Pross is also correct in his assertion that parliament does more. Whether the proportion of policies influenced by parliament is greater is, however, doubtful. Growth of government and an accelerating rate of change have made policy-making into a much larger part of politics and administration, and parliament is still only dealing with a small part of a much larger total. The dominant voice in policy-making is still the executive, and within the executive the main issue is still political control by cabinet, prime minister, and central agencies over the bureaucracy. In the outside world, the critical question is to achieve consent and legitimacy for policies and programmes. Here parliament plays an important, though often frustrating, role.

PARLIAMENT AND THE MOBILIZATION OF CONSENT

Policy-making in Canada consists of not one but many processes, each with its particular traits. But the most important processes, including rational policy-making, bureaucratic pluralism, and executive federalism, are executive-centred. Executive-centredness leads to difficulties in building consent. Policy-making is in private, below the level of public visibility, and often policies, when they emerge, are sprung full-blown on a surprised, unsuspecting and sometimes non-too-pleased public. It is hard to link the inside, private sphere of government with the outside public world of politics. Executive-centred policy-making does not lead to the mobilization of consent while policies are being developed. Parliament is unimportant. It ratifies and authorizes decisions worked out elsewhere.

Although the intention of the Trudeau reforms was to improve the ability of government to create policies directed towards a general public interest, the impact on structure and process was to distance policy-making and government from general public and often interest-group participation. The reliance on royal commissions of the Diefenbaker and Pearson governments might well have produced ad hoc and uncoordinated policies, but it did also, simply through the process of consideration by commission, ensure a high level of public participation and understanding. The commission process, because it was outside the secretive enclosed structure of the executive, was an effective tool for mobilizing consent.

Efforts of the Trudeau government to increase participation by citizens in policy-making were not successful. Consequently, the remarkable strengthening of central agencies after 1968 was not balanced or complemented by new methods for mobilizing consent. The centralized power structure was reinforced, but the deference and acquiescence to leadership that developed during the war and the immediate post-war years vanished, as did the consensus on Keynesianism-cum-collectivism, leaving the government with the unhappy problem of having to persuade a divided and uncertain public of the attractiveness of policies without the mass parties and other instruments of collectivist politics to organize and mould consent.

On the one hand the government can rely on interest-group interaction and bartering to produce policies agreeable to organized groups. This process is especially effective when the agreement is also supported by a parliamentary committee. The structure of organized interests, however, means that these policies will often be especially helpful to the already advantaged. On the other hand, the government, through its centralized machinery of political leadership, co-ordination, and policy-making, creates policies which it believes are directed towards a more general interest. The process of creating these policies, because it is private, within government, neither educates the public nor encourages consent formation. As such, it leaves the government with a difficult selling job once it has decided upon and announced its policy intentions. Experience with constitutional reform, the National Energy Program, the tax changes in MacEachen's budget of 1981, and the changes to the Crow's Nest rates amply illustrate this problem. The Mulroney government has found the same sort of problems in its efforts to negotiate free trade with the United States. These policies were new, important, reformist, and hostile to entrenched interests. They had emerged from the private womb of bureaucracy and cabinet, not from the dialectic of party or public discussion. Consent and understanding had not been developed for them before they became fixed government policy. Their revolutionary nature, and their sometimes obvious harms to powerful interests, made this consent difficult to win.

The burden of mobilizing consent is placed on post-decision processes. Here, the government is in the unenviable situation of having to gain support from an uninformed public for policies created in private, in the face of particular interests which stand to lose, and a hostile opposition in parliament. One way of winning consent is to use the techniques of mass communication, including advertising and publicity campaigns. Although not to be ignored, these have been found for the most part to be crude and unsatisfying. They are better adapted towards encouraging choices between brands of beer or toothpaste than for developing understanding and support for complex policies, especially when these cause obvious harm to specific, interested, groups.

But the main forum for mobilizing consent is parliament. To the extent that the previous policy-formulating process has been in private this does not work well. A policy choice, decided in private by the government and embodied in a bill (and usually already discussed and agreed to by the government caucus), is laid before parliament. This is frequently the first time the opposition, media, and public are made aware of the direction, let alone the details of the government's policy. Parliamentary discussion begins. The parliamentary format is confrontation and debate between opposing and rigidly disciplined teams. All policy proposals have some faults, and all important ones take away from some and give to others. Policies oriented towards a general, often unassignable, public interest are especially vulnerable on this score. Frequently the groups which stand to lose are readily identifiable and clearly aware of their potential losses, while those who stand to gain are not easy to identify, nor are their prospective gains specific.

In the Trudeau era, the opposition parties in parliament were particularly sensitive to the losing groups, which in turn found lobbying the opposition a ready route to publicity. Because it was not in the position of government and therefore was not forced to think of the nation as a whole, the opposition was far less sensitive to the collective public interest. These tendencies were exacerbated by the strange mixture of disparate regional, economic, and other groups that formed the opposition. The opposition was a collection of minorities, not an integrated whole. If roles stay reversed, and the present Conservative government remains in power and the Liberals become the perpetual opposition, the Liberals would soon come to behave like the chronic Conservative opposition.

The Conservative opposition could see only the harms in legislation, not the good. And they quite logically perceived it to be to their advantage to respond to the pressures on them and to castigate the government. They were a true, and essentially negative, opposition to the governing coalition of the centre. The opposition was supported by losing groups. The media, with their inherent tendency towards drama and their negative stance, gave great weight to criticisms. In turn, because the government had prepared its policies in secret, it had often not adequately taken into account the negative impact of proposals, and was vulnerable to criticisms. The government was faced with the difficult task of mobilizing support from an uninformed, indeterminate mass electorate, while the opposition had the advantage of clearly defined, well-informed, and powerful supporters.

Under these conditions the parliamentary legislative process became warfare. The government, so long as it enjoyed the support of a majority, could win a vote in the House, so the opposition's objective was to delay the vote. It discovered, used, and refined an extraordinary number of devices to achieve this end. Although the dramatic instances of prolonged parliamentary battle are the most memorable – the debates on the constitution, the National Energy Program, the tax changes in the budget of 1981, the changes to the Crow's Nest rates, and the Mulroney government's backtracking on de-indexing old age pensions – this atmosphere of obstruction, delay, and confrontation also slows the passage of minor legislation. It makes the timetabling of government business a crucial problem to both government and parliament. It means that the government, where possible, does everything in its power to avoid parliament.

The reasons usually offered for Canadian problems in timetabling include the relative newness of pressures on the parliamentary timetable in Canada and the pigheadedness of the chronic opposition. The line of analysis presented here suggests that a third explanation is as important: the centralized, secretive nature of policy-creating in Canada places an excessive burden on the parliamentary stages, and the delays and difficulties the government faces in getting its business through parliament serve an important function in mobilizing consent.

It can be seen that there is an intimate relationship between the internal processes of policy-making, the kinds of policy initiatives the government wishes to pursue, and the way parliament and parliamentary committees handle government business. During the parliamentary stages the public is informed, for the first time, of policy proposals. Prolonged warfare in parliament then moulds and creates public opinion, and, further, mobilizes consent. At the end of the war, bloodied but triumphant, the government has its legislation and the opposition, although it has lost, has fought the good fight. The media report the parliamentary struggle as a game, a contest between two teams. The government victory is acceptable because the game was fought well and hard. The government's willingness to suffer and endure the combat is proof of its sincerity.

Parliament is a far from negligible tool for mobilizing consent, but the present processes of policy-making place an unnatural and heavy burden on it. Confrontation and conflict, posturing for the media, oversimplification and trivialization, transmutation of issues of policy into conflicts of personality, the subordination of every other aspect of parliament or approach to the legislative process to the demands of partisan warfare, all follow from parliament's strange role. Government, opposition, and parliament itself are brought into disrepute by the prolonged, brutal, boring, degrading, and generally unproductive parliamentary processes. The roots of the problem lie far deeper than the normal explanation in terms of poor procedural rules or bad attitudes of government and opposition.

The Trudeau government was unable to find a satisfying role for parliament in policy-making. To find one remains one of the greatest challenges facing our parliamentary system. It is intimately tied to the closely related problems of national unity and mobilizing consent. The change of government in 1984 has done nothing to resolve the problem. The Mulroney cabinet has not yet developed enough policies to put the system to test; when it does, the problem of obstruction will emerge again. It is most unlikely that a Liberal opposition, once it finds its feet, will be more tractable and less obstructionist than the previous Conservative opposition. Approval by parliament is an essential step in gaining consent and achieving legitimacy. Governments have to pay a high price to earn it. The option of consensual agreement through endorsement by a parliamentary committee, although it has its place, is also a potentially dangerous route to consent and legitimacy: it can emphasize particular groups and interests to the expense of the more general public ones, and consequently weaken the government.

THE ELEMENTS OF CONSENSUS AND COMBAT

To reformers the worst characteristics of Canadian parliamentary government come together in policy-making. The process is dominated by government, parliamentary proceedings are dominated by obsessive confrontation and small-mindedness, and the elected members of the representative assembly do not have a useful role. The route to reform most often proposed is to emphasize the consensual aspects of parliamentary proceedings, particularly in committees and to diminish the confrontational ones.

Two recent sets of proposals for reform will illustrate this point. As we have seen, the 1985 special committee on reform proposed a loosening up of party discipline and a strengthening of committees. The thrust of the committee's recommendations was to de-emphasize confrontation and adversarial combat, and to emphasize the consensual and non-partisan aspects of parliamentary proceedings. In arguing for the loosening of confidence conventions, the special committee claimed that backbench dissent might: 'have a direct and sometimes observable impact on public policy. As a result of defeated measures, the threat of defeat, or simple dissent not entailing defeat, governments might modify or withdraw certain measures. This opens the way for the House to become more vital and significant in influencing policy than it has been for a long time and a more accurate reflection of Canadian public opinion.'[17] What the committee did not point out was that at present many legislative proposals of the government are substantially modified during consideration by parliament. Many others, as much as 30 per cent, are not passed. Canadian governments at present have less success than their British counterparts in getting legislation through parliament, even though confidence conventions have been relaxed in Britain but have not been in Canada. A strong case could be made that Canadian governments at present do not have adequate powers to get their programmes through. Further weakening of their powers might have a disastrous effect on the cabinet's ability to control departments and the bureaucratic-pluralist nexus.

The recent Royal Commission on the Economic Union and Developmental Prospects for Canada also wanted the House of Commons to have a much larger role in making policies. It argued for:

the formation of a permanent Economic Policy Committee of the House of Commons. The Committee would hold annual pre-budget hearings; take testimony about the nation's economic prospects from the Department of Finance, the Bank of Canada and the Treasury Board, and from related agencies such as the Economic Council of Canada and the Science Council; and gather the views of major groups, including business and labour associations. In addition, the committee could hold hearings on other important economic issues throughout the year. Its hearings should be televised and should become part of the annual cycle of economic policy formation.

Such a committee could inform public and parliamentary debate, and become an instrument for collective debate about the economy ... A permanent Committee would integrate economic interests into the policy-making processes of the House of Commons, the central representative body of Canadian life. In moving from specific problems to the more general issues of economic policy making, it becomes increasingly appropriate to link consultative mechanisms to Parliament, through which the government is ultimately responsible for its decisions.[18]

As a reform to the budget process, the same committee should, the commission proposed, 'hold an annual series of pre-budget meetings timed to allow its work to influence budget preparation. During televised hearings, it would analyse the government's performance.'[19]

Implicit in these proposals and their discussion by the commission is the assumption that a committee of the House of Commons could consider the most important annual policy business of the government in a non-partisan way, with the various interests in the nation making presentations to a deliberative, impartial, investigative committee. The committee might not make recommendations, but it would certainly 'influence budget preparations' and 'analyze the government's performance.'

Attractive as these proposals might appear to be on surface, they nevertheless have severe flaws. One is that nothing in past experience or present practices suggests that a committee of the House of Commons can operate in this manner. Parliamentary attention is fickle, and there are no examples of a committee consistently paying attention to major partisan policy issue year after year in the way the commission proposes. Another flaw is that the debate on the budget is a central partisan issue. The government proposes, the opposition criticizes. Perhaps pre-budget parliamentary discussion could be non-adversarial and consensual. The commission, however, makes no proposals or suggestions as to how this might occur. The commission identifies a problem. It proposes a committee. How this committee is to fit into the realities of parliamentary life, or how it ties into existing activities, is not considered. These weaknesses are all too common to proposals to reform parliament's role in policy-making.

Also ignored is the problem of the inadequacy of the manpower resources of the House of Commons. Not only are MPs for the most part to the right of the Canadian public in perceptions, they are also in a fundamental sense unaccountable because they are in office for a short term, have low commitment to a parliamentary career, and are less important than parties and leaders in affecting voter choice. Further, the demands of the work world of parliament do not except on rare occasions permit the sort of attention, focusing of energy, and reflection by MPs which a thorough examination of policy issues requires. In the past twenty years, if anything, the pressures and problems of the career and workworld of MPs have grown worse. Turnover is still severe. The present committee system stretches the resources of manpower to its limits.

It is not reasonable to expect parliamentary committees to be much more influential in policy-making until some of these factors change. It could be argued that changes in the confidence conventions and improvements to committees will make parliament such a delight that MPs will want to make their careers there, and that the new role will give them such visibility and importance that the voting choices of the electorate will become directly related to the behaviour of the MP, creating solidly based representation, and real responsibility and accountability from citizens to representatives. That would be reform indeed. But to believe that it will happen requires a strong act of faith, confounding the lessons of more than a hundred years of parliamentary tradition in Canada.

The advocates of more independence for MPs and stronger, non-partisan committees make a judgment that the adversarial system is bad. But a strong defence can be made of it. The important influence of parliament is not in its direct effect on legislation and policies. Rather, its influence is indirect. Parliament normally wields power through the deterrent effect of bad publicity. A government, to be successful, must anticipate criticism, and ensure that its policies, budgets, and proposals are defensible as a good balancing of special interests, and an expression of a public interest. The opposition will be quick to pounce on flaws and errors of omission and commission. The adversarial system thus puts strong inducements on a government to consult widely, deliberate carefully, and present well–thought-out policy proposals. Governments, of course, often fail to do so – MacEachen's budget of 1981 is a notorious example – and they then suffer the consequences. They lose an election. Their adversaries become government and have a chance to do better. No system can ensure perfection. But the adversarial elements of the parliamentary system place a high premium on careful, sensitive preparation, place responsibility squarely on the shoulders of a government, ensure that mistakes are punished, and provide an opportunity for another team to replace the losers.

The adversarial practices of the parliamentary system also have hidden elements of consensus in them. The disagreements and confrontations are exaggerated and, as in a competitive school debate, serve to illustrate varying aspects and views of truth, rather than assert a single monolithic view. When the government ultimately wins, the opposition accepts the outcome. In fact, many of the proposals it has fought so bitterly are ones it might well have introduced if it were government. The Canadian populace is probably better aware of these symbolic and gaming aspects of the adversarial combat than critics realize.

The key problem in the policy-making process lies in mobilizing consent and in the pre-decision and consultation phases of policy-making. Secrecy, on budgets in particular, as the royal commission on the economic union noted, but on other questions of policy development as well, prevents the moulding of a public opinion before decisions are taken. In these pre-decision stages the government faces a difficult challenge in balancing the various private and public interests. These are especially important in tax and budget issues. Experience with revisions to tax law in the early 1970s shows that, because of the biases in the parliamentary and interest-group systems, consideration by parliamentary committee does not guarantee a fair and equitable outcome. The problem with the pluralist heaven, as has been remarked, is that the choir sings with an upper-class accent. Examination of issues by an influential parliamentary committee could, in many instances, produce a result which, although it had the approval of interest groups and the support of the media, was in fact inimical to the more general public interest. More influential committees could lead to parliamentary pluralism, reinforcing bureau-cratic pluralism and weakening political control over departments and agencies. That is what happens in the United States, where the 'iron triangle' of congressional committee, interest group, and executive agency dominates policy-making. Apparent consensus can prevent very important differences of opinion and interest from being exposed and discussed.

Within parliament three systems of representation are at work. One is through the individual members. As we have seen, the average member is well to the right of the average Canadian in perceptions and opinions. This is especially true of the Progressive Conservative party. There is also representation through prime minister and cabinet, who are responsible for governing the whole of Canada, and are ultimately accountable to the country in an election. Third is the variety of opinions and interests in the political parties, which is expressed through the combat between the parties. Proposals for parliament-centred reform tend to extoll and emphasize only the first of these three systems, and ignore or denigrate the other two.

But the one that is being emphasized, the individual member, is the weakest and in many ways the least representative. A government truly concerned with the well-being of all Canadians is often going to find itself at odds with its own supporters, with the caucus to the right of government. The present system of party discipline and adversarial combat has the virtue of giving the government a strong hand in controlling its caucus. Adversarial combat ensures that the government is exposed in public to a wide range of criticisms. A shift of decision-making power from cabinet to private members and parliamentary committees, as is proposed in the parliament-centred rhetoric of reform, would weaken both government control and adversarial combat, and would have implications for policy choices and the distribution of power that discussion of reform do not come to terms with. It would strengthen the already strong, and weaken the already weak. In so doing, it is also likely to harm a government's chances of re-election.

Reformers perhaps focus on parliament-centred reforms because the political parties do so little in policy development. Ideally opposition parties between elections would discuss and propose a political agenda. But this is not how Canadian parties operate. In the years leading up to the 1984 election the Progressive Conservative party established many small task forces to examine policy areas such as agriculture, transportation, youth employment, Crown corporations, and productivity in the workforce and to make proposals for change.[20] One of the noteworthy features of the 1984 election campaign was that the party kept these proposals well hidden. Most did not become part of its election platform. The exception was energy policy, where the new Conservative government followed its promises to Alberta and dismantled the Liberals' National Energy Program. Whether this helped win them public support is doubtful. Not the least of the reasons for burying the other proposals was that the election was fought on the record of the Liberal government. For the Tories to have introduced numerous new policy proposals would have diverted attention from this primary focus, and at the same time would have given the Liberals a target to attack. Another reason was that the policy proposals were flawed. An opposition party is normally sensitive to, and hears, mostly the voices of those who are hostile to the government. Therefore, it is likely that it gets a distorted picture of the real impact of and satisfaction with policies. This problem was a severe handicap to the short-lived Clark government. Doubtless having profited from this unhappy experience, the Mulroney government entered office unencumbered by specific promises and policy proposals.

It is increasingly apparent that in many instances it is to a party's advantage to avoid making commitments to policies. Thus, it seems that in future Canadians are more likely to see bold policy proposals put forward (if at all) by a government in power than by an opposition party, or by either party during an election campaign. It is a curious paradox that political parties are by far the most powerful determinant of the behaviour of elected representatives, yet they give virtually no guidance to the electorate on what they are going to order their captive MPs to do once they are elected.

A few elections in Canada have been fought on matters of substance. Important in the campaign of 1911 which led to Laurier's defeat were the naval question and trade reciprocity with the United States.21 The main issue in 1963 was a very real question of the competence of John Diefenbaker as prime minister. But it is at the provincial level that on occasion issue and ideology have been most important. The election of the CCF government in Saskatchewan in 1944 brought in a government dedicated to social and economic reform, and during the twenty years of its life this government made fundamental policy innovations, in many of which, such as universal hospital and medical care insurance, it led the way for reforms later adopted throughout Canada.22 The Social Credit government elected earlier in Alberta also had a platform of visionary reform. The Parti Québécois won the election of 1976 in Quebec on a platform based mainly on independence for Quebec although it also included social-democratic elements. These are exceptions, however, and for the most part election campaigns at the provincial as well as at the federal level are run on amorphous issues of image, leadership, and sentiment.

Nevertheless, many policy innovations in Canadian politics have come from the parties. The New Democrats, and more particularly their predecessor the CCF, inspired many of the policies for social and economic reform of the post-war period. The opposition Liberal party under Lester Pearson held a conference on national problems in 1960 which provided Mr Pearson with much of his government's programme for the rest of the 1960s. J. Wearing offers some hope that the Liberal party will again find this sort of inspiration:

Looking at the history of the Liberal Party in perspective, one can clearly see a cyclical pattern of decay and renewal; the decay coming after a number of years in power and the renewal prompted by electoral defeat, either threatened or actual. During the periods of decline, the parliamentary party and the leader have become progressively more isolated from opinion in the party and in the country at large, while the volunteer or extra-parliamentary wing have grown disillusioned and uninterested. The sobering reality of electoral losses has then prompted the parliamentary leadership to take the volunteer wing more seriously, as King did after 1930 and 1943, as Pearson did after 1958 and as Trudeau did after 1972. The extra-parliamentary wing has subsequently become the source of new ideas and fresh faces; but, with the party safely back in power, the whole cycle starts again within a few years.[23]

G. C. Perlin is less optimistic about the Tories: 'The party can be expected to win elections from time to time ... [but] any Conservative government can expect to go through an extended period in which it is vulnerable to disruption from within. The party's ability to avoid this danger and survive in office long enough to change its competitive position would appear to require exceptionally adroit leadership and some considerable luck.'[24] Such a party is not going to be noted for developing policies while in opposition.

Reformers for the most part do not have much good to say about royal commissions, which however remain a vital part of the policy-making process in Canada and perform many of the functions that are expected of reformed parliamentary committees. There is nothing wrong with having royal commissions examine and make recommendations on major issues of policy. On the contrary, there is much to be said for their capacity to devote time and energy to an issue, to support research, to encourage public discussion, and to ensure that all viewpoints are heard. They have a better record than committees of the House of Commons. An intelligently chosen and managed royal commission has been, and in future will still be, one of the most effective instruments for clarifying issues and leading to the formation of public opinion. Senate committees also have a far better record than is generally appreciated. Executive task forces and advisory committees, although normally smaller and less formal than royal commissions, are also extremely important in clarifying issues, proposing solutions, and stimulating public discussion. Many are at work at any given time, and their total contribution to the consideration of policies and mobilization of consent is impressive.

The analysis in this chapter might appear to be unfairly hard on proposals for strengthening the House's role in policy-making. It might also appear to be pessimistic, and to suggest that nothing will ever work. This is not my intention. Rather, I have tried to describe some of the often unappreciated ways in which the present system works successfully, and some of the usually ignored constraints on the possibilities of reform. Policy-making is neither a technology nor a technical question. It is an intensely human process involving countless people in the articulation of their wants, needs, and values, and translating them into living government policies and programmes. It is not reasonable to expect that all people will agree or that politics will be sweetness and light. Universal and all-encompassing consensus is not possible. Consent, however, is. The parliamentary battles are a very real manifestation and expression of the deep cultural, geographic, and economic divisions within the country. Most times, when a battle is over and the dust settles, an advance has been made towards clarifying and defining national identity and values. Real political life is neither smooth nor easy. The Canadian press (and probably the public as well) likes a good parliamentary battle, and can live with the outcome, provided both sides have fought long, hard, and earnestly, and provided the government makes a good case, and accommodates reasonable criticisms. The parties are central to policy-making in Canada, but primarily as contestants less so as devisers and formulaters. The government is the chief policy-maker and the central initiating, energizing body.

Both the adversarial and consensual elements have their place, and they are not always in competition. They often complement rather than detract from each other. Sometimes consent comes from agreement, sometimes from combat. Parliament's main role in policy-making is as the focus for a continuing national debate on big and small issues. The adversarial system forces a discipline on the government. It must be able to defend what it has done in terms of a general public interest. This serves to counter the extremes of particularism in Canadian politics. Parliament is not primarily an investigative, consensual body, though its committees have been useful on many minor non-partisan issues, and on the large one of constitutional reform, where the main adversary of the federal government becomes the provinces, not the opposition parties in parliament.

Policy-making is strongly executive-centred in Canada. For most of Canadian history this has produced satisfactory results. The system breaks down, however, when the basis of consent erodes, or parliament fails to perform its crucial task of mobilizing consent. It also fails when the government itself is in disarray; when the prime minister and cabinet are unable to impose vision and direction on the executive, when a sense of collective, national concerns is subverted by excessive concern with particular, venal, and patronage matters, or when there is mistrust and misunderstanding between politicians and public servants. Domination of power by a government party, through which there is close connection and interchange between political and bureaucratic levels, has been the Canadian way of coping with these dangers. When, however, political and bureaucratic power do not mesh satisfactorily, as often occurs when a chronic opposition party is elected to power, or when a government party too long in power loses its vision, the system breaks down in loss of sense of national direction, confusion, and chaotic, unsatisfactory policy-making.

11

Accountability

Nothing could be simpler than the theory of parliamentary accountability. Its essence is ministerial responsibility, which means that 'each minister is responsible to Parliament for the conduct of his Department. The act of every civil servant is by convention regarded as the act of his minister.'[1] This responsibility includes political accountability for policies and other political acts and decisions, administrative accountability for management and administration, and financial accountability for the use of funds. One of the great strengths of the theory of the parliamentary cabinet system is that it locates responsibility in the ministry, so that a small, clearly identifiable group of individuals not only has complete responsibility, but is held directly accountable to parliament. Parliament, in turn, exposes wrong-doing, omissions, and lapses in any of the three areas, and the cumulative results of this exposure are made manifest by the electorate when they support or reject a government in an election. But, as in most areas of politics and government, reality is much more complex and less satisfying than the theory. A seminar held by the Canadian Institute of Public Administration concluded: 'there is indeed a serious problem related to the power and responsibility of the public service,' and 'ministerial responsibility is no longer real or even practical as an ideal.'[2]

There is a simple reason for the gap between theory and reality. The theory of parliamentary government, as it was developed in the nineteenth century, was based upon the existence of and linkages between two systems: the representative system which created the elected House of Commons; and the executive system of departments headed and controlled by ministers. The cabinet, with its members being both ministers of government and members of parliament, was the link between the two, and parliamentary control consisted of two key phases: first, the assigning of responsibility and authority through statutes and appropriation; and second, accountability through scrutiny in the house and its committees.

The reality of modern government is more complex than this simple model, and the main change is the emergence of the administrative branch as a separate, semi-autonomous system. So where the model postulates only one boundary between systems over which linkages, controls, and accountability must function, the modern reality is that there are two, and in many ways it is the boundary between the cabinet and the public service which is the difficult one. On the one side is a small number of elected politicians who for the most part will hold a portfolio for only a few years, whose political careers are not likely to last more than ten or fifteen years, and who are amateurs in the work of their departments. On the other side are hundreds of thousands of public servants, most of whom are likely to spend the bulk of their working careers within one department, and who are the professional experts in their field of responsibility.

One challenge in accountability is for parliament (and the executive) to come to terms with the reality of the size and diversity of the administrative structure. Another is to handle the variety of policies, rapid policy changes, and the confusing multiplicity of objectives which policies try to accomplish. Accountability is all the more difficult in non-departmental agencies, where the board, or its executive head, has statutory authority for which they are not responsible to a minister. The problems are serious. The recent Royal Commission on Financial Management and Accountability reported: 'After two years of careful study and consideration, we have reached the deeply held conviction that the serious malaise pervading the management of government stems fundamentally from a grave weakening, and in some cases an almost total breakdown, in the chain of accountability, first within government, and second in the accountability of government to Parliament and ultimately to the Canadian people.'[3]

Accountability, in all its ramifications through parliament, cabinet, central agencies, civil service, Crown corporations, and other non-departmental agencies, is too big a topic to be covered in one chapter. Here the focus must be on parliament, and in particular accountability for financial administration and management. But before we pursue the questions relating to the role of parliament, it is necessary to get some sense of the overall system.

THE DIFFUSION OF RESPONSIBILITY

One of the classic arguments in the study of public administration is the Friedrich-Finer dispute, so named after the two eminent scholars who more than forty years ago engaged in an academic dog fight over responsibility and accountability.[4] C.J. Friedrich argued that employment in the public service ought to be a profession in itself, with its own internal standards and accountability. In addition, the public servant ought to be responsible to the standards and ideals of the community which he serves. H. Finer argued that this was a very dangerous approach, and that responsibility and accountability ought to be formal and direct to elected politicians, the legislature, and the electorate. Each finally agreed that the accountability he proposed was not absolute, but needed to be balanced by the other system; nevertheless each remained adamant that his approach was the essential one. Like most interesting arguments, the Friedrich-Finer dispute has never been resolved. It remains important not only as a splendid duel between two academics but also because it portrays brilliantly the constant dilemma in administration of how to balance the different elements of responsibility.

Friedrich, himself from Germany, was well aware of the problems of the Nazi regime. Hitler demanded absolute personal obedience and loyalty not only from his direct subordinates and the public service as a whole, but also from teachers, professionals, and other persons in public employment. The whole state service became an instrument for executing the Nazi political will, even when this perverted normal standards of justice and common humanity. The normally valuable ideal of obedience became part of the problem when it was not counterbalanced by adherence to moral standards, or by a political system which exposed and punished diseased leadership and administrative behaviour. After the Second World War Friedrich's viewpoint found support in the Nuremberg trials, which found not only Nazi political leaders but underlings and bureaucrats many levels down the hierarchy guilty of crimes against humanity. In effect the bureaucrats were punished for failing to disobey lawfully given orders. The courts ruled that they should have followed their consciences to the point of wilfully disobeying their superiors.

Discussions of accountability in modern Canadian public administration use the same concepts, but label the Finer and Friedrich approaches as 'objective' and 'subjective' accountability, respectively. In objective accountability someone is responsible *for* something and accountable *to* some person or body in a formal way, through clearly defined rules and mechanisms. In subjective accountability a person feels a duty towards the profession of public service or a sense of the public good and the nation which determines and defines conduct even though there are no formal mechanisms or processes through which this accountability can be enforced.[5]

Much of the attraction of responsible government as a theory is found in its linking of the comfort of appointing mature people with a sense of the public good to power as cabinet ministers with the safeguard of the institutional mechanisms of accountability to parliament. Public servants also are expected to be responsible and trustworthy people, and to be accountable both for the performance of routine work and for the ideals and values which they bring to this work, and which affect the discretionary decisions they make and the policies they propose. The subjective element is an essential part of the skills, knowledge, and wisdom which is brought to bear on the great issues of governance. Growth of government means that the problem now is to ensure accountability to parliament of a huge and complex executive where discretion is exercised at many levels, and ministers can make, or even be aware of, only a small portion of decisions.

The beguilingly simple theory of responsible government suggests that parliament approves a mandate for the government in the form of statutes and budget; the public service then executes this mandate under the control and direction of ministers who are then accountable for their stewardship to parliament. The reality is that both statutes and the budget are loose frameworks which often are more like permits for the government to engage in activities than instructions and directions on how it must act. Ministers have a great deal of freedom and discretion in applying their subjective values and sense of what is important. Public servants similarly exercise a great deal of discretion, and in semi-autonomous boards, commissions, and Crown corporations opportunities for exercising subjective judgment will be even greater.

To put it bluntly: in modern governance it is not possible for ministers to exercise direct control over the public service, or for parliament to exercise direct control over ministers. Both the cabinet and the public service have substantial autonomy. Parliament is only one of the pressures and influences to which they respond, and not always the most important one. Accountability is different from control, and a good audit system will encourage responsible, autonomous judgment rather than a plethora of detailed controls.

This point can be illustrated by describing briefly how accountability looks from four positions in the parliamentary-cabinet system.

First, for an opposition member of parliament, there is no doubt that the government ought to be fully accountable to the House of Commons. In question period he demands that ministers, including the prime minister, answer for any aspect of their own conduct or that of persons under them. In committee the member questions ministers and public servants. If he is a member of the public accounts committee, the MP takes advantage of the report of the auditor general, and pursues mismanagement with the expert help of this servant of parliament. Although committee reports have no power by themselves to reward or punish, they, like question period and debates, form part of that climate of opinion and background of knowledge by which the government is judged, and if the opposition are effective in their criticisms, the government will ultimately pay a price in loss of support.

Opposition members recognize no limits in the questions they are entitled to ask and demand answers to. They also make no distinction between those aspects of administrative responsibility which are subjective and those which are objective, or those which might more properly be considered as administrative. The target is the minister. Everything is fair game, as long as it helps in the parliamentary battle. The main improvements the opposition MPs would like to see implemented would be better ways of making ministers and public servants accountable through more powerful committees and more publicity for debates and question period.

In stark contrast to this clear insistence that all of government is accountable to him in parliament, the opposition MP will sense his own accountability to be much more diffuse. He will be aware of a responsibility to his constituency, yet he will also be aware that what he does as an MP does not have as much effect on his chance of re-election as what his party, and his party leader, does. He will be in contact with a restricted range of constituents through direct contact and the correspondence handled by his office. He will keep a close eye on newspapers and other media reports to learn what their reaction is to his own and his party's behaviour and attitudes. He will have contacts with other MPs, and with representatives of interest groups, who will similarly react to his performance. The whips will reward him if he serves the party. Apart from party, the elements of objective accountability for the MP are weak, while the less formal elements, and those in which the only real accountability is to his own conscience, are comparatively strong. The brief careers of most MPs make even the external sanction of electoral disapproval of small importance. Opposition MPs find no paradox in expressing their general feeling that the formal objective processes by which they hold the government accountable ought to be strengthened, while their own accountability is for the most part subjective and informal. An unusually reflective member might on occasion wish that there was a closer correlation between his conduct and the way his constituents vote, but MPs are busy, practical persons, and for the most part accept the system as given and operate within it.

Second, for a minister in the government, accountability is to many bodies, and parliament is only one of several important forums. Much of his time, far more than he spends in parliament, is spent with his ministerial colleagues in cabinet and cabinet committees. His ability to explain and defend his department, and to get what his department wants, is an important measure of his power. A minister has a responsibility to his department, to be an effective spokesman for it, and a defender of its interests in parliament, cabinet, and public. Since most ministers stay in an office for less than two years, their main function is to act as a spokesman rather than as a policy initiator or administrative leader, and the minister's prestige and esteem (i.e., how he is assessed) in large part depend on his ability to perform the spokesman's role, and on his status in the eyes of his colleagues and the inner circle of senior bureaucrats, including those in his department. Part of the minister's job is to deal with influential interests and pressure groups, and his status with them is also a measure of his performance. The caucus of his own parliamentary party is also an important and useful forum for explanation and accountability.

Parliament has its peculiar characteristics for a minister: it is very public, and can be either a powerful and useful means of reaching the media and the public with a message or an arena in which a reputation is destroyed. To a minister, the opposition, far from looking like defenders of the public and minority interests, are a pack of hostile and, on occasion, vicious and unscrupulous opponents who will use any means at their disposal, fair or foul, to discredit him and his colleagues. Accountability to parliament is not a matter of getting a fair hearing, but rather a confrontation and contest in which points can be scored by low blows as well as clean jabs. Ministers might be quick to argue that parliamentary control and accountability ought to be strengthened, but not if that strengthening means simply giving the opposition more tools with which to obstruct the government, and more opportunities to score points in an atmosphere of hostile confrontation. A thoughtful minister might point out that it was his party, not the opposition, that was elected to govern, and that the opposition represents those who lost, and the pressure groups which influence it are those who failed to get their way with the public service and the minister himself. These groups, and the opposition itself, do not represent the interests of the public as a whole, but rather peculiar disaffected elements. Some ministers enjoy the rough and tumble of parliament, others do not; but few would say that accountability to parliament is the most effective and useful control over them and their departments. The minister's ultimate accountability is not to parliament but to the prime minister who appoints and dismisses him, to cabinet colleagues, and to the electorate. Modern governments take every opportunity to reach the electorate directly, in part because this helps reduce the biases and distortions of the parliamentary processes.

Third, the deputy minister is the public servant who, under the minister, heads the department. In theory the deputy minister has only one master, the minister, whom he or she serves loyally and impartially. But in practice he has many masters and many accountability relationships. Deputy ministers are, like ministers, appointed by the prime minister, not the departmental minister, and therefore they have a sense of direct accountability to the prime minister, who can dismiss as well as appoint them. In recent years, in fact, turnover among deputy ministers has been comparable to that of ministers, so the power to reward and punish through dismissal and transfer has been by no means unimportant. The privy council office makes annual assessments of the performance of deputy ministers which determine salary among other things, so in a very real sense they are also held accountable to this central agency. Michael Pitfield, as clerk of the privy council, was very powerful because of the influence he had over the careers of key bureaucrats. The Financial Administration Act and the Financial and Asset

Management Act give implicit recognition to the management role of deputy heads by assigning responsibility in a number of important areas to them rather than to ministers.[6] Deputy ministers are also members of a community of other senior civil servants and are informally evaluated by them. Their standing in this peer group is of importance. They are members of departmental management teams and leaders of employees and have a responsibility to them to provide leadership and motivation. Most deputy ministers also have formal and informal responsibilities for and towards Crown corporations, and agencies and advisory bodies within their minister's portfolios.

Deputy ministers are also influenced by a sense of accountability to the public. Part of this accountability is a subjective sense of commitment to public service and the public interest, but a great deal of it is part and parcel of their direct relationships with the clientele and interests whom their department serves, and to whom the quality of that service is a prime concern. The Lambert Commission found that 'some deputies maintain that they are, in effect, accountable only to themselves, and claim to measure their performance against their own standards of excellence.'[7]

Although deputy ministers frequently appear as witnesses before parliamentary committees, parliament is not the most important forum for their accountability. They are normally witnesses on behalf of their ministers and speaking for them. Ministerial responsibility means that the deputies are not normally held accountable by committees, but simply provide information.

Where the ultimate accountability for ministers is external, to the electorate, public opinion, and parliament, that of the deputies is internal, to central agencies and their minister. The relationships between deputies and ministers are closer to being a two-way street between equals with differing concerns and responsibilities than a formal master-servant structure. The position of the deputy minister is one of the most important places where the immense and powerful bureaucratic system meshes and interacts with the system of political power (others being the privy council office, treasury board, the department of finance, and other central agencies), and a deputy minister must perform a difficult act in juggling the various pressures and interests while walking the tightrope between political and bureaucratic power. In both responsibilities and accountability no sharp distinction is made between the deputy minister's role in administration and his role in policy, and for the most part there is more overlap than separation between the roles.

Fourth, for a public servant in the middle or lower levels of the administrative hierarchy, parliament is a distant and unimportant control. Responsibility and accountability relationships are largely with the immediate supervisor, and with the peer group of other employees performing similar jobs. It is the supervisor who sets tasks and makes assessments of performance, although these powers are usually hedged by departmental and central-agency regulations to ensure fair and adequate review. Also, for much of the public service, unions serve to protect employees from arbitrary discrimination. The peer group, and the informal organizations which flesh out the formal bureaucratic hierarchies, are at least as important as rules and regulations and supervisors in determining the norms of behaviour in such areas as workload and how discretion is to be exercised. The many public servants who belong to professions, such as law, nursing, medicine, engineering, accountancy, also are in some measure accountable to their profession. Civil servants who deal directly with the public, especially when contact is on a face-to-face and personal basis, also often develop a strong sense of accountability to their clientele.

Most public servants are located in the lower and middle ranks of the bureaucracies. Organizational structures and personnel are very stable at these levels. An average public servant has a career in government of twenty to thirty years, and in this period would likely have no more than two or three promotions or changes of jobs. With this sort of stability, the mores and personal relationships within the work group become very important, and external controls less so. This situation is what makes bureaucratic behaviour itself so stable and resistant to change, which has its good points in consistency and dependability, and its bad points when the informal mores are counterproductive, as they have become in the post office. It is not much of an exaggeration to say that, for the bulk of the public service, parliament, central agencies, ministers, and deputy ministers are not normally direct or even powerful controls. Life in the workplace continues much as it has in the past regardless of what has been discussed or decided at those levels. Accountability to parliament and ministerial responsibility are remote, mythical, and largely irrelevant to day-to-day work.

THE REQUIREMENTS FOR PARLIAMENTARY CONTROL

Parliament cannot specify what every minister and every public servant must and must not do. Rather, parliament must ensure that a framework and system are developed which ensure that the mandate and intentions of programmes and policies are adequately stated, and that the financial system includes proper budgeting, management, and accountability. To this end, the following requirements should be met:

1 There should be a legislative framework that defines intentions and authorizes and restricts the powers of the executive.
2 There should be an annual comprehensive budget that includes the amounts to be spent on each programme.

3 The actual use of funds and making of expenditures should be the responsibility of the executive.
4 The monies collected and spent must be accounted for and reported to parliament.
5 There should be an audit process that ensures that parliament is aware of the problems, important exceptions, and instances of maladministration.
6 Parliament itself should be able to examine the auditor's report and the accounts of the government and ensure that problems are dealt with.

There are four important bodies involved in the audit process. Parliament is the central legislative and legitimating institution and the body to which the government is accountable. The central agencies of government are responsible for the overall budget and financial control systems. The departments are responsible for programme administration and actual expenditures. The legislative auditor (auditor general) is responsible for examining the accounts and financial systems of the government and reporting on them to parliament.

In practice the system becomes more complex. Because the government, not parliament, has the power to introduce money bills (those proposing taxes or expenditures), parliament's role in the budgetary process is severely limited. Within the executive, a balance must be found between the responsibilities of central agencies, ministers, civil servants, and other agencies such as Crown corporations and boards and commissions, which are non-departmental in form and over which ministers do not have their customary responsibilities. The auditor must establish his kind of audit and its purposes, whether it is simply an audit to ensure that funds have been accounted for and spent legally, or whether it will also examine economy, efficiency, value for money, and other less easily measurable factors. Parliament cannot itself consider the auditor's report and investigate the questions it raises, but delegates this task to the public accounts committee. The organization, work procedures, and effectiveness of this committee directly affect the quality of accountability and parliamentary control.

In the development of accountability to parliament in Canada, many weak links have been found in the delegation of responsibility and functions. There has been slow but steady improvement, however, and the present system is a vast change from what existed even as recently as the early decades of this century.

From confederation until the First World War, 'the distribution of patronage was the most important single function of the government.'[8] Both decisions on personnel within the civil service and decisions on expenditure of funds were political. The opposition in parliament not unnaturally hunted for scandals in administration, while the government used its majority to prevent disclosure and investigation. There was no effective system of audit and accountability and administration was conducted on the basis of executive discretion rather than rules. This system foundered in inefficiency during the First World War. In 1918 patronage was reduced in the civil service through the introduction of a strict merit system controlled through a powerful independent civil service commission.[9] Ministers lost their responsibility for personnel administration, and accountability within the civil service for this function (and much of the actual administration as well) was assigned to the commission. In theory the commission reported to parliament, but in practice parliament exercised no control over it.

Patronage and other abuses continued to pervade financial administration until the crisis caused by the great depression forced reform in the 1930s. Control over the use of funds was then, as personnel administration had been before, brought under the aegis of a new central agent, here the comptroller of the treasury. Departmental responsibility for making expenditures was diminished, and internal accountability was to the comptroller rather than to departmental management. Although the auditor general reported to parliament, the public accounts committee was weak, and accountability to parliament for the use of funds was still virtually non-existent. The rigid controls within government stifled good management. Most additions to the administrative structure were in corporations and other forms of non-departments, until there were in effect two civil services: one under the Finance Administration and Civil Service acts; another, equally large, outside these controls. Part of the reason for this wholesale use of non-departments was to permit freer and more efficient management. Part also was to permit patronage to be exercised by politicians in the less tightly controlled non-departments.

In the 1960s, under the stimulus of a royal commission on efficiency in government, a move began towards reducing these central controls because they were stifling administration and reducing efficiency.[10] 'Let the managers manage' became a slogan. The issue was not accountability so much as autonomy and creativity, on the assumption that the delegation of increased responsibility for personnel and finances would encourage efficiency and effectiveness. The position of comptroller was abolished, and the treasury board and its secretariat were strengthened so that they could serve as the central control agencies of government. Controls over departments were to be like those over non-departments. The Glassco Commission had proposed that controls should be strengthened through the system of appointing and monitoring chief financial officers of departments. But this system was never satisfactorily implemented, and in later years, much of the movement was in the direction of increased control through regulation.

Collective bargaining now also limits management's discretion. Conditions of work, pay, grievance, and many other matters have come under collective agreements. As R.B. Bryce pointed out, 'it is very difficult to remove an individual for incompetence in the performing of his duties. This is particularly important in the case of supervisors and middle management. The laws, and now the collective agreements, provide so much protection against unfair dismissal that they make efficient management much more difficult.'[11] In so far as management decisions are covered by collective agreements, accountability for them is as much through the grievance and bargaining processes as it is through internal-management lines of accountability and responsibility.

Central agencies and departmental management have to strike a balance between control through detailed regulation and control through relying on management's desire to achieve economy and efficiency. The intention from the time of the Glassco Commission to the mid-1970s was to reduce central-agency regulations and to place greater reliance on the sense of frugality in departmental management, bolstered by sanctions and rewards in the career development of senior civil servants. But the growth of government and the strengthening of central agencies in the Trudeau years directed attention away from programme management and towards policy-making. At the same time, the treasury board, far from reducing paper work and regulations, increased them. The Lambert Commission wanted to strengthen departmental planning capacity, which they thought was lamentably weak. Far too much of management resources was consumed in responding to central agency demands for more form-filling and mute compliance with barely understood objectives. Control in Canada has been through detailed regulation and centralization. It has attempted to prevent inefficiency and waste before they happen. The cost has been cumbersome, unresponsive administration, and departmental management with a weak sense of responsibility. The system has been directed towards prevention of misdeeds rather than towards the encouragement of good management.

It would be preferable to give departments more administrative autonomy, but it is difficult with this sort of decentralization to ensure that the bad managers are detected and punished and the good ones rewarded. In recent years deputy ministers (and assistant deputies as well) have tended to stay in one office for so short a time that their sins did not catch up with them. A reputation was made by having policy proposals accepted – and not necessarily even implemented – rather than by good management. Until recently, the buoyancy of government revenues meant that the ability to spend money was more appreciated than frugality. Also, the public service has become a series of large, separate agencies. There was a weakening of the cohesion and collegiality created by a small band of senior mandarins who had worked together for decades, who controlled the management of the public service, and who had an innate concern for economy. A new breed of public servants has emerged with an ethos less oriented to public interest and frugality than towards career advancement and making a mark through bold plans and expenditures.

One crucial issue is attitude, and changing the ethos of the public service so that frugality is rewarded. Another is that increased delegation of authority must be balanced by some technique for disclosing how that authority has been used and for revealing and punishing misuse and abuse. This technique must involve a system of audit and accountability. Regardless of how strong managers' sense of responsibility and frugality is, an awareness that sins will be detected is a powerful and necessary persuasion to propriety. An audit process with ultimate accountability to parliament closes the circle of control. For much of Canadian history accountability to parliament has not been effective enough to deter government from unwise, improper, or uneconomical uses of funds and personnel.

THE ROLE OF THE AUDITOR GENERAL AND THE PUBLIC ACCOUNTS COMMITTEE

After confederation the new government of Canada took over many of the institutions and personnel of the old colony of United Canadas. These transfers included both the position of legislative auditor and the incumbent, John Langton.[12] As he had in the earlier colonial period, Langton continued to have responsibilities towards both the legislature and the executive. As legislative auditor he had the task of reporting to parliament on the results of his audit of how the government had used and spent the monies granted it by parliament. But he also held the senior administrative position of deputy minister of finance and secretary to the treasury board. As a result he wore two hats: he was an officer of the government and responsible for the use of funds; and he was an officer of parliament responsible for auditing and criticizing the government's handling of funds. These two functions were incompatible. The audit was not effective because while wearing one hat Langton was, in effect, criticizing decisions he had made wearing the other. Executive control of financial administration was not effective because a parliamentary official, the legislative auditor, was responsible for much of the handling of funds, and would often come into conflict with the government. Accountability to parliament suffered. The public accounts committee met only sporadically, and when it was active, it was usually after a change of government when the new majority party used the committee to uncover scandals in the previous administration's use of funds.

Canadian practice differed markedly from that in Britain where the auditor general (although his full title was comptroller and auditor general) had only trifling executive functions in issuing funds, and was, in reality, an officer of parliament, independent of the executive, concerned solely with examining how the government had handled its stewardship of government finances and reporting on his audit to parliament. The British public accounts committee was a strong and influential voice in improving financial management and accountability because of the circumstances of its development.

In Canada the legacy of this early period continued in the unfortunate mixing of incompatible functions until well into the twentieth century. It was not until the great depression, when Prime Minister R.B. Bennett found that he was unable to ascertain the financial state of the government because accounting and management procedures were in such disarray, that the auditor lost most of his control over disbursement of funds. The Consolidated Revenue and Audit Act of 1931 created the position of comptroller of the treasury, an officer of the government responsible for the handling of funds. The auditor general's functions became those of an officer of parliament examining the accounts of the government and reporting on them to parliament.

These changes enabled the government to improve internal financial management. They also for the first time gave parliament a truly independent legislative auditor. But, even though the auditor general reported to parliament every year, his reports were neglected. The public accounts committee rarely met and for the most part was ineffective. Not until 1958, when Prime Minister Diefenbaker appointed for the first time an opposition member chairman, did the committee begin to meet on a regular basis. But even as recently as 1967 the committee did not meet because the house did not refer the auditor general's report to it. Nevertheless, adopting the British precedent of an opposition chairman was an important reform. An opposition member has a strong motive for criticizing the government, while a government backbencher is equally concerned with defending it. The opposition chairman is balanced by a government majority in the membership of the committee.

The auditor general and the public accounts committee must work hand in hand to ensure effective accountability. Without the auditor and his report the committee is unable to dig into government's finances, or to choose from among the millions of transactions and thousands of issues those which are important and deserve study. Without the committee the auditor general can only report and express an opinion; he has no backing or guidance by parliament, and his findings have less publicity and attention without the media interest in proceedings of the public accounts committee. In the period since 1958 the committee and the auditor general have gradually developed and improved their working relationship, so that now they are important parts of the system of accountability and control. Much of this evolution can best be understood in terms of the successive auditors general, who have been more influential than the committee members or chairmen.

Maxwell Henderson, who was appointed auditor general in 1959, was the first chartered accountant to hold the post. He sought to adapt some of the practices of accountants in the private sector to government. One of them was to prepare detailed confidential reports for the management of departments, Crown corporations and other agencies which would offer comments and suggestions on weaknesses in internal control, savings that might be achieved, and other matters noted during the audit. The public accounts committee, however, felt that there could be problems if the auditor were to make reports to management that were not available to parliament, including the spectre of the auditor once again becoming involved in administrative matters, and the idea of presenting special reports to management was dropped.

Although Henderson's tenure was marked by a spirit of co-operation between auditor and committee, his relationship with the Liberal government was one of 'bitter and unceasing controversy.'[13] The two aspects of the controversy were Henderson's belief that the government was denying him the quality and numbers of staff he needed, and the question of how far the audit ought to go. There was no question that a legislative auditor ought to be concerned with accountability, that is, to ensure that the government has adequately kept track of and accounted for funds, and that the audit also ought to include legality, to determine whether funds have been spent for the purposes and within the limits which parliament approved in statutes and appropriations.[14] The problem concerned the extent to which the auditor ought to investigate a third area, that is, propriety, or 'unproductive expenditure.' Here the government resisted because it felt the auditor was intruding into questions of political judgment and policy which were not his concern. This issue was not resolved during Maxwell Henderson's regime. Nevertheless, Henderson helped make the audit and accountability function much more visible and important. The Toronto *Globe and Mail* annually published a series of excerpts from his report entitled 'Horrible Stories,' and arguments over the scope of his audit were held on the national television network.

In 1973 James J. Macdonell, a vigorous and colourful chartered accountant and management consultant who, like Henderson, came from the private sector, was appointed auditor general. One of his first acts was to appoint an independent review committee to evaluate the role of his office, composed of two eminent chartered accountants and a former president of the Canadian Bar Association. This committee recommended that the auditor general be given the powers to classify, select, and appoint his own staff. It recommended that the auditor continue to report on issues of accountability and legality, and that he should also report on any case where he felt that 'value for money' had not been obtained for any expenditure. The committee recognized that:

Value for money, as a concept, is complex and poses problems of judgment for the person making its evaluation. It encompasses three interrelated components: whether the money is expended *economically* and *efficiently* and whether the program on which it is expended is *effective* in meeting its objectives. The first two components, economy and efficiency, are susceptible to reasonably objective definition and measurement, and there should be no discrepancy between a policy approved by Parliament and the carrying out of this policy by the administration in an economic and efficient manner.[15]

The committee concluded that the auditor general's office should gradually develop expertise in the audit of questions of effectiveness, and then should report to the house on instances where measures of effectiveness could be, but were not, being used.

The government accepted the recommendations of the review committee, and in 1977, a new act was passed which gave the auditor general clear powers to examine questions of economy, efficiency, and effectiveness. He was directed to bring to the attention of the House of Commons any case where he observed that:

1 accounts had not been faithfully and properly maintained or public money had not been fully accounted for;
2 essential records had not been maintained or the rules and procedures applied had been insufficient to safeguard and control public property, to secure an effective check on the assessment, collection and proper allocation of the revenue and to ensure that expenditures had been made only as authorized; or
3 money had been expended other than for the purpose for which it was appropriated by Parliament. In addition, the Auditor General was directed to report any case in which he had observed that:
4 money had been expended without due regard to economy or efficiency; or
5 satisfactory procedures had not been established to measure and report the effectiveness of programs, where such procedures could appropriately and reasonably be implemented.[16]

Macdonell gathered a team of senior chartered accountants from across Canada to examine all aspects of financial management and control in government, including statutes and treasury-board regulations, financial systems and procedures in departments and agencies, monitoring and information producing systems, and the duties of financial and accounting managers. He told parliament: 'The study leads to one clear conclusion: the present state of the financial management and control systems of departments and agencies of the Government of Canada is significantly below acceptable standards of quality and effectiveness.'[17] His report for 1976 again re-reinforced this conclusion. The treasury board secretariat and departments had failed to grasp fully the significance of the major deficiencies. Nor had they identified ways to remedy the situation. They were making only minor changes, where a drastic overhaul was needed. 'Financial management and control in the Government of Canada is grossly inadequate,' Macdonell concluded, and 'furthermore, it is likely to remain so until the Government takes strong, appropriate and effective measures to rectify this critically serious situation.'[18] He was 'deeply concerned that parliament – and indeed the government – has lost, or is close to losing, effective control of the public purse.' As remedy he proposed that a chief financial officer for the government, with the title of 'Comptroller General of Canada,' be created, with responsibility for financial management and control.

The media, and the opposition in parliament, goaded the government until, in November 1976, a royal commission on financial management and accountability (the Lambert Commission) was appointed. And before the commission had reported, the government adopted the auditor general's recommendation and appointed a comptroller general, with deputy-minister status, responsible to the treasury board for the quality and integrity of the government's financial-control system and for administrative practices and policies. The commission, which reported in 1979, recommended far-reaching changes within the government to strengthen financial management, particularly increasing the responsibility of deputy ministers and clarifying the role of treasury board and the comptroller. They also, like most examiners of parliamentary government in Canada, recommended that the committee system of the House of Commons be strengthened.[19]

The question of the type of audit the auditor general should make remained a source of controversy. Macdonell introduced the concept of a 'comprehensive audit,' which has been described as:

A shorthand phrase referring to a systematic, systems-based audit encompassing the traditional elements of information for the legislature, opinions on financial statements, adherence to legislative authorities, and safeguarding and controlling assets, as well as the value-for-money elements of regard for economy and efficiency in operations and procedures to measure and report on the success of programs in achieving their objectives.[20]

To perform these functions the auditor general has received vast increases in staff and funds. The audit office has been one of the fastest growing of government offices in recent years. A controversy remains over the scope of the audit. The statutory power is carefully worded so that the auditor general does not report on how well programmes have achieved their goals, but only on instances where the government has not established methods for discovering whether programmes are effective, and then only where such a system of measurement could reasonably be expected to be in use.

Nevertheless, there are numerous critics. S.L. Sutherland has criticized the comprehensive audit both for its costs and for entrenching political conservatism inside government.[21] R.B. Bryce, former deputy minister of finance and clerk of the privy council, similarly has been concerned that there might be disproportionate emphasis on justifying everything on paper and knowing and counting the costs. He is sceptical of:

elaborate systems of goal-setting and the evaluation of efficiency and effectiveness in many fields where these defy measurement. More than a quarter-century ago as Secretary of the Treasury Board I tried to find ways of measuring output of departments and judging efficiency objectively, but in the end I found I had to rely on detailed knowledge and judgment of what was being done and of the ability and (to use a good phrase from the reports) 'the sense of frugality' of those in charge. Can we create a system to replace detailed knowledge and a sense of frugality both at the centre and at the top of departments?[22]

The royal commission on the economic union felt there was an imbalance between the vast increases in resources for the comprehensive audit by the auditor-general's office and the low level of support for members of parliament, who 'lack adequate resources to scrutinize policy as their job demands.' The commission would have preferred:

to see the Office of the Auditor General focus on the more traditional auditing functions, that is, checking honesty, profits and efficiency in government finances. Broader aspects of policy and program should be the concern of elected Members of Parliament. These politicians should emphasize social and political values, as well as fiscal values, while looking at the political goals which underlie spending and taxation, and while maintaining financial efficiency as a primary criterion.[23]

The commission wanted the politicians to make the critiques of policy and the auditor general to evaluate administration. Underlying the commission's remarks is a concern over the weakness of public discussions of policy. The auditor general's office is certainly not an appropriate centre for policy discussion.

The comprehensive audits performed by the auditor general have for the most part been constructive and useful. Their criticisms and recommendations have been modest and have not often trespassed into contentious political areas. They have dealt with issues for which administrators could legitimately be held accountable. Under Macdonell's successor, Kenneth Dye, the auditor general's office has become less colourful. Long gone are the lists of 'horrible stories.' In their place are sober, thoughtful, and restrained evaluations of the financial management of the government, departments, and agencies, and equally temperate responses from the government. Now well over a hundred years old, the audit function is finally reaching a stage of stability and maturity.

The public accounts committee has not improved its procedures and powers to the same extent as has the auditor general. It now meets regularly, considers the auditor general's report and the responses of departments, and reviews action on previous recommendations. But its recommendations and investigations do not receive the same sort of attention as the auditor general's report, and its recommendations often appear to be a rubber-stamp of those of the auditor. The interests and concerns of parliament are not the same as those of the auditor, and the committee has not yet found the power or means to express its own voice. The committee is the weaker partner in the relationship.

The weaknesses of the public accounts committee stem from the same sources as the weaknesses of other committees: shortages of competent long-term members; frequent changes in membership and chairmanship; excessive competing demands on members' time and energy; unsatisfactory work procedures; and a tradition of weakness and lack of influence. Nor, despite its opposition chairman, is the committee always non-partisan.[25] The committee is much better than in the past, but there is still vast room for improvement.

WHO SHOULD BE HELD RESPONSIBLE AND ACCOUNTABLE?

The doctrine of individual and collective ministerial responsibility makes it a principle that only politicians, not public servants, are responsible and to be held accountable. But in Britain there is one major exception. The 'Accounting Officer' is the person who signs the accounts for a department, defends them before the public accounts committee and is held responsible for faults the committee finds in them. The accounting officer is normally also the 'Permanent Secretary,' or deputy minister, of the department. The separation of responsibility for financial administration from political control means that in Britain there is a clear separation both in law and practice between ministerial responsibility for policy choices and the exercise of political discretion and the civil service's responsibility for administration.

In Canada much of this formal division of responsibility and accountability between politicians and public servants exists in law, but there has been a singular reluctance to apply it in practice. Ministers here are held responsible and accountable to parliament for all aspects of policy and administration, with no acceptance of allocation of responsibility to public servants. The privy council office argued against adopting the British approach: 'As government has learned through the blurring of individual responsibility by the imposition of central controls, responsibility shared tends to be responsibility shirked.'[26] The Lambert Commission did not agree, and recommended that deputy heads of departments be held accountable before parliament through the public accounts committee for the probity and legality of expenditure, the economy and efficiency with which programmes are run, and their effectiveness in achieving policy goals.[27]

The commission noted that most of the time it was the deputy rather than the minister who was witness before the public accounts committee and pointed out that circumstances have changed since the nineteenth century:

Today, ministers are not necessarily held responsible for all the mistakes or failings of public service subordinates unless they clearly knew about and ignored them, or ought to have known about them. Even in cases where fault has been found, ministers are not really expected to resign unless they have been personally involved. Moreover, the imposition of the ultimate sanction, Parliament's withdrawal of confidence, is highly unlikely under a system of governments [*sic*] based on disciplined political parties and legislative majorities.[28]

Ministers, the commission stated, ought to recognize that they may, and likely will, be called upon to answer in parliament for all matters relating to their departments. Nevertheless:

Ministerial delegation of management authority is essential. Ministers face heavy demands on their time. They are members of a political party, constituency representatives, members of the Cabinet and its committees, and Members of Parliament. The obligations attendant on these roles must be balanced with departmental responsibilities, and it is unrealistic to expect that ministers will be able to devote to their departments the time necessary to gain a detailed knowledge of their operations.

Many ministers are severely overworked. This is especially true for ones like the minister of employment and immigration who, by law, must personally review and decide on many hundreds of appeals each week, in addition to carrying the normal ministerial workload. The Special Committee on Reform of the House of Commons of 1985 also supported the assignment of responsibility to deputy ministers.[29]

So far the government has not shown much interest in making this change in the allocation of responsibility and accountability. Perhaps the primary reason is that the distinction between politics and administration is not as clear in Canada as it is in Britain. Patronage, whether in appointments, contracts, purchases of goods, or other spheres, in Canada affects many management decisions and low-level matters involving small amounts of money. Regional and cultural diversity has, for much of Canadian history, made the important political questions detailed administrative choices of where and on whom money is spent rather than questions of broad policies. The a-philosophical, pragmatic, patronage-oriented nature of the major political parties is a testimonial to this pronounced overlap of political and administrative spheres, which means that, unless the nature of Canadian politics were to change dramatically, a division of responsibility like that proposed by the Lambert Commission might not reflect accurately the real-world functions of either politicians or administrators. Perhaps this was in the privy council office's mind when it commented in its submission to the Lambert Commission:

Formal and *direct* accountability of officials to parliament for administrative matters would ... require the establishment of firm practices governing the sorts of questions for which ministers as distinct from officials would be answerable ... Experience indicates that such distinctions, are artificial and that Parliament prefers not to recognize the informal division between the answerability of officials and of ministers for the very reasons that ministers are constitutionally responsible and the extent of their answerability is defined by political circumstance.[30]

In practice, however, ministerial responsibility remains a contentious issue. In 1982 Mr Ian Stewart, the deputy minister of finance, asked to be relieved of his post after serving two and a half years in this demanding position. In his letter of resignation he took full responsibility for policy advice tendered to the minister and cabinet by the department. It was not his subordinates, but he himself, who was responsible for advising. Mr Stewart, in taking this responsibility, intended to affirm his belief in the tradition of an objective and politically neutral senior public service. He expressed his concern with the personal criticisms levied in the media against civil servants, to which they, because of the requirements of anonymity, are unable to respond. Prime Minister Trudeau, in accepting Mr Stewart's resignation, re-asserted his belief in the fundamental principle of responsible government that the public service carries out the policies of the duly elected government. It is the government, not the public service, that is accountable to parliament and ultimately to the Canadian people. Civil servants are responsible for the advice, not the decisions.

In spite of these clear statements of proper constitutional principles, the *Globe and Mail*, and other media reports, construed Mr Stewart's letter and resignation as though he were accepting responsibility for the much-maligned budget of November 1981. One academic observer, accepting this misinterpretation by the media, concluded that 'despite the undoubtedly high-minded intentions of the deputy, both the doctrine of ministerial responsibility and the convention of a politically neutral senior civil service took another body blow.'[31] Perhaps it did, but this was not because of the realities of the resignation but because of the misrepresentations in the press. The false reality presented by the media, rather than the true contents of the letter of resignation and its acceptance, became the prevailing version of what had happened.

In March 1984, after six months of opposition attacks on Revenue Canada, Prime Minister Trudeau dismissed the deputy minister of the department, Mr Bruce MacDonald. Several members of the Liberal caucus had asked for his removal. Chris Speyer, a Conservative spokesman, said that Mr MacDonald was being made a scapegoat for the minister's failure to control the department. The revenue minister, Pierre Bussières, retained his post. Here, in practice, it was the deputy minister who bore the responsibility for problems in the department, while the minister was untouched.

In 1985 Mr Edmund Clark was forced out of his job as associate secretary of the treasury board by Prime Minister Mulroney because Mr Clark, formerly a middle-ranking bureaucrat in the ministry of energy, was identified as a leading author of the Liberals' National Energy Program. The Alberta premier Peter Lougheed had demanded Mr Clark's head as the price for his co-operation in a new energy agreement, and prime minister Mulroney had complied. The chairman of the public service commission, Mr Edgar Gallant, commented in his report to parliament:

Public servants make an important contribution to the development of government policy, but the final decision rests with ministers who bear the responsibility.

There will be far-reaching implications for the future quality of the public service if those who are seen to be examples of dedication in providing loyal, professional advice and service to their ministers are subjected to punitive measures because of their association with policies or programs regarded as unacceptable to a new government.[32]

These events turned the doctrine of ministerial responsibility on its head. The civil servants, not the ministers, were held responsible and punished for policy choices. The time is overdue for the theory and formal structure of responsibility and accountability to come to terms with the practice, and for a clear distinction to be made between the political responsibility of ministers and the administrative responsibility of deputies. Despite the peculiarities of Canadian politics and administration, the Lambert Commission was right.

Nevertheless, it must be recognized, as Ian Stewart stated, that the responsibilities of deputy ministers extend beyond administration to advice on policy matters. A recent conference concluded that:

... public servants are more than mere tools to implement the instructions of ministers. The official may also be guardian of certain facts of life of which the politician as salesman may be only dimly aware. Some things ministers propose to do may be inconsistent with statutory obligations of the administration, such as dismantling the apparatus designed to permit the discharging of duties laid down in legislation. Some things may have predictable adverse long-term consequences. Some things may be incompatible with fundamental rights. Some may be inconsistent with etablished conventions or basic social traditions. One assumes that parliamentary democracy is not intended to confer on politicians the authority to rewrite the social contract in a fundamental way each day. It is worth recalling that responsible government is based on the responsibility of the executive to Parliament, which surely implies that the public service is also broadly responsible to the legislature and indirectly to the public, not solely to the minister directly.

Nevertheless, the conference also concluded that 'when conflict arises between the public interest as interpreted by the minister, and the public interest as seen by the public servant, what must be implemented is the view of the minister. If such implementation creates insuperable difficulties for the official involved, then it is time to move on.'[33]

The Lambert Commission felt that a deputy's personal responsibility for financial management should go along with him when he moves to another department. It found that in June 1978 the median time for a deputy minister in office was one and a half years, and that mobility had been increasing. Twice as many changes were made in the five years up to 1978 as had been made in the same departments in the five years up to 1963. This high rate of mobility of deputy heads had become a major management problem. By breaking management continuity it undermined morale in departments. The commission found that: 'Claims cannot be made that wide experience helps make up for the high mobility of deputies. Nearly 80% of present deputies received their initial appointments as deputy heads since 1971, and about half have neither worked at the lower levels in the department they administer, nor had the benefit of significant similar experience in related fields before joining the federal government.'[34] Senior management in departments experienced all too often the replacement of deputy, which meant reorientation, a pause in decision-making, possibly new priorities and reorganiza-tion, new relationships, and some anxiety before the necessary mutual trust could be created. The fact that departments had to undergo this trying process so often was a vital part of the explanation for low morale in the civil service and for drifting departments and the lack of a sense of direction in management. Moreover, deputies who changed frequently were not able to settle into managing their department, nor did they need to live with the consequences of their actions. Rapid turnover would create problems for making the concept of 'accounting officer' work. The commission thought this problem to be so serious that they recommended that deputy heads be expected to serve for three to five years after appointment.

Turnover is comparably rapid for ministers, and creates similar problems both in the possibility of a minister acting as anything but a figurehead and exerting real influence in his department and in the problem of responsibility and accountability in parliament. When problems were being disclosed in the security service of the RCMP, the minister, new to the job, refused to answer questions about events under the tenure of his predecessors. At the same time the speaker ruled that questions could not be asked of the predecessors, making it impossible for parliament to obtain answers to questions about the critical period when the problems occurred.

These issues of the individual responsibility and accountability of ministers and deputies are closely related to questions of the role of central agencies and of collective ministerial responsibility. Historically, the evolution of the concept of individual ministerial responsibility in Britain preceded that of collective cabinet responsibility. The development of strong cabinets and party discipline served to protect individual ministers from censure by parliament, but at the expense of some of their power and autonomy. The strengthening of central agencies under the Trudeau and Mulroney governments has further reduced the power of ministers both in terms of what they can or cannot do without the collective approval of cabinet and in terms of their ability to control and direct a deputy minister who has his own relationships with and controls by central agencies. Some of the murky confusion of responsibility and accountability in Canada comes from this strengthened role of central agencies that operate in secret below the level of parliamentary scrutiny and put severe limits on the individual powers of ministers and deputies alike. Central agencies have no real public or parliamentary accountability.

The strengthening of central agencies and the frequent shuffling of minister and civil servants from post to post like inconsequential bit players leave a strong impression that the real power is not in the visible political and management levels of departments, but hidden in central agencies and middle management.

The saving grace of parliamentary government is that collective responsibility can, unlike individual responsibility, be a powerful force. The whole-scale rejection of the Liberal government by the electorate in 1984 was as much a rejection of a style of governing and handling power as it was anything else. The government was held accountable by the electorate and suffered the consequences of its behaviour. This sort of political accountability is very effective; accountability to parliament by individual ministers and administrators is not.

CORPORATIONS AND NON-DEPARTMENTS

The Lambert Commission found that Canada had in effect two public services: one, in the traditional departments, employed about 300,000 persons; the other, in non-departmental agencies such as Crown corporations, was nearly as big, employing more than 200,000.[35] Non-departmental agencies are needed for many of the new roles which government has adopted during the twentieth century, including independent sources of policy advice, the regulation of important sectors of the economy, adjudication and the determination of rights through quasi-judicial bodies, and outright ownership or partial ownership by government of businesses and business-like undertakings. These agencies are necessary and useful not only for lightening the burdens on ministers caused by the growth of programmes and added responsibility within conventional departments, but also because many government activities, whether because they are business-like or because they are quasi-judicial, need to be handled impartially and at arm's length from government without political interference. But there is a paradox in their control and accountability: on the one hand, non-departmental agencies are autonomous and independent; on the other, they are instruments of government and responsive to the concerns and needs of government.

By definition a non-departmental agency has a different structure of responsibility from departments because tasks are directly assigned to the agencies rather than to ministers. Ministers are neither responsible nor accountable for them. The constitutional principles of ministerial and collective responsibility do not apply to them. The framework for their management and accountability has been primarily concerned with financial controls, and the larger issues of accountability to parliament and government have not been systematically dealt with. As a result, Crown agencies in recent years have received numerous criticisms from the auditor general, the public accounts committees, and even from ministers who have felt they have lost control of them. The problems included criticism of Air Canada's establishment, operating, and reporting of subsidiaries, claims of separatist influence in the CBC, and cost overruns and doubtful payments to sales agents by Atomic Energy of Canada Limited. There were questions of how objectives and policies are set for agencies, their probity in financial management, and the way they are (or are not) held accountable by both government and parliament.

The Lambert Commission found the structure of accountability and responsibility for non-departments weak at all stages. It was strongly opposed to any set of solutions to the problems of management and accountability of Crown agencies which would tend to reduce their responsibility by increasing control by government and parliament. Instead, it felt that the mandate given them and the power they have should be clearly stated. The control exerted by government should be clear and limited. Improved procedures for evaluation and reporting would ensure performance by the agencies and satisfy the requirements of accountability to parliament.

One major problem lay in the appointment of chairmen and board members. In view of the need for autonomy in non-departmental agencies, the commission felt that the government ought to heed Lord Macaulay's dictum that the essence of responsible government is 'to choose wisely and confide liberally.' The government had often been remiss in 'choosing wisely,' and had shown reluctance to 'confide liberally' by asserting controls that countermanded the original direct delegation of power to the agency. Recent spectacles such as the Mulroney government's firing of all part-time directors of Air Canada, whose chief qualification for appointment was service to the Liberal party, and replacing them with new members whose chief qualification was service to the Conservative party, only emphasize the importance of selection of personnel, albeit by default.

Although legislation has now been passed codifying controls and accountability over Crown agencies, many of the problems are still unresolved. Some are rooted in ideological questions of the role of government in the economy. Canada has a mixed economy in which approximately one-quarter of industrial capital is owned by federal and provincial government-owned corporations. The Mulroney government hopes to 'privatize' some government corporations, but many will remain; as long as they do, there will be disagreement about what their roles and purposes are, the extent to which they should be autonomous and the extent to which some should operate like private businesses. As long as these questions are not resolved, neither their mandates nor their accountability will be entirely satisfactory to everyone.

PARLIAMENT AND ACCOUNTABILITY

Between the reforms of the 1930s and the defeat of the St Laurent government in 1957 Canada had strong, stable ministerial leadership. There were close relationships between ministers and senior civil servants. A system developed of rigorous administrative and financial controls of departments through central agencies. At the upper levels the distinction between the administrative and political systems became blurred, with many senior civil servants advancing to the cabinet and seats in the house. Administration was cautious and parsimonious. The public accounts committee was a negligible force, although it did have its brief day in the sun when it looked at the questions of horses on the payroll at Petawawa and other improprieties which the auditor general, Watson Sellar, had uncovered. In a normal year the committee would not meet. Also, during the twenty-two years from 1935 to 1957, the opposition in parliament was weak, and parliament itself retained the part-time avocational character of the previous century. Effective though it was, the centralized system of control was stifling to management, and without the support of review by the public accounts committee, neither parliament nor public had assurance of legality and propriety. The circle of control was not closed. It was also limited because it excluded the new civil service which had grown in non-departments to escape the confines of central-agency regulations.

This strong control by the political executive broke down in the post-1957 decades, partly through the difficulties of the Diefenbaker government and its lack of trust of the civil service, and partly through the changes taking place in government and administration. The strengthening of the privy council and prime minister's offices under Prime Minister Trudeau was an effort to exert better central control and direction over departments. But there was a price to be paid for these developments in terms of weakened concern for economy and efficiency, and a general weakening of financial and administrative control and accountability, was the situation which caused so much distress to successive auditors general. The end result was most visible in weaknesses in the government's accountability to parliament, but the underlying problem was weaknesses in internal accountability within the executive, because there cannot be effective accountability to parliament without effective internal accountability, except in the limited sense that parliament can expose the internal weaknesses – which, with the help of the auditor general, it has done.

The questions of what sort of audits ought to be done, and the role of the auditor general, were a counterpoint during the 1960s and 1970s to changes in administration and questions of the role of government. The thrust of the Glassco Commission was to reduce the detailed controls by central agencies and give power and responsibility to departmental management. But at the same time there was a growth of collective bargaining in the public service, which created strong unions and curtailed management's powers over personnel. Bilingualism affected career patterns, the qualifications for appointment and promotion, and the composition and work procedures of the public service. Like collective bargaining it added new criteria for evaluation of performance that had nothing to do with normal standards of administrative efficiency and in some ways were opposed to them. The reforms to central agencies and policy-making under the Trudeau government reduced the autonomy and power of departmental management and created new, complex processes for making decisions. Senior management personnel were shifted frequently in the effort to assert central control and weaken the power of the department–interest-group nexus. These changes both reduced concern for efficiency and weakened departmental management along with departmental autonomy. They helped to create the situation which successive auditors general criticized so harshly.

At the same time government activities and revenues grew at an unprecedented rate. Before 1974 the booming economy and revenues made the issue in policy-making more a question of how to spend money plausibly rather than a difficult choice of how to allocate scarce resources between competing needs. New policies were introduced and old ones changed at a rate so rapid that for many programmes there was little stability in administrative practices and procedures. Much more money is saved or lost through policy choices than through administrative efficiency. Continuous policy changes meant that the logical focus of efforts to ensure that money was spent wisely was policy rather than administration. This problem, plus those of mobilizing consent and understanding for policies, meant that policies were a ripe and ready target for criticism. Opposition MPs often expressed their desire to see the auditor general go even further in questioning value for money and policy effectiveness. In this way, the problems in policy-making identified in the previous chapter create further problems in the audit process.

Government spending is now the single most important factor affecting the economy. Its size has been a concern to many politicians, especially in the Conservative party, who in opposition felt government spending to be unproductive and a drag on the private sector. More recently government deficits have raised similar concerns. A not unnatural hope has been that the audit could uncover areas where large reductions in expenditure could be made. The auditor general has expressed interest in auditing 'tax expenditures.' R.B. Bryce pointed out that 'the government payroll is between one fifth and one quarter of the budgetary expenditures, capital expenditures are only about one thirtieth of the expenditures (as distinct from loans through certain agencies), and that over one half of the expenditures are transfer payments and grants and contributions.'[36] In his opinion not more than one-fifth of the deficit in 1979 (it would be a much smaller proportion in 1985) could be saved through improved financial and personnel management. A large reduction to the deficit can only come with a major improvement to the economy, with decisions by parliament and government to eliminate programmes, by eliminating tax expenditures, or by raising taxes. The audit, unless it begins second-guessing major policy decisions approved by parliament, is not likely to help much in identifying where the debt can be reduced.

It is still too soon to tell whether there will be much improvement in internal accountability and control as this depends in large part on the pressures to which government is subjected. If the current problems of slow economic growth and a large deficit persist the pressures the pressures on the government will be towards getting maximum benefits from strictly limited resources, which should help to encourage efficiency, economy, and effectiveness. If, however, there are severe pressures on government for large-scale, rapid innovation and change, then financial administration and accountability will suffer. If there is one thing that the experience of the past decades proves, it is that there are severe limits to what government can do, to how much change it can digest, and to how many different and sometimes conflicting administrative and policy goals it can juggle and balance. In'particular, competent senior personnel are a scarce commodity, and the number of things they can concentrate on at one time is limited. An emphasis on policy-making and programme change must inevitably lead to less emphasis on other things, like economy and propriety.

Canadian experience with big government, and what can be done both by the political executive to hold the administration accountable and by parliament to hold the government accountable, is now sufficiently extensive and documented that the main contours of issues of accountability can be descried.

First, there is a need for a clearer division between the political and the administrative. The administrative branch has an ethos and modus operandi quite different from that of the political sector, and it is by no means obvious that political will should in every instance dominate the bureaucratic will. The bureaucratic norms are impartiality, effectiveness, efficiency, and adherence to rules; the political norms are partiality, sensitivity to differences, personal relationships and rewards. Much of the criticism of Canadian governments for corruption, or excessive patronage and partisanship, come from the intrusion of political norms into areas such as hiring, the letting of contracts, and allocation of resources, where the bureaucratic norms ought to prevail.

Also, the stability of structure, procedures, and attitudes of a bureaucracy is a necessary part of the framework of private activity in a mixed economy, and too much change can mean that businesses and individuals are uncertain as to what to expect from government, an uncertainty which reduces their capacity to plan and to handle the future. In Canada, because of the amateurism of politicians and the weakness of party and public discussion of policies, there is a danger of the political will being capricious, and a partly autonomous bureaucratic sector can counterbalance this danger.

For the most part, deputy ministers are now in effect the persons held answerable and accountable to the public accounts committee. The numerous and prominent non-departmental agencies create a clear divide between politics and administration. The direction of much of central agency activity has been to link the two together rather than to divide them, through increasing politicization of the position of deputy minister, and through making the deputies responsive and accountable to the prime minister's office and privy council offices. The Lambert Commission and others have proposed assigning financial and administrative accountability to deputy ministers, and making it separate from political, ministerial, accountability. This proposal has not yet received enough attention.

Second, there is a need for a balance between autonomy and control. The role of parliament is not to review and second-guess every administrative act, but to ensure that power is exercised within the limits set by parliament, and within acceptable standards of economy, propriety, and justice. Thus, parliament must ensure that legislation and appropriations give clear limits to authority and guidelines as to how it is to be used. The audit process must expose deficiencies in these parliamentary mandates as well as in the internal executive control system. The audit must also disclose where authority and funds have been abused. The audit must not, however, be so rigorous and exacting that it stifles innovation, creativity, and judgment. Rather it should offer guidelines that encourage the wise exercise of discretionary powers.

Third, the House of Commons has been instrumental in exposing problems and demanding improvement in financial administration and management. The auditor general has been an active and powerful voice, and the public accounts committee has been the forum in which his reports have been discussed, and where the publicity has been generated which has forced response from the government. The joint committee on statutory instruments has made inroads into questions of delegated legislation.

Unlike during the 1930s, when the pressure for administrative improvement came from within the executive, in recent years the stimulus has been from outside, from parliament. There has also been a response from the government, including the formation of a royal commission and the creation of the position of comptroller general. Recently critics, including the auditor general, have concluded that financial administration is improving. Much of the credit for this improvement belongs to parliament.

Fourth, there is still room for improvement in the system of accountability to parliament. Members of parliament are deluged with information and government documents such as annual departmental and agency reports, financial documents such as the estimates and accounts, white and green papers, publicity pamphlets, and briefs from pressure groups. The auditor general, with his large professional staff and powers to investigate, plays a vital role in pursuing issues and digesting information to the point where it is understandable and handleable by the public accounts committee. He and the committee have also contributed to making the estimates and the public accounts more comprehensible. Other committees could benefit from this sort of assistance.

In proposing and envisaging improvement there must, however, be some recognition of the very real limitations set by the parliamentary system. Criticism and calling to account are mainly the function of opposition MPs. A large number of these will, at any point in time, be frontbench spokesmen, concerned more with matters of policy than administration. The demands on a member's time are severe, and only a few out of the already small number available have the time or the inclination to pursue complex, and to most people uninteresting, questions of systems of financial administration and review of discretionary powers. The experience of Senate committees shows that a highly motivated, persistent few can be effective, but much of the time even this core is lacking in the public accounts committee and other commons committees.

The central focus of the modern House of Commons is the contest between government and opposition. The time and energy consumed in this battle is formidable. For opposition members, or government backbenchers, to devote more time to unglamorous processes of financial and administrative accountability they would have to find rewards from these activities, either in terms of prestige or improving assurance of re-election. So far the system has not provided these rewards.

Fifth, accountability and responsibility are diffuse, and include the courts, unions and their grievance procedures, peer groups, the community, the media, clientele and public servants' professional ethics and individual conscience. Accountability to parliament is only a part of the process.

Last, there was no golden age of accountability. The audit by the auditor general and the public accounts committee has steadily improved during the past thirty years, and is better now than ever before. To say that accountability to parliament has declined over the years is simply wrong. The golden age is the present. Public awareness of weaknesses is largely to the credit of the improved public accounts committee and the powerful auditor general. There was no assurance in the good old days that financial and administrative accountability within government was adequate. Perhaps it only looks better in retrospect because faults that were hidden then are now exposed.

12

The Question of Reform

In studying the Canadian parliament not one but two subjects require attention: the parliamentary system itself and the literature about parliament. The two have gone in different directions. The parliamentary system has retained the executive-centred characteristics it developed during its early years. In modern times it has become the vehicle for the creation of collectivist policies, and the development of these policies, and strong government intervention in culture and the economy, are directly related to the strength of this executive-centredness. Its central mode of operation is adversarial combat between government and opposition. The literature about parliament argues, with a few notable exceptions, that parliament is in desperate shape and needs reform, and that the direction reform should take is to lessen executive-centredness and to make the system more parliament-centred. Proposals for reform also emphasize the consensual elements, and neglect or denigrate the adversarial. The reality of how parliament functions is so different from the ideal proposed in reform that the two are difficult to reconcile. This contradiction has led to exaggeration of the faults of the present system, overstatement of the possibilities of reform and what reform is likely to accomplish, and failure to appreciate the strengths of the present system.

These contradictions, as we have seen, prevented many of the recommendations of the 1985 special committee on reform from being translated from intention into successful change. The committee's membership included neither the House leaders of the parties, nor any cabinet minister, nor the party whips. It was truly a committee of backbenchers, and its work was directed towards their concerns. Its final report is the strongest statement yet produced by a parliamentary committee in favour of a parliament-centred approach. Some of the obstacles encountered in making the committee's proposals work are simply difficulties inherent in making complex changes (like, for example, the awkward but much-improved procedures for electing the speaker, and the unnecessary proliferation of legislative committees), although even these show a dangerous amateurism in those responsible for implementing reform. Others, however, like the difficulties in improving private-members' business, or in weakening the conventions on confidence, have arisen because the committee's recommendations did not adequately consider how parliament really functions, or appreciate the variety of important interests that need to be taken into account in reform.

The main argument put forward by the special committee in support of its recommendations was that strengthening the position of the private member would 'restore' powers to parliament. Parliament, it argued, in the past had a more powerful role, but this power had been taken from it. There is a superficial appeal to an argument for restoring to its rightful owners something that has been improperly taken away, but it is not a very good way of coming to terms with the political problems of the late twentieth century. Also it is not correct. In most ways, including committees, accountability, facilities available to members, and resources of the House, parliament was weaker in the past than it is now. Only in the unusual period of the first few years after confederation did members have more independence from party. The public accounts committee and the auditor general are more active and effective now than ever in the past.

Parliamentary reform, including the report of the special committee, has its rhetoric and accepted conventions of discourse and argument. Such are the myth of 'restoring' lost powers, and the presumption that the need for more autonomy for private members and stronger committees is self-evident. But these are, in fact weak arguments. The problem with this rhetoric is not so much that it includes bad arguments as that these are accepted uncritically, and divert attention from the real issues in reform, questions of political power, who shall have it, and for what purposes, collective or particular, power has been and should be used.

The special committee identified a serious problem in the role of the backbench member. Cabinet ministers have fulfilling and challenging jobs governing the country. Opposition frontbench spokesmen have lesser though still important roles. But the backbench members function mainly as supporters for their side. They are caught between two sorts of pressure: those from the electorate which make the position unstable and subordinate the identity and opinions of the member or candidate to party label and party leadership, and those within parliament which force MPs to conform to party discipline and subordinate autonomy and judgment to the adversarial combat between the front benches. The end result is that the average MP does not stay long in parliament, and frequently does not enjoy his stay while there. The backbench member is all too often an unhappy, underpaid, overworked, and anonymous foot soldier in the battle between the parties. In a lopsided parliament like the one elected in 1984, discontent is particularly a problem on the government side. Most of the opposition is busy in the party battle.

Almost unnoticed, and despite constant rhetoric to the contrary, the past twenty years have seen a pronounced increase in the control the parliamentary parties exert over the fundamental essentials of an MP's life in parliament. Party control now includes assignment of office space, participation in debate, question period, and committees; and representation on international delegations. An MP cannot now function effectively without the support of a party.

MPs lack power because their base in constituencies is weak. The electorate votes on the basis of party and party leadership, not on the basis of the record of the local candidate or MP. This is a deeply embedded part of Canadian political culture. The danger in giving more power to backbench MPs is that influence is being transferred to transient individuals who are not held accountable in elections. Worse, they do not want to stay in parliament, nor do they. To leave parliament is a release and a reward, not a penalty. MPs are to this very real extent neither accountable nor responsible to the electorate. Until Canada has a large number of MPs who want to remain in parliament for several decades, whose base in both constituency associations and electorate is secure, and who not only want to but can pursue a career as parliamentarians even though they defy party, the legitimacy of the MP as a representative is weak.

These comments should not be interpreted as a mean-spirited attack on members of parliament and their legitimate aspirations. The point is, rather, that the process of representation through constituencies and individual members is insubstantial and ephemeral, especially compared with the clarity of the contest between government and opposition, the stability and permanence of the parties themselves, and the solid power of the executive. This feature permits the dominance of executive over parliament, and of party over elected member. It cannot be changed by procedural reform, or by wishing it away. The electorate votes on the basis of party and leader, not on the record or promises of local candidates. Public opinion surveys can, and do, find that the electorate might wish the individual member to be less obedient to party, but the same electorate does not vote in a way that permits the MP to be independent.

The proposals of the special committee expressed the discontent among backbenchers. They did not come to terms with problems faced by cabinet or opposition front bench. Failure to examine the crucial issue of timetabling is one glaring omission. The failure to take into account the relationship between government and parliament is another. The responsibility for creating policies, and for balancing general and particular interests, rests with prime minister and cabinet. The opposition, as its name suggests, has the function of criticizing and offering alternatives. Canadian politics has a collectivist orientation, especially in comparison with the United States. The more prominent role of government in culture and the economy and the existence of such programmes as universal, prepaid medical and hospital insurance and a comprehensive safety net of welfare measures are manifestations of this trait. Unlike most countries with collectivist policies, these did not emerge in Canada through broadly based, powerful, social-democratic parties. Rather they emerged through the electoral dialectic of a powerful, centralized cabinet and a mass electorate. This executive-centredness is a powerful force in determining policies.

A Canadian government already finds it difficult to get its programme through parliament. Diffusion of power to committees, and increased autonomy of private members, will likely exacerbate these difficulties. The capacity of powerful, entrenched interests, whether in the bureaucracy or outside, to oppose change, will likely increase because committees and private members are generally more sensitive to particular than collective concerns. Making the system more parliament-centred as the special committee proposed will make it more permeable to powerful, particular interests and less responsive to cabinet direction. It is not unlikely that one of the more important outcomes of the present spate of reforms will be increased tension between a cabinet which realizes it must pursue collectivist policies to ensure re-election, and private members of parliament who are more sensitive to special interests. In the parliament elected in 1984 this tension might manifest itself through disagreement between the cabinet and its massive collection of backbenchers, most of whom have come from small business, half of whom are new to parliament, and at least half of whom are not likely to be there after the next general election. The government, not the individual members, will ultimately be held accountable by the electorate. Cabinet control over the bureaucracy might become weaker, and consent more difficult to mobilize, as members and committees go their own idiosyncratic ways.

The special committee's efforts at reform, like most others, attempt to strengthen the consensual aspects of parliament. Many have already floundered, or will, on the realities of the adversarial nature of the parliamentary system. The electorate sees political argument in adversarial terms, as do MPs for most of the time. The adversarial system has important virtues which are ignored; the consensual has serious weaknesses which are also ignored. Government in parliament, not by parliament, is the central feature of responsibility and accountability.

By ignoring these broader issues in reform, and by using weak arguments to defend its proposals, the special committee indulged in an all-too-common tendency of presuming that there is a technical fix to political problems. This problem can be seen more explicitly in discussion of proposals to improve financial and administrative accountability, such as those that were considered by the special committee of 1982. Many of the criticisms of accountability arise because critics think that government is too big, and tries to do too much. Accountability, especially through a 'value for money' audit, is expected to uncover ineffective programmes and policies. The danger here is of pretending that what are essentially political decisions can be treated as technical, value-free decisions. Answers to the most important questions about government, including, for example, how much the government should intervene in the economy and society, and whether the amounts spent on various programmes such as welfare, unemployment insurance, defence, research, foreign aid, or support to business are adequate and in proper balance, are in essence unquantifiable judgments. An audit which attempts to determine answers to such questions will only remain the opinion of auditors; it cannot state final truth. But critics of big government and of collectivist policies, instead of arguing the merits of reducing expenditures as a political and value question, which it is, attempt to change it into a technical one, which it is not, and claim that it is weaknesses in accountability and audit processes which permit these presumed excesses to occur. Reform based on such false assumptions as these can never succeed. Worse, it misdirects attention away from real, political issues and towards spurious, pseudo-technical ones. Policy-making and policy-criticizing are the essence of politics.

Reform to parliament must balance the interests of backbenchers with other legitimate concerns, including those of the government, the parties, and the party leadership. The most recent series of reforms has done a great deal to strengthen the position of backbenchers. The system of standing and legislative committees is now the limits of the manpower resources of parliament to handle. The concerns of government and opposition, particularly in the difficult tasks of arguing, explaining, criticizing, defending, and proposing policies, are at present at least as in need of reform as is the position of the individual member of parliament.

It has not been the purpose of this book to present yet another agenda for the reform of parliament. Quite the contrary, one of the main thrusts of the argument has been that parliament is more in need of understanding than of change, and that change based on simplistic assumptions, and too much change, are dangerous. Several popular proposals for reform have been rejected. One which was rejected is proportional representation which I have argued, would strengthen the already exaggerated control of parties over members, and harm the House by creating two classes of MPs. A second is a drastically altered or elected Senate, which would do nothing to eliminate the causes of problems in confederation, and might do a great deal to make the system more unworkable. A third is a strongly enhanced role for committees.

Some other reforms have, however, been found to be potentially useful. Three, in particular, were concerned with making the career of MP more attractive, and encouraging the development of long-term, secure members with more legitimacy as representatives and hence more capable of asserting their own authority against party. One of these was the question of pay. Successive commissions have been united in discovering that members of parliament are severely underpaid in comparison with other demanding jobs. Better pay would be a form of public recognition of the importance of the job, and an expression of appreciation for the very real sacrifices public life demands. The second was the possibility of additional pay for the chairman of committees. This would be evidence that service to parliament itself is as valuable as service to government as a parliamentary secretary. This reform should only be made, however, if chairmen of both standing and legislative committees were to be selected in a balanced way from all parties, and only if selection of chairmen were truly to be in the hands of backbench members, or the speaker, rather than the party whips. Otherwise it would inevitably become another instrument for party control over members.

A third is the size of the House. This deserves detailed attention. Under the Representation Act, 1974, the House would have grown to 310 members after the next election, and to 369 by early in the next century. The new legislation of 1986 will keep the House much smaller, at 295 seats. The arguments put forward by the Progressive Conservative government to support this change were that it would save money and help maintain the collegial atmosphere of the House. Not expressed by the government, but perhaps at the back of their minds, was the argument that a government with a large majority has problems in keeping idle and restive backbenchers under its control. The larger the majority the larger the problem. And the larger the House the larger the problem. J.R. Mallory has pointed out that Prime Minister Diefenbaker discovered this problem after 1958, and:

The tendency of the Trudeau government to move as many backbenchers as possible through two-year stints as parliamentary secretaries and committee chairman is a symptom of the problem. The life of a government backbencher can be frustrating. The whips need him on the floor and in committee but they do not hesitate to remind him that he is there to vote, not to delay proceedings by speaking, and above all not to criticise the government. The prospect of even more members in this mute but mutinous state no doubt daunts both the whips and a prime minister.[1]

An argument that was not given much attention in consideration of the bill was that the most severe problem in Canadian parliamentary government is the shortage of competent manpower. This has shown up in many ways during our examination of parliament and its workings. Opposition parties can, as at present, be so small that they have difficulty finding effective frontbench spokesmen let alone manning parliamentary committees. This shortage drastically weakens the capacity of parliament to criticize and comment on policies and programs and diminishes the quality of political debate between the opposition and government.

Spreading the heavy demands of constituency business among more MPs would free up more members for committee and other work. At present there are too few MPs to man all the committees properly. Shortage of interested, able MPs with time to devote to committee work is the greatest handicap to improvement of committees. A prime minister in choosing his cabinet is severely restricted by the limitations of the talent available in his caucus, and a larger House of Commons would give him more choice, and ensure better ministers and political direction of the executive. Because the constituency would be smaller in size and numbers of electors, a larger House of Commons could well mean closer contact between an MP and his constituents, leading to greater stability in representation and more satisfaction in the job. The greatest natural obstacle which Canadian politics has to overcome is geography, and a larger House would be a step towards resolving the problem of large constituencies.

A larger House of Commons would lead to better regional representation in the caucuses of the parties. Proportional representation has been proposed by many, including the recent royal commission on the economic union, as a way of resolving the imbalances caused by the single-member, simple-plurality system. But these imbalances would also become smaller as the size of constituencies is reduced, enabling geographic variations in voter support for parties within each province to be more adequately expressed in variations in party composition of elected members.[2] This system would surely be preferable to an untried one of proportional representation, with its problems, including the creation of two classes of MPs and stronger control over MPs by parties.

A larger House would mean greater distance between back and front benches. It might, though this might be too optimistic a hope, consequently mean that Canada could develop a substantial number of elected members who would see their careers within parliament as being a private member, and who would not be concerned with advancement to the cabinet and front benches. This change might do more to reduce the domination of whips and parties than a change directed at standing orders and conventions of confidence.

A larger House would, indirectly, lead to remodelling of the chamber itself. As there would no longer be room for desks for all members, the chamber would become a more intimate and exciting place in which to debate and discuss the nation's business. At present the chamber is far too large to be satisfactory for most parliamentary occasions, apart from question period.

Expansion of the House is the right direction for change. The recent reduction in the rate of growth was a false economy, and will reduce the future effectiveness of parliament and parliamentary government. A substantially larger House would mitigate many of the problems in the role of the private member and would enhance the capacity of the House and the cabinet to do their jobs properly.

These three changes would help the House serve better as a representative institution. They would involve some increases in cost, though the increases would be an insignificant drop in the very large bucket of government expenditure. If the changes helped parliament and its members perform their representation function better, they would be value for money indeed. These suggestions, and those on the Senate in chapter 9, do not add up to a large and comprehensive agenda for reform. Again it must be emphasized that it was not my intention to do this. Rather I have tried to show that constant reform itself can be as much an unthinking reaction as passive acceptance of the status quo, and that far too many proposals for change are simplistic in their assumptions and uncritically optimistic in their faith in change. It is also well to remember that democratic politics are more often messy and unsatisfying than beautiful. As J.A. Corry perceived, the democratic state

is not an exalted communion in which men lose themselves gladly and spend themselves prodigally. That calls for spontaneity and there is little spontaneous enthusiasm left after the processes of discussion and compromise necessary for defining the sphere of state action have been carried through. The compromises reached seem to many to be tainted with mediocrity. Decisions reached by compromises are rarely executed with single-minded devotion.[3]

Parliamentary politics are not at the grand scale of an exalted communion between nation and leader. They are at a much smaller, and much more human scale. This is one of their virtues. The Canadian parliamentary system has other virtues which also often go unappreciated. Some of these have already been mentioned. Others, and some of the weaknesses as well, will become evident in a summary and review of how well the system performs its proper functions.

PARLIAMENT AND ITS FUNCTIONS

Four main functions were postulated for parliament in chapter 1: to make a government; to make a government work; to make a government behave; and to make an alternative government. In addition, two further functions were suggested: to recruit and train political leaders; and to inform, to teach, and to express through political communication.

The essential basic function of parliament is to make a government. The Canadian parliament does this well. In spite of the lack of policy identity of and differences between the two major parties, elections are hard fought. They generate a great deal of interest. They are genuine battles, and what is being fought over is clear: who gets to be government. Once elected, and regardless of whether they have a majority or a minority, the prime minister and cabinet have the power to govern and the responsibility for doing so. When things go wrong the government is blamed, when things go right they claim the credit. The opposition are critics, not holders of power. Parliamentary government is a great simplifier, especially in creating a stark distinction between those who hold power and those who do not. In so doing it resolves one of the most difficult things to achieve in a political system: to ensure accountability by binding responsibility to power. Parliamentary cabinet government is a system of concentrated power and authority in which prime minister and cabinet control the executive and lead parliament. The parliamentary-cabinet system, according to Bagehot, 'is framed on the principle of choosing a single sovereign authority, and making it good; the American upon the principle of having many sovereign authorities, and hoping that their multitude may atone for their inferiority.'[4] Ours is not a system of checks and balances, but of fused, concentrated, centralized power.

The parliamentary system binds power and responsibility together. Neither can be evaded by a cabinet. This virtue is underappreciated, for it is more typical of human societies that those who exercise power over others seek to deny or hide it:

When we see the conceptual connection between the idea of power and the idea of responsibility we can see more clearly why those who exercise power are not eager to acknowledge that fact ... For to acknowledge power over others is to implicate oneself in a position where *justification* for the limits placed on others is expected. To attribute power to another, then, is not simply to describe his role in some perfectly neutral sense, but is more likely *accusing* him of something, which is then to be denied or justified.[5]

This conceptual connection is translated into a strong institutional conjunction through the concentration of power and responsibility in the cabinet. The electorate is faced with a clear choice between government and opposition.

Contrary to common rhetoric the Canadian parliament does a reasonably good job in the function of holding the government accountable and making it behave. Financial and administrative accountability have shown steady improvement. Question period and debates are effective weapons in the hands of the opposition for focusing attention on problems and demanding actions from government. More often than is generally appreciated the populace expresses its displeasure with the government in elections. Of the eleven elections since 1953, seven have chastised the government (five defeats, two reductions of a majority to a minority), one has been neutral in returning a minority with a minority, and only three have registered approval by changing a minority to a majority. No majority has been returned with a majority. Since the goal of the parties is to get, use, and keep power, the sanctions by voters in elections have been, and are, no trivial judgments.

The Canadian parliamentary system also, through its adversarial format, creates an alternative to the government – the official opposition. The apparent stability of the Liberals in recent years masks a reality of an often effective opposition and considerable change. Since 1953 the Conservative party has replaced the Liberals in power three times, while the Liberals have replaced the Conservatives twice. Liberal governments have been more adept in keeping power once they get it. The problem is not that the parliamentary system has failed to enable the alternative to attain power, but that once in power the alternative, the Conservative party, has been unable to govern to the satisfaction of Canadians and governs for only a short time before being rejected by the electorate. The roots of this problem lie deep within Canadian political culture and the Conservative party itself, and cannot be resolved through reform of parliament.

The Canadian parliamentary system is not quite as successful in the function of making a government work. A chronic opposition in particular finds it difficult to create policies once in power. Another aspect of this weakness is the problem in parliamentary timetabling, and the triviality and negativism of much of the discussion in parliament. Factors which contribute to these difficulties include the imbalance between a long-lived government party and a chronic and habitually negative opposition; the way the government prepares its policies in secret, with a heavy burden of informing the public and gaining understanding and consent placed on the primarily adversarial stages of parliamentary discussion; the constant concern of promoting national identity and unity; and the problems all modern industrial nations face in adapting to changing economic, technological, and social forces. The weakness of the political parties both as policy-makers, and as representative institutions which aggregate the concerns of varied regions and groups are central causes of weaknesses in policy-making. The two weaknesses are closely related.

The function of recruiting and training political leaders is also not well done. The short-term, amateur MP is a severe problem. So also is the weakness of resources available to prime minister in forming a cabinet and to leader of the opposition in creating a credible alternative. Nevertheless, the best ministers in a new government are likely to have served an apprenticeship in parliament, which will have given them more sensitivity to political realities, constraints and demands than their numerous neophyte colleagues. Improvements to the pay of MPs, a larger House, and enhanced independence and prestige for committee chairmen will help to improve parliament's ability to serve as a recruiting and training ground. Politics is an excessively demanding job, and one that involves real sacrifices from MPs. The often sharply critical rhetoric used to describe politicians and politics is also, perhaps, one of the factors leading to difficulties in recruiting and training political leaders.

The final function of communication could be done better. Under the pressures of parliamentary gamesmanship and the demands of the media, especially television, adversarial politics do not have much content. Nor do the platforms of the two main political parties, or debates between their leaders. The literature on reform of parliament is filled with discussions of the constraints of party discipline on backbench MPs, and how this ought to be changed. Equally severe, but usually undiscussed, are the constraints that the requirements of the media place on party leadership. Oppositions are expected to oppose, and when they fail to do so, or, worse, support the government (as their common sense and conscience might dictate), they get bad publicity or none at all. Opposition leaders must posture in public to satisfy the media where their real inclination would be to be less simplistic and negative. Poor media coverage of debates means that many important issues are debated poorly if at all in the House. The interesting debates – and there are far more of these than is generally realized – rarely are noticed. These characteristics and problems of the relationship between the media and the House of Commons are the most important single factor contributing to weakness of parliamentary discussion and parliament as a centre of national politics. The media are now a crucial part of parliamentary government. Their coverage of parliament does not serve the institution, the public, politics, or politicians well.

This performance of functions is a far from perfect record, but in the real world human institutions do not achieve perfection. By comparison with most other political systems it is a very good record indeed. Canada is still in the process of nation-building, and the stability and coherence of a society with many centuries of development and evolution cannot be found in it. The institutions of parliamentary government have more than adequately enabled the process of nation-building to be undertaken, and for the variety of opinion and interest in the country to be expressed and taken into account. There is room for improvement. But there is also a need for caution. There is no point in making change after change if reforms are based on superficial concerns or deal with peripheral effects rather than root causes. Reform of this sort cannot be successful. Much discussion of the Canadian parliament, because it is so obsessed with criticism and reform, fails to recognize the strengths and virtues of the present system. It is also filled with unreasonable expectations of both how well a political system can function and what can be accomplished through reforms.

Much of the discussion of reform, especially to the senate, committees, and the role of the private members, is based, implicitly or explicitly, on comparison with the United States. This comparison is not a good one. The parliamentary and the congressional systems are quite different in terms of representation of power, of decision-making, and of balancing collective and special interests. The policy outcomes are also very different. Our political system is Canadian and parliamentary, not American and congressional.

Conventional explanations attribute the different orientations of government in the United States and Canada to differences in political culture: Canada has a collectivist tradition of both socialist and Red Tory thought, while the United States is more individualistic and nineteenth-century liberal. This difference in political culture is real, but at least equally important to differences in policy outcomes is that the parliamentary system, with the dominant role it gives the cabinet, enables the executive to express a public interest beyond party and pressure group, and gives it a strong motive to govern so that it appeals to general rather than particular interests. This institutional feature has permitted Canadian governments to be more activist and welfare-oriented than u.s. governments have been. Our institutions as well as our buildings shape us.

Proposals for movement towards the u.s. model in Senate and other reforms must be viewed with caution. Such changes would entrench particularism and make the federal government less capable of responding to general public concerns. Government would be less able to promote equality, justice, economic development, and other collective ideals. It is puzzling that the policy successes of our parliamentary system are attributed to political culture rather than to institutions, while problems in political culture such as weak national unity and the absence of content in partisan politics are blamed on the institutions of parliamentary government. The parliamentary-cabinet system deserves much of the credit for the successes, and much of the remedy for many of the problems lies in political culture, outside the capacity of institutionalized reform to improve. Change will only come through political action and political leaders.

Canada is not an easy country to govern. The huge land mass, two languages, many regional economies, strong provincial governments, the prevailing shadow of the United States, all create centrifugal tensions. The central government, parliament, the executive, and especially prime minister and cabinet, are the main institutions and forces holding the country together and asserting a national purpose, national standards, and national concerns over and above those of provinces, regions, and particular groups. The federal government has a critical role as the central expression of the nation as opposed to the numerous bodies expressing the concerns of its parts. There are periodic oscillations between assertion of a strong centre and assertion of strong parts. But when the federal government fails to exert leadership and sense of purpose, its support drops. The parliamentary-cabinet system has a unique virtue in combining authority and responsibility within an elected government, and in forcing that government to choose, and explain and defend its choices. The final judge of its success is the nation as a whole.

In 1983 the Canadian public told the Gallup poll that they would like to see reform to parliament, and that the reform they most wanted to see was a change of government. The public made their wish come true in no uncertain terms in the general election of 1984. The question then became how well the new Conservative government would handle its stewardship and governance of the country, and how well the opposition would do its job of criticizing the government and proposing alternative policies and programmes. If a new government fails, the parties again change position. This is, as the public implied, an essential and true process of reform, though it is not the sort usually discussed. It is change *through* parliament, not reform *of* parliament. That this kind of change can take place is a virtue of the parliamentary system. That the change too often means more of the same is a defect. The main functions of the House of Commons are to create a responsible government and to hold that government accountable. Debate and party competition are the heart and soul as well as the blood and guts of our system of representative, responsive, and responsible government. The next challenge is to improve the quality, relevance, and reportage of this vital central core of our democratic processes.

Notes

CHAPTER 1: INTRODUCTION: PARLIAMENT IN AN AGE OF REFORM

1 Canada, Privy Council Office, *Submission to the Royal Commission on Financial Management and Accountability* (Ottawa: 1979), Submission 1, 'Responsibility in the Constitution,' i–xi
2 Canada, House of Commons, Special Committee on Reform of the House of Commons, *Report*, June 1965, xi
3 Peter C. Dobell, 'Some Comments on Parliamentary Reform,' in Peter Aucoin, ed., *Institutional Reforms for Representative Government* (Toronto: University of Toronto Press, 1985), Studies for the Royal Commission on the Economic Union and Development Prospects for Canada, vol. 38:43

CHAPTER 2: APPROACHES TO PARLIAMENTARY GOVERNMENT

1 A useful discussion of this complex term can be found in: A.H. Birch, *Representative and Responsible Government* (London: Allen and Unwin, 1964).
2 L.S. Amery, *Thoughts on the Constitution* (London: Oxford, 1964), 30–1
3 Walter Bagehot, *The English Constitution*, with an Introduction by R.H.S. Crossman, The Fontana Library Edition (London: Collins, 1963), 65
4 A good discussion of this can be found in: Gordon Reid, *The Politics of Financial Control: The Role of the House of Commons* (London: Hutchinson, 1966), 35–45
5 J.A. Corry and J.E. Hodgetts, *Democratic Government and Politics*, 3rd ed. (Toronto: University of Toronto Press, 1959), 188
6 Samuel H. Beer identified five successive types of politics in Britain from the sixteenth century to the present, each of which had its own identifiable and distinctive political formation and style of parliamentary government. As they emerged successively over the centuries these are: Old Tory, Old Whig, Liberal, Radical, and

Collectivist. See S.H. Beer, *Modern British Politics: A Study of Parties and Pressure Groups* (London: Faber, 1965), chaps. 1–3.

7 John B. Stewart has made this suggestion in correspondence with the author. Also see his 'Commons Procedure in the Trudeau Era,' in John C. Courtney, *The Canadian House of Commons: Essays in Honour of Norman Ward* (Calgary: University of Calgary Press, 1985), 21–42. A.H. Birch describes the viewpoints of the ins and outs as 'Whitehall' and 'Liberal' respectively. *Representative and Responsible Government*, 164. A recent provocative study which uses the court-country division is: Gordon T. Stewart, *The Origins of Canadian Politics: A Comparative Approach* (Vancouver: University of British Columbia Press, 1986).

8 Beer, *Modern British Politics*, 8. The best study of the House of Commons in this period is J.E. Neale, *The Elizabethan House of Commons*, revised ed. (Harmondsworth: Penguin, 1963). Excellent too is Wallace Notestein, *The House of Commons, 1604–1610* (New Haven: Yale University Press, 1971).

9 Canada, Privy Council Office, *Submissions to the Royal Commission on Financial Management and Accountability*, Submission 1: 'Responsibility in the Constitution,' 1–5

10 Walter Bagehot, *The English Constitution*, 97

11 J.S. Mill, *Representative Government*, chap. 8, 'Of the Extension of the Suffrage,' in *Utilitarianism, Liberty, Representative Government* (London: Dent, 1910)

12 Bagehot, *The English Constitution*, 67–9

13 J.S. Mill, *On Liberty*, in *Utilitarianism, Liberty, Representative Government*, 72–3

14 See A.V. Dicey, *Law and Opinion in England: Lectures on the Relation between Law and Public Opinion in England during the Nineteenth Century*, 2nd ed. (London: Macmillan, 1930).

15 Quoted in Beer, *Modern British Politics*, 62

16 In correspondence with the author. See his 'Government Defeats in the Canadian House of Commons, 1867–73,' *The Canadian Journal of Economics and Political Science* 29, 3 (August 1963), 364–7.

17 Escott Reid, 'The Rise of National Parties in Canada,' in Hugh G. Thorburn, ed., *Party Politics in Canada*, 4th ed. (Scarborough: Prentice-Hall, 1979)

18 Frederick W. Gibson, ed., 'Conclusions,' in *Cabinet Formation and Bicultural Relations: Seven Case Studies*, Studies of the Royal Commission on Bilingualism and Biculturalism, Study No. 6 (Ottawa: Information Canada, 1970), 171

19 See C.E.S. Franks, 'The Legislature and Responsible Government,' in Norman Ward and Douglas Spafford, eds., *Politics in Saskatchewan* (Toronto: Longmans, 1968), 20–43.

20 Patrick Weller, 'The Vulnerability of Prime Ministers: A Comparative Perspective,' *Parliamentary Affairs* 36, 1 (Winter 1983), 96–117, compares the security of a prime minister in Australia, Canada, and the United Kingdom.

21 David Pring, 'The New Select Committee System at Westminster,' *The Parliamentarian* 64, 2 (April 1983), 57–63
22 See E. Watkins, *R.B. Bennett: A Biography* (Toronto: Kingswood House, 1963), chap. 15: 'Reaping the Whirlwind.'
23 R. MacGregor Dawson, *The Government of Canada*, 5th ed., revised by Norman Ward (Toronto: University of Toronto Press, 1970), 12
24 Joseph Schull, *Edward Blake: The Man of the Other Way (1833–1881)* (Toronto: Macmillan, 1975), 34
25 Dawson, *The Government of Canada*, 31
26 Corry and Hodgetts, *Democratic Government and Politics*, 179, 168
27 Dawson, *The Government of Canada*, 366
28 Richard J. Van Loon and Michael S. Whittington, *The Canadian Political System: Environment, Structure, and Process*, 3rd ed. (Toronto: McGraw-Hill Ryerson, 1981)
29 Canada, House of Commons, Special Committee on Reform of the House of Commons. James A. McGrath, Chairman, *Report* (June 1985)
30 See J.E. Hodgetts, *Pioneer Public Service: An Administrative History of the United Canadas, 1841–1867* (Toronto: University of Toronto Press, 1955).
31 See, for example, Robert Presthus, *Elite Accommodation in Canadian Politics* (Toronto: Macmillan, 1973), and Wallace Clement, 'The Corporate Elite, the Capitalist Class, and the Canadian State,' in Leo Panitch, ed., *The Canadian State: Political Economy and Political Power* (Toronto: University of Toronto Press, 1977).

CHAPTER 3: PARLIAMENT AND THE PARTY SYSTEM

1 Arend Lijphart, *Democracies: Patterns of Majoritarian and Consensus Government in Twenty-One Countries* (New Haven: Yale University Press, 1984), 108.
J.A. Corry, *Democratic Government and Politics* (Toronto: University of Toronto Press, 1946), 266
2 Hugh G. Thorburn, ed., *Party Politics in Canada*, 4th ed. (Scarborough: Prentice-Hall of Canada Ltd., 1979), 45–6
3 Richard Van Loon and Michael S. Whittington, *The Canadian Political System: Environment, Structure, and Process* (Toronto: McGraw-Hill Ryerson Limited, 1981), 626–8
4 Maurice Pinard, 'One Party Dominance and Third Parties,' *Canadian Journal of Economics and Political Science* 33, 3 (August 1967), 358–73, and Reginald Whitaker, *The Government Party: Organizing and Financing the Liberal Party of Canada 1930–58* (Toronto: University of Toronto Press, 1977)
5 Lijphart, *Democracies*, 108–10
6 Ibid, 23

7 Ibid, 93

8 Whitaker, *Government Party*, 405–6

9 Ibid, 407

10 Arend Lijphart, *Democracy in Plural Society: A Comparative Exploration* (New Haven: Yale University Press, 1977)

11 Whitaker, *Government Party*, 408

12 Ibid, 420

13 Escott Reid, 'The Rise of National Parties in Canada,' in Thorburn, ed., *Party Politics in Canada*, and Norman Ward, 'The Formative Years of the House of Commons, 1867–91,' *Canadian Journal of Economics and Political Science* 18, 4 (November 1952), 431–51

14 George Perlin, *The Tory Syndrome: Leadership Politics in the Progressive Conservative Party* (Montreal: McGill-Queen's University Press, 1980)

15 Jeffrey Simpson, *Discipline of Power: The Conservative Interlude and the Liberal Restoration* (Toronto: Personal Library Publishers, 1980), 159–74

16 Hugh G. Thorburn, 'Interpretations of the Canadian Party System,' in Thorburn, ed., *Party Politics in Canada*, 45

17 Perlin, *The Tory Syndrome*

18 John Meisel, 'Development of the Liberal Style: The Growth of Arrogance,' in *Working Papers on Canadian Politics*, enlarged ed. (Montreal: McGill-Queen's University Press, 1973), 237

19 Good sources on minority parliaments include: Eugene Forsey, 'The Problem of "Minority" Government in Canada,' *Canadian Journal of Economics and Political Science* 30, 1, (February 1964), 1–11; Linda Geller-Schwartz, 'Minority Government Reconsidered,' *Journal of Canadian Studies* 14, 2 (Summer 1979), 67–79; Vernon P. Harder, 'A House of Minorities: Parties and Party Behaviour in the Canadian House of Commons: A Case Study,' Master's Thesis, Queen's University, 1980. See also, Ian Stewart, 'Of Customs and Coalitions: The Formation of Canadian Federal Parliamentary Alliances,' *Canadian Journal of Political Science* 13, 3 (September 1980) 451–79.

20 This section is based on many sources, among which three particularly useful ones have been: John Meisel, *Working Papers on Canadian Politics*; Harold D. Clarke, Jane Jenson, Lawrence LeDuc, and Jon H. Pammett, *Political Choice in Canada* (Toronto: McGraw-Hill Ryerson, 1979); and Barry J. Kay, Steven D. Brown, James E. Curtis, Ronald D. Lambert, and John M. Wilson, 'The Character of Electoral Change: A Preliminary Report from the 1984 National Election Study,' a paper presented to the 1985 Annual Meeting of the Canadian Political Science Association, University of Montreal, May–June 1985.

21 A detailed study of the implications of this election for parties and the party system can be found in my: 'Plus ça change, Plus c'est la même chose: Reflections on the

Canadian General Election of 1984,' *American Review of Canadian Studies* (Spring 1986), 1–16.

CHAPTER 4: THE HONOURABLE MEMBERS

1 Norman Ward, *The Canadian House of Commons: Representation*, 2nd ed. (Toronto: University of Toronto Press, 1963), 3
2 A.F. Pollard, *The Evolution of Parliament*, 2nd ed. (London: Longman's, 1926), 152
3 Michael Brock, *The Great Reform Act* (London: Hutchinson, 1973), 29
4 Quoted in Ward, *The Canadian House of Commons*, 5
5 Ibid, 6–7
6 Pollard, *The Evolution of Parliament*, 152
7 This evolution is admirably discussed in Ward, *The Canadian House of Commons*, chap. 1: 'The Nature of Representation in Canada,' and more briefly in R. MacGregor Dawson and Norman Ward, *The Government of Canada*, 5th ed. (Toronto: University of Toronto Press, 1970), chap. 16: 'The House of Commons: Representation.'
8 See J.A.A. Lovink, 'Parliamentary Reform and Governmental Effectiveness in Canada,' *Canadian Public Administration* 16, 1 (Spring 1973), 35–54.
9 See Dawson and Ward, *The Government of Canada*, 322–7, and J.R. Mallory, *The Structure of Canadian Government* (Toronto: Macmillan, 1971), chap. 5: 'The Electorate.'
10 Joseph Wearing, *The L-Shaped Party: The Liberal Party of Canada, 1958–1980* (Toronto: McGraw-Hill Ryerson, 1981), 238–9
11 See Alan C. Cairns, 'The Electoral System and the Party System in Canada, 1921–1965,' in *Canadian Journal of Political Science*, 1, 1 (March 1968), 55–80.
12 Donald V. Smiley, 'Federalism and the Legislative Process in Canada,' in William A.W. Neilson and James C. MacPherson, eds., *The Legislative Process in Canada: The Need for Reform* (Toronto: Butterworth, 1978), 85
13 These and other proposals are summarized in 'Canada's Electoral System: Assessments and Alternatives,' *Parliamentary Government*, 1, 4 (Summer 1980), 2. A thorough and scholarly analysis of proportional representation is: William P. Irvine, *Does Canada Need a New Electoral System?* (Kingston: Institute of Intergovernmental Relations, 1979). See also: Irvine, 'A Review and Evaluation of Electoral System Reform Proposals,' in Peter Aucoin, ed., *Institutional Reforms for Representative Government* (Toronto: University of Toronto Press, 1985). Studies for the Royal Commission on the Economic Union and Development Prospects for Canada, vol. 38.
14 J.A.A. Lovink, 'On Analysing the Impact of the Electoral System on the Party System in Canada,' *Canadian Journal of Political Science* 3, 4 (December 1970), 499, 514
15 Other criticisms of proportional representation can be found in: Allan Kornberg,

Harold D. Clarke, and Arthur Goddard, 'Parliament and the Representational
Process in Contemporary Canada,' in Harold D. Clarke, Colin Campbell, F.Q. Quo,
and Arthur Goddard, eds., *Parliament, Policy and Representation* (Toronto:
Methuen, 1980), 17–22, and Peter McCormick, Ernest C. Manning and Gordon
Gibson, *Regional Representation: The Canadian Partnership* (Calgary: Methuen,
1981), 53–8.

16 See David E. Smith, *The Regional Decline of a National Party: Liberals on the
Prairies* (Toronto: University of Toronto Press), 1981.

17 See Arend Lijphart, *Democracies: Patterns of Majoritarian and Consensus Government in Twenty-One Countries* (New Haven: Yale University Press, 1984), chap. 9:
'Electoral Systems: Majority and Plurality Methods vs. Proportional Representation.'

18 Ward, *The Canadian House of Commons*, 115.

19. The classic study of the characteristics of MPs is Ward's *The House of Commons:
Representation*, chap. 7: 'The Personnel of Parliament.' Other important studies are:
David Hoffman and Norman Ward, *Bilingualism and Biculturalism in the Canadian
House of Commons* (Ottawa: Queen's Printer, 1970), Allan Kornberg, *Canadian
Legislative Behaviour: A Study of the 25th Parliament* (New York: Holt Rinehart and
Winston, 1967), chap. 3, 'The House of Commons of the 25th Parliament'; Allan
Kornberg and William Mishler, *Influence in Parliament: Canada* (Durham, NC: Duke
University Press, 1976), chap. 2: 'The M.P.'s: An Overview'; and Robert Presthus,
Elite Accommodation in Canadian Politics (Toronto: Macmillan, 1973), and *Elites in
the Policy Process* (London: Cambridge University Press, 1974). Other useful studies
include: Allan Kornberg, Harold D. Clarke, and Arthur Goddard, 'Parliament and
the Representation Process in Contemporary Canada,' in Clarke, Campbell, Quo, and
Goddard, eds., *Parliament, Policy and Representation*; Allan Kornberg, David J.
Falcone, and William Mishler, 'Legislatures and Societal Change: The Case of Canada,'
Sage Research Papers in the Social Sciences 1 (#90-002) (Beverly Hills: Sage
Publications, 1973); Dawson and Ward, *The Government of Canada*, 5th ed.,
chap. 17: 'The House of Commons: Personnel'; Richard J. Van Loon and Michael S.
Whittington, *The Canadian Political System: Environment, Structure, and Process.*
3rd ed. (Toronto: McGraw-Hill Ryerson, 1981), 471–6; and John McMenemy and
Conrad Winn, chap. 9: 'Party Personnel – Elites and Activists,' in McMenemy and
Winn, eds., *Political Parties in Canada* (Toronto: McGraw-Hill Ryerson, 1976), 152.

20 Dawson, *The Government of Canada*, 304

21 John Porter, *The Vertical Mosaic: An Analysis of Social Class and Power in Canada*
(Toronto: University of Toronto Press, 1965), chap. 12: 'The Canadian Political
System,' and chap. 13: 'The Political Elite'

22 Examples are: Leo Panitch, 'The Role and Nature of the Canadian State,' in Panitch,
ed., *The Canadian State: Political Economy and Political Power* (Toronto: University
of Toronto Press, 1977); Dennis Olsen, 'The State Elite,' and Wallace Clement,

'The Corporate Elite, the Capitalist Class, and the Canadian State,' 199–224 and 225–48, the same volume; and Olsen's full-length study, *The State Elite* (Toronto: Macmillan, 1980).

23 *The Government of Canada*, 317

24 Robert J. Jackson and Michael M. Atkinson, *The Canadian Legislative System: Politicians and Policymaking*, 2nd ed. (Toronto: Macmillan 1980), 159

25 Peter A. Hall and R. Peter Washburn, 'Elites and Representation: A Study of the Attitudes and Perceptions of M.P.'s,' in Jean-Pierre Gaboury and James Ross Hurley, eds., *The Canadian House of Commons Observed: Parliamentary Internship Papers* (Ottawa: The University of Ottawa Press, 1979), 294. The study was completed in June 1975.

26 Ibid, 308

27 Dawson and Ward, *The Government of Canada*, 317. The words are Ward's addition to the earlier text.

28 Winn and McMenemy, 'Party Personnel – Elites and Activists,' 155–6

29 See, for example, John Meisel, 'Howe, Hubris and '72: An Essay on Political Elitism,' in *Working Papers on Canadian Politics*, enlarged ed. (Montreal: McGill-Queen's University Press, 1973), 217–52. The literature on 'clientelist' politics, such as Sid Noel's *Politics in Newfoundland* (Toronto: University of Toronto Press, 1971), suggests a strongly deferential political culture in some regions of Canada. Simeon and Elkins found only a small proportion of the electorate to be deferential: *Small Worlds: Provinces and Parties in Canadian Political Life* (Toronto: Methuen, 1980), 45.

30 Presthus, *Elites in the Policy Process*, 350

31 Ward, *The Canadian House of Commons*, 121–4

32 David Hoffman and Norman Ward, *Bilingualism and Biculturalism in the Canadian House of Commons* (Ottawa: Queen's Printer 1970), 63

33 Ibid, 62

34 *Canadian Legislative Behaviour*, 54. The analysis in Kornberg and Mishler, *Influence in Parliament: Canada*, 63–73, does not alter these findings.

35 V. Peter Harder, 'Career Patterns and Political Parties at the National and Sub-National Levels in the United States and Canada,' in Gaboury and Hurley, eds., *The Canadian House of Commons Observed*, 338

36 See Norman Ward, *The Canadian House of Commons: Representation*, 115–18, and J.A.A. Lovink, 'Is Canadian Politics too Competitive?' *Canadian Journal of Political Science*, 6, 3 (September 1973), pp. 341–79.

37 Thomas W. Casstevens and William A. Denham III, 'Turnover and Tenure in the Canadian House of Commons, 1867–1968,' *Canadian Journal of Political Science* 3, 4 (December 1970), 655–61

38 See Charles S. Bullock III and Burdett A. Loomis, 'The Changing Congressional Career,' in Lawrence C. Dodd and Bruce I. Oppenheimer, eds., *Congress Reconsidered*, 3rd ed. (Washington: Congressional Quarterly, 1985), 65–84.

39 See, for example, William P. Irvine, 'Does the Candidate Make a Difference? The Macro-Politics and Micro-Politics of Getting Elected,' *Canadian Journal of Political Science* 15, 4 (December 1982), 755–82.
40 Lovink, 'Is Canadian Politics too Competitive?' 358
41 See Harold D. Clarke, Jane Jenson, Lawrence LeDuc, and John H. Pammett, *Political Choice in Canada* (Toronto: McGraw-Hill Ryerson, 1979).
42 See Kornberg and Mishler, *Infuence in Parliament*, 96–8. See also Harder, 'Career Patterns and Political Parties,' 335.
43 Both MPs (anonymous) are quoted in Canada, *Report of the Commission to Review Salaries of Members of Parliament and Senators* (Ottawa: Supply and Services, 1980), 4–5.
44 Ward, *The Canadian House of Commons*, 145
45 Ibid, 147
46 Porter, *The Vertical Mosaic*, 403–5
47 Kornberg and Mishler, *Influence in Parliament*, 97

CHAPTER 5: THE WORKWORLD OF PARLIAMENT

1 This and the following quotations are from: C.G. Power, 'Career Politicians: The Changing Role of the MP,' *Queen's Quarterly*, 63, 4 (Winter 1957), 478–90.
2 The reports were by Alfred D. Hales, Commissioner, 1980 (appointed in 1979): *Report of the Commission to Review Salaries and Allowances of Members of Parliament and Senators*; Dr Cliff McIsaac and Hon. Leon Balcer, 1980 (appointed in 1980): *Report of the Commission to Review Salaries of Members of Parliament and Senators*; and William H. Clarke and Coline Campbell, same title, 1985. The arguments over payment of MPs are well covered in Norman Ward, *The Canadian House of Commons: Representation,* 2nd ed. (Toronto: University of Toronto Press, 1963), chap. 6: 'The Payment of Members.'
3 McIsaac and Balcer, *Report*, 8
4 Hales, *Report*, 4
5 McIsaac and Balcer, *Report*, 5
6 Ibid, 7
7 Ibid, 22
8 Ibid, 34–5
9 A useful discussion of some aspects of an MP's staff can be found in: Robert Finbow, 'Private Member's Staff: Current Assessments, Future Needs,' *Parliamentary Government* 1, 3 (Spring 1980), 7–10. See also Alistair Fraser, 'Legislators and Their Staffs,' in Harold D. Clarke, Colin Campbell, F.Q. Quo, and Arthur Goddard, eds., *Parliament, Policy and Representation* (Toronto: Methuen, 1980), 230–40.

10 A.H. Hanson and Malcolm Walles, *Governing Britain: A Guide-book to Political Institutions*, 4th ed. (London: Fontana, 1984), 91

11 See Grant Mitchell, 'Research Facilities and the Backbench Member of Parliament,' in Jean-Pierre Gaboury and James Ross Hurley, eds., *The Canadian House of Commons Observed* (Ottawa: The University of Ottawa Press, 1979), 155–63.

12 Douglas Roche, MP, *The Human Side of Politics* (Toronto: Clarke Irwin, 1976), 201

13 David Hoffman and Norman Ward, *Bilingualism and Biculturalism in the Canadian House of Commons* (Ottawa: Queen's Printer, 1970); and Allan Kornberg, *Canadian Legislative Behavior: A Study of the 25th Parliament* (New York: Holt, Rinehart and Winston, 1967)

14 Hoffman and Ward, *Bilingualism and Biculturalism*, 97

15 The work of Heinz Eulau and John Wahlke was especially influential. See John Wahlke, et al, *The Legislative System: Explorations in Legislative Behavior* (New York: John Wiley and Sons, Inc., 1962).

16 Roche, *The Human Side of Politics*, 60

17 Gordon Aiken, *The Backbencher: Trials and Tribulations of a Member of Parliament* (Toronto: McClelland and Stewart, 1974), 92

18 Hoffman and Ward, *Bilingualism and Biculturalism*, 110–11

19 Aiken, *The Backbencher*, 93. The following quotations referring to Paul St Pierre came from the same location.

20 Roche, *The Human Side of Politics*, 41

21 See Finbow, 'Private Member's Staff.'

22 Aiken, *The Backbencher*, 113

23 Hoffman and Ward, *Bilingualism and Biculturalism*, 94–5

24 Aiken, *The Backbencher*, 86–7

25 Ibid, 91

26 James Gillies and Jean Pigott, 'Participation in the Legislative Process,' *Canadian Public Administration* 25, 2 (Summer 1982), 260

27 Aiken, *The Backbencher*, 95

28 Ibid, 127

29 See A. Paul Pross, *Canadian Pressure Groups in the 1970's: Their Role and Their Relationship with the Public Service* (Toronto: Institute for Public Administration, 1974), 1. See also Robert Presthus, *Elite Accommodation in Canadian Politics* (Toronto: Macmillan, 1973).

30 Gillies and Pigott, 'Participation in the Legislative Process,' 256

31 Quoted in William T. Stanbury, 'Lobbying and Interest Group Representation in the Legislative Process,' in W.A.W. Neilson and J.L. MacPherson, eds., *The Legislative Process in Canada* (Toronto: Butterworth, 1978), 188

32 Gillies and Pigott, 'Participation in the Legislative Process,' 256

33 Abbie Dann, 'New Rules Change the Game: The Bank Act Hearings, 1978–79,' *Parliamentary Government* 2, 1 (Autumn 1980), 5

34 Quoted in 'Is Lobbying MPs Worth the Effort?' *Parliamentary Government* 2, 1 (Autumn 1980), 11

35 Bill Kempling, MP, quoted in Dann, 'New Rules Change the Game,' 7

36 Gillies and Pigott, 'Participation in the Legislative Process,' 260

37 A. Paul Pross, 'Parliamentary Influence and the Diffusion of Power,' *Canadian Journal of Political Science* 18, 2 (June 1985), 235–66

38 See Aiken, *The Backbencher*, 89–91.

39 Colin Campbell and George Szablowski, 'The Centre and the Periphery: Superbureaucrats' Relations with MPs and Senators,' in Clarke et al, *Parliament, Policy and Representation*, 209

40 Quoted in Norman Ward, 'Responsible Government: An Introduction,' *Journal of Canadian Studies* 14, 2 (summer 1979), 3

41 Aiken, *The Backbencher*, 89

42 Ibid, 8

43 Philip Norton, *The Commons in Perspective* (Oxford: Martin Robertson, 1981), 227–32

44 See Lynda Rivington, 'Sanctum/Sanctorum: The Role of Caucus,' *Parliamentary Government* 4, 1 (1983), 6–7.

45 Gillies and Piggott, 'Participation in the Legislative Process,' 263; Thomas d'Aquino, G. Bruce Doern, and Cassandra Blair, *Parliamentary Government in Canada: A Critical Assessment and Suggestions for Change* (Ottawa: The Business Council on National Issues, 1979), 40

46 Canada, House of Commons, Special Committee on Reform of the House of Commons, *Report* (June 1985), 5–10

47 Among the best sources on the party caucuses is *Parliamentary Government* 4, 1 (1983). This whole issue was devoted to the question of caucuses. See also Guy Chevrette, 'The Government Member: His Relations with Caucus and Cabinet,' *Canadian Parliamentary Review* 4, 1 (Spring 1980), 5–8; and Paul Thomas, 'Parliamentary Reform through Political Parties,' in John C. Courtney, ed., *The Canadian House of Commons: Essays in Honour of Norman Ward* (Calgary: University of Calgary Press, 1985), 43–68. Also Paul G. Thomas, 'The Role of National Party Caucus,' in Peter Aucoin, ed., *Party Government and Regional Representation in Canada* (Toronto: University of Toronto Press, 1985); Studies for the Royal Commission on the Economic Union and Development Prospects for Canada, vol. 36.

48 All quotations are words of Liberal MPs quoted in Rivington, 'Sanctum/Sanctorum.'

49 Ibid

50 Howard Gold, 'Revitalizing Caucus: Enhancing the Role of Private Members,' *Parliamentary Government* 4, 1 (1983), 11

51 Two excellent studies of the whips are: *Seminar on Whips and Discipline* (Ottawa: Canadian Study of Parliament Group, 1983), and Michel Juneau, 'Le Whip,' in Gaboury and Hurley, eds., *The Canadian House of Commons Observed*, 273–92.

52 Aiken, *The Backbencher*, 97, 101

53 Parts of the story of the evolution of this practice can be found in: James Jerome, *Mr Speaker* (Toronto: McClelland and Sewart, 1985), chap. 3: 'Question Period.'

54 Charles Turner, quoted in *Whips and Discipline*, 11

55 Both quotes are from Rivington, 'Sanctum/Sanctorum,' 3.

56 Juneau, 'Le Whip,' 276 (my translation)

57 *Seminar on Whips and Discipline*, 6–7

58 Quoted in *The Globe and Mail*, 2 Jan. 1985, 'MP Roman Enjoys Playing the Wolf in Sheep's Clothing,' 10

59 Aiken, *The Backbencher*, 100

60 Elmer MacKay, MP (PC), quoted in Rivington, 'Sanctum/Sanctorum,' 6

61 These figures are taken from: Michael Rush, 'The Members of Parliament,' in S.A. Walkland and Michael Ryle (for the Study of Parliament Group), *The Commons Today* (revised edition of *The Commons in the Seventies*) (London: Fontana, 1981), 40–1.

62 A.H. Hanson and Malcolm Walles, *Governing Britain: A Guidebook to Political Institutions*, 4th ed. 58

63 Norton, *The Commons in Perspective*, 232–3. See also: Canadian Study of Parliament Group, *Confidence: The British House of Commons and the Ontario Legislature*, Report on Seminar of 20–21 March 1986. Ottawa.

CHAPTER 6: PROCEDURE

1 Motions are discussed in more detail in: John B. Stewart, *The Canadian House of Commons: Procedure and Reform* (Montreal: McGill-Queen's University Press, 1977), 37–8, 62–4. This book is the best avilable source on procedure of the House. Also available is W.F. Dawson, *Procedure in the Canadian House of Commons* (Toronto: University of Toronto Press, 1962), and Alistair Fraser, G.H. Birch, and W.F. Dawson, *Beauchesne's Rules and Forms of the House of Commons of Canada*, 5th ed. (Toronto: Carswell, 1978). James Jerome's *Mr Speaker* (Toronto: McClelland and Stewart, 1985) is a very readable and useful introduction to procedure.

2 Canada, House of Commons, Special Committee on Standing Orders and Procedure, *Fourth Report*, 3 December 1982. Another useful source on the speakership is: Dennis Smith, 'The Speakership of the Canadian House of Commons: Some Proposals,' in Frederick Vaughan, Patrick Kyba, and O.P. Dwivedi, eds., *Contemporary Issues in Canadian Politics* (Scarborough: Prentice-Hall, 1970), 177–92. James Jerome's *Mr Speaker* is another excellent source.

3 I am indebted to Eugene Forsey for this last piece of information.
4 A good discussion of some of the difficulties Bosley faced as Speaker can be found in: Charlotte Gray, 'Animal House,' *Saturday Night*, July 1986, 9–12.
5 The Special Committee on Reform in 1985 recommended that nominations of persons to be appointed to fill these positions by order in council should be examined by a parliamentary committee (*Report*, 33). I prefer a stronger role for the speaker.
6 See also Jerome, *Mr Speaker*, chap. 3: 'Question Period.'
7 Quoted in Bob Miller, 'The Hon. John Bosley, an Interview with the Speaker of The House of Commons,' *Parliamentary Government* 5, 4 (1985), 7
8 Canada, House of Commons, *Debates*, 4 December 1985, 9162
9 The pipeline debate is discussed by Jerome in *Mr Speaker*, 11, 14, 136–7.
10 J.W. Pickersgill, *My Years with Louis St Laurent: A Political Memoir* (Toronto: University of Toronto Press, 1975), 299
11 See C.E.S. Franks, 'Procedural Reform in the Legislative Process,' in W.A.W. Neilson and J.C. MacPherson, eds., *The Legislative Process in Canada: The Need for Reform* (Toronto: Butterworth, 1978), 253. A valuable summary of procedural reform can be found in: John Stewart, 'Commons Procedure in the Trudeau Era,' in John C. Courtney, ed. *The Canadian House of Commons: Essays in Honour of Norman Ward* (Calgary: The University of Calgary Press, 1985).
12 Canada, House of Commons, Standing Committee on Procedure and Organization, *Minutes*, 20 November 1975, 9:10
13 The editors of the *Debates*, in an extreme understatement, say 'The ringing of division bells continued past the hour of adjournment.' *Debates*, 2 March 1982, 15539.
14 19–20 March 1984. The bill was c-9, to establish the Canadian Intelligence Service.
15 *Debates*, 30 March 1984, 2570
16 Ibid, 2574
17 Canada, House of Commons, *Report of the Special Committee on Reform of the House of Commons* (the McGrath Committee), June 1985, 1
18 Richard Cleroux, 'Death Penalty Bill Could Scuttle House Reform,' *The Globe and Mail*, 29 March 1986
19 *Report*, 9. A useful discussion of these conventions of confidence can be found in: Peter C. Dobell, 'Some Comments on Parliamentary Reform' in Peter Aucoin, ed., *Institutional Reforms for Representative Government* (Toronto: University of Toronto Press, 1985); Studies for the Royal Commission on the Economic Union and Development Prospects for Canada, vol. 38, 42–52
20 Special Committee, *Report*, 9–10
21 Ibid, 1 (both quotations)

CHAPTER 7: DEBATE AND QUESTION PERIOD

1 Quoted in Frederick Rose, 'Hurling Brickbats Is Just Good Sport in Canada's House,' *Wall Street Journal*, 14 February 1983

2 John Reid, 'Notes for an Address to the Seminar of the Canadian Study of Parliament Group in Vancouver, 6 June 1983,' 4 (unpublished)
3 United Kingdom, House of Commons, *Debates*, 28 October 1943
4 A detailed analysis of the use of time in the House can be found in John B. Stewart, *The Canadian House of Commons: Procedure and Reform* (Montreal: McGill-Queen's University Press, 1977), chap. 8: 'Doing the Government's Business.'
5 Canada, House of Commons, Standing Committee on Organization and Procedure, *Minutes*, 20 November 1975, 9:10
6 I have discussed these problems in more detail in C.E.S. Franks, 'Procedural Reform in the Legislative Process,' in W.A.W. Neilson and J.C. MacPherson, eds., *The Legislative Process in Canada: The Need for Reform* (Montreal: Institute for Research on Public Policy, 1978). See also Stewart, *The Canadian House of Commons*, chap. 9: 'Closure and Time Allotment.'
7 Canada, House of Commons, Debates, 17 June 1977, 7:6793
8 Ibid, vol. 8, p. 7365, 6 July 1977
9 Useful sources on these events are: David Milne, *The New Canadian Constitution* (Toronto: Lorimer, 1982); Robert Sheppard and Michael Valpy, *The National Deal: The Fight for a Canadian Constitution* (Toronto: Fleet Books, 1982); Edward McWhinney, *Canada and the Constitution, 1979–1982: Patriation and the Charter of Rights* (Toronto: University of Toronto Press, 1982); and Keith Banting and Richard Simeon, *And No One Cheered: Federalism, Democracy and the Constitution Act* (Toronto: Methuen, 1983).
10 See David R. Harvey, *Christmas Turkey or Prairie Vulture?: An Economic Analysis of the Crow's Nest Pass Grain Rates* (Montreal: The Institute for Research on Public Policy, 1980).
11 An interesting comment on political myths can be found in: Northrop Frye, *Anatomy of Criticism: Four Essays* (Princeton: Princeton University Press, 1971), 186.
12 Canada, House of Commons, *Debates*, 4 December 1985, 9157 (Mr Penner)
13 Special Committee on Reform of the House of Commons, *Minutes and Proceedings* 6, 7 February 1985, 26
14 Ibid, 38
15 *Debates*, 4 December 1985, 9175 (Mr Halliday)
16 Special Committee on Reform, *Minutes and Proceedings*, 7 February 1985, 45
17 Special Committee on Reform, *Report* 53
18 *Minutes and Proceedings*, 7 February 1985, 37
19 Ibid, 24 January 1985, 20
20 Ibid, 7 February 1985, 37

CHAPTER 8: COMMITTEES

1 See John B. Stewart, *The Canadian House of Commons: Procedure and Reform,*

(Montreal: McGill-Queen's University Press, 1977), chap. 7: 'The Standing Committees: The Pattern Established.'

2 This history is chronicled in Norman Ward, *The Public Purse: A Study in Canadian Democracy* (Toronto: University of Toronto Press, 1964).

3 Canada, House of Commons, Special Committee on Procedure, 1968, *Third Report*, para 12

4 I discussed this in more detail in C.E.S. Franks, 'The Dilemma of the Standing Committees of the Canadian House of Commons', *Canadian Journal of Political Science* 4, 4 (December 1971), 461–76.

5 See Michael M. Atkinson and Kim Richard Nossal, 'Executive Power and Committee Autonomy in the Canadian House of Commons: Leadership Selection, 1968–1979,' *Canadian Journal of Political Science* 13, 2 (June 1980), 287–308

6 Ibid, 305–6

7 Maxwell Henderson, *Plain Talk: Memoirs of an Auditor General* (Toronto: McClelland and Stewart, 1984), 269–74

8 A good analysis of attendance can be found in Dorothy Byrne, 'Some Attendance Patterns Exhibited by Members of Parliament during the 28th Parliament,' *Canadian Journal of Political Science* 5, 1 (March 1972), 135–41. Attendance is also discussed in: Royal Commission on Financial Management and Accountability, *Final Report* (March 1979), 397–9.

9 'Committee Substitution: Seeking a Cure for the Revolving Door Syndrome,' *Parliamentary Government* 1, 2 (January 1980), 7–8

10 House of Commons, *Debates*, 15 October 1970, 15–16 (Marcel Lambert)

11 See Frans F. Slater, *Parliament and Administrative Agencies* (Ottawa: Law Reform Commission of Canada, 1982), 146–7, n. 149.

12 See Peter C. Dobell, 'Some Comments on Parliamentary Reform,' in Peter Aucoin, ed., *Institutional Reforms for Representative Government* (Toronto: University of Toronto Press, 1985); Studies for the Royal Commission on the Economic Union and Development Prospects for Canada, vol. 38, 56–8.

13 Quoted in 'The Committee Track Record: A Limited Pay-Off,' *Parliamentary Government* 3, 4 (Autumn 1982), 7

14 Quoted in ibid

15 See C.E.S. Franks, 'The Committee Clerks of the Canadian House of Commons,' *The Parliamentarian* 50, 2 (April 1969).

16 Standing Committee on Public Accounts, *First Report*, 27 February 1978

17 Many of these problems are discussed in 'Staffing a Parliamentary Committee: Bridging the Gap,' *Parliamentary Government* 2, 4 (Autumn 1981), 8–11. See also Peter C. Dobell, 'Committee Staff: What Else is Needed?' a paper presented at the Conference on Legislative Studies in Canada, Simon Fraser University, 16 February 1979.

18 Royal Commission on Financial Management and Accountability, *Final Report,* 389. See also John B. Stewart, 'Strengthening the Commons,' *Journal of Canadian Studies* 14, 2 (Summer 1979), 35–47

19 J.R. Mallory, 'The Two Clerks: Parliamentary Discussion of the Role of the Privy Council Office,' *Canadian Journal of Political Science* 10, 1 (March 1977), 18–19

20 See Grace Skogstad, 'Interest Groups, Representation and Conflict Management in the Standing Committees of the Canadian House of Commons,' *Canadian Journal of Political Science* 18, 4 (December 1985), 734–72.

21 *Eighteenth Report,* 18. The original White Paper was called 'Proposal for Tax Reform' and was intended for discussion before the government stated its final policies. Using British terminology now current in Canada it would more appropriately have been called a 'green paper.'

22 A good general discussion of the process of tax reform can be found in: W. Irwin Gillespie, 'Tax Reform: The Battlefield, the Strategies, the Spoils,' *Canadian Public Administration* 26, 2 (Summer 1983), 182–202. The Tax Legislative Process Committee of the Canadian Tax Foundation not only saw no difficulties of the sort discussed above in the examination of tax reform, but recommended much more use of such committees. See their report, 'The Tax Legislative Process,' *Canadian Public Administration* 21, 3 (Fall 1978), 324–57.

23 James Gillies and Jean Pigott, 'Participation in the Legislative Process,' *Canadian Public Administration* 25, 2 (Summer 1982), 259

24 'The Tax Legislative Process,' 337

25 Canadian Study of Parliament Group, *Parliament and Foreign Affairs,* Ottawa, 30 April, 2 May 1984, 11

26 Abbie Dann, 'New Rules Change the Game: The Bank Act Hearings, 1978–9,' *Parliamentary Government* 2, 1 (Autumn 1980), 3–8

27 'Looking toward Committee Reform: What Have the Task Forces Proved?' *Parliamentary Government* 2, 4 (Autumn 1981), 4

28 These task forces are usefully discussed in Nora S. Lever, Barbara Plant Reynolds, and Philip Rosen, 'The Parliamentary Task Forces: Committees of the Future?' *Canadian Parliamentary Review* 4, 1 (Spring 1981), 15–20.

29 See J.R. Mallory and B.A. Smith, 'The Legislative Role of Parliamentary Committees in Canada: The Case of the Joint Committee on the Public Service Bills,' *Canadian Public Administration* 15, 1 (Spring 1972), 1–23. A useful discussion of the committees' handling of legislation in general can be found in Paul Thomas, 'The Influence of Standing Committees of the Canadian House of Commons on Government Legislation,' *Legislative Studies* 3, 4 (November 1978), 683–704.

30 See also Gary Levy, 'Delegated Legislation and the Standing Joint Committee on

Regulations and Other Statutory Instruments,' *Canadian Public Administration* 22, 3 (Fall 1979), 349–65.
31 These reforms are discussed in John A. Holtby, *The Work of the Special Committee on Standing Orders and Procedure: A Background Summary Prepared for a Meeting of the Canadian Study of Parliament Group* (Ottawa: Fall 1984). The British example has been discussed in the academic literature, but there is little percolation in Canada from academic to parliamentary discussion. See C.E.S. Franks, 'Procedural Reform in the Legislative Process,' in W.A. Neilson and J.C. MacPherson, eds., *The Legislative Process in Canada: The Need for Reform* (Toronto: Butterworth, 1978), 256–7.
32 See David Pring, 'The New Select Committee System at Westminster,' *The Parliamentarian* 64, 2 (April 1983), 57–63.
33 The chairmen of the committees combined to produce an assessment of the work of the committees in their first three years: Britain, House of Commons, Liaison Committee, *The Select Committee System*, First Report, HC 92, 1982–3.
34 Pring, 'The New Select Committee System,' 63
35 See John M. Reid, 'The Backbencher and the Discharge of Legislative Responsibility,' in Neilson and MacPherson, eds., *The Legislative Process in Canada*. Royal Commission on Financial Accountability and Reform, *Final Report*, 398.
36 Canada, House of Commons, *Report of the Special Committee on Reform of the House of Commons*, June 1985, 16–17
37 *Debates*, 4 December 1985, 9163

CHAPTER 9: THE SENATE AND REFORM

1 R.A. MacKay, *The Unreformed Senate of Canada*, revised ed. (Toronto: McClelland and Stewart, 1963). First published in 1926
2 Derived from *Canadian Parliamentary Guide* (Ottawa: Normanding, 1985)
3 MacGregor Dawson, *The Government of Canada* (Toronto: University of Toronto Press, 1954), 338–9
4 Much of the material for this section is derived from: Beverley D. MacLean, 'What Does the Senate of Canada Do That Is Useful?' B.A. Hons. thesis, Queen's University, Department of Political Studies, 1985. Other recent studies of the Senate include: F.A. Kunz, *The Modern Senate of Canada: A Re-appraisal, 1925–1963* (Toronto: University of Toronto Press, 1965); and Colin Campbell, *The Canadian Senate: A Lobby from Within* (Toronto: Macmillan, 1978).
5 Canada, Senate, Standing Committee on Legal and Constitutional Affairs, *Report on Certain Aspects of the Canadian Constitution*, 1980, 54
6 J.R. Mallory, 'Curtailing "Divine Right": The Control of Delegated Legislation in Canada,' in O.P. Dwivedi, ed., *The Administrative State in Canada: Essays in Honour of J.E. Hodgetts* (Toronto: University of Toronto Press, 1982), 145

7 See C.E.S. Franks, 'The Political Control of Security Activities,' *Queen's Quarterly* 91, 3 (Autumn 1984), 565–77.

8 See Kunz, *The Modern Senate of Canada*, 313–15.

9 Campbell, *The Canadian Senate*

10 Dawson, *The Government of Canada*, 331

11 P.E. Trudeau, *The Constitution and the People of Canada* (published by the Government of Canada on the occcasion of the Second Meeting of the Constitutional Conference, Ottawa, 10, 11, 12 February 1969)

12 Quoted in Dawson, *The Government of Canada*, 339. His change of mind is recorded in Grattan O'Leary: *Recollections of People, Press and Politics* (Toronto: Macmillan, 1977), 165–80.

13 Senator Joan Neiman, quoted in Nancy Pawelek, 'The Conscience of Parliament: The Second Chamber Contemplates Its Future,' *Parliamentary Government* 5, 1 and 2 (1984), 8

14 Useful books on this topic include: Donald V. Smiley, *Canada in Question: Federalism in the Eighties* (Toronto: McGraw-Hill Ryerson, 1980); Roger Gibbins, *Regionalism: Territorial Politics in Canada and the United States* (Toronto: Butterworth, 1982); Richard Simeon, *Federal Provincial Diplomacy: The Making of Recent Policy in Canada* (Toronto: University of Toronto Press, 1972); and Garth Stevenson, *Unfulfilled Union: Canadian Federalism and National Unity*, revised ed. (Toronto: Gage, 1982).

15 See, for example, R.J. May, *Federalism and Fiscal Adjustment* (Oxford: Clarendon Press, 1969).

16 See: Donald V. Smiley, 'Central Institutions,' in Stanley M. Beck and Ivan Bernier, eds., *Canada and the New Constitution: The Unfinished Agenda*, vol. 1 (Montreal: The Institute for Research on Public Policy, 1983).

17 Alberta, Select Special Committee on Upper House Reform, *Strengthening Canada: Reform of Canada's Senate* (March 1985)

18 Canada, Report of the Special Joint Committee of the Senate and the House of Commons on Senate Reform (January 1984)

19 Canada, Royal Commission on the Economic Union and Development Prospects for Canada, *Report*, Vol. 3 (Ottawa: Supply and Services, 1985), 86–92. The research study which covered this area is: D.V. Smiley and R.L. Watts, *Intrastate Federalism in Canada* (Toronto: University of Toronto Press, 1985).

20 See Stevenson, Unfulfilled Union, chap. 6: 'The Consequences of Province-Building.' Some discussion of these problems can be found in Roger Gibbins, *Senate Reform: Moving towards the Slippery Slope* (Queen's University: Institute of Intergovernmental Relations, 1983), Discussion Paper 16.

CHAPTER 10: PARLIAMENT AND POLICY-MAKING

1 A.V. Dicey, *Law and Opinion in England. Lectures on the Relation between Law and*

Public Opinion in England during the Nineteenth Century (London: Macmillan, 1930)

2 Robert Stanfield, 'The Present State of the Legislative Process in Canada: Myths and Realities,' in W.A.W. Neilson and J.C. MacPherson, eds., *The Legislative Process in Canada: The Need for Reform* (Toronto: Butterworth, 1978), 47

3 See J.L. Granatstein, *Canada's War: The Politics of the Mackenzie King Government, 1939–1945* (Toronto: Oxford University Press, 1975), chaps. 7 and 10.

4 Useful sources on policy-making in Canada include: G. Bruce Doern and Richard W. Phidd, *Canadian Public Policy: Ideas, Structure, Process* (Toronto: Methuen, 1983); Richard D. French, *How Ottawa Decides: Planning and Industrial Policy-Making, 1968–1980* (Toronto: Lorimer, 1980), and James Gillies, *Where Business Fails: Business-Government Relations at the Federal Level in Canada* (Montreal: Institute for Research on Public Policy, 1981).

5 M.J.L. Kirby, H.V. Kroeker, and W.R. Teschke, 'The Impact of Public Policy-Making Structures and Processes in Canada,' *Canadian Public Administration* 21, 3 (Fall 1978), 407–17

6 A good discussion of this can be found in Richard Gwyn, *The Northern Magus: Pierre Trudeau and Canadians* (Toronto: McClelland and Stewart, 1980), 176–7.

7 See previous chapter, fn 14. Also, Allan Cairns, 'The Governments and Societies of Canadian Federalism,' *Canadian Journal of Political Science* 10, 4 (December 1977), 695–725.

8 Fred Schindeler and C. Michael Lanphier, 'Social Science Research and Participatory Democracy in Canada,' *Canadian Public Administration* 12, 4 (Winter 1969), 490

9 A. Paul Pross, 'Parliamentary Influence and the Diffusion of Power,' *Canadian Journal of Political Science* 18, 2 (June 1985) 248

10 Ibid, 264

11 Canada, Royal Commission on the Economic Union and Development Prospects for Canada, *Report*, vol. 3 (Ottawa: Minister of Supply and Services, 1985), 37

12 Canada, House of Commons, Special Committee on Indian Self-Government, *Report*, October 1983

13 See C.E.S. Franks, 'The Political Control of Security Activities,' *Queen's Quarterly* 91, 3 (Autumn 1984), 565–77.

14 A useful consideration of the committee stage of this process can be found in Grace Skogstad, 'Interest Groups, Representation and Conflict Management in the Standing Committees of the House of Commons,' *Canadian Journal of Political Science*, 18, 4 (December 1985), 739–72.

15 This section is based on: John M. Reid, 'The Backbencher and the Discharge of Legislative Responsibilities,' in Neilson and MacPherson, eds., *The Legislative Process in Canada*, 139–45.

16 Ibid, 145

17 *Report* (June 1985), 10
18 *Report*, vol. 3, 64–5
19 Ibid, 67
20 Paul G. Thomas, 'Parliamentary Reform through Political Parties,' in John C. Court-ney, ed., *The Canadian House of Commons: Essays in Honour of Norman Ward* (Calgary: University of Calgary Press, 1985)
21 Useful discussion of each election up to 1968 can be found in: J. Murray Beck, *Pendulum of Power: Canada's Federal Elections* (Scarborough: Prentice-Hall, 1968).
22 The first stages in this story are well described in S.M. Lipset, *Agrarian Socialism: The Cooperative Commonwealth Federation in Saskatchewan: A Study in Political Sociology* (Berkeley: University of California Press, 1950).
23 Joseph Wearing, *The L-Shaped Party: The Liberal Party of Canada, 1958–1980* (Toronto: McGraw-Hill Ryerson, 1981), 235
24 George Perlin, *The Tory Syndrome* (Montreal: McGill-Queen's University Press, 1980), 201, and 'The Progressive Conservative Party,' in H.G. Thorburn, ed., *Party Politics in Canada*, 4th ed. (Scarborough: Prentice-Hall, 1974), 167

CHAPTER 11: ACCOUNTABILITY

1 Sir Ivor Jennings, *The Law and the Constitution*, 5th ed. (London: University of London Press, 1972), 207–8
2 David M. Cameron, 'Power and Responsibility in the Public Service: Summary of Discussions,' *Canadian Public Administration* 21, 3 (Fall 1978), 358, 364
3 Royal Commission on Financial Management and Accountability, *Final Report* (the Lambert Commission Report) (Ottawa, March 1979), 21
4 C.J. Friedrich, 'Public Policy and the Nature of Administrative Responsibility,' from C.J. Friedrich and E.S. Mason, eds., *Public Policy* (Cambridge, Mass: Harvard University Press, 1940) and Herman Finer, 'Administrative Responsibility in Demo-cratic Government,' *Public Administration Review* (Summer 1941). Both reprinted in Francis E. Rourke, ed., *Bureaucratic Power in National Politics*, 2nd ed. (Boston: Little, Brown, 1972)
5 Kenneth Kernaghan, 'Responsible Public Bureaucracy: A Rationale and a Framework for Analysis,' *Canadian Public Administration* 16, 4 (Winter 1973), 572–603; and 'Power, Parliament and Public Servants in Canada: Ministerial Responsibility Re-examined,' in Harold D. Clarke, Colin Campbell, F.Q. Quo, and Arthur Goddard, *Parliament, Policy and Representation* (Toronto: Methuen, 1980), 124–144. Also Colin Campbell, *Governments under Stress: Political Executive and Key Bureau-crats in Washington, London and Ottawa* (Toronto: University of Toronto Press, 1983), 294
6 Royal Commission on Financial Management and Accountability, *Final Report*, Part

III: 'Departments,' especially chap. 9: 'Responsibility and Accountability for Departmental Management'

7 Ibid, 189

8 Quoted in Frederick W. Gibson, ed., 'Conclusions,' in *Cabinet Formation and Bicultural Relations: Seven Case Studies*, Studies of the Royal Commission on Bilingualism and Biculturalism, Study No. 6 (Ottawa: Queen's Printer, 1970), 171

9 See J.E. Hodgetts et al, *The Biography of an Institution: The Civil Service Commission of Canada, 1908–1967* (Montreal: McGill-Queen's University Press, 1972).

10 Canada, Royal Commission on Government Organization, *Report* (the Glassco Commission Report), vol. 1: *Management of the Public Service* (Ottawa: Queen's Printer, 1962)

11 R.B. Bryce, 'Reflections on the Lambert Report,' *Canadian Public Administration*, 22, 4 (Winter 1979), 578. This issue has a series of excellent articles on the Lambert Report.

12 The history of the office of the auditor general is succinctly discussed in Herbert R. Balls, 'The Watchdog of Parliament: The Centenary of the Legislative Audit,' *Canadian Public Administration* 21, 4 (Winter 1978), 584–617. The classic study of audit control is Norman Ward's *The Public Purse; A Study in Canadian Democracy* (Toronto: University of Toronto Press, 1961).

13 Balls, 'The Watchdog of Parliament,' 606. See also Maxwell Henderson's memoirs, *Plain Talk: Memoirs of the Auditor General* (Toronto: McClelland and Stewart, 1984).

14 A good discussion of the role of the auditor can be found in: John J. Kelly and Hugh R. Hanson, *Improving Accountability: Canadian Public Accounts Committees and Legislative Auditors* (Ottawa: Canadian Comprehensive Auditing Foundation, 1981), chap. 3: 'Legislative Auditors.'

15 Independent Review Committee on the Office of the Auditor General of Canada, *Report* (Ottawa, 1975), 33

16 Balls, 'The Watchdog of Parliament,' 609

17 *Report of the Auditor General of Canada to the House of Commons for the Fiscal Year ended March 31, 1975*, 4

18 Ibid, 1976, 9

19 Royal Commission on Financial Management and Accountability, *Final Report* (Ottawa: Ministry of Supply and Services, 1979). A good discussion of the report can be found in Kenneth Kernaghan, ed., 'Symposium on the Report of the Royal Commission on Financial Management and Accountability,' *Canadian Public Administration* 22, 4 (Winter 1979), 511–80.

20 Kelly and Hanson, *Improving Accountability*, 59–60

21 S.L. Sutherland, 'On the Audit Trail of the Auditor General: Parliament's Servant, 1973–1980,' *Canadian Public Administration* 23, 4 (Winter 1980), 643–4

22 Bryce, 'Reflecting on the Lambert Report,' 573
23 *Report*, vol. 3, 66
24 See Sharon L. Sutherland, 'The Politics of Audit: The Federal Office of the Auditor General in Comparative Perspective,' *Canadian Public Administration* 29, 1 (Spring 1986), 118–48.
25 See Henderson, *Plain Talk*, 269–74, 269 et seq, 294, and 342.
26 Privy Council Office, *Submissions to the Royal Commission on Financial Management and Accountability* (Ottawa: Supply and Services, 1979), 'Submission 1': 54
27 *Report*, 374–5
28 Ibid, 180. The quote that follows is from the same source.
29 *Report*, 21
30 *Submissions to the Royal Commission*, 54
31 Ted (J.E.) Hodgetts, 'The Deputies' Dilemma,' *Policy Options* 4, 3 (May 1983), 17. I am grateful to Mr Ian Stewart for showing me the correspondence on his resignation, and for discussing this matter with me.
32 Quoted in Hugh Winsor, 'PCs Warned about Bureaucrat Bashing,' The *Globe and Mail*, 16 May 1985
33 A. Rodney Dobell, 'Responsibility and the Senior Public Service: Some Reflections in Summary,' *Canadian Public Administration* 27, 4 (Winter 1984), 621–6
34 *Report*, 194
35 Their *Report*, Part IV: 'Crown Agencies,' thoroughly discusses the problems of this accountability.
36 Bryce, 'Reflections on the Lambert Report,' 579

CHAPTER 12: THE QUESTION OF REFORM

1 J.R. Mallory, 'Parliament: Every Reform Creates a New Problem,' *Journal of Canadian Studies* 14, 2 (Summer, 1979), 30
2 See John C. Courtney, 'The Size of Canada's Parliament: An Assessment of the Implications of a Larger House of Commons,' in Peter Aucoin, ed., *Institutional Reforms for Representative Government* (Toronto: University of Toronto Press, 1985), Research Studies for the Royal Commission on the Economic Union and Development Prospects for Canada, vol. 38, 1–39.
3 J.A. Corry and J.E. Hodgetts, *Democratic Government and Politics,* 3rd ed. (Toronto: University of Toronto Press, 1959), 42
4 Walter Bagehot, *The English Constitution* (London: Collins, 1963), 63
5 William E. Connolly, *The Terms of Political Discourse* (Lexington, Mass.: Heath, 1974), 97

Index

130, 133–4; private, 19, 191–2; private
members, 137–8; success rate, 112,
130, 219, 260
Blake, Edward, 28, 42
Board of Internal Economy, 136, 137
Bosley, John, 122, 124, 137
Britain
– accounting officer, 244
– audit process, 238–9
– committee system, 24, 113, 162,
178–81; membership, 166
– Conservative party, conception of parliamentary government, 17–20; role
of pressure groups, 94
– constituency associations, 111–12
– government, defeats in House, 113–14
– House of Commons, 4
– Labour Party, collectivist ideology,
19; role in government, 45–6; role of
pressure groups, 94
– members of parliament: backbench,
140–1; equality of expectations, 45–6;
frontbench, 140–1; political careers,
23–6, 74–6, 140
– parliamentary system, 15–20, 30, 60,
67
– party caucuses, 101–2
– party discipline, 99–115, 140–2
– party leaders, frequent change, 112
– procedure, 113
– question period, 146
– safe seats, 76
– speaker, 106, 124, 141
British Columbia, 37, 51, 65
British North America, 28
British North America Act, 149–50
Broadbent, Ed, 109, 148, 150–1
broadcasting, films, and assistance to arts
committee, 167
Bryce, R.B., 236–7, 242–3, 253

budgets, 230, 234; preparation, 11, 174,
210, 218, 220–1, 222
bureaucracy: big, 204, 254; political, 211;
see also public service
bureaucratic pluralism, 209–10, 220, 222
Burke, Edmund, 57–8, 143
Bussières, Pierre, 152–3, 247
by-elections, 61

cabinet, 11, 44, 222–3, 227–8, 231;
control of bureaucracy, 211, 227–8; loss
of power, 211; power and responsibility, 11, 127, 265; supported by
House, 11–13; tensions with backbenchers, 260
cabinet ministers, 257, 262; accountability, 231–2, 247–9, 250; attitudes, 69;
control of departments, 211; exits from
office, 77, 248–9; leadership, 251–2;
members of government caucus, 45,
232; power, 98; relations with pressure
groups, 13, 93, 231; responsibility to
departments, 231; responsibility to parliament, 232, 248–9; socio-economic
status, 66; turnover, 248–9; witnesses
before committees, 167, 168
Cairns, A.C., 62–4
Canada Elections Act: chief electoral officer, 61; funds to national parties for
election expenses, 100
Canada Oil and Gas Act, 191
Canada West, 41
Canadian Banker's Association, 168
Canadian Bar Association, 198, 199, 240
Canadian Broadcasting Corporation, 158,
159, 250
Canadian Labour Congress, 103
Canadian Pacific Railway, 26
Canadian Press, 157
Canadian Study of Parliament Group, 107–8

118–20; principles of, 118–28; quorum, 119; reform, 132–42, 259; speaker, 121–4; times of sittings, 120; and turnover, 14; voting, 119–20
professions, accountability to, 234
Progressive Conservative government of Ontario, 39, 40, 208–9
Progressive Conservative governments. *See* entries under names of prime ministers, Macdonald, Bennett, Diefenbaker, Clark, Mulroney
Progressive Conservative party: caucus, 103–4; as government, 54, 223–4, 266; ideology, 30, 69; language policy, 43, 109; as opposition, 41–8, 217–18, 219; policy-making, 223–6; problems in office, 31, 71; refusal to accept Leonard Jones as candidate, 100; representation in parliament, 61–6, 73–4; selection of leader, 79
Progressive party, 37
proportional representation, 58, 62–6, 261, 263
Pross, A.P., 96, 211–12, 215
provincial governments, 13; *see also* federal system; federal-provincial relations
public, accountability to, 232, 233
public accounts committee, 230, 235, 236, 238–44, 250, 254, 255, 256, 258; opposition chairman, 45, 163, 164, 183, 239; role of auditor general, 185, 243–4; study of nuclear power station exports, 170, 250; work procedures, 243–4, 251
public servants: accountability, 232–4, 237–8, 244–9, 254; responsibility, 226, 246–8, 254; turnover, 232, 234, 237, 248; witnesses before committees, 167, 168, 254

public service: autonomous system, 7, 13, 78, 227–30; bilingualism, 252; politically neutral, 98, 246–8; relationship to MPs, 96–9; relationships to politics, 233, 246–9; relationships to pressure groups, 13, 210–12; response to MPs' demands, 91–2; role in policy-making, 209–10, 222, 260–1; senior, 98, 152–3, 211, 237, 244–9, 253; *see also* deputy minister

Quebec: constituents' attitudes to MPs, 91; Créditistes, 42, 51; electoral volatility, 52, 73; Liberal party role in nomination of candidates, 100; number of seats, 59; referendum, 149; role in confederation, 201; role in Macdonald's government, 21; security service, 147–9; separatism, 198, 207, 224; support for Liberal party, 42, 73, 74, 76; support for Progressive Conservative party, 43, 61; support for Social Credit party, 37, 42
question period, 120, 123, 145–6, 214, 265; media coverage, 155–60; selective, 154; supplementaries, 145; uses of, 153–60

RCMP, security service. *See* security service
Reagan, president, 18, 156
reform. *See* electoral system; committee system; parliament; procedure; Senate; etc.
regionalism: in Canada, 16, 245; in political parties, 51–5; in representation in parliament, 61–6, 263; Senate reform, 196–201
regulations and other statutory instruments, joint committee, 178, 182, 191, 255